HODGES UNIVERSITY
LIBRARY · NAPLES

ALSO BY DAVID K. SHIPLER

The Working Poor: Invisible in America

A Country of Strangers: Blacks and Whites in America

Arab and Jew: Wounded Spirits in a Promised Land

Russia: Broken Idols, Solemn Dreams

The Rights of the People

The Rights of the People

HOW OUR SEARCH FOR SAFETY
INVADES OUR LIBERTIES

David K. Shipler

Alfred A. Knopf · New York · 2011

THIS IS A BORZOI BOOK
PUBLISHED BY ALFRED A. KNOPF

Copyright © 2011 by David K. Shipler
All rights reserved. Published in the United States by Alfred A. Knopf,
a division of Random House, Inc., New York, and in Canada by
Random House of Canada Limited, Toronto.
www.aaknopf.com

Knopf, Borzoi Books, and the colophon are
registered trademarks of Random House, Inc.

Library of Congress Cataloging-in-Publication Data
Shipler, David K., date.
The rights of the people : how our search for safety invades
our liberties / David K. Shipler.—1st ed.
p.   cm.
A Borzoi book.
Includes bibliographical references and index.
ISBN 978-1-4000-4362-0 (alk. paper)
1. Civil rights—United States. 2. Law enforcement—United States.
3. Rule of law—United States. I. Title.
JC599.U5S495 2011
323.0973—dc22   2010034255

Jacket design by Jason Booher

Manufactured in the United States of America

First Edition

For Madison, Ethan, Benjamin, Kalpana, Dylan,
and those of their generation yet to come.

CONTENTS

THE BILL OF RIGHTS

FIRST AMENDMENT

Congress shall make no law respecting an establishment of religion, or prohibiting the free exercise thereof; or abridging the freedom of speech, or of the press; or the right of the people peaceably to assemble, and to petition the Government for a redress of grievances.

SECOND AMENDMENT

A well regulated Militia, being necessary to the security of a free State, the right of the people to keep and bear Arms, shall not be infringed.

THIRD AMENDMENT

No Soldier shall, in time of peace be quartered in any house, without the consent of the Owner, nor in time of war, but in a manner to be prescribed by law.

FOURTH AMENDMENT

The right of the people to be secure in their persons, houses, papers, and effects, against unreasonable searches and seizures, shall not be violated, and no Warrants shall issue, but upon probable cause, supported by Oath or affirmation, and particularly describing the place to be searched, and the persons or things to be seized.

FIFTH AMENDMENT

No person shall be held to answer for a capital, or otherwise infamous crime, unless on a presentment or indictment of a Grand Jury, except in cases arising in the land or naval forces, or in the Militia, when in actual service in time of War or public danger; nor shall any person be subject for the same offence to be twice put in jeopardy of life or limb; nor shall be compelled in any criminal case to be a witness against himself, nor be deprived of life, liberty, or property, without due process of law; nor shall private property be taken for public use, without just compensation.

SIXTH AMENDMENT

In all criminal prosecutions, the accused shall enjoy the right to a speedy and public trial, by an impartial jury of the State and district wherein the crime shall have been committed, which district shall have been previously ascertained by law, and to be informed of the nature and cause of the accusation; to be confronted with the witnesses against him; to have compulsory process for obtaining witnesses in his favor, and to have the Assistance of Counsel for his defence.

SEVENTH AMENDMENT

In suits at common law, where the value in controversy shall exceed twenty dollars, the right of trial by jury shall be preserved, and no fact tried by a jury, shall be otherwise re-examined in any Court of the United States, than according to the rules of the common law.

EIGHTH AMENDMENT

Excessive bail shall not be required, nor excessive fines imposed, nor cruel and unusual punishments inflicted.

NINTH AMENDMENT

The enumeration in the Constitution, of certain rights, shall not be construed to deny or disparage others retained by the people.

TENTH AMENDMENT

The powers not delegated to the United States by the Constitution, nor prohibited by it to the States, are reserved to the States respectively, or to the people.

PREFACE

Most of the people in this book are powerless until they find a handhold on the Bill of Rights. There, embedded in the first ten amendments to the Constitution, are the words the framers gave them to climb and counter the mighty state, to keep their speech free, their confessions true, their trials fair, their homes and files sealed from cavalier invasion by police. If the rights were solid, all of the people's stories would be uplifting.

But parts of the Bill of Rights are eroding—dramatically in the war on terrorism and less obviously, more gradually, in the war on drugs and other common crime. In courtrooms where hardly anybody goes to watch, violations of the same rights undermined by counterterrorism are evident, if less flagrant: searches without warrants, coerced confessions, punishment before judgment, the near extinction of jury trials, and legal defenses impaired by poverty and unreasonable procedure. In criminal justice as in counterterrorism, the executive branch has grabbed immense authority, distorting the process of determining guilt or innocence. All these are breaches of our founding principles.

The principles remain, compromised but not abandoned. They rescue some of the people in these pages and leave others to suffer from government's abuse. Those who are violated, whose rights lose force, tell a cautionary tale to those of us who have not been victims, yet.

I decided to do this book on the morning of September 11, 2001. Sometime around 11 a.m. I finally loosened myself from the grip of the awful images on television, stepped outside into the dappled sunshine of a brilliant day, and in a moment of extreme clarity had an extreme thought: There go our civil liberties.

It was a rash prediction, I knew, and I quickly re-formed it into a question about how firmly we would hold our liberties in such a time of testing; whether the Bill of Rights would sustain us. I figured there would be deterioration, but how much? Where would we come out at the other end? That was about as far as my thinking could progress on that dreadful day.

I had another book to finish first, which took me another two years, and by then my curiosity had broadened beyond counterterrorism onto much larger ground: What happens when rights are denied to individuals who dissent, protest, or run afoul of the law? How do the Constitution and the key elements of the Bill of Rights play on the lives of citizens and immigrants in everyday America?

That has been the framework of this exploration. When I told people I was writing about civil liberties, I was peppered with wisecracks: "Oh, remember them?" "Better hurry, there won't be any left." "You're doing a history!" At a luncheon in Washington during the administration of George W. Bush, retired generals and ambassadors at my table jumped in with a raucous round of one-liners: "I guess it won't be a long book." "It's getting shorter and shorter." "You'll be a pamphleteer!" Ha ha.

I couldn't keep it short, a sign of the complexity of our constitutional culture—for it is a culture as well as a body of law, containing not only rules and regulations but also values and mores. This makes a landscape too vast for a single volume, so I've divided it into two books, with the second to be published a year after the first. This one focuses mainly on the element of liberty most severely affected by the spasm of fear following 9/11: the physical boundary between the individual and the state, guarded by the Fourth Amendment, which guarantees "the right of the people to be secure in their persons, houses, papers, and effects, against unreasonable searches and seizures." The second book will assess the risks to rights protected by the First, Fifth, and Sixth Amendments, and the implications for accused criminals, legal immigrants, and ordinary citizens seeking to practice democracy and maintain individual liberty.

The boundaries of this journey encompass some issues and exclude others, according to a logic that I hope seems sensible.

The first limit is geographical. The domestic arena is the subject here. Wherever certain counterterrorism tactics have been used, whether at home or abroad, controversy has erupted when they violate constitutional principles central to life inside the country. Yet by and large, the Constitution does not apply outside the United States unless a defendant is questioned by American officials or their agents and is then brought to the

United States for prosecution. My focus is not our behavior overseas—at our naval base in Guantánamo Bay, Cuba, or in secret CIA prisons—unless it implicates law and justice on American soil, as it sometimes has.

The second boundary is drawn to emphasize constitutional rights whose denial inhibits free discussion, undermines privacy, or impairs the truth-finding process that can lead to imprisonment. Starkly damaged by the government's campaign against terrorism, they are the same rights that have long been subjected to daily stress in our schools, our streets, and our criminal courts. They include the right to speak and the right to be silent (in the First and Fifth Amendments, respectively); the right to be free from unreasonable searches (in the Fourth Amendment); and the constellation of due process rights (largely in the Sixth Amendment)—to confront the evidence, to summon witnesses, to retain counsel, and to be tried by a jury—all designed to produce reliable determinations of fact. They also include the checks and balances created by the Constitution's separation of powers, undermined most vividly by excessive claims of presidential authority and less visibly by prosecutors' authority to manipulate charges and sentences.

Third, because the Bill of Rights restricts only government, not private entities, I focus here on the powers of the state, not the intrusions of the private sector. There is some overlap, to be sure, especially in the area of data collection and surveillance, where information collected privately can be obtained by government. That interface is examined, but most nongovernmental impact on the constitutional culture is not.

By concentrating on these three areas of geography, consequential rights, and governmental actors, I set aside certain issues. No writer enjoys making difficult omissions, so I take no pleasure in the minimal discussion of the right to bear arms in the Second Amendment, for example, and the ban on cruel and unusual punishment in the Eighth Amendment—worthy topics but tangential to the human and legal struggles illuminated here.

It is easier to exclude provisions of the Bill of Rights that have not been central to constitutional conflict. We have not seen violations of the Third Amendment, which prohibits soldiers from moving into private houses during peacetime without owners' consent, or of the Seventh Amendment, which guarantees the right to jury trials in civil suits. There has been judicial jockeying around federalism and states rights but arguably no serious defiance of the Ninth and Tenth Amendments, which provide that the people and the states reserve rights that are not enumerated or delegated.

. . .

To search and seize, officers of the law must touch you and your possessions, either with their hands or, increasingly, with computer software
that intrudes into digital files. Uncontrolled, the authority to search "is
one of the first and most effective weapons in the arsenal of every arbitrary government," Justice Robert H. Jackson wrote in 1949. And so the
Fourth Amendment's shield belongs "in the catalog of indispensable freedoms," he declared. "Among deprivations of rights, none is so effective
in cowing a population, crushing the spirit of the individual, and putting
terror in every heart."

Today, the government's powers to probe into your private life have
been arranged along a broad spectrum. If you stand at the end most faith-
ful to the Constitution, you see the traditional search warrant, which
is supposed to follow an exacting requirement: a sworn affidavit from
the executive branch, and endorsed by the judicial branch, that probable
cause exists to believe that a particular piece of evidence of a particular
crime will be found in a particular place at a particular time. This is
where the brightest sunshine illuminates the actions of law enforcement.

Take a few steps from the Constitution and you find yourself in the
twilight of crime-ridden neighborhoods where cops frisk pedestrians and
search cars without warrants, on the officers' sole determination that
they have reasonable suspicion or probable cause. Their actions may be
reviewed by the courts, so you can still watch government at work, but
dimly.

Traveling along the continuum, you plunge into a darkness where the
secret Foreign Intelligence Surveillance Court issues clandestine warrants authorizing stealthy break-ins at homes and offices, collections of
phone and e-mail communications, and sweeps through financial and
travel and medical records. You may never know that you've been a target,
but at least a neutral judge has reviewed the surveillance request.

Finally, toward the furthest end of the spectrum, most distant from the
protections of the Constitution, you are subject to searches and monitoring at the whim of middle-level agents in the executive branch, without
probable cause, without public knowledge, without a judge to check and
balance the voracious appetite of law enforcement for vast quantities of
information. The flood of unverified intelligence has overwhelmed analysts and investigators, distorting their work. From lightness to darkness,
this continuum is mapped by the chapters that follow.

The intimate intrusions are part of a long history, and while this book is about the present, it comes with some perspective on the past. Chapter One, "Saving the Constitution," sketches America's deviations from constitutional principles in six episodes from the eighteenth century into the current post-9/11 era.

The next three chapters go into the streets to watch narcotics police, gun squads, and cops on the beat honor or ignore the Fourth Amendment's guarantee against unreasonable search as they try to hold down common crime. These issues predate 9/11, of course, but stand on the same spectrum as the more insidious violations of privacy since then. Each chapter describes the intricate literature of evolving court opinions governing what police may see and seize.

Chapter Two, "Another Country," portrays the interaction between that body of case law and officers' behavior toward citizens in dangerous neighborhoods. Chapter Three, "Defending the System," explores the temptation for cops to fudge the facts, and defense attorneys' efforts to get evidence suppressed by exposing police lies in court. Chapter Four, "With Warrants and Without," assesses the current health of the search warrant, which is the key protection of the Fourth Amendment. The section examines the Supreme Court's accelerating campaign to emasculate the exclusionary rule, that longstanding practice of protecting rights by excluding evidence seized in violation of the Constitution.

The three following chapters explore the hidden mechanisms, enhanced since September 11, 2001, now being used to collect personal information without meeting the standards set by the Fourth Amendment. Chapter Five, "Patriotic Acts," describes the impact on several Americans of secret surveillance under the Foreign Intelligence Surveillance Act (FISA), as expanded by the Patriot Act. Chapter Six, "The Law Falls Silent," reports on the human costs and legal damage of gag orders and warrantless subpoenas called National Security Letters, of computerized monitoring by the National Security Agency, and of privacy laws now riddled with exceptions. Chapter Seven, "The Right to Be Let Alone," examines the inaccuracies of no fly lists, the privatization of personal data collection, and the rising tyranny of technology.

Chapter Eight, "Life, Liberty, and the Pursuit of Terrorists," explores the latitude of the executive branch in prosecuting those accused of terrorism, the strengths and failures of the federal courts, the protection of classified evidence, the designation of Americans as enemy combatants, and the dangerous legacy of the Military Commissions Act, which authorizes a parallel judicial system wholly within the executive branch. The chapter offers illustrations of the state of mind that can corrupt investigators in a time of fear. The Epilogue considers the differences between democracy and dictatorship, reflecting on the importance of the constitutional structure in restraining officials who display behavior more typical in authoritarian systems.

Woven into these chapters is the flow of legal history, for the present cannot be understood and the future cannot be envisioned outside the background of constitutional struggles that have gone before. The statutes and court opinions that trace the lines of liberty across the decades are the means of our hardships and our benefits, so it is worth knowing about them. Furthermore, every Supreme Court case is a human story. It decides a person's fate. It also creates precedent for the next individual, and the next, and so on until the scope of rights is adjusted for all. This is the magic of the rule of law.

As I researched, it became evident that to understand how constitutional rights are maintained and damaged, it helps to know something about the law and its mechanisms, just as in maintaining your car and listening to your mechanic, it helps to know something about internal combustion engines and how brakes work. So I've included some legal detail in this book, sufficient for better understanding.

I am not an attorney. I have had no legal training, just informal teaching by numerous lawyers and judges in answer to my questions. The long learning process has brought me a certain understanding of the law, but the result has no pretensions of constitutional scholarship. It is a layman's attempt to knit together legal and personal narratives that define the evolving limits of our constitutional protections. I have tried to give legal context to the human stories. If it informs lawyers as well as laymen, as it may, that's to the good, and I've included extensive footnotes helpful to professionals. But the law is too important to be left to the lawyers, to paraphrase Georges Clemenceau about war and generals. We laymen know too little about our Constitution and think too superficially about its influence on the qualities of American life. Civic duty requires more.

The best view of American freedoms may be from a country without them, as I learned in Moscow, where I lived for four years as a *New York Times* correspondent in the Soviet era of the 1970s. Devoid of the intricate balances and protections that preserve individual rights, the Soviet system sent many of my friends to prison camps and Siberian exile after sham trials for the mildest political dissent. The conforming population, cowed and conditioned, did not quite know what they were missing, just as many Americans don't see clearly what they have. The clarity I gained there about the mechanisms that preserve our rights helped guide me through this project, so I occasionally use the Soviet Union as a method of illumination. I wish those who made policy in post-9/11 Washington had spent time in Moscow.

There are many ways to honor America. This book is mine. I have completed this journey of self-education in the belief that the most terrifying possibility since 9/11 has not been terrorism—as frightening as that is—but the prospect that Americans will give up their rights in pursuing the chimera of security.

ACKNOWLEDGMENTS

So many skilled attorneys displayed so much generosity to educate me in the law that if their time had been reckoned in billable hours, it would have cost a small fortune. They talked with me in person, by phone, and by e-mail, and sent me volumes of indictments, briefs, motions, and rulings to document my work. They answered my uninformed questions with precision and patience. Many who deserve gratitude are mentioned in the text, but others contributed much more than their brief appearances in the book suggest, so they are named here.

My friend David Tatel, a federal appeals court judge, opened doors to valuable people on the bench and in the bar, helped me understand aspects of the law and the Constitution, and provided useful comments on drafts of chapters. A. J. Kramer, the Federal Public Defender in Washington, D.C., kindly lent me an office, where I spent many weeks learning from him and his crew of superb lawyers, poring over case records, attending motion hearings and trials, and watching the Bill of Rights play out where it matters most acutely — in the criminal courts. Kramer also read part of the manuscript to check facts and give feedback. Assistant public defenders Tony Axam, David Bos, Beverly Dyer, Neil Jaffee, Jonathan Jeffress, Tony Miles, Shawn Moore, Michelle Peterson, Mary Petras, Lara Quint, Gregory Spencer, Robert Tucker, and Carlos Vanegas spent considerable time leading me through the complexities of criminal law. Other helpful defense attorneys included Whitney Boise, James Brosnahan, Frank Dunham, Richard Foxall, Steve Kalar, Larry Kupers, Bob Luskin, Jerome Matthews, James McCollum, Andrew Patel, Gregory L. Poe, Barry Portman, Jay Rorty, Elden Rosenthal, Marc Sussman, Bryan Stevenson, and Kristen Winemiller. Most prosecutors and some judges, except those named in the text, preferred anonymity, so my thanks to them must remain private.

William B. Wiegand, an assistant U.S. attorney, patiently explained legal issues on many occasions over the years, referred me to relevant case law, and introduced me to D.C. police officers who allowed me to accompany them as they went on operations. Sergeant G. G. Neill (now retired), Sergeant J. J. Brennan, and the men and women of their gun and narcotics units, respectively, were welcoming and open, providing me with a rare window into police work on the streets. My observations and conclusions are entirely my own, however. Neither the officers nor the others who assisted me should be held responsible for anything I have written, with which they may or may not agree.

Anthony Lewis and David Cole oriented me at the outset, offering overviews of important issues. Kenneth Ballen, Ann Beeson, Michael Bromwich, Alan Davidson, Mary Holper, Jameel Jaffer, Joe Onek, Paromita Shah, Judge Scott Vowell, and James Woodford helped with contacts, cases, and insights, as did many others who are cited in this book. Alan Hirsch, an expert on confessions, read several chapters and offered helpful feedback. Joe Polski, chief operations officer of the International Association for Identification, graciously provided FBI reports on fingerprint misidentification. Martha Gies put me in touch with relatives of some of the Portland Seven.

For police and other government documents, I relied heavily on those obtained in lawsuits by the American Civil Liberties Union under the Freedom of Information Act. The ACLU was also a treasure trove of information on current constitutional cases being litigated around the country. Details on various rights violations that did not always reach court were accessible through the First Amendment Center, the Constitution Project, and the libertarian Cato Institute. My friend David Burnham provided data on various issues through TRAC, the Transactional Records Access Clearinghouse, which processes digital records it obtains—usually against great resistance—from the federal government. Of the many fine books I used to educate myself, two stood out as especially helpful: David M. O'Brien's *Constitutional Law and Politics* and Geoffrey R. Stone's *Perilous Times*. The reporting on warrantless surveillance by Eric Lichtblau and James Risen of *The New York Times*, which exposed a major violation of the Fourth Amendment, threw light on the shadowy end of the continuum of abuse. Jane Mayer's articles for *The New Yorker* and her probing book *The Dark Side* helped open the scourge of torture to public view. My epilogue's title, "The High Court of History," comes from a speech by John F. Kennedy to a joint convention of the General Court of Massachusetts on January 9, 1961.

All people in this book are real. There are no composite characters, a device I deplore, and all who were willing are identified. Actual names are used except for those few clearly labeled as pseudonyms or nicknames, sometimes with quotation marks around them on first reference. Many of the notes at the end of the book explain the law or describe the case beyond simple sourcing, and those whose superscript numbers in the text are underlined contain significant elaboration.

My agent, Esther Newberg, and my longtime editor, Jonathan Segal, have been unfailingly supportive and helpful during this extended project. Jonathan's criticisms and suggestions have improved the book. So have the comments and insights of my son Michael Shipler and my wife and toughest editor, Debby Shipler, both of whom read the entire manuscript and gave me sound advice, as always.

Finally, I owe thanks to my seminar students at Dartmouth, where I taught in 2003. Their research under the rubric "Civil Liberties in a Time of Terrorism" helped sharpen my thinking and illuminate the land scape I was beginning to travel. When I asked them on the last day of class to summarize their thoughts about Americans and their rights, Elliot Olshansky quoted Dylan Thomas: "Rage, rage against the dying of the light."

The Rights of the People

CHAPTER ONE

Saving the Constitution

As nightfall does not come at once, neither does oppression. In both instances, there is a twilight when everything remains seemingly unchanged. And it is in such twilight that we all must be most aware of change in the air, however slight, lest we become unwitting victims of the darkness.

— Justice William O. Douglas

THE STATE RELIGION

THE GLASS THROUGH which Americans could see their Constitution was gradually losing clarity. Small, superficial cracks and microscopic crystals, discovered by National Archives technicians in 1995, would eventually bring opaqueness, and the handwritten codes of freedom would disappear from view.

Behind the cloudiness, moreover, the huge pages were endangered by the slightest of threats: an incremental rise in humidity inside the massive cases, which had been constructed in 1952 to house the Declaration of Independence as well as the Constitution and its Bill of Rights.

So, with the most advanced technology applied to preserving the nation's most venerable treasures, new encasements were designed and tested against extremes. Sealed with materials developed for space flight, prototypes were submerged in ice and subjected to heat. Bases were fabricated of aluminum, and frames of titanium were plated with nickel and gold. When the modern containers were ready, in 2003, the founding documents were carefully placed under thick, tempered glass. The cases were filled with the inert gas argon and fitted with ports and sensors for constant monitoring to keep the humidity at 40 percent, the temperature at 67 degrees Fahrenheit.

The seals, designed to last longer than a century, admit no outside air and no tiny insects that might gradually eat away at the precious sheets of parchment. If sheer science is sufficient, the Constitution will survive even the subtlest assault.

In the rotunda of the National Archives in Washington, D.C., hushed and calmed in the dim glow of a dusky light, the sacred documents are laid out as if on an altar, with the Constitution's four enormous pages in the center, flanked on the left by the Declaration of Independence and on the right by the Bill of Rights, its script now faint and barely legible.

That these faded marks on the parchment's surface have reached so deeply into the human experience makes this a place of pilgrimage, inspiring a worshipful mood. If America has a state religion, as the historian Robert Kelley used to say, it is constitutional democracy. Among all the rancorous arguments in the American landscape, no call to abandon the Constitution can be heard. Across the entire sweep of the political and social spectrum, no rejection of the Constitution can be seen. No threat to the nation, no fear of insecurity has been enough to provoke such apostasy. Instead, every departure from constitutional principles has been excused, rationalized, or justified by assertions that the Constitution is actually being observed—that the document awards or withholds powers, that it permits or prohibits or requires, that its meanings derive literally from its authors' original intent, or that its provisions transcend the bonds of history. The Constitution is reinterpreted and sometimes stretched grotesquely, but no political actor so far has had the brazen arrogance to discard it explicitly.

Indeed, the Constitution is still being discovered. Like any holy text, this one is what its followers need it to be. It is malleable but not equivocal, principled but not brittle: It can bend without breaking. The rights it enshrines are fundamental but not absolute, and they expand and contract as they are debated and rethought with time and circumstance. The Constitution's pages may be embalmed in argon, but its ideas live and breathe the same air that we citizens do.

Those ideas have proven greater even than the men who put them on paper, men who could be small and parochial in their mutual suspicions and partisan bickering. The liberties they originally inscribed, in an era when women had no vote and blacks were enslaved, continue to awaken values and sensibilities that our national ancestors did not imagine.

The framers, state delegates to the Constitutional Convention in the sweltering Philadelphia summer of 1787, were fairly young men for the most part who championed rights mainly for themselves and their kind— for propertied males of their race. Yet the seed they planted could not be contained. It was too brilliantly conceived, and so it grew and spread beyond the confines they envisioned.

Jealously holding the powers of their respective states and suspicious of the central authority they were creating, the framers deftly divided the government against itself, with each of three branches checking and balancing the others. This avoided placing liberty's fate in the hands of individuals, for as James Madison observed at the Constitutional Convention, "All men having power ought to be distrusted to a certain degree."[1]

The framers built the constitutional structure on a critical concept: the assumption that individual rights exist as a natural condition, that government cannot bestow rights on the people, for the people already possess them. They are the people's to relinquish in careful measure as they choose. So basic was this conviction that the delegates saw no need to codify the people's rights, and they adjourned the convention without doing so. It was considered sufficient to include the venerable principle of habeas corpus (literally, "you have the body"), by which a prisoner could petition a court for a writ to summon his jailer to defend and justify the incarceration.

This right, with roots in Anglo-Saxon common law predating the Magna Carta of 1215, was regarded by Madison and others as an impregnable shield of liberty. No other rights needed enumerating. If no jailer could keep a person without the oversight of an independent court, it was believed, autocracy was thwarted. So the framers made sure that access to the "Great Writ," as it is known, could not be curtailed lightly. "The Privilege of the Writ of Habeas Corpus shall not be suspended," they wrote in Article I of the Constitution, "unless when in Cases of Rebellion or Invasion the public Safety may require it."

Relying on habeas corpus was not enough for those in the political class who were apprehensive about governmental abuse of power. Evangelical Christian voters demanded from Madison, a candidate for Congress, support of an amendment protecting religious freedom by separating church from government.[2] Only later, mainly as a price of ratification demanded by the states, did the Bill of Rights, the first ten amendments, strike the great chords of liberty that have reverberated for more than two centuries.

This was accomplished with a distinctive choice of words. In many other constitutions, governments give rights; in the United States Constitution, the people do the giving, by retaining their rights and granting government limited powers. In the First Amendment, Congress does not award the people freedoms of religion, speech, assembly, and the press. Rather, "Congress shall make no law . . . abridging" those existing rights. Government does not magnanimously donate the right to be secure against "unreasonable searches and seizures" in the Fourth Amendment. Instead, "The right . . . shall not be violated." The most positive forces in the Constitution are the negatives.

Every constitutional right has been kindled by its violation. That men could torture other men to extract confessions led to the Fifth Amendment's guarantee that no person "shall be compelled in any criminal case to be a witness against himself." The writs of assistance issued by the British as blanket authorizations for unlimited searches led to the Fourth Amendment's ringing declaration of "the right of the people to be secure in their persons, houses, papers, and effects." Religious persecution, both in England and America, generated the First Amendment's ban on any law "respecting an establishment of religion, or prohibiting the free exercise thereof." Our liberties are rooted in their opposites: the separation of powers in the autocracy of monarchs, freedom of speech and the press in censorship, the right to counsel and due process in the Star Chamber of the sixteenth and seventeenth centuries.[3]*

The framers built a bold bulwark against ingenious methods of oppression, and were driven not only by the violations on American soil under British rule but also by long patterns of action and reaction in England itself. They tended to see the abuse of rights in America as a deviation from British principles, unfaithful to English tradition. They honored English common law—that largely unwritten body of rules and precepts that had taken on the weight of custom and consensus in the absence of a written constitution. As codified and explained by Sir William Blackstone, a British judge who published his *Commentaries on the Laws of England* the decade before the American Revolution, common law remains an underlying presence in the contemplations of American lawyers and judges today, a complement to constitutional provisions, statutes, regulations, and the detailed court opinions that make up judicial precedent. A statue of Blackstone stands in a square near the U.S. Supreme Court.

To a degree, then, the framers' work on the Constitution represented an effort to revive the liberties embedded in the legal heritage of England, and much of that legacy came down intact into the founding documents. More than half a millennium before, in reaction to abuses by King John, the Magna Carta had outlawed forced and false confessions by providing that "in future no official shall place a man on trial upon his own unsupported statement, without producing credible witnesses to the truth of it." The same goal was adopted by the Fifth Amendment. The 1689 English Bill of Rights, which placed the monarchy under the rule of parliamentary law, contained a ban on "excessive bail," "excessive fines," and

* Underlined note numbers indicate that significant information beyond sourcing can be found in the corresponding notes at the end of this book.

"cruel and unusual punishments." Those exact words were carried into the Eighth Amendment a century later.

The poetry and the power of the Bill of Rights are enhanced by brevity. The Eighth Amendment demands humaneness in merely sixteen words. With a single sentence, the First Amendment chisels the keystone of a free society. The authors wrote so concisely that generations of argument have ensued over the meaning of "excessive" or "unreasonable," and every era has put its mark on the interpretations.

At one extreme, "originalists" seek to understand the framers' original intent and limit the Constitution's meaning accordingly; at the other, "activists" of both liberal and conservative persuasions see the Constitution through their personal and political lenses. More responsibly, those who might be called "purists" distill the essence of the principles and rights the framers set down, then apply them faithfully to the present.

That is the beauty of the sparse text: that it does not shackle today rigidly to yesterday, that it allows constitutional protections to broaden as consciousness evolves and values mature. Unlike the voluminous constitutions of many other countries, this one avoids most details, offering the most basic sketches of liberties. The succinct style minimizes the risk of spelling out rights and procedures so specifically that those omitted are assumed to be absent. Just the opposite is the case. As the Ninth Amendment states: "The enumeration in the Constitution, of certain rights, shall not be construed to deny or disparage others retained by the people."

For over two centuries, then, America has enjoyed and endured an intriguing fluidity within the walls of its constitutional ideals. From time to time, courts and legislatures have enlarged or curtailed the scope of liberty. On the one hand, they have come to see certain rights, such as privacy, implicitly protected even while going unmentioned in the text. On the other hand, especially during times of national stress and fear, they have narrowed and compromised rights that are explicitly delineated by the Constitution. Later, to its credit, the country has looked back on the violations with shame.

To take a measure of any society, any legal system, any institution that aspires to justice or decency or just plain efficiency, watch how self-correcting it can be. The constitutional structure promotes that virtue, facilitating an interplay of politics, morality, and jurisprudence that tends to pull the country back from its departures, at least after a while. If a minority's rights to political speech and association are curbed by a spasm of suspicion in one era, those rights can eventually find constitutional protection from the majority's tyranny in another time. The courts may rule too late for the victim of the moment, but as the law professor David Cole observes, "They often reach results which constrain in the next crisis what can be done."[4] That this can happen even while the public's anxieties flow into the halls of power sets up a curious interplay between expediency and principle, calibrated by the law and nourished in the souls of citizens.

When composed, the Bill of Rights was envisioned mainly as a barricade against the new federal entity. Only over generations, and quite recently, has most of it come to stand as a defense against governmental authority in every form. The states' own constitutions, while written in general harmony with the U.S. Constitution, were implemented inadequately, leaving the Supreme Court to invoke the federal protections step by step.

Central to this evolution was a controversial expansion of authority known as "judicial review," the power of the courts to strike down any law or governmental action deemed in violation of the Constitution. Judges routinely presided over trials and interpreted laws and regulations by applying them to actual cases. But to rule on the validity of a law itself, to overturn a statute passed by the legislature and signed by the executive, was to add a layer of judicial power unsettling to none other than Thomas Jefferson. He wrote firmly that "each of the three departments"—executive, legislative, and judicial—"has equally the right to decide for itself what is its duty under the Constitution, without any regard to what the others may have decided for themselves."[5]

His argument was rejected in the late eighteenth century by some early Supreme Court justices who claimed the power of judicial review, but the matter was not fully settled until the unanimous 1803 landmark decision in *Marbury v. Madison,* in which Chief Justice John Marshall saw "no middle ground" between the propositions "that the constitution controls any legislative act repugnant to it; or, that the legislature may alter the constitution by an ordinary act." The choice was clear: The Constitution was "a superior paramount law, unchangeable by ordinary means," and legislative acts in violation could be ruled invalid.[6]

Still, the Court trod softly. Not until the United States was well into its second century did the Bill of Rights become a true shield against the awesome police power of government—first the federal government, then gradually the state and local governments as the Supreme Court incorporated individual amendments into the umbrella of protections. This took many decades after the ratification in 1868 of the Fourteenth Amendment, which followed the Civil War and declared: "No state shall . . . abridge the privileges or immunities of citizens . . . deprive any person of life, liberty, or property, without due process of law; nor deny to any person within its jurisdiction the equal protection of the laws."[2]

Converting this promise into reality became an arduous task of litigation. Not until 1925 was the First Amendment's guarantee of free speech deemed applicable to the states,[8] and freedom of the press was applied to state laws only in 1931.[9] Not until 1936 did the Supreme Court outlaw physical force during interrogation, an implicit purpose of the Fifth Amendment.[10] Not until 1949 was the Fourth Amendment's requirement for search warrants, based on probable cause, applied to the states,[11] and not until 1964 did the states have to observe the Fifth Amendment's protection against self-incrimination.[12] No penalty existed for illegal searches by state authorities until 1961,[13] when the Supreme Court ruled that evidence thus obtained would be inadmissible in trial. Not until 1963 was the right to a lawyer, in the Sixth Amendment, guaranteed for defendants too poor to hire attorneys.[14] Coerced confessions were not effectively barred by law until 1966, when the famous Miranda warning, "You have the right to remain silent . . ." was fashioned by the Court.[15] Trial by jury was not required of the states until 1968.[16]

Such has been the gradual, belated process of self-discovery. In mining the great document for the core freedoms it contains, we have advanced and retreated and wandered. During at least five periods before September 11, 2001, the United States strayed from its principles dramatically. After the attacks on that day, we lost our bearings for the sixth time in our history.

DEVIATIONS

Americans had scarcely found their constitutional footing before they slid off course the first time, in 1798, just seven years after ratifying the Bill of Rights. The country had not yet gained comfort with its new experiment in constitutional democracy when the French Revolution of 1789, threatening a domino effect against European monarchies, triggered declarations of war on France by a coalition of states, Britain among them. Napoleon turned the tide, expanded French dominion across the continent, and was poised to cross the English Channel against England. The United States, seeking to protect its fledgling trade by sea, sought neutrality, but in vain. Hundreds of American ships were seized by both

Britain and France; Britain closed most ports of its empire to American shipping, and France did the same to neutral shipping, further declaring that any vessel carrying British-made goods would be captured.

The United States barely avoided war with Britain by signing a conciliatory peace, but a virtual war with France arose, leading to exaggerated fears of French subversion and invasion. In an atmosphere of "tumult and fear," David McCullough writes,[17] Congress passed the Alien and Sedition Acts, and President John Adams signed them into law. Under the Alien Enemies Act, whose powers remain in the U.S. Code today, citizens of a country in a declared war with the United States could be detained and deported;[18] under the Alien Friends Act, the president could seize and remove any foreign citizen, even of a friendly nation, without anything resembling due process. Many French were driven from the United States by a poisonous mood of suspicion and the threat of arrest.

The Sedition Act then made it a crime "to write, print, utter or publish . . . any false, scandalous, and malicious writing or writings against the government of the United States, or either House of Congress, or the President, with intent to defame . . . or to bring them . . . into contempt or disrepute, or to excite against . . . the hatred of the good people of the United States. . . ."[19] This was "perhaps the most grievous assault on free speech in the history of the United States," in the assessment of the constitutional scholar Geoffrey R. Stone.[20] Several influential American editors were imprisoned for acerbic criticism of President Adams. So was a Republican Congressman from Vermont, Matthew Lyon, who had voted against the act and became its first victim after skewering the Federalists in office with biting attacks that seem mild today: He accused Adams of "a continual grasp for power" and Alexander Hamilton of "screwing the hard-earnings out of the poor people's pockets." Indicted for malicious intent "to bring the President and government of the United States into contempt," he was found guilty by a jury, fined more than he could pay, and sentenced to four months in prison.[21]

The young democracy proved self-correcting. Both the Alien Friends Act and the Sedition Act expired at the end of Adams's term in 1801. By then the Sedition Act in particular had contributed to an upsurge of public resentment, which helped the Republicans drive the Federalists out of power. Everyone who had been convicted under the act was pardoned by Jefferson, the new president, who in his inaugural address enumerated the "essential principles of our Government," calling them "the creed of our political faith," and "the bright constellation which has gone before us and guided our steps through an age of revolution and reformation," He urged that "should we wander from them in moments of error or of alarm, let us hasten to retrace our steps and to regain the road which alone leads to peace, liberty, and safety."[22]

That road to liberty, which the country then followed quite faithfully until the second great departure during the Civil War, was open only to white men, of course, not to enslaved blacks, disenfranchised women, or displaced Native Americans. Those groups suffered violations too fundamental in early America to figure in the shifting index of civil liberties. When history documents the periodic trampling and restoration of constitutional rights, it speaks of the rights of white men, who—unlike the others—had rights to lose.

White men's speech was suppressed on both sides of the Civil War. Southern states outlawed abolitionist campaigning out of fear that it might stir slaves to rebel; the Confederate president, Jefferson Davis, suspended the writ of habeas corpus and declared martial law. In the North, several hundred newspapers were closed down for various periods, at least eight major papers were banned from the U.S. mail for criticizing the war policies, and some white men were seized by the Union army under martial law as suspected secessionists. A few were Northern editors who opposed the draft and the war, and advocated negotiation with the Confederacy; one was a prominent politician.[23] President Abraham Lincoln, who tolerated considerable vitriolic dissent, nonetheless suspended habeas corpus to evade due process for alleged Confederate sympathizers, thereby denying prisoners the basic right to challenge their incarceration before a neutral judge.

In the rising war, Lincoln saw "Cases of Rebellion" as the Constitution required to justify suspension. In April of 1861, when a Massachusetts regiment passing through Baltimore came under attack by Confederate partisans and rioting ensued, the city's mayor ordered bridges to the north destroyed, and Lincoln confronted the specter of the nation's capital cut off from troops and supplies. He suspended habeas, imposed martial law in Maryland, and had the army set about arresting men thought to be in league with the Confederacy, including one John Merryman, who was accused of severing telegraph wires and burning bridges.

Merryman petitioned for a writ of habeas corpus, and won his argument before Chief Justice Roger Taney. Since the framers had located the authority to suspend in Article I, which denotes the powers of the legislature, not the executive branch, Taney ruled that only Congress, not the president, could interrupt the right. And since civilian courts were operating, he added, they had jurisdiction, not the military.

In one of the earliest presidential rebuffs to the rule of law, Lincoln defied the chief justice. Soldiers at Fort McHenry, where the prisoner was jailed, blocked a U.S. marshal from entering to serve the writ on the commander, and in a sorrowful admission, Taney conceded that in the face of "a force notoriously superior" to the marshal service, "the Court has no power under the law." Unable to exercise his right to appear before a judge, Merryman fared well nonetheless, given the circumstances. He was released after several weeks and never tried, "because the government recognized that no Maryland jury would convict him," as Stone observes. Two years later, Congress resolved the constitutional clash by granting Lincoln the authority to suspend habeas corpus.[24] (A suspension was also authorized by Congress during Reconstruction, in the Ku Klux Klan Act of 1871, and was used by President Ulysses S. Grant to put down a rebellion in nine counties of South Carolina.)[25]

Again, after the war, the Supreme Court found that if civilian courts were functioning, they could not be replaced by military tribunals. It ruled unconstitutional the trial, conviction, and death sentence by a military commission in Indiana of Lambdin Milligan, a civilian who had been arrested with four others for conspiring to steal weapons and free Confederate soldiers from a P.O.W. camp. In *Ex parte Milligan*, whose relevance extends into the post-9/11 era of military commissions, the Court unanimously declared that the Constitution "is a law for rulers and people, equally in war and in peace, and covers with the shield of its protection all classes of men, at all times, and under all circumstances." The opinion was written by Justice David Davis, a close friend of Lincoln's who had managed his 1860 campaign—and this time, the executive branch obeyed the Court. Milligan was released and never subjected to civilian prosecution. He won a suit against the military for false imprisonment, with an award of five dollars.[26]

The third major departure from constitutional principles came against a groundswell of protest over the United States' entry into World War I. Leading a campaign of paranoia, President Woodrow Wilson portrayed the antiwar opposition as threatening the ability to raise an army and protect national security. He warned Congress that German spies, infiltrating American communities and government agencies, had "set criminal intrigues everywhere afoot against our national unity." He turned his intense resentment of criticism into the force of law—the first since the Sedition Act—arguing for "a firm hand of repression" against the "disloyal," who, he declared bluntly, "had sacrificed their right to civil liberties."[27]

He proposed the 1917 Espionage Act, which passed Congress and facilitated the prosecution of 2,000 activists, with German-Americans, labor union leaders, socialists, and anarchists among the most convenient targets. The government effectively barred socialist newspapers from the mail, sometimes by removing their second-class postage privileges, which raised their rates prohibitively. Then, in 1918, Congress added the Sedition Act—an echo of the 1798 version—which criminalized "any disloyal, profane, scurrilous, or abusive language about" the American form of government, the Constitution, the flag, the military, or its uniforms. The law penalized those who "by word or act oppose the cause of the United States" during wartime.[28]

More than 1,000 people were convicted under the acts, and those prosecutions that reached the Supreme Court were upheld, most of them unanimously. It was a period of acute intolerance. The suppression of speech was endorsed by the American Federation of Labor, the American Association of Universities (urging that professors be fired for anti-war statements), and the American Bar Association (which condemned attempts "to hinder and embarrass the government" as "giving aid and comfort to the enemy").[29] The scope of permissible debate narrowed on other issues as colleges came under pressure from donors, religious leaders, and government to dismiss faculty who were on the "wrong" side of Prohibition, immigration, and Darwinism. In reaction after the war, universities adopted tenure to protect faculties against intrusions into academic freedom.[30]

The victims of the time were both famous and obscure. Among the best known were Jane Addams, the founder of Hull House for the poor in Chicago, whose speaking engagements were canceled as she was vilified and threatened for her pacifism; Eugene Debs, the Socialist Party's presidential candidate and labor leader, who was jailed; and Emma Goldman, the anarchist advocate of "liberty unrestricted by man-made law," who was arrested and then deported for organizing rallies against the draft.

Among the lesser known was Thomas Aloysius "Red Tom" Hickey, a socialist in Texas who opposed U.S. involvement in the European fighting, calling instead for a "war from within" against capitalism, an economic system he colorfully labeled "a secretive, elusive, Janus-faced foe that besmirches our judiciary, corrupts our congress, debauches our legislatures, muzzles our press, mammonizes our teachers and preachers, and even seeks to degrade the electorate." As he left a post office on the afternoon of May 17, 1917, after mailing copy for his newspaper, *The Rebel*, Hickey was seized by a Texas Ranger and three gun-wielding deputies. By the time he was bailed out of an Abilene jail by his wife, over fifty small businessmen and tenant farmers had been locked up for "seditious conspiracy," writes his biographer, Peter H. Buckingham. Their crime? Their organization had narrowly approved peaceful resistance to the planned draft, a protest the government exaggerated as "an armed uprising." The criminal cases went nowhere. A jury found all but three of the businessmen and farmers not guilty, and those convicted were later pardoned.

Hickey was never prosecuted, but authorities had other ways to silence him, and strong motives for doing so. He had run afoul of the postmaster general, Albert Sidney Burleson, by reporting in *The Rebel* the eviction of thirty tenant farmers from land owned by Burleson and his brother-in-law. The farmers had been replaced with convict labor—a thinly disguised form of slavery in those years.

On the eve of the Espionage Act's passage—but six days before it became law—the U.S. Post Office employed the prospective statute to ban *The Rebel* from the mails "for publishing treasonable matter," Buckingham reports. Hickey protested that the government could not invoke a law not yet in force, but to no avail. He was hounded the rest of his life; his barn was burned down by a mob, and his county's local newspaper recommended that those who schemed against America be awarded "a nice little plot of their own, about seven feet long, three feet wide and four deep." Residents of his Texas town of Brandenburg changed its German name to Old Glory, as it is still called today, a monument to xenophobia.[31]

World War I's conclusion segued smoothly into the Red Scare of 1919–20, an ideological war with Lenin's Russia: American union organizers were branded Bolsheviks, leftist foreigners were deported, and state laws were generated to prosecute people for displaying the red flag of worker internationalism. At least 1,400 flag-flyers were arrested, and 300 received sentences of up to twenty years.[32] Some 6,000 people, mostly immigrants, were swept up as alleged anarchists in the 1919 Palmer Raids after a series of bombings was punctuated by an explosion on the porch of Attorney General A. Mitchell Palmer's home. The usual suspects were rounded up.

Looking back at this history, you have to marvel at the sense of fragility endured by those at the pinnacle of power. In practically every war, it seems, those wielding the authority of the state were gripped with a galvanizing fear, not just of the enemy abroad but of an imagined virus of resistance and subversion at home. Or they cynically mobilized the fear. Hitler's deputy Hermann Goering thought such manipulation possible in every political system. Ordinary people never want war, he told an American psychologist questioning him in 1946, after his capture. "Why would some poor slob on a farm want to risk his life in a war when the best that he can get out of it is to come back to his farm in one piece?" Goering asked. "It is the leaders of the country who determine the policy, and it is always a simple matter to drag the people along, whether it is a democracy or a fascist dictatorship or a parliament or a communist dictatorship." Even where the citizens have a voice? the psychologist asked. "Voice or no voice," Goering argued, "the people can always be brought to the bidding of the leaders. That is easy. All you have to do is tell them they are being attacked and denounce the pacifists for lack of patriotism and exposing the country to danger. It works the same way in any country."[33]

Wartime anxieties in the United States tend to focus first on non-citizens, then spill easily into the ranks of Americans who are outspoken, who have foreign names, or whose race or class makes them readily identifiable as "others." As if the country were not stable enough to withstand strident dissent or even the silent presence of people ethnically akin to the enemy, those who seem different become convenient targets. That has happened during every detour from constitutional principles.

"Safety from external danger is the most powerful director of national conduct," wrote Alexander Hamilton in *The Federalist Papers*. "Even the ardent love of liberty will, after a time, give way to its dictates." Even "nations the most attached to liberty" will resort to institutions that destroy their rights. "To be more safe, they at length become willing to run the risk of being less free."[34]

And so for the fourth time, during World War II, individual rights succumbed to national fear. There were scattered prosecutions on both the right and the left of the spectrum, using the Espionage Act of 1917 and a new measure, the Smith Act of 1940,[35] whose prohibition against advocating the overthrow of the government "by force or violence" was stretched to cover mere membership in communist or fascist organizations. (It is still on the books.) President Franklin D. Roosevelt, a civil liberties supporter in the abstract, repeatedly pressed his reluctant attorneys general to arrest his isolationist critics.

More than two dozen leaders of the Socialist Workers Party in Minneapolis were indicted for opposing entry into World War II and organizing work stoppages in the defense industry; about the same number of fascist leaders were prosecuted in the Great Sedition Trial, which ended without convictions but effectively curbed speech on the extreme right.[36] German-born Americans who expressed sympathy for Germany were stripped of their U.S. citizenship in 146 cases.[37] State laws outlawed the uniforms of the pro-Nazi German-American Bund and the employment of communists, resulting in the dismissal of about thirty New York City schoolteachers alleged to be communists. In fifteen states, Communist Party candidates were barred from the ballot.[38]

After Pearl Harbor was attacked, on December 7, 1941, Roosevelt invoked the 1798 Alien Enemies Act to designate 900,000 Japanese, Italians, and Germans as enemy aliens required to register, to stay within five miles of their homes, and to observe a nighttime curfew.[39] They could be searched without warrants and were prohibited from owning guns, cameras, and shortwave radios. Some 120,000 ethnic Japanese, about 80,000 of them American citizens, were expelled from their homes and locked up in ten camps from California to Arkansas, out of suspicion that they *might* aid Japan. They were implicated by their race and national origin alone, not by anything they had actually done. Not a single such charge was ever brought, yet the Supreme Court upheld their internment.[40]

SECRET SUPPRESSION

After the Allied victory, the Cold War against Soviet-led communism sowed fear into fertile ground. For the fifth time in its history, the United States swerved dramatically away from its protection of individual rights. It was a time of flourishing imagination, seeing in respectable political and economic criticism the specter of internal subversion. Leftists, whether communist or not, were promoting workers' rights, condemning capitalism's exploitations, and urging an agenda of public policies that triggered high-level anxiety in the political class. To those in power, being a communist was neither a benign intellectual exercise nor a legitimate political position. It was more than an embrace of Marxism's theory that the stages of history would progress inevitably from feudalism to capitalism to socialism to communism. It was "un-American," and its proponents were seen as advocates of the Soviet Union's designs on American security and independence. As David Cole has noted, the suspicions and tactics of the first Red Scare after World War I were now applied against American citizens. "The link between internal enemy—the Communist Party of the

United States—and external foreign threat—the Soviet Union—helped to collapse the distinction between foreign national and citizen."[41]

The House Un-American Activities Committee, which compiled dossiers on one million suspected communists, ruined many loyal Americans' professional lives by summoning them to testify under oath, then berating them with the question "Are you now or have you ever been a member of the Communist Party?" An affirmative answer would doom their careers, whether in Hollywood or at universities, and might expose them to prosecution; taking the Fifth Amendment's shield against self-incrimination, however, put them on blacklists that excluded them from jobs. One hundred of three hundred people who were named as communists and "fellow travelers" in 1950 were fired. Some 3,000 were interrogated publicly from 1945 to 1960. Senator Joseph McCarthy waged a crass and cunning campaign of character assassination against supposed communists in government and the army. And President Harry Truman's loyalty program permitted the FBI to collect unchallenged rumors and innuendo about millions; an estimated 6,300 employees of private firms, and 11,000 of federal, state, and local governments, were dismissed for allegations of disloyalty that they were never allowed to see or rebut.[42]

Beginning in this era of the Cold War, and stretching through the Vietnam War into the 1970s, government actions descended underground. In the previous four periods, which began around 1798, 1861, 1917, and 1941, the violations of constitutional rights had been committed mostly in the open, for the public to see and the victims to challenge. During the postwar anxiety over communist infiltration, however, federal agencies evaded the law covertly, and their targets spread exponentially beyond suspected communists to political, labor, civil rights, and antiwar organizations that dared to push against the status quo.

We know the details thanks mainly to Senator Frank Church of Idaho, who chaired a relentless investigation in 1976, collecting testimony and documents that exposed the remarkable breadth of the government's surveillance, disinformation, and dirty tricks against legitimate and constitutionally protected political activity.[43]

Not only the FBI—through its infamous Counterintelligence Program called COINTELPRO—but also the CIA, the National Security Agency (NSA), the Internal Revenue Service, and army intelligence were secretly mobilized against dissident groups and individuals. The FBI routinely requested tax files on activists, and the IRS, through its Ideological Organizations Audit Project, selected for audits and investigations about

8,000 people and 3,000 groups "of predominantly dissident or extremist nature," as the assistant commissioner for compliance told the FBI director in a 1969 memo. The targets included such grave national security threats as the American Library Association, the American Civil Liberties Union, the National Association for the Advancement of Colored People (NAACP), and the National Urban League.

From 1947 to 1975, the NSA intercepted "millions" of private telegrams going into and out of the United States, just as it has done with e-mails and phone calls since 9/11. Nearly 250,000 first-class letters were secretly opened and photographed by the CIA from 1953 to 1973, and the FBI did the same with at least 130,000 from 1940 to 1966.

In addition, using secret informants, warrantless wiretaps, hidden microphones, and clandestine break-ins of homes and offices, various agencies "swept in vast amounts of information about the personal lives, views, and associations of American citizens," the Church committee found. The CIA compiled an index of 1.5 million names; the FBI had 500,000 intelligence files in headquarters alone, with uncounted numbers in field offices; and the army put 100,000 people in its records from the mid-1960s to 1971. The army monitored protests by welfare mothers in Milwaukee, infiltrated church youth groups in Colorado, dispatched operatives to a meeting of priests on birth control, and even sent agents to a Halloween party for children in Washington, D.C., following a report that a "dissident" might be there.

All this was done for more than curiosity's sake. The FBI had a list of 26,000 suspicious Americans to be rounded up in case of a "national emergency," the Church committee discovered. Dossiers were assembled on student activists in case they someday applied for government jobs. "Groups and individuals have been harassed and disrupted because of their political views and their lifestyles," the report concluded. "Unsavory and vicious tactics have been employed—including anonymous attempts to break up marriages, disrupt meetings, ostracize persons from their professions, and provoke target groups into rivalries that might result in deaths."

The FBI sent unsigned letters to wives of Black Panthers and others alleging infidelity, a ploy that worked to destroy at least one marriage, the bureau's files showed. It sent letters to employers trying to get activists fired for their political views. It falsely identified certain members of antiwar organizations as FBI informants so that they would be expelled or isolated, a technique that succeeded in ostracizing at least one draft-resistance counselor.

The dirty tricks got very dirty indeed. Stokely Carmichael, the fiery advocate of black power, flew to Africa the day after the FBI shocked his mother by calling her with an invented report that the Black Panthers were out to kill him. Agents also tried to incite a preemptive strike against the group by telling the head of a Chicago gang that the Panthers had "a hit out for you."

Martin Luther King, Jr., was under surveillance for many years. In the strangely twisted world of federal law enforcement, he was seen as a communist sympathizer, a subversive threat. King's inspiring "I Have a Dream" address at the 1963 March on Washington may be ranked with the greatest oratory in American history, but the FBI's Domestic Intelligence Division worriedly called it a "demagogic speech" that made King "the most dangerous and effective Negro leader in the country."

The FBI campaign, termed a "war" by one official, was designed to "neutralize" King: "No holds were barred," one bureau document declared. When hidden microphones in a hotel room caught King in a compromising situation, the FBI mailed him the tape with a note that he and his aides interpreted as suggesting that the recording would be made public unless he committed suicide.

In this mental framework, facts were not allowed to get in the way of a good investigation. Nonviolent peace and civil rights activists were seen as national security threats; the women's liberation movement, Senator Adlai Stevenson, and the NAACP were categorized as dangerous enough to rate expensive surveillance. "The NAACP was investigated to determine whether it 'had connections with' the Communist Party," the Church committee stated. "The investigation lasted for over twenty-five years, although nothing was found to rebut a report during the first year of the investigation that the NAACP had a 'strong tendency' to 'steer clear of Communist activities.'"

The truth is, presidents of both parties liked seeing the information. Truman received intelligence on the inside negotiating positions of labor unions and on journalists' upcoming articles. President Dwight D. Eisenhower got reports on "purely political and social contacts with foreign officials" by Eleanor Roosevelt and Supreme Court Justice William O. Douglas, among others. The administration of John F. Kennedy ordered FBI wiretaps on "a Congressional staff member, three executive officials, a lobbyist, and a Washington law firm." His brother Attorney General Robert F. Kennedy saw the results of the King taps. President Lyndon B. Johnson got the FBI to provide intelligence on certain senators; do electronic surveillance at the 1964 Democratic Convention; and report on the staff of his opponent in the presidential campaign, Senator Barry Gold-water.

Extensive wiretapping provided President Richard Nixon with con-siderable personal and political information "unrelated to national secu-rity," according to the Church committee. At one point, the CIA asked to renew its mail-opening program, which it falsely told Nixon had been halted. Nixon said yes, then five days later reversed himself, but the program continued anyway. And then, during the 1972 presidential cam-paign, Nixon's operatives broke into the Democratic National Committee offices at the Watergate office complex to plant bugs. His cover-up led to his downfall as he resigned to avoid impeachment.

Such cavalier disdain for both presidential authority and the rule of law typified intelligence gathering for many decades, as the official who headed the FBI's intelligence division for ten years told the Church com-mittee: "Never once did I hear anybody, including myself, raise the ques-tion: 'Is this course of action which we have agreed upon lawful? Is it legal? Is it ethical or moral?' We never gave any thought to this line of reasoning, because we were just naturally pragmatic." Such pragmatism, the committee concluded, meant that intelligence officials proceeded as if governed by "a higher law," their own interpretation of the interests of national security.

As in the wake of earlier deviations, the country came back. After the Church committee's stunning report, Congress passed a series of privacy laws, including the Foreign Intelligence Surveillance Act (FISA), which imposed a modicum of judicial review on wiretapping, bugging, and other spying directed against agents of foreign powers inside the United States. An administrative wall was erected to prevent intelligence information, which was gathered under loose controls, from seeping into criminal investigations, where constitutional rights had to be observed. A clandes-tine court was established to hear secret applications for warrants—not an ideal way to check executive authority, but some oversight nonetheless.

Since September 11, 2001, even that inadequate process has been weak-ened and evaded while the United States has strayed seriously for the sixth time in its history. The American experience demonstrates how permeable the barriers of time can be in the ebb and flow of individual rights. The past is not walled off from the present; the virtues and the violations come forward.

International frontiers are also porous boundaries. They cannot seal American soil from contamination by lawless American behavior in the outside world: Some of the toxic disrespect for rights in the "war on terror" has seeped into the domestic criminal justice process. Nor can our practices on civil liberties be defined as neatly as we might think by the lines dividing political parties or types of crime, Republicans from Democrats or terrorism from narcotics.

The neoconservative Republicans who dominated the administration of George W. Bush after September 11 strayed egregiously from constitutional principles essential to democracy, a detour made ironic by their evangelical passion for spreading democracy worldwide. Yet they got plenty of cooperation from Democrats, only one of whom in the Republican-led Senate—Russ Feingold of Wisconsin—opposed the 2001 Patriot Act, which undermined the protections enacted after the Church committee's exposure of domestic spying. Even as a majority in both houses, Democrats in 2008 passed a measure legalizing much of the National Security Agency's warrantless eavesdropping, for which Bush had been so vilified when it was exposed two years earlier. The new law got the vote of Barack Obama, then a senator in the midst of a heated presidential campaign.

Civil liberties had not been protected under the Democratic president Bill Clinton, who endorsed amendments that undermined various privacy laws, for example, by circumventing normal subpoena and warrant requirements. In 1994 he signed into law an expansion of the Foreign Intelligence Surveillance Act, with its secret courts and secret warrants, to allow not only clandestine electronic surveillance but physical searches as well. Two years later, he broadened the law to apply not just to foreign intelligence but "to international terrorism." In 1995 he authorized "extraordinary renditions," secret transfers, of suspected terrorists to Egypt after they were captured by the CIA in Croatia, Albania, and possibly elsewhere.[44] He signed an immigration law in 1996 that expanded retroactively the list of relatively minor crimes for which noncitizens had to be deported, even if committed decades before. He put his pen to a 1996 antiterrorism act establishing Special Administrative Measures under which certain prisoners—not only terrorists—are so closely restricted that privileged attorney-client conversations are monitored by the government, legal documents are screened before going to defendants, and lawyers are barred from conveying their clients' statements to third parties. Clinton thereby laid the groundwork for some of the abuses that followed 9/11.

In the period that Bush labeled "the war on terror," America lived at a juncture formed by historical coincidence: a terrorist threat driven by religious militance, a right-wing administration bolstered by another brand of religious militance, a Congress controlled by the administration's party, and a national consensus dissolved by corrosive polarization. This permitted extra-constitutional policies, both secret and overt, both outside the country and within.

Obama's election in 2008 shook the kaleidoscope sharply but did not discard all pieces of the troubling pattern. His administration released documents on torture but withheld photographs of abuse in Abu Ghraib prison, transferred some terrorism suspects to criminal courts but reserved the option of indefinite detention, and continued widespread monitoring of Americans' communications. He sought legislation to force companies to give government the keys to their codes, in effect to facilitate surveillance by requiring that encrypted networking Web sites such as Skype and Facebook, and e-mail devices such as BlackBerry, be redesigned to empower the FBI and intelligence agencies to unscramble conversations and messages. His Justice Department invoked state secrecy (in one case using language identical to the Bush administration's) to block lawsuits by those who had been spied on or subjected to "extraordinary rendition."[45] In fact, Obama continued the practice of capturing suspects overseas and spiriting them to other countries, and fought their efforts to gain access to federal courts. He rejected calls to investigate the torture and surveillance programs, an investigation that could have been as self-correcting as the Church committee's work more than three decades before. Clearly, it would be a long way back from the country's sixth major detour.

CRIMINAL ACTS

As no one can forget, the morning of September 11, 2001, had a deceptively beautiful beginning, heralding one of those crystal days between late summer and early autumn. The clarity of the air provided unlimited visibility, deadly visibility. In Boston, New York, and Washington, a total of nineteen men, some carrying box cutters, passed through airport security. They boarded four passenger jetliners fully loaded with fuel, and after takeoff seized control of the cockpits. Two planes were driven at high speed, one after another, into the two looming towers of the World Trade Center in lower Manhattan, bringing the symbols of financial might down in a whirlwind of fire and debris. A third rammed the Pentagon, carving a cavernous wound in the fortress of American military power. The fourth, recaptured by passengers who had learned by cell phone about the other attacks, plunged to earth in Pennsylvania before it could reach its supposed target of the Capitol or the White House.

The hijackers were quickly identified as Muslim followers of Osama bin Laden, the militant son of a wealthy Saudi family, whose al-Qaeda movement had been training jihadists in Afghanistan to strike at the promiscuous, crusading American empire, as he saw it. His success surely surpassed his plan. In the end, he did more than destroy buildings and kill nearly 3,000 people. He traumatized the nation and provoked Americans into damaging their own moral enterprise, at least for a time.

Government officials never show fear, but they feel it, as they often confess in later memoirs and interviews. Sometimes it's for a good cause, as during Mikhail Gorbachev's liberalization of the Soviet system. "Fear" was the word that one of his closest colleagues, Politburo member Aleksandr Yakovlev, used when I asked what he had been feeling at the time. I thought he might say pride or exhilaration, but no, he had feared the unknown consequences of their uncharted path. "I am surprised I am still alive," Yakovlev declared. It got me wondering if Václav Havel felt fear as he brought Czechoslovakia out of communism, and if Nelson Mandela, beneath his inspirational assuredness, endured fear as he led South Africa from its bondage of apartheid. Perhaps if you're not at least a little scared, if you do not go to the edge of your comfort zone and beyond, you are not doing anything worthwhile.

In other circumstances, though, fear in high places can infect values, as it did following September 11. With heavy responsibility for preventing further attacks, those in powerful offices moved rapidly into a wartime mentality, with all the world a battlefield. Vice President Dick Cheney was frequently secreted in "an undisclosed location," probably Mount Weather, the underground command complex fifty miles west of Washington, to keep him apart from the president so the government could not be decapitated. Cofer Black, who headed the CIA's Counterterrorist Center, was so convinced that more was coming, possibly with black-market nuclear weapons, that "he warned a colleague not to travel to New York for the weekend," Jane Mayer reports in her book *The Dark Side*. "His wife told [a] friend that when Black came home, he would turn off the lights and just sit there in the dark with a glass of something to drink and a cigar, lost in apocalyptic gloom."[46] Systematically terrified early each morning with the scariest intelligence organized into the so-called Threat Matrix, President Bush and other top officials were "plunged into a state of controlled panic," in Mayer's words, especially after the attacks were followed by powdered anthrax mailed to a few victims. When you start every day seeing a list of dire threats to national security, it must be hard to keep your equilibrium.

The immediate targets of governmental reaction were Muslim residents of the United States, mostly those here illegally, but some legal immigrants as well. In the first seven weeks, at least 1,182 foreigners were seized on little more than hunches, rumors, and vindictive calls from estranged spouses or hostile neighbors. Their names were kept secret, and their families and lawyers had trouble finding them in scattered jails, where they were held with common criminals and abused by guards who presumed them guilty of terrorism, which none turned out to be.

Thereafter, immigration authorities gave priority to finding and deporting 6,000 Muslims among the 300,000 foreigners who had defied previous orders to leave the country. In addition, over the objection of James W. Ziglar, the commissioner of Immigration and Naturalization, the Justice Department commanded "nonimmigrant" male adult citizens of twenty-five predominantly Muslim countries to register with the immigration agency. Several thousand who dutifully appeared, but lacked legal immigration papers, were arrested before the program was dropped as ineffectual: No terrorists hastened to register.[47] Then, during the 2004 presidential election campaign, sloppy intelligence from the CIA about "priority leads" to possible plots sent federal agents scurrying to interrogate more than 2,500 foreigners, 79 percent of whom were from Muslim countries. They were peppered with astute questions about their opinions of America, the mosques they attended, and whether they had chemical or biological weapons. Some were detained, those with expired visas were deported, but none was charged with national security offenses.[48]

It got worse. The Fourth Amendment's promise of individual privacy was gravely compromised, both by the Patriot Act and by President Bush's secret order to the National Security Agency to intercept huge volumes of communications by phone and the Internet, from Americans and non-Americans alike. Ignoring the Constitution's separation of powers, Bush—driven by Cheney and his zealous counsel David Addington—authorized the sweeping surveillance without approval by the legislative branch or oversight by the judiciary.

Basing his decrees on tendentious legal reasoning in memos he tried to keep out of public scrutiny, the president signed secret executive orders authorizing commando raids, kidnappings, clandestine imprisonment, and the torture of suspected al-Qaeda members around the world. He unilaterally declared the Geneva conventions on the treatment of prisoners inapplicable to terrorism suspects, creating a lawless landscape without boundaries. The military and the CIA conducted missions in fifteen or twenty different countries, often without their governments' knowledge.[49] If the targets were not killed, they were captured, stripped, forcibly sedated with suppositories, and flown in executive jets to an American ship or secret CIA "black sites" overseas, or to a country the State Department listed as a premier human rights violator, usually Egypt, Syria, Jordan, Uzbekistan, Morocco, or Afghanistan, where questioning was not known for being gentle.[50]

In the government's Orwellian lexicon of euphemisms, this kidnapping was called "extraordinary rendition." Torture by Americans was termed "enhanced interrogation." Prisoners locked up for years without charges or definite sentences at the American naval base in Guantánamo Bay, Cuba, were "detainees," as if they had been merely delayed inconveniently for a while on their way somewhere. "Waterboarding," named as if it were some fun sport, was a medieval technique deemed acceptable in the new era. The prisoner was strapped to a board and tipped with his head down. A cloth was held over his mouth and nose, and as water was poured onto it, he gasped and gagged and in seconds descended into utter panic that he was drowning. Two years after leaving office, Bush wrote that he had personally approved waterboarding, prompting the ACLU to call for a criminal investigation into the former president.

There seemed to be no moral brakes, or legal ones, either. As Mayer tells it in *The Dark Side*, even pragmatism fell away. Despite early success in getting information with soft methods, and strong evidence from experienced interrogators that torture produces false confessions and erroneous leads, al-Qaeda suspects were crammed and folded painfully into tiny boxes, deprived of sleep for days at a time, kept naked and doused with water in the cold, humiliated sexually by female questioners, and forced to stand for up to eight hours with wrists shackled so high that if they so much as bent their knees they would hang in excruciating positions. Wearing black goggles and earplugs or kept in pitch-dark cells, they were assaulted with complete sensory deprivation—or the opposite, with blaring music and unending bright lights. Their meals were served irregularly, with varying amounts of food, to disable their sense of routine or predictability. One said he had been told that a recording he heard of a woman's scream was his wife's. Some were slapped on painful wounds.

Despite the Bush administration's go-it-alone tactics in foreign and military policy, its officials tapped the international community for torture methodology. Six of the fourteen highest-ranking al-Qaeda prisoners, including the supposed mastermind of 9/11, Khalid Sheikh Mohammed, told the International Committee of the Red Cross independently, without the opportunity to coordinate their stories, that towels wrapped around their necks had been used to smash them into walls (while preventing whiplash, one of the Justice Department memos asserted)—a technique suggested by the Israelis, according to a CIA official Mayer interviewed. The Americans adopted stress positions and other approaches that the army had been teaching soldiers to resist, because they had been used by the Russians, Chinese, North Koreans, North Vietnamese, and other despotic regimes.[51]

A few died along the way, but nobody in the CIA was prosecuted. Neither would President Obama authorize criminal investigations after he took office, nor—more significantly—support a systematic study to find the facts and propose remedies to prevent recurrences.[52] Wishing away history had bipartisan support.

Bush also arrogated to himself the power to designate anyone— whether inside the United States or not, whether citizen or not—as an "enemy combatant" eligible for indefinite imprisonment without charge or trial. Three "U.S. persons" were so classified—an American who had been captured during the war in Afghanistan, and two arrested in the United States, one a citizen, the other a legal immigrant. Two of the cases were transferred to criminal court just before the Supreme Court could step in; the third man, who won his habeas corpus appeal in the Supreme Court, was released to Saudi Arabia after he relinquished his American citizenship.

Bush tried to suspend habeas corpus for such prisoners to deny them access to federal courts. He took it upon himself, ignoring the legislative branch, to establish military tribunals to process Guantánamo "detainees" and others, dodging and weaving in and out of a series of adverse Supreme Court rulings, finally enlisting Congress in the sordid business of denying habeas rights and creating military commissions. These commissions could admit coerced confessions, hearsay evidence, and the fruits of illegal searches. The Supreme Court struck down the habeas denial and left the rest of the law in doubt—but on the books.

The Military Commissions Act of 2006 was potentially one of the most repressive statutes in American history and remains a grave legacy of the country's sixth major deviation from constitutional values. While public attention centered on how it applied to the suspected terrorists in Guantánamo, the law recognized no geographical limits, in fact; it could be used inside the boundaries of the United States as well as outside. Obama refused to call for its repeal, just its revision, which was effected in 2009 to restore significant rights to defendants. Still, if a president were to employ its full powers, America would become a very different place.

LAWYERS VERSUS THE RULE OF LAW

From 1798 on, these episodes of history had several notable characteristics. First, the abuses derived from lawmakers and laws or had the blessings of lawyers; most were not the product of some rogue vigilantism. Second, they were not the rule but the exception: aberrations against a background of liberty and justice. Finally, every one of the steps, justified at the time by threats to the nation's security, is now viewed as a disgrace. Looking back into history through the smoke from the World Trade Center and the Pentagon, to take the latest example, many Americans feared a massive roundup of Arabs and made urgent calls to avoid repeating the crime of the Japanese internment.

It remains to be seen how history will judge the violations after September 11, and how lasting the legal corruptions in constitutional protections will be. In general, George Bush based his actions on a sweeping interpretation of his constitutional powers, under Article II, as commander in chief of the military. An astonishingly small coterie of lawyers—mobilized by Cheney's Addington with the collusion of Jay S. Bybee, head of the Justice Department's powerful Office of Legal Counsel; his assistant John Yoo; and the Defense Department's general counsel, William J. Haynes II—was able to invent rationales in memos and opinions giving the president virtually unfettered authority to arrest, imprison, torture, and murder. A few other lawyers in the Justice Department, the military, and the CIA who tried to resist this juggernaut of legal aggression were ridiculed, marginalized, dismissed, or subjected to threatening investigations. They were quiet heroes who risked their careers out of public view.

One infamous legal opinion was the so-called torture memo of August 1, 2002, written mainly by Yoo and endorsed by Bybee for then White House Counsel Alberto R. Gonzales. It interpreted so narrowly the federal law enacted to implement the international Convention Against Torture that nothing illegal was found in the CIA's methods. Even that limited prohibition, they argued, would be unconstitutional if used to restrict a president in wartime. They advised that anyone prosecuted for torture could defend himself with the opening sentence of Article II of the Constitution: "The executive Power shall be vested in a President of the United States of America." In an attempt to expand Bush's latitude, the lawyers read this as a "sweeping grant" of "unenumerated 'executive power.'" They saw no limits, no checks, no balances. "In wartime," the Bush lawyers declared ominously, "it is for the President alone to decide what methods to use to best prevail against the enemy. . . . One of the core functions of the Commander in Chief is that of capturing, detaining, and interrogating members of the enemy."[53]

In another official opinion, Yoo and a colleague determined that the Constitution permits the president "to deploy the military against international or foreign terrorists operating within the United States," superseding law enforcement agencies. On that basis, Cheney proposed (and Bush rejected) using the military to arrest a group of suspected terrorists in upstate New York. "The Fourth Amendment would *not* apply in these circumstances," Yoo's finding declared. "Thus, for example, we do not think that a military commander carrying out a raid on a terrorist cell would be required to demonstrate probable cause or to obtain a warrant."[54]

Under these authoritative interpretations, practically everything that a Soviet leader in the 1970s had ordered the KGB to do in the name of "national security" would have been legal under the United States Constitution.

The American system is structured to restrict and restrain. Yet the small group of lawyers who wielded momentous power to overcome those restrictions and restraints came from the mainstream legal establishment, remained there, and even advanced within it. Addington had gone to law school at Duke and worked in the CIA's general counsel's office; Bybee, from Brigham Young, was nominated by Bush and confirmed by the Senate to a lifetime appointment as a federal appeals court judge (before his torture memo was publicized); Haynes, a graduate of Harvard Law, was nominated four times by Bush to the federal bench but was blocked by Democratic senators; and Yoo, who had graduated summa cum laude from Harvard and then from Yale Law School, had clerked for Supreme Court Justice Clarence Thomas. After leaving the Justice Department following his permissive memos on torture, Yoo returned to teach constitutional law at Berkeley, where he survived demands for his ouster. The Obama Justice Department refused to recommend his or Bybee's disbarment.[55]

It is not the lawyers or the law that protects us, then, but rather the "rule of law," a habit derived from the most intricate impulses of political culture and history, enforced by the mechanisms of adjudicating disputes and dividing power, and driven by the incessant idealism of the nation. Countries that lack those attributes can use laws and courts and constitutions of convenience to imprison political opponents and persecute religious and ethnic minorities. That is not the rule of law but "the terror of law," as former president Emil Constantinescu of Romania labeled it.[56]

The military governments of Brazil and Uruguay duly brought to court prisoners who gave graphic testimony on how false confessions had been extracted by torture—and the courts sentenced them on the basis of their confessions. Every element of the U.S. Bill of Rights had its counterpart in the constitution of the communist Soviet Union, where no element of the Bill of Rights existed in practice. My favorite was Article 56: "The private life of the citizen, the secrecy of letters, telephone conversations, and telegraph communications are protected by law." I once heard that a dissident who cited his rights under the Soviet constitution during a KGB interrogation was interrupted by the agent, who said with a patronizing smirk, "Please. We're having a serious conversation."

The rule of law is less easy to define than it might seem, but the World Justice Project, organized by the American Bar Association, has identified four "universal principles" applicable across an array of political and social structures: First, officials don't make up rules as they go along to suit the purpose of the day; they and the government are account-able under the law. Second, the laws are not obscure or ambiguous, and they don't change from moment to moment; they are "clear, publicized, stable, and fair," and protect personal and property rights. Third, laws are enacted and enforced in a transparent, accessible process. Fourth, "ethi-cal" police, lawyers, and judges exist in "sufficient number," are indepen-dent, and "reflect the makeup of the communities they serve."[57]

Clarity and stability are fostered by the courts' reliance on precedent, known in legal parlance by the Latin phrase *stare decisis* ("let the decision stand"), in which judges look to established principles in previous rulings to guide them in current cases. The most assiduous judges observe prec-edent even when they disagree, applying the law as handed down over generations. This can be frustrating for them, but it provides predictabil-ity and encourages consistency. It doesn't necessarily produce stagnation. While no reputable opinion fails to cite precedent extensively, the "case law," as it's called, is varied enough to offer openings for reinterpretation and incremental change. One slight shift leads to another and another until the earlier precedent dims. The Supreme Court has the authority to overturn precedent dramatically, albeit often with fancy legal footwork that seems to honor what has gone before.

The United States has wandered outside the rule of law during its six departures from constitutional principles, but not only then. Denying women the vote made the process of enacting laws inaccessible to them. De jure segregation hobbled an entire people in the South by using the law oppressively, without respecting the rule of law. Today, under the law but not the rule of law, immigrants are routinely jailed without due process, the poor are often imprisoned without effective lawyers, and all of us are subject to search without probable cause. The Bill of Rights labors under burdens more lasting than the war on terror, whose violations of rights are nothing new, only new variations of old problems faced by the republic throughout its history.

TAKING CHANCES

Freedom demands a certain risk. We risk the open spread of racial hatred by protecting free speech. We risk the release of a murderer by presuming innocence and by protecting his rights to the privacy of his home, to silence during interrogation, to counsel, to confront witnesses against him. We risk terrorism (if we are willing) by restricting the police power of the state to search, to interrogate, to jail without sufficient evidence or proper trial. It is the police state, not the open society, that strives to abolish risk. We do not want massive wiretapping and sweeping home invasions, confessions obtained by torture, secret testimony, and kangaroo courts—or do we?

Our system is founded on the premise that it is far worse to convict wrongly than to fail to convict at all, that imprisoning the innocent is more heinous than freeing the guilty. And while that ideal is not always met—innocents populate death row and other wings of American prisons—the model stands as a benchmark for measuring performance. It confronts us with a biting question: How much risk are we willing to absorb to preserve liberty?

Waves of common crime tend to generate surges against individual rights. Drug trafficking has thinned the Fourth Amendment's shield against police searches. Organized crime has sharpened the little-known tool of asset forfeiture, in which the punishment precedes the proof as police empty bank accounts and seize property before a trial.

But is terrorism a crime or an act of war? As in periods of wartime, tolerance for risk plummeted after September 11. "Don't let this happen again," President Bush instructed his attorney general, John Ashcroft, and with that command, the massive apparatus of government gathered momentum and swerved onto an uncharted course. Instead of waiting and trying to solve a crime after it is committed—which has been difficult enough for the police and the courts—the new strategy aims to solve the crime of terrorism before it occurs.

That requires predictions, and predicting who might be plotting attacks has taken intelligence and law enforcement into a netherworld of guesswork and nefarious techniques, not just abroad but inside the borders of the United States: ethnic and religious stereotyping, guilt by association, warrantless surveillance, shady informants, secret arrests, entrapment, deportation, and prosecution at such an early stage of an alleged conspiracy that many of those arrested have possessed no weapons, laid no detailed plans, and progressed no further than idle bragging and brainstorming in what they thought were private conversations. True, it's better to nab "bad guys" while they're still talking, before they start shooting—but are the guys you're nabbing really bad? Several juries have been unconvinced, given the prosecution's scant evidence.

Prevention is demanded because terrorism imposes a sensation of risk more pervasive than most common crime. The impression of vulnerability spreads and lingers far beyond the place and time of the murders. The three planes flown into the World Trade Center and the Pentagon on 9/11 killed nearly 3,000 but terrified millions; a suicide bomber in Israel or Pakistan kills dozens but galvanizes a nation, and in Iraq or India sends a shiver of alarm through an entire religious sect. In sheer numbers, terrorism's casualties are relatively minor. "About the same number of children worldwide die of preventable causes every twelve hours as people die in acts of terrorism in an entire year," writes David Rothkopf. "The same number of people around the world die of HIV/AIDS every three days as die of terrorism annually."[58] In the United States, where nearly 43,000 a year die in traffic accidents and 5,000 from food-borne illnesses, 14 of the 14,000 murdered in 2009 were killed in two attacks that might loosely be considered terrorism—13 by an army psychiatrist at Fort Hood, Texas, and one at a recruiting station in Arkansas.[59]

Fear is not a mathematical calculation, however. It is more like an illness, infiltrated into emotions with techniques carefully crafted. First, terrorism mixes politics with violence by making bloodshed the instrument of a larger purpose: a political goal, a religious dispute, a cause of revenge. So it is driven not by deranged individuals who can be dismissed as aberrations, as a disturbed school shooter might be. It is the tool of a movement—a quality that can turn citizen against citizen by sowing suspicion toward certain attitudes and beliefs, as during the communist witch hunts of the 1950s. The Muslim who prays in an airport, the professor who rails against Israel, the imam who preaches fundamentalism, are all subjects of unwelcome scrutiny.

Second, terrorism turns the common artifacts of everyday life into weapons: a passenger jet becomes a high-speed missile, an automobile becomes a bomb, a shopper in a crowded market becomes a suicidal explosion. Third, it is ugly and dramatic, devoid of rules and boundaries, willing to rain havoc on a Passover Seder, a wedding, or a Shiite mosque on a holy day. It recognizes no taboos. It can seem ubiquitous by disguising itself to penetrate any zone of safety.

Therefore, it plays into the imagination differently from ordinary street crime. You may think you can avoid getting mugged or murdered by avoiding certain parks at night and some neighborhoods at any time. But persistent terrorism steals that sense of choice. You may create the illusion of control with little tricks, as in Israel during bus bombings in 2001, when some drivers stayed as far from buses as possible. You may reach for power with vigilantism, as after 9/11, when a few Americans attacked turban-wearing Sikhs who were mistaken for Arabs. But you cannot entirely fill the hollow sense of helplessness.

Applying the preventive model to terrorism, then, may reduce the sensation of immediate risk for the public at large. But it increases danger in other forms. It is seductive: If terrorism is so serious as to justify prevention, why not school shootings? Why not drug smuggling? Why not the sexual abuse of children? If certain rights can be waived to head off terrorism, why not other crimes? Once shortcuts are approved to investigate one kind of offense, they gain acceptability for others. Precisely that argument was adopted by the Foreign Intelligence Surveillance Court of Review, which justified the Patriot Act's permissive monitoring by noting that exceptional circumstances already permit random or wholesale searches in school drug testing, drunken driver checkpoints, and border security inspections. These are all encroachments on the Fourth Amendment's protections. They are all on a continuum.

Prevention can replace one risk with another. For targeted groups, it raises the risk of arbitrary search and arrest. It undermines the rules and rights of criminal procedure, which are designed to protect not only individual liberty but the fact-finding exercise of gathering evidence and testing it in a fair trial. Without the adversarial justice system pushing the police toward careful investigation, mistakes are more likely, and the threat to society is obvious: If an innocent man is arrested for murder, the real killer remains on the loose.

So the notion that we must give up some liberty for more security, that somehow our safety and our freedom are juxtaposed in a zero-sum game, looks like a false premise. Only after the Soviet Union collapsed, for example, and courts gained a modicum of independence, did Russia's police have to learn the basics of investigating a crime, compiling evidence, and proving a case. They had little idea how to do it, because "telephone justice" had been dispensed by calls from Communist Party officials instructing judges on how to rule. There was no jury system—just a judge and two party apparatchiks, called lay assessors, who usually found defendants guilty.

Crime will not be investigated thoroughly unless it has to be. That is the truth across all political systems, from dictatorships to democracies. If evidence cannot be challenged, cops will not check out and nail down the facts. If no right to remain silent is enforced, they will use coercion and base their prosecutions on confessions that may be false. Only a hard, demanding system separating powers and requiring proof can overcome that human impulse to take shortcuts. And if it's not in place, if the wrong people are locked up, the society is hardly safer.

But the Soviet Union *felt* safe, because the absence of free speech kept real dangers out of sight, festering below the calm surface of censorship. When I lived in Moscow during communism, Russians' sense of risk was artificially low. Street crime was kept secret. Police didn't report it publicly, newspapers didn't cover it, and statistics were classified. "If we wrote about crime in Moscow every day," a columnist for the government paper *Izvestia* told me in the late 1970s, "there would be as much fear as there is in New York." Without that fear, Muscovites wandered naïvely at night into high-crime areas where they were sometimes mugged or raped.

Perceived risk and actual risk, then, do not always coincide; one is obvious, the other can be hidden. Just as the freedom to speak openly risks the spread of racial hatred, for example, its suppression only drives bigotry underground, preventing it from being turned out into the sunlight, examined, and possibly cured. Healing does not occur in dark places, and Soviet society did not eliminate racial and ethnic tension by banning the subject of bigotry from public speech. Undiscussed and largely out of sight, it stayed virulent enough to contribute to the Soviet Union's 1991 breakup along ethnic lines into fifteen separate countries.

This is the paradox of fear. The risks required by liberty are far preferable to what Alexander Hamilton called "the risk of being less free."

The jarring violations of constitutional principles that have earned the public's attention during this time of terrorism are hardly unique in the American experience. They are extreme versions of those routinely suffered by people arrested for ordinary crime. Those everyday infringements, less dramatic yet dangerous, slowly erode individual rights by working gradually into precedent and practice. The infringements are similar, the specific cases located at different points along the same spectrum.

- While Internet and telephone users have seen their Fourth Amendment shield against warrantless searches chipped away to catch terrorists, for example, so have motorists and pedestrians, to catch gun-toting drug dealers.
- While captives held at Guantánamo Bay and the navy brig in Charleston were initially denied lawyers, so are foreigners who are jailed on administrative immigration charges and cannot afford attorneys. Impoverished Americans charged with crimes get lawyers hired by the government, but in states without well-funded public-defender systems, the attorneys are underpaid, overworked, and often inadequate.
- While terrorism suspects rarely get trials, neither do most ordinary criminal defendants.[60] The Bush administration sought to hold hundreds of prisoners indefinitely at Guantánamo without trial, Obama has continued the practice of unending detention, and prosecutors in the United States seek to avoid trials of criminal defendants as well, pressing them for guilty pleas by invoking tougher laws and sentencing guidelines to threaten long imprisonment if they're convicted in court. They have a choice, at least, but the playing field is tilted so severely that nearly all forfeit their right to trial and take the pleas.
- The separation of powers has been undermined both in counterterrorism, where presidential authority has been enhanced at the expense of the legislative and judicial branches, and in the criminal justice system, where prosecutors' immense clout represents a shift toward the executive branch.
- Preventive detention, an inviting antiterrorism tool, has also been practiced in the criminal justice system, although not under that name. Many defendants accused of dangerous crimes are held for long periods before they are proved guilty; they are denied bail, unable to raise bail, or subjected to the delays of overloaded courts.
- Finally, torturing terrorism suspects for information stands at the most severe end of a scale of coercion. In a more moderate place on the spectrum, police periodically evade the Fifth Amendment's protection against forced self-incrimination. Notwithstanding the Miranda warning, people in custody are sometimes tricked and hounded into confessing to crimes they did not commit.

Opposite ends of the spectrum are not the same just because they occupy the same spectrum, of course. The difference between torture and trickery is obvious. To think otherwise is to make the argument of the beard: the fallacy that since one cannot say how many hairs a man must grow before they add up to a beard, there is no real distinction between the bearded and the clean-shaven.

There are distinctions. Yet the continuum of violations represents a gradation of risk to the constitutional enterprise. Even in nonterrorism cases, those who are poor, members of a minority group, foreign-born, or unable to negotiate through the labyrinth of the law are especially vulnerable to being profiled by ethnicity, searched illegally, denied effective lawyers, maneuvered into dubious confessions, blocked from adequately challenging prosecution witnesses, and unable to gather sufficient evidence in their defense. Their rights are damaged less spectacularly than in counterterrorism cases, but damaged they are. Therefore, so are everyone's.

How far America will stray from its freedoms in confronting both terrorism and common crime is not yet known. How deeply it will invade liberties in search of safety is not resolved. In the past, the country has regained its footing after a time, and even now, amid the threat, those who would enhance the power of the state are meeting the force of those who would defend the rights of the people. Such is the unending struggle of a nation built not on territory or religion or ethnicity, as so many other nations are, but on an idea that requires constant tending.

CHAPTER TWO

Another Country

I don't think that there's much left of the Fourth Amendment in criminal law.

—Federal District Judge Paul L. Friedman

There is no Fourth Amendment for most of our clients.

—Tony Axam, assistant federal public defender, Washington, D.C.

FRISKING PEDESTRIANS

DEEP IN THE NIGHT, no more than a mile or two from the Supreme Court, a wiry police sergeant named G. G. Neill went hunting. He wedged a 12-gauge shotgun between the front seats of his patrol car, cradled a handheld radio on his knee, and watched closely for telltale reactions by black men as his driver cruised through their impoverished neighborhood.

He and his squad traveled openly, not undercover. They wore uniforms and drove marked police cars, trying to trigger behavior that Neill could read. He was looking for guns, and he knew that men concealing guns often betrayed themselves when they saw cops sweep into view.

It was early June, the air was cool and seductive, and the pleasant weather had lured people from their decaying apartments into the darkened streets. As Neill's car slowed down on a somber block, two young men began to walk away—a simple act and a sign of guilt, he believed. He said a few words into his radio and got out. Three other patrol cars materialized, and six other officers, "jump-outs" in police slang, spilled onto the street.

The pair of men looked younger now, like scared boys in their late teens. Neill strode in their direction and wished them good evening.

What happened next was a portrait of the Constitution's standing in the hidden corners of society—less than a five-minute drive from where the Supreme Court justices sat, but so far from their world of sterile legal briefs and abstract oral arguments that it might have been another country.

In a string of cases beginning with *Terry v. Ohio* in 1968,[1] the Court had been sketching blurry lines defining how far police could go before hitting the limit of "unreasonable searches and seizures" barred by the Fourth Amendment. For fast-moving encounters that were often confusing and dangerous, the justices had loosened the amendment's strict requirement that police have "probable cause" to justify a search, finding instead that if "reasonable grounds" or "reasonable suspicion"[2] existed to believe that someone was armed, officers without a warrant could, on their own authority, stop and frisk him on the street. This was justified on safety grounds, for the cops' own protection.

In so doing, the Court interpreted the Fourth Amendment as if it were not a single sentence but rather two separate parts: the clause requiring probable cause for a warrant, and the clause barring unreasonable searches. If a search was once "unreasonable" unless the police could show "probable cause," that was no longer the case. *Terry* disconnected the two, setting in motion an accelerating redefinition of "unreasonable" to fit the crime-fighting purposes of the day.

To a couple of young men standing on a sidewalk, the difference between "probable cause" and "reasonable suspicion" may seem slight, but it has moved the bulwark that protects the citizen's right to be free of the state's prying eyes. The Court has defined "reasonable suspicion" as stronger than a hunch but a good deal weaker than the "probable cause" demanded by the authors of the Constitution.[3] Probable cause requires a preponderance of evidence, "a fair probability that contraband or evidence of a crime will be found," the justices ruled in 1983.[4] By contrast, reasonable suspicion requires only "some minimal level of objective justification for making a stop," the Court stated in 1989,[5] and the "minimal level" has become an expanding loophole allowing Sergeant Neill and other law enforcement officers to look in the pockets, cars, and purses of people on the margins of society.

Patting down nonwhites on the streets is the crude, intimate version of a wide enhancement of police power, a broad intrusion on personal privacy that has grown technologically sophisticated as government has probed computerized medical records, e-mail messages, credit-card transactions, financial transfers, and other digital information. Whether the search is an antiseptic invasion by electronic gadgets or a midnight frisk by groping hands, the individual in America is losing a precious ingredient of a free life, especially in the twilight wars against terrorism and in the deep night of mean neighborhoods. Those are the places, most distant from those who make the rules, where the limits on police action grow less and less visible.

When *Terry* was decided, the lone dissenter on the Court, Justice William O. Douglas, worried about an oppressive result. "The term 'probable cause' rings a bell of certainty that is not sounded by phrases such as 'reasonable suspicion,'" he warned. "If the individual is no longer to be sovereign, if the police can pick him up whenever they do not like the cut of his jib, if they can 'seize' and 'search' him in their discretion, we enter a new regime."

Terry's looser standards applied only to a stop and frisk, not to the search of a house. So, a policeman acting on mere "reasonable suspicion" could now pat down a pedestrian with less evidence than the stricter "probable cause" that was still required for a judge to sign a search warrant. This struck Douglas as a chilling irony. "To give the police greater power than a magistrate is to take a long step down the totalitarian path," he declared. "Perhaps such a step is desirable to cope with modern forms of lawlessness. But if it is taken, it should be the deliberate choice of the people through a constitutional amendment."

No such amendment has been needed in the gritty life of the streets. So common have warrantless searches become in the neighborhoods worked by Neill that when the "jump-outs" arrive, certain blocks and courtyards are suddenly torn away from the fabric of American liberties and hurled into scattered moments of "a new regime."

Neill had nothing close to probable cause when he saw the two young men walking away, but he felt reasonable suspicion that they had something to hide. They were doing exactly what he had described during a class I had watched him teach at the police academy three weeks earlier, so he flashed me a foxy grin. "Just like training," he said.

In the training, Neill and two detectives had shown videos and played roles to teach nineteen experienced officers how to spot clues that someone might be carrying a weapon. Race, an undercurrent, went unmentioned, although Neill was white, one of the two detectives was white, most members of the class were white, and their targets were generally black. On the street, though, race seems less of a divide than the line between officer and civilian: Black cops are perfectly capable of hassling black citizens.

"A good policeman is what?" Neill began.

"Nosy," said one of the two black women in the group.

"A good policeman is nosy," Neill declared, making it sound like a motto that should be posted over the door of every precinct.

"Anybody here ever chased a person with a gun?" asked one of the detectives, Curt Sloan. Nearly all raised their hands. "What's the first thing they do?" Grab it, several said. Yes, Sloan noted: Even police officers unconsciously touch their guns a hundred times a day, although those guns are safe in holsters. Someone with a pistol tucked in his waistband is going to touch it much more often, adjust it, make sure it's secure and accessible. Watch the hands. Figure out which is the dominant side: Wristwatches are usually worn on the weak side; a right-handed person usually smokes a cigarette with the right hand and begins walking by pushing off with his right foot, leading with his left. Over 90 percent of people are right-handed, so the right hand will touch the waistband.

When the gunman walks, the instructors explained, his gun hand doesn't swing as far from his weapon as his other hand, and the asymmetry increases with the speed of his gait, until, running, he's holding on to the gun in the waistband. If he suddenly begins to run normally, both arms pumping identically, he's probably thrown down the gun. Look near the place where his running becomes symmetrical.

"Crap games offer an excellent opportunity to spot individuals who are carrying firearms," said a handout distributed to the class. "Because the participants bend over during the game, and stand after each roll of the dice, a loosely worn firearm will have a tendency to move. These subjects will be constantly attempting to turn from view to make the adjustment, and will also tend to pull their pants up constantly."[6]

Clothing can be a good tip-off, Neill and the others explained. A jacket with a gun in a pocket hangs in a lopsided way, the wrinkles and folds askew, the empty side's fabric clinging to the front of the pants. The side holding the firearm hangs away from the trousers and swings like a pendulum when the gunman walks. A bag with a gun may tilt markedly in one direction.

Look for clothing that seems designed to conceal a weapon, the class was told: a tailored shirt that's not tucked in, a baggy coat too warm for the weather, a loose windbreaker over unmatching garments such as suit pants and tie, a belt around pants with no belt loops. Someone who wears only one glove may be keeping his gun hand bare for quick action.

And watch the reactions when you arrive on a scene, Neill said. The guys standing on a corner may all turn to look at the guy with a gun, who may walk away or run. The gunman may turn one side away, if there's a protrusion where he's stuck the firearm. He may hold his girlfriend tightly against his weapon—Sloan happily demonstrated with a female officer—or lean on that side against his vehicle, or turn his gun side away during a pat-down.

With that technique, Neill told me later, he saved his life in Iraq, where he spent a year as a first sergeant in an army reserve intelligence unit. A report that someone had thrown a grenade led American soldiers and Iraqi policemen to search the house of a man who struck Neill as uncommonly bold as he walked past four infantrymen. Neill stepped toward him. The man turned a side away and put a hand on his pocket. "I thought it was a grenade," Neill said, "and I grabbed it, and as his hand was goin' to grab it, my hand got underneath his hand, and I felt the grenade in his pocket, pushed him up against the wall, and the last guy in the infantry squad helped me secure him, and we got a couple of more grenades out of his house, some AK-47s and some currency, some powder to make the grenades hotter, some BBs to fill it up with more pellets. So in that instance the police work came in good." He won a bronze star.

In other ways, too, he transported tactics from Washington to Baghdad. "I was teaching the same thing to the guys who were teaching the soldiers, and also to my soldiers," he said. "When you ride up the street, look for the guys outside to be moving. . . . Look for people to react to you, look for cars that try to cut into your convoys. And most importantly, look for those guys [who] start movin' to the cars when you pull up—somethin's goin' on. They start runnin' out of there when somethin' pulls up, better start hittin' the brakes, buddy, cause somethin's gettin' ready to happen."

In Washington, the class of police officers was told to make sure the pat-down was thorough. A black instructor, Detective Ali Ramadhan, assumed the frisk position with his back to the class and his hands on the chalkboard. "Check his hands. Take them off the wall. One guy had a derringer in his palm," he said. "I could have been killed."

"In every cellblock in this city," Sloan warned, "there's been a gun making it to the cellblock. A derringer was found in the shoe of a guy in the cellblock." An officer in the class told of a new model that folds, looks like a cell phone or a pager, and can fire four .22 rounds. Others had heard about it.

The crotch is a favorite hiding place, Sloan told them. "Put your fingers between the belt and the waistband. He may say, 'I'm sensitive down there.' Well, aren't we all. Or, 'I have a colostomy bag.' Well, don't we all. 'I just had surgery.' Don't let him bullshit you. You continue, no matter how much he runs his mouth. Do a good search."

Under *Terry*, a frisk is supposed to be brief and superficial, restricted to feeling outer garments based on the suspicion that there's a dangerous weapon, not drugs or other criminal evidence. That led one young, well-spoken uniformed cop in the class to wear a puzzled look as he listened to story after story about doing pat-downs. "How is it you patted him down?" he finally asked.

"For his safety and my safety," said Ramadhan, using the standard justification.

The young cop declared: "Under *Terry v. Ohio* you have to have articulated suspicion."

"I know he's a drug dealer," Ramadhan replied. "I know he's got a gun. I pat everybody down."

"I'm not saying we don't, and we all do," the cop confessed. "But legally we can't."

"If I'm in [mostly white] Georgetown and the guy's in a business suit," Ramadhan noted, "I'm not gonna pat him down." It was an unusual admission to profiling. Later, I asked him if he really frisked everybody he encountered in the rough neighborhoods. No, he said, only when "something in the back of my head says danger."

Neill had another take on this. "Making a stop of cars in these neighborhoods, you'll more than likely get a gun," he told the class. It was a wild exaggeration, based on what I saw in my nights with his unit. "I ask them if they got drugs or guns in the car. What do they always say? 'No.' Then I say, 'Can I search your car?' Ninety-nine point nine percent of the time they say, 'Yes.' When they say, 'No,' I got to decide whether to search them anyway."

"Do you savagely search?" an officer asked.

"We savagely search," Neill replied.

In effect, the Court has given permission for this, as summed up by the Metropolitan Police Department's handout for the class: "For too long police officers have been trained to view the Constitution of the United States and its judicial interpretations as placing rigid restrictions on what law enforcement personnel can do on the street while shielding criminals from detection. . . . The members of the . . . Gun Recovery Unit have viewed the Constitution and its associated case law as a law enforcement sword rather than a shield. It is a sword because it provides police officers with a lesser standard than probable cause, i.e. 'reasonable suspicion' to better enable them to identify individuals who carry illegal firearms."

. . .

I came away thinking that the *Terry* stop was morphing from merely protective into investigative. A federal narcotics prosecutor confirmed my hunch: "We've gotten now to the point where we can stop if we think they've got drugs only. It's not necessary to have guns. Now it's not reasonable suspicion that they've got something dangerous, but just reasonable suspicion."

This position is adopted by some conservative judges, true judicial activists, such as Brett M. Kavanaugh and David B. Sentelle of the United States Court of Appeals for the D.C. Circuit, who misstated *Terry* in a 2007 gun and search case as a way of giving police more latitude. After a pedestrian had reported being robbed by an armed man wearing a blue fleece, officers stopped a differently dressed man walking nearby, took him to the scene, and unzipped his outer jacket so the victim could see what he was wearing underneath. He was not identified as the robber, but an officer felt a hard object as he opened the jacket, and a further pat-down revealed a gun.

Unzipping the jacket just to see the color of his shirt was upheld by the judges as legitimately investigative, a reading of *Terry* that reached beyond its original rationale. The police had neither reasonable suspicion that he was armed nor probable cause to believe that he was the robber, yet to bolster their argument, the judges distorted the meaning of a 1985 Supreme Court opinion, reading into an ambiguous sentence an expansion of *Terry* that the Court had neither rejected nor accepted. On appeal, they were slapped down by the full federal Court of Appeals in D.C., seven to four.[7]

Rarely are judges so intellectually dishonest. Many more look scrupulously to precedent. Yet however precise their opinions try to be, in the real life of the street the *Terry* stop has gradually spread beyond its initial concept. Legally, officers still have to suspect someone of carrying a weapon to justify the search, but if the frisk turns up drugs instead of a gun, the drugs can be used as evidence provided the judge believes that the police followed certain rules.

The key to expanding the scope of *Terry* frisks is the "plain-view" concept, devised in 1969 by the liberal Court of Chief Justice Earl Warren to end the common police practice of searching entire homes and offices when an arrest was made. In *Chimel v. California*, the Court overturned precedent and ruled that only criminal evidence "in plain view" could be seized without a search warrant.[8]

Then, in 1993, the conservative Court of Chief Justice William H. Rehnquist stretched "plain view" into "plain feel." As long as reasonable suspicion of danger exists to permit a stop and frisk to check for weapons, the justices held in *Minnesota v. Dickerson,* an officer who finds no gun but feels something that he immediately recognizes as drugs can seize them as if they were in plain view. The Minnesota Supreme Court had refused to allow the expansion, noting that a search using "the sense of touch is far more intrusive into the personal privacy that is at the core of the Fourth Amendment." But the U.S. Supreme Court accepted the corollary. "We think that this [plain-view] doctrine has an obvious application by analogy to cases in which an officer discovers contraband through the sense of touch during an otherwise lawful search," wrote Justice Byron R. White.[2]

It was an unusual opinion, because even as the Court established the principle, it suppressed the evidence and overturned the guilty verdict against Timothy Dickerson, who had been spotted leaving a crack house by two Minneapolis police officers. When he saw their squad car, he quickly turned away into an alley, so they stopped him and patted him down. An officer found no weapon but felt a small lump. So far, so good, the Court decided. Then, however, because the policeman wasn't sure what the lump was, he squeezed it and slid it around until he could tell it was crack cocaine; it turned out to be a plastic bag containing one-fifth of an ounce. If he had been able to identify the object immediately, the justices ruled, the evidence would have been admissible as plainly felt during a pat-down for a weapon. But his further manipulation, after he knew there was no gun, took the search beyond the bounds allowed in a *Terry* stop. Under the resulting opinion, "nonthreatening contraband," if detected instantly by touch or smell during a *Terry* stop, can be introduced at trial. This has made it easy for the police to look for drugs by inventing a suspicion about guns and then displaying remarkable tactile ability. In such cases, the skeptical judge is a rare breed.

In the decades since *Terry,* the Court has also made it easier to justify the suspicion needed for a warrantless stop. The *Terry* case arose after a veteran officer in Cleveland observed two men strolling back and forth individually, peering into store windows, then coming together for brief conversation, and peering again, then being joined by a third for more consultation. The officer knew the neighborhood, did not recognize the men, watched them case the stores for ten to twelve minutes, and finally approached them to ask their names. When they "mumbled something," the policeman thought they might be armed, so he grabbed Terry first, patted him down, felt a gun, and then found a pistol on one of the others as well. State courts and the Supreme Court judged the frisks legal.

By 2000, a divided Court was endorsing frisks with minimal cause. In *Illinois v. Wardlow,* the justices split five to four in ruling that police could chase, seize, and search a man who did nothing more than run from them in a drug-trafficking area of Chicago.[10] He was carrying a white plastic bag, which turned out to contain a .38-caliber handgun that he sought to have excluded as evidence. The bare majority held that his flight, plus the high-crime location, added up to a "totality of the circumstances"[11] creating "reasonable suspicion" justifying the search.

Wardlow's running man was close but not identical to the situation that Sergeant Neill faced when he saw those two teenagers walking away. The boys were walking, not running, and they weren't carrying a bag. But they were in a high-crime neighborhood afflicted by drugs and guns, which was where Neill's gun unit operated. The squad, carrying the macho nickname Power Shift because of the intense, perilous time of night it worked, never entered the affluent, largely white areas of Georgetown or Northwest D.C. It concentrated on Southeast and other sections where most residents were black and poor.

Under *Wardlow,* the rules here were different from those in wealthier, whiter parts of town; the Court had included this sort of neighborhood in the "totality of the circumstances," and so had legalized a brand of profiling, ostensibly one based on geography and crime rates but producing targets by race and class. Yes, Neill conceded, there were probably plenty of illegal guns in Georgetown, but with a difference: The rich folks there weren't using them to murder each other.

Neill greeted the boys politely: "Good evening, gentlemen." Against the intimidation of four squad cars and seven cops, his courtesy struck an odd counterpoint. It was his practiced method, his seasoned play at finding a quick rapport within the sudden tension of a confrontation. It was designed to induce "subjects" to consent to the search, thereby waiving their Fourth Amendment rights and avoiding a constitutional test. And most of the time, it worked.

The teenagers were obviously no strangers to this kind of police muscle, and they seemed no more eager than Neill to step up to the line between their rights and his. Anyone who had read the Supreme Court decisions and followed the intricate arguments between defendants and the police might have thought that battalions of idealistic citizens were out fighting for their rights. Anyone with that view of America would have been stunned by what these hastily departing young men did next.

After Neill said, "Good evening, gentlemen," they stopped. They raised their hands. Then they pulled up their T-shirts to show that no guns were tucked in their waistbands.

It was the last gesture that was most striking. Nobody had ordered them to lift their shirts. They did so as routinely as airline passengers remove their shoes. The decades of litigation through the courts had loosened the legal leash on officers until all the articulate calibrations of personal rights and police powers now vanished in a swirl and a rush. Even if these young men had studied the case law, they could not have been sure that they had provoked "reasonable suspicion," and the Supreme Court justices nearby would surely have disagreed among themselves on whether Neill could constitutionally have stopped and frisked the boys against their will.

The officers patted them down and found the reason for their move to leave—two small plastic bags of marijuana—but just confiscated the drugs and let the boys go on their way. The Power Shift was after guns, not weed.

So, the encounter became an invisible incident without a name or a case number, an erosion of the Fourth Amendment never scrutinized by a prosecutor, never challenged by a defense attorney, never adjudicated by a judge, never reviewed by the Supreme Court—but an episode nonetheless, an unrecorded police action that characterized life on the streets of a thousand poor neighborhoods in America.

Again and again, in the nights I traveled with Sergeant Neill, black men who were sitting on stoops, strolling on sidewalks, or standing on corners just lifted their T-shirts when a squad of policemen approached. Some tried to ingratiate themselves with the officers, joking with them, boasting that they had jobs as if to flash a badge of respectability that distanced them from local drug dealers and thieves. Others wore the sullen expressions of men long abused by surly cops and bosses and prison guards. The ritual gave the lie to the Supreme Court's noble line in *Terry*: "This inestimable right of personal security belongs as much to the citizen on the streets of our cities as to the homeowner closeted in his study to dispose of his secret affairs." As I watched men raise their shirts without being asked, I wondered what the justices would have thought of the situation they had helped to create. No Supreme Court justice had ever traveled the nights with Sergeant Neill.

He was now fifty-two years old with twenty-six years on the force, a white man in a black part of town. He was not strapping, but he was sinewy, stronger and faster than he looked in his baggy blue police fatigues. He wore a sandy gray moustache and spoke his own dialect, a mixture of rural Southern and black ghetto, a patter as rapid as that of a pitchman selling a phony cure.

"How y'all this evening, gentlemen?" he would usually begin affably. Typically, his detail of four to six cars had wheeled into the block and parked at crazy angles in the street. Six or eight officers were approaching the "subjects." Emerging into the lead would be Neill, such a familiar presence that some residents greeted him: "Gee Gee," they'd say, or just "Gee."

"We're keeping the brothers alive in 2005," he'd tell his makeshift audience on the street, and then after the turn of the year, he used a colleague's suggestion: "Stay in the mix in 2006." Subsequent years had subsequent rhymes, until he retired. Peppering the folks with chatty greetings and coaxing, he'd ask, as casually as if he were angling to bum a cigarette, "Got any drugs or guns this evening?" To the inevitable denial, he'd go on, "So, it's OK if we search real quick?" If the pedestrian or the driver hesitated, Neill coaxed. "Let's just get this done real quick, OK?" But he hardly waited for answers. The introduction to a pat-down—"For your protection and mine, OK?"—was less of a question than part of a monologue, and a second of silence between the question and the search was deemed consent. By this standard, Neill prided himself on being able to talk just about anyone into permitting a search, and if there is voluntary consent, then the search is legal even without a warrant, probable cause, or reasonable suspicion.

"You know, the citizens have a right not to be searched," he told me one afternoon before he hit the street. "You know," he repeated with the insistent lilt of indignation that a civil liberties lawyer might use, "they have a right not to be searched. If they tell you no, you don't have any of the indications that there's guns or drugs in the car, then no is no, and you gotta let 'em go.

"I'm sure we've all been on dates where, you know, you try to get a kiss and she says no and then you wait a little while and try to kiss her again and she says no again, and then finally she says, 'OK.' No isn't really no. So sometimes you talk to these guys who said no. 'Well, you said there was nothin' in the car, right?' The guy's like, 'Yeah.' 'Well, if there's nothin' in the car, why can't I search? You know, what's the problem?' You know, you kind of look at the guy like, what's up?" And that works? "Yeah, a lot of times."

About 9 p.m., the officers of the Power Shift, some white, some black, some Latino, strolled out of First District on Fourth Street SW, just three blocks from the U.S. Department of Education, and gathered among their squad cars in a nearby parking lot, smoking and joking. They were not rookies. Most were seasoned enough to seem relaxed, although they were about to go hunting in darkness for deadly weapons. When Neill arrived, they mounted up and headed out.

In their lingo, the police officers wouldn't just look around. They'd "peep the bandits." They wouldn't pull over a car. They'd "cut shorty"— swerve in front to cut off the vehicle. If they set up a checkpoint for ostensible safety checks while looking for guns, they'd "pop the block."

The first stop, to peep the bandits, would be through a couple of alleys off K Street SE, leading into a courtyard among the apartments of a public housing project, Neill explained. "That's a good spot. It's where I like to start. I got three guns there."

The courtyard was full of kids and families relaxing in the summer evening, barbecuing, holding a large birthday party. They gave no cheerful greetings when six patrol cars drove in from all sides and jump-outs flowed through their festivities, but they seemed unfazed, as if this happened every other night. Officers selected a few young men for pat-downs and came up with nothing.

"They used to call guys on the other side on cell phones and tell them we're coming," Neill remarked.

"Too many people out here in the summertime," said his driver, Officer Matthew LeFande, who's a lawyer as well as a cop.

"In wintertime, it's better 'cause people are in their cars," Neill added. Searching cars has its own legal rules, but if you can get somebody for a traffic violation, you can gaze into the passenger compartment while checking his license and registration, and if you see anything suspicious "in plain view"—an open drink that could be alcoholic, for example—you might get consent or have probable cause for a full search.

The Power Shift was quick and efficient, focused and fast. Four squad cars careened to a stop beside a black man in a football jersey. Neill frisked him and found nothing. In another courtyard, three men sitting on a stoop were approached and patted down. Nothing. "Stand up, let me check, bro," Neill said to another three on another stoop. "No guns or drugs?"

The indignant answer came from one: "No, we don't got no guns or drugs." He put on a disgusted face at the outrageous suggestion. Neill and a couple of colleagues patted them down, running their hands over and under their arms, along their sides, squeezing lumps in their pockets, down the inside and outside of their legs. LeFande stood by, cradling a shotgun over an arm, like a prison guard making sure inmates in the chain gang didn't run off from their highway jobs.

Walking to and from their cars, the cops took little detours to peer into bushes, along walls. "We were told they keep the guns in the alley," Neill said. "We ain't never found them."

Suddenly we spotted a sedan stopped in the middle of the street, a black woman standing nearby. "Baby, got anything in the car?" Neill asked. He and LeFande looked with flashlights through the windows but didn't search, just checked her license and registration. Blocking traffic is arrogant, a way of stating your status, Neill said as we pulled away. "You can't do that unless you got a gun in the car." But the Power Shift almost always let "girls" go without a search; Neill played the odds, and the odds were that the guns were with the men. When we cruised up beside an expensive-looking white sedan, Neill saw that the driver was a woman and moved on.

Neill's team profiled vehicles as well as people. If they spotted something expensive—a Cadillac, a big SUV—or the opposite, a broken-down old car, they'd try to find some minor violation to excuse a stop: tinted windows, decorative lights, a hanging air freshener blocking vision, all infractions of the D.C. code, designed to give cops maximum latitude to investigate suspicious drivers. In fact, the Power Shift carried a handy tool in the search for guns: a tint meter. When the edge of a car window is inserted into a groove, the meter displays the percentage of light getting through. The law requires at least 70 percent for side windows in the front, 50 percent in the back.[12]

Next came a demonstration of how the Power Shift stopped vehicles in these poor, black neighborhoods—nothing as tame as approaching from behind with flashing lights and a siren. LeFande followed a white Cadillac as it turned a corner and slowed at the next intersection. Then he cut shorty, hitting the gas, wheeling around in front, and blocking the vehicle. All the while, Neill was chattering on his handheld radio, instructing his squad on how to converge on the Cadillac.

Inside, a black man sat smoking a cigarillo and trying to look casual. Neill leaned through the driver's window, chatted him up while looking around the passenger compartment for anything "in plain view." Six patrol cars pulled up one by one to fill the block, but the driver seemed to stay cool.

LeFande, standing aside with me, offered a running commentary. Neill was hovering to restrict the driver's movement, he explained, and other officers needed to stay out of the "kill zone," where a bullet could reach them should the driver pull a gun. It's best to put a vehicle, preferably the engine block, between you and the subject. Notice, LeFande said, how the spotlights and headlights from behind are designed to reflect off his rearview mirror into his face to place him under stress and destroy his concentration. "You see," LeFande said, "he's trying to find his documents, but he can't see. He's under stress."

And in this atmosphere a driver is supposed to make an uncoerced, voluntary decision on waiving his Fourth Amendment rights. Having created stress, Neill tried to read the level of nervousness and make his judgments accordingly. When he asked for consent to search the white Cadillac, he told me later, the driver came back sharply: "You got probable cause?"

"I said, 'I don't have probable cause. I'm asking your permission,'" Neill reported.

"I don't give it," the driver replied, according to Neill. So Neill tried to soften him up. He got talking with him about his Cadillac, what year it was, how he had maintained it so well, while another officer took the man's license back to a patrol car equipped with a computer system called WALES, the Washington Area Law Enforcement System, which taps into a criminal database to check for outstanding warrants. The driver came up clean, so Neill let him go with a cheery farewell and a "Have a good evening." He didn't think he missed anything by not searching. "He was too calm. He wasn't nervous."

How the most upstanding citizen, blinded by spotlights and surrounded by cops, could seem anything but nervous was a mystery to me, but Neill was sure he could tell. "If I ask him the questions, 'Are you carrying any guns or drugs?' and he immediately breaks into a sweat, that's a clear indication that he has a weapon and he may get to that weapon, and what you want to do is—you're allowed to protect yourself," Neill said. Indeed, the line of cases from *Terry* is predicated on a safety concern: that an officer should not have to endanger himself by refraining from a search if he believes the subject is armed.

"We take it instinctively," Neill said. "You're in a situation, you can kind of get that hair or chill coming up your back. Kind of like, your caution is aroused for whatever reason. And so it's hard to explain that situation in paperwork. And then come to a jury and also explain the same thing?" He shrugged at the impossibility of conveying the nuances of a policeman's labors to a layman. "While people may want you to do your job, they may not necessarily want to know *how* you do your job."

Some judges think Neill's telltale signs of gun possession are enough for reasonable suspicion, others do not. Those keen to expand police power may credit a cop's perception of someone's jitters. But the opposite view was taken by the federal appeals court in the D.C. Circuit, which ruled in 2007 that suspecting a person of carrying a gun "must be based upon something more than his mere nervousness. A person stopped by the police is entitled to be nervous without thereby suggesting he is armed and dangerous or, indeed, has anything to hide," the court said. "Were nervous behavior alone enough to justify the search of a vehicle, the distinction between a stop and a search would lose all practical significance, as the stop would routinely—perhaps invariably—be followed by a search."[13]

Cops are nervous, too, since 109 of the 578 officers murdered nationwide from 1999 through 2009 were killed during traffic stops.[14] The police, and even some of their targets, tend to see a search as defusing danger. "The frisk doesn't just protect the officers," Neill said one day. "It also protects the person you're friskin' because you eliminate the possibility that they may have a weapon so you can relax a little bit more. You know, it's for their protection and our protection, 'cause we don't want to be standing there talking to an armed suspect and have to worry about gettin' shot or havin' to shoot somebody. You don't want to—you never want to have to shoot anybody. But sometimes you have to." Neill had done it twice, once wounding a fleeing man who raised a gun, once killing an unarmed man high on PCP who tried to carjack Neill's vehicle. So, the frisk had become standard operating procedure.

Patting down people in such circumstances gave Justice Antonin Scalia constitutional misgivings, suggesting that had he been on the Court when *Terry* was decided in 1968, he might have authorized the stop but not the frisk before a full arrest. "I frankly doubt," he wrote in 1993, "whether the fiercely proud men who adopted our Fourth Amendment would have allowed themselves to be subjected, on mere suspicion of being armed and dangerous, to such indignity."[15]

Although the indignity of searches wasn't mentioned by Scalia in 2008, when he wrote a landmark opinion on the Second Amendment right to keep guns at home, the ruling—if gradually expanded through litigation—could eventually reduce or eliminate such confrontations with the police on the street, while raising the dangers from firearms.

It was the Supreme Court's first comprehensive decision on the scope of the Second Amendment. The justices in *District of Columbia v. Heller* found narrowly, five to four, that the framers meant the right as an individual one, not restricted to members of state militias, as the minority believed. The Second Amendment was poorly written: "A well regulated Militia, being necessary to the security of a free State, the right of the people to keep and bear Arms, shall not be infringed."

Parrying each other with intricate grammatical and historical arguments, the justices on both sides left a good deal open to further challenge. At first, the Court ruled only that people in a federal jurisdiction had the right to functioning guns in their own homes. Two years later, the same five-to-four majority applied the Second Amendment to state and local governments. The rulings left intact Washington, D.C.'s and other jurisdictions' laws against carrying firearms on the street. "Although we do not undertake an exhaustive historical analysis today of the full scope of the Second Amendment," Scalia wrote in *Heller,* "nothing in our opinion should be taken to cast doubt on longstanding prohibitions on the possession of firearms by felons and the mentally ill, or laws forbidding the carrying of firearms in sensitive places such as schools and government buildings, or laws imposing conditions and qualifications on the commercial sale of arms." This language was repeated in the 2010 opinion, indicating how far states could go in limiting gun possession.[16]

The District of Columbia complied with the *Heller* decision by enacting a strict licensing law for guns at home. Firearms in the street remained illegal, and defense attorneys discerned no shift in the gun arrests being prosecuted. Nor did the police change the tactics they had used before the Court's ruling, during my nights with the Power Shift.

The political spectrum gets scrambled out on the street. Liberals who favor strict gun control oppose the intrusive searches, which erode the Fourth Amendment but facilitate police in finding guns. Conservatives who oppose gun control favor more police power to search, which helps them find guns. You might say that the rights under the Second and Fourth Amendments rise and fall together.

A radio call came about an SUV in the left lane behind us. LeFande slowed down and stopped in front of the vehicle, which was trapped by another patrol car behind. The black driver was told to get out, and he was frisked. "What are you patting me down for?" he protested.

"That's routine for us, dude," said a black cop. "You got a car with tinted windows." The meter showed only 17 percent of the light getting through.

"You want to search the car?" asked the driver, spitting it out as a challenge and a curse. Neill said OK, was joined by two or three officers in the search, and found nothing. The driver looked bitterly victorious, part of a school of black men, frequently hassled by the police, who offer the search as a means of defiance to prove the cops wrong, to show them up as stupid or ineffective. Sometimes, people would lash the officers with the consent as if it were a righteous demand: "Search the car!"

LeFande pulled up beside a red sedan. "That's a girl," Neill said dismissively, and we moved on. What drew them to check the car? It came out of a high crime area and didn't make a full stop, Neill explained.

He then got out and approached two black men, in their twenties, wearing long white shirts. They pulled up their shirts before the cops even asked, and then submitted to pat-downs.

The next target was a black Mustang with tinted windows. A young black man was ordered out from behind the wheel and was patted down while he kept explaining, "I live right here." The tint meter showed only 16 percent, and Neill asked permission to search. "There ain't nothin' in there, man," said the driver. "Let's just get it done," said Neill. They did and found nothing. They are careful to say they want to "search," not "check," to be sure the consent is clear and legal.

"We've got a guy walking to the front of the building," Neill said into his radio. The jump-outs surrounded him, put his hands up against an iron fence, frisked him, and found nothing. Through the darkness I could not see any reasonable suspicion. As an officer swept the ground with the beam of his flashlight, however, he discovered a black plastic bag of weed packaged in tiny ziplock bags. The officers made no arrest; there was no proof connecting the man to the marijuana, and besides, the Power Shift was looking for guns.

A lone man sat behind the wheel of a parked car. "Any drugs or guns in the car?" Neill asked affably. "How was your day?" They got him out, searched him, and seated him on the ground. LeFande had him stretch his legs out straight so he couldn't run, at least not without sending an obvious warning by pulling up his knees before jumping to his feet. The officers searched his car (if he gave consent, I didn't hear it) and found no weapons, but a sack full of packing materials presumably used for ten-dollar bags of crack—not enough for an arrest.

Down the block, another driver, alone in a parked car, got Neill's attention. "Any guns or drugs in the car tonight?" Neill asked in a bantering tone. LeFande had the driver sit on the curb behind the car while the officers searched the trunk, which had only a few jackets and a toolbox. Once, Neill recalled, he'd looked in a trunk and found a safe.

At Sixteenth and C Streets SE, he spotted a couple walking. "Wha's up?" he said in his best ghetto accent. The man pulled up his shirt and answered, "No guns, no guns." Neill patted him down and remarked afterward, "If you talk to 'em good and don't violate 'em too hard, they all right."

After eighteen frisks and seventeen vehicle searches, no guns had turned up, just a few telltale signs of the drug trade, probably not much different from what Neill's squad would find on a college campus. The only difference would be the explosive uproar from congressmen and bankers and judges if their children were patted down by a police squad roaming late at night among the hallowed walkways and quads of, say, Princeton or Harvard. Of course, to cite Neill's argument, those kids wouldn't be carrying guns around. In Southeast D.C., the nineteenth man of the night was doing just that.

Neill figured it out before I realized that anything was amiss. Traveling the streets with him reminded me of going through Sinai with a Bedouin who notices what the newcomer never sees, or of journeying in Lebanon with an old soldier whose instincts are remarkably alert, or in Vietnam with a local interpreter whose eye is keen and ear attuned to nuance and danger. That didn't make Neill a hero, just a specialist, and it certainly didn't make him always right; he had been wrong eighteen times so far tonight. But he was well accustomed to watching in a way that laymen never do.

So I noticed nothing when a white Ford SUV slowed toward the end of the block and pulled over to park, and when the driver, a lean black man of about forty, got out and walked across the street in front of us and back our way down the sidewalk on the opposite side. To my eyes, he didn't seem in a rush. He lit a cigarette and strode purposefully but not hastily.

To Neill, however, he seemed too much in a hurry to get away from his car.

"Hey, sir, what's up?" Neill asked cheerfully. The man turned and stopped. "This your car?" The back side and rear windows were very dark, and Neill said something about illegal tint. It was done in the factory, the driver protested, and walked back to his SUV. Other officers arrived.

Through the windshield, Neill could see a cup in the center console. "Is that a drink?" He was fishing for a violation—open alcohol—that would get him inside the vehicle.

Now the driver was fully engaged in proving his innocence, so he unlocked the door and picked up the cup to show that it was empty. Underneath, Neill spotted a little bag of crack, he said later, at which point, based on the "plain view" doctrine, he had the right to search the car without consent. So he did, poking his head inside and rummaging around while the driver argued. "What have I done? I done nothing! I do not give you permission to search."

On the floor in front of the passenger seat, Neill came up with a black gym bag. He unzipped it and reached inside and pulled out a very mean-looking TEC-9 machine gun with a short barrel wrapped in an air cooler. "You're free to go," Neill said, which was code that night for "Gun!" The officer nearest the driver grabbed his wrists and handcuffed them behind his back. You never let a suspect know in plain language that you've found a gun, Neill said, because he may have another one and be tempted to use it. On the Power Shift, "Let's get a cup of coffee" or "I need a smoke" can mean "I've found a gun."

So, I said, legally the guy didn't have to stop when you asked him if that was his car, right? Right, Neill said. And he didn't have to walk back to his car, right? Right, Neill answered. And he certainly didn't have to unlock the door, open it, and pick up the cup, right? Right, Neill said, and quipped, "He could have done better." There was the slight smile and twinkle of a man who had just won a little contest.

In the end, though, the assistant U.S. attorney refused to "paper the case," as they say around the station house, because the vehicle search seemed vulnerable to challenge by the defense. Neill might have gone beyond the "plain view" limit by standing on tiptoes to gaze through the windshield and spot the crack cocaine. He was philosophical. There was one less gun on the street—his unit had confiscated ninety-three in the last eight months—and besides, characters like this always make more mistakes. "We'll get him next time," Neill said.

The rest of the night was anticlimactic but still instructive. On Twenty-first Street NE, we stopped face-to-face with a car containing four young black men, a couple of them wearing their hair in cornrows. Neill seemed to think he'd hit a gold mine. He got everybody out of the car, patted them all down, had them sit on the curb, and searched the car. Nothing. Neill reached out his hand to help all of them up, one by one. He thought these little nice-guy gestures eased the humiliation, but the glum, angry expressions on his victims' faces rarely changed.

One fellow, though, grinned as the cops walked to their cars and called after them, "Anybody need some tile work done? I do tile work." He was shining his badge of honor.

On Twenty-fourth and E Streets NE, a Cadillac and a Lincoln pulled over and parked as soon as the squad car came into view, a standard maneuver to minimize the chance of getting nabbed for a moving violation. Neill took a lone man from the Lincoln; other officers got a woman out from behind the wheel of the Cadillac. The cops searched inside the passenger compartments, then asked for the keys and opened the trunks, which were full of bags and backpacks. The officers pushed their meaty hands around inside the bags and found nothing criminal.

The faces of the two drivers were an artist's challenge: a mixture of sorrow, fear, smoldering anger. I wondered if these policemen ever thought about the fact that a lot of the people they hassled were going to end up on juries. The country that these citizens live in is not the kind of country that I would want to live in. But then, I wouldn't want to live in a neighborhood crawling with armed drug dealers, either.

"There's all kinds of illegal shit on that car," said LeFande, nodding toward an Isuzu Trooper at Eighteenth and D NE. Two little red lights twinkled above the windshield, for decoration. Neill was about to try to talk his way into a search of the vehicle when the driver revealed the interesting fact that he worked for the Department of Corrections. Neill told him the lights were against the law, then let him go.

The next targets, a few blocks away, were five black men all wearing white undershirts with straps. "Wha's up, gentlemen?" said Neill. "How y'all doin' today? Mind if I check you over?" He never quite waited for an answer. The whole process flowed from gesture to gesture, sentence to sentence, a monologue and an athletic play and a magician's sleight of hand all at once. He'd be chatting everyone up, folksy like, and moving in for the search, cajoling people to open the legal door, even a crack, so he could joke and push his way in. He didn't break it down, he just shoved a little, or slid in through whatever opening existed. So, these five responded by raising their hands and getting frisked, and then they strolled quickly down the street and around the corner while the cops searched the ground with their flashlights and found nothing.

When the officers looked up, they noticed a couple of cars parked nearby—one a red sedan, behind it a dark sedan with a Maryland license plate on the rear and another on the dashboard. The red car was unlocked, so the officers just opened the doors and did a search. With probable cause, a car parked on a public street can be searched without a warrant, based on the logic that unless police guard the vehicle while a warrant is obtained, it can be driven away, and the evidence along with it. One of the five men who had just been searched reappeared from around the corner, and shouted, "You can't search my vehicle!" He was legally correct, because no probable cause was evident. But the cops ignored him and finished rummaging around inside. Had they found anything and charged the owner, a judge would have been right to exclude the evidence as the fruit of an unconstitutional search.

They then moved to the car behind. They figured that this one's unattached front plate gave them probable cause to suspect that the car was stolen, and while one officer radioed headquarters to check, LeFande tried to open the door. He wedged a plastic block between the window and the frame to make room for an oddly shaped metal bar, which he inserted and twisted toward the manual lock. "I got the key!" a voice called out. The owner, coming up the block, was dangling a keychain. "Don't break the lock! I have the key!" Neill taunted him merrily, saying, "Come on, we'll see who can open it first." The winner was LeFande.

The plates came back stolen. "Stolen?" the owner shouted. "Where would I steal tags from?"

"That's what we'd like to know," Neill said.

The man stumbled around in a rage, as if he were high on either indignation or drugs. "Y'all search it. You accusing me of stealing tags, y'all search it." So they did. Nobody could come up with a registration. There were no guns or drugs in the car. The officers took the tags and let the man go stalking and cursing down the street.

That was the end of the shift, which added up to twenty-nine people frisked, twenty-two vehicles searched, and one gun. After we drove back to the First District station house, Neill got out, and as he walked inside, he turned and said over his shoulder, "It's addictive, isn't it?"

PROFILING CARS AND DRIVERS

Profiling is common throughout the country. "We would pull over cars that had college bumper stickers, because we knew college kids often partied with marijuana," said Barry Cooper, a former narcotics agent in Texas. "We would pull over 'Vietnam Vet' plates, because a lot of our vets developed a habit over there. I feel bad about it," he told NPR. "I would look for Mexicans. I would look for black people. It works."[17]

White, black, and Hispanic drivers were stopped at similar rates in 2005, a survey by the Bureau of Justice Statistics found, but what happened to them afterward was quite different. Vehicle searches were done on 9.5 percent of the black drivers, 8.8 percent of the Hispanics, and only 3.6 percent of the whites. Just 11.6 percent of 854,990 searches nationwide uncovered evidence of a crime, and black drivers were twice as likely as whites to be arrested (4.5 versus 2.1 percent). Fewer blacks than whites thought they'd been stopped legitimately.[18]

Since the Power Shift operated in virtually all-black neighborhoods, geography determined the race of the "subjects," and the profiling was more refined: age, gender, dress, hair style, type and condition of vehicle. The gun squad mixed more car searches into the blend one night, setting up roadblocks, questioning drivers, patting some of them down, and pushing for permission to look through passenger compartments and trunks. The techniques were supported by an evolving structure of legal precedents that have left people's cars virtually unprotected by the Fourth Amendment.

As early as 1925, the Supreme Court distinguished automobiles from houses, holding in *Carroll v. United States* that warrantless searches of cars were not "unreasonable" if based on probable cause. The reasoning was simple: Cars could be moved; buildings could not. The distinction had roots in law written "contemporaneously with the adoption of the Fourth Amendment," the Court noted, which recognized the difference between items "concealed in a dwelling house or similar place, and like goods in course of transportation and concealed in a movable vessel where they readily could be put out of reach of a search warrant." Autos were considered akin to the ships, beasts, and wagons that had been susceptible to warrantless searches for illegally imported items during the late 1700s and early 1800s.

So the legal concept has remained fairly constant as the contraband has changed over time, from smuggled goods two centuries ago, to liquor during Prohibition, to drugs and handguns today. In 1925, federal agents doing a sting operation against a bootlegger happened to see him driving his Oldsmobile Roadster between Grand Rapids and Detroit. Figuring that he must be transporting alcohol, they pulled up beside him, and, as one agent testified, "I stepped out on the running board and held out my hand and said, 'Carroll, stop that car.'" The feds tore open the rumble seat's upholstery and discovered sixty-eight bottles of gin and whiskey.

Finding probable cause, the Court admitted the bottles into evidence but warned, "It would be intolerable and unreasonable if a prohibition agent were authorized to stop every automobile on the chance of finding liquor, and thus subject all persons lawfully using the highways to the inconvenience and indignity of such a search."[19]

Since then, the boundary between the individual and the state, between privacy and law enforcement, has been tested by the collision of two forces: the nature of criminal activity (liquor, drugs, terrorism) and the advance of technology (the automobile, the telephone, the Internet). Sometimes the courts succeed at adapting the constitutional principles to the shifting circumstances of the modern world. But when the judges fail, the line defining constitutional freedoms blurs and meanders in a confused landscape.

So it has been with respect to vehicles, where courts have wrestled with two key questions: What circumstances justify a stop and a warrantless search, and how extensive can the search be?

If a stop is illegal, so is the subsequent search, and judges have therefore been drawn into parsing the circumstances of case after case to assemble a jigsaw puzzle of rules. Many devised by the pro-police Rehnquist Court are permissive, but one bedrock standard remains from 1925: To pull a car over, police must have probable cause or reasonable suspicion to believe that a law has been broken. This was redefined in 1990 to include an anonymous tip, plus some corroboration.[20] But it precludes just picking vehicles for random checks, or "suspicionless stops," a tactic that often involves racial or ethnic profiling.[21]

That's the theory. In practice, it's easy enough to find virtually anybody in a traffic violation, since hardly anyone obeys speed limits, for example, or comes to a full halt at stop signs. In neighborhoods where the Power Shift operates, there is no shortage of other infractions as well, from tinted windows to broken taillights to beads hanging from rearview mirrors. In effect, the police can find cause to pull over practically any driver they choose, a tactic permitted under a long line of Supreme Court cases allowing traffic stops for ulterior purposes.[22]

Purely suspicionless stops, however, are allowed only if everyone gets stopped, as at a checkpoint, and only to investigate certain noncriminal matters. The Court has approved police roadblocks to check for drunken drivers,[23] for illegal immigrants,[24] and for invalid licenses and registrations,[25] but not for drugs.[26] The exception to these rules comes during "exigent circumstances" after a crime, when police can use checkpoints to capture an escaping car.

Then comes the question of what police can do once they make a stop. They can look through the windows, and if they see something illegal "in plain view," such as a bag of crack or the handle of a gun, they have probable cause to search the vehicle. They can take a good whiff and if they smell marijuana, for example, they may search on that basis—"plain odor,"[27] a variation of the "plain view" and "plain feel" concepts. They can even bring a drug-detecting dog to the scene, if they do so promptly.

In 2005, the Court ruled that a car stopped for speeding could be checked by a dog without probable cause, because that alone was not a "search" as long as it was done without delaying the motorist unduly. Roy I. Caballes had been pulled over for speeding by an Illinois state trooper, who was writing a warning ticket when another trooper arrived and walked his drug-sniffing dog around the car. The Illinois Supreme Court ruled that use of the dog converted a traffic stop into a drug investigation without justification. But the U.S. Supreme Court decided six to two that when the dog smelled drugs, probable cause was established for the trunk to be opened and searched and the marijuana found inside introduced as evidence.[28]

Since warrantless searches were based on the rationale that cars could be driven away, containers inside were another issue altogether. They could be held unopened while police obtained a judge's signature, and so they enjoyed Fourth Amendment protection. That was the ruling in a 1977 case involving Joseph Chadwick, who was arrested by federal agents, after arriving by train in Boston, on a tip that his heavy, double-padlocked footlocker was leaking talcum powder, often used to neutralize the smell of marijuana. Meeting the train, narcotics agents brought in a dog, which signaled the presence of drugs in the footlocker. They waited until Chadwick claimed his chest, put it in the trunk of his car, and drove off. When they stopped him and seized his car, they did not bother with a search warrant, but ninety minutes later simply opened the footlocker. It contained marijuana, which the Court excluded as evidence, declaring, in the opinion by Chief Justice Warren Burger, "No less than one who locks the doors of his home against intruders, one who safeguards his personal possessions in this manner is due the protection of the Fourth Amendment Warrant Clause."

The original intent of the framers rested on a principle that transcended the circumstances of their time, Burger decided. They had neither limited the warrant requirement to the home nor explicitly applied it "in public places," he wrote, "because, aside from searches incident to arrest, such warrantless searches were not a large issue in colonial

America. Thus, silence in the historical record tells us little about the Framers' attitude toward application of the Warrant Clause to the search of respondent's footlocker. What we do know is that the Framers were men who focused on the wrongs of that day but who intended the Fourth Amendment to safeguard fundamental values which would far outlast the specific abuses which gave it birth."[29]

The Court brightened this clear line between a vehicle and its containers in 1979,[30] and again in 1981,[31] excluding evidence in warrantless searches of suitcases and bags inside cars. But the following year, the Court began to dim the line and finally erased it altogether. First, in *United States v. Ross*, the justices ruled in favor of Washington, D.C., police officers who received a call from an informant about a dealer selling drugs from the trunk of his car, searched the vehicle, and, without getting a warrant, opened a paper bag containing heroin. The search of the bag was deemed a logical part of the search of the vehicle. "Contraband goods rarely are strewn across the trunk or floor of a car," Justice John Paul Stevens wrote for the majority. "Since by their very nature such goods must be withheld from public view, they rarely can be placed in an automobile unless they are enclosed within some form of container."[32] By inference, this set up a contradiction: A container could be searched without a warrant if there was probable cause to search the vehicle, but if the probable cause applied to the container only, a warrant was still required.

Then, in 1985, the Court went a step further in *United States v. Johns* by extending warrantless searches to packages that had been seized from a vehicle three days earlier. Federal agents had spotted two pickup trucks driving to an Arizona airstrip fifty miles from the Mexican border, and had seen two small planes land and then take off again. Agents approached the trucks and arrested the alleged smugglers. They later claimed to have smelled the odor of marijuana coming from taped packages wrapped in dark green plastic, so they seized the vehicles and the packages, and took them to headquarters in Tucson. The agents never applied for a search warrant, and when they finally opened the packages, they found pot. Seven justices reasoned that since, under *Ross* three years earlier, the agents could have done a warrantless search when the packages were first seized, they could do so after three days.[33]

With that decision, the rationale of mobility did a vanishing act. A vehicle could be driven away, but a package in the hands of drug-enforcement agents could not. "There is simply no justification for departing from the Fourth Amendment warrant requirement under the circumstances of this case," Justice William J. Brennan, Jr., wrote in dissent. "No exigency precluded reasonable efforts to obtain a warrant prior to the search of the packages in the warehouse."

The succession of rulings had incrementally expanded the warrantless search, in steps deceptively small, until it had spread far beyond its original logic. This case was only slightly different from the last, the scope of this search only slightly broader than the one before, and so principles were nibbled away under the guise of pragmatism and common sense. Yet the result for a time was confusion in police departments and lower courts about how far warrantless searches of automobiles could go.

To end the uncertainty, the final restriction on searching containers disappeared in 1991, when *California v. Acevedo* removed all distinctions between a vehicle and the bags, boxes, and suitcases within. Police knew that marijuana had been delivered to an apartment, so when they saw Charles Steven Acevedo take a paper bag from the dwelling to the trunk of his car, they had probable cause to search the bag—but not the vehicle itself. The Court ruled that no warrant was required to search the bag, and the marijuana discovered inside was admissible into evidence. It was surely no comfort to Acevedo that the Court accompanied its decision with this ringing declaration: "It [is] a cardinal principle that searches conducted outside the judicial process, without prior approval by judge or magistrate, are *per se* unreasonable under the Fourth Amendment—subject only to a few specifically established and well-delineated exceptions."[34]

In adding this exception, the Court was solving a problem that it had created in *Ross,* namely, the separate rules that governed container searches depending on whether the container alone, versus the entire vehicle, was the target. "Until today," Justice Harry A. Blackmun wrote in the majority opinion, "this Court has drawn a curious line between the search of an automobile that coincidentally turns up a container and the search of a container that coincidentally turns up in an automobile. The protections of the Fourth Amendment must not turn on such coincidences."[35]

But in adopting "one clear-cut rule to govern automobile searches," the Court now legalized its basic error. Gone was the notion that the police should be exempted from getting a warrant only when the evidence could be removed. Gone was the expectation of privacy in one's luggage, so forcefully defined by Burger in *United States v. Chadwick,* just fourteen years before. The justices, so focused on giving law enforcement the license of simplicity, let slip away the principle of checks and balances that requires the police to be overseen by a neutral magistrate in the intrusive act of searching through personal possessions.

"The Fourth Amendment is a restraint on Executive power," wrote Stevens, now dissenting in *Acevedo*. "The Amendment constitutes the Framers' direct constitutional response to the unreasonable law enforcement practices employed by agents of the British Crown." And then he pointed to a new paradox created by the majority's ruling: "It is anomalous to prohibit a search of a briefcase while the owner is carrying it exposed on a public street yet to permit a search once the owner has placed the briefcase in the locked trunk of his car. One's privacy interest in one's luggage can certainly not be diminished by one's removing it from a public thoroughfare and placing it—out of sight—in a privately owned vehicle."[36]

If a policeman wants to search your car without your consent, and he can't justify reasonable suspicion that it contains a weapon or probable cause that it contains drugs, he can use another legal approach. If he actually arrests you and takes you into custody for a traffic offense and then impounds your car, he may inventory the contents of your vehicle, as well as your pockets.[37] For many years, until the Supreme Court refined the rules in 2009, he could usually search even without impounding. The tactic has turned a good many traffic stops into narcotics cases.

In 1987, the Court found that Colorado police arresting a drunk driver and impounding his van could search a backpack as part of their normal routine of conducting an inventory of the vehicle's contents. The list is ostensibly made to protect against pilferage—protection that became this driver's undoing: His backpack contained drugs, cocaine paraphernalia, and a large amount of cash.[38] In a similar case three years later, Brennan in dissent warned of "a prime danger of insufficiently regulated inventory searches: Police may use the excuse of an 'inventory search' as a pretext for broad searches of vehicles and their contents."[39]

The Court drew a limit in 1998, unanimously declaring unconstitutional an Iowa law allowing police to do a full search of a vehicle when issuing only a traffic ticket without an arrest. No arrest, no search, the justices declared. Patrick Knowles, pulled over for speeding, could have been taken into custody under state law, but the trooper chose to write a citation and then performed a warrantless search of the vehicle—unconstitutionally, the justices decided. The marijuana and "pot pipe" that the officer discovered were suppressed as evidence, and the drug conviction was overturned. If the trooper had used his prerogative to lock

Knowles up for speeding, then the search would have been legal, the evidence admissible.[40]

Three years later, the Court expressly allowed just such arrests for misdemeanors that carried maximum penalties of nothing more than small fines. As a result, if you're driving along in Texas, for instance, and you commit an infraction punishable by no prison time, you can be taken to jail for up to forty-eight hours, and your vehicle impounded and thoroughly searched.[41]

It was a close decision, five to four, with Justice David Souter writing for the majority and Justice Sandra Day O'Connor for the dissenters. The case involved Gail Atwater, who was driving her children home from soccer practice in the Texas town of Lago Vista when one of their beloved toys flew out the window. She turned her pickup truck around, retraced her route at fifteen miles an hour, and unbuckled the seat belts so the kids—Mac, three, and Anya, five—could peer out the windows and help in the search.

Driving without a seat belt was a misdemeanor carrying a fine of twenty-five to fifty dollars, and no imprisonment, but Texas law gave a police officer discretion either to write a ticket or arrest an offender. The officer who pulled Atwater over, Bart Turek, took the harder approach. Three months earlier he had stopped her because he thought Mac wasn't wearing a seat belt, but saw when he approached the car that, in fact, the boy was strapped in, albeit unsafely on an armrest. He gave Atwater a warning.

This time, according to the court record, Turek immediately started yelling at the mother, and when she asked him to lower his voice because he was scaring the children, he poked his finger in her face, saying, 'You're going to jail!'" Then, when she couldn't produce her license and insurance card because her purse had been stolen the previous day, Turek replied, "I've heard that story two hundred times."

In a sharp dissent, O'Connor recounted what followed: "Atwater asked if she could at least take her children to a friend's house down the street before going to the police station. But Turek—who had just castigated Atwater for not caring for her children—refused and said he would take the children into custody as well. Only the intervention of neighborhood children who had witnessed the scene and summoned one of Atwater's friends saved the children from being hauled to jail with their mother." He handcuffed her and took her in a squad car to the police station. "Ironically," O'Connor noted, "Turek did not secure Atwater in a seat belt for the drive." She was put in a cell for an hour, until a magistrate released her on bond.

Mac, her three-year-old, was so traumatized that "after the incident," O'Connor wrote, "he had to see a child psychologist regularly, who reported that the boy 'felt very guilty that he couldn't stop this horrible thing . . . he was powerless to help his mother or sister.' Both of Atwater's children are now terrified at the sight of any police car. According to Atwater, the arrest 'just never leaves us. It's a conversation we have every other day, once a week, and it's—it raises its head constantly in our lives.'"

Atwater and her husband sued the town for damages, and as the case made its way up to the Supreme Court, their lawyers assembled an expansive historical argument. They contended that English common law and the framers' intent confined misdemeanor arrests to breaches of the peace. The Court's slim majority rejected the assertion. The historical record was mixed, at best, Souter wrote. He found no evidence that the framers sought such limitation. On the contrary, state legislatures at the time authorized nonviolent misdemeanor arrests. In early years after independence, American laws permitted arrests for profanity and violating the Sabbath. And he found much in English statutory law, some dating back to the thirteenth century, to riddle any common-law protection. A 1285 act authorized the arrest of nonviolent minor offenders, such as "nightwalkers," strangers who happened to walk through town at night. "One 16th-century statute, for instance, authorized peace officers to arrest persons playing 'unlawful game[s]' like bowling, tennis, dice, and cards, and for good measure extended the authority beyond players to include persons 'haunting' the 'houses, places and alleys where such games shall be suspected to be holden, exercised, used or occupied.'" Centuries later, Americans might fairly shudder as antiquated indignities are absorbed into modern jurisprudence.

The majority noted that all fifty states and the District of Columbia permitted arrests for misdemeanors that carried no jail time, and that those measures had withstood judicial challenges. (D.C. had changed the law and exempted most traffic offenders from arrest, frustrating old-timers on the police force who remembered nostalgically the days when a couple of outstanding tickets got you busted and your car searched.) Souter's key point was not that the Atwater arrest was justifiable—indeed, he and the majority found it full of "gratuitous humiliations imposed by a police officer who was (at best) exercising extremely poor judgment." But the justices did not think that one policeman's overreaction should induce the Court to ban all such misdemeanor arrests and thus "mint a new rule of constitutional law."

The fudge factor in the text of the Fourth Amendment is the word "unreasonable," which presents judges with latitude for indulging their predilections for or against police power. Courts have held that to be reasonable, an arrest must balance two competing factors: its intrusion on personal privacy versus its weight in promoting government interests, as O'Connor noted in her *Atwater* dissent. She was known as a pragmatic justice, rooted as much in the real-life impacts of decisions as in their constitutional principles. Unlike Souter, she saw no problem deciding each case individually, and she accused the majority of minting its own "new rule" permitting an arrest for "even a very minor criminal offense," as the majority itself had characterized the seat-belt incident.

But seven years later, in 2008, she joined a unanimous Court in giving the police latitude to arrest and search drivers even where the law authorized nothing more than a summons. A Virginia man, taken into custody for driving on a suspended license, was personally searched— standard procedure incident to an arrest—and crack cocaine was found. He lost his argument to have his arrest declared illegitimate and the drugs excluded from evidence.[42]

Traffic stops and car searches have been among the most confusing and difficult areas for the courts. Case law holds that warrantless searches accompanying arrests are justified for two purposes only: either to preserve evidence or to protect officers from hidden weapons. But these are fragile limits on police power, drawing support from only a slim majority of five justices in 2009. They barely ruled for an Arizona man who had turned into his driveway, parked, gotten out, and was then arrested for driving with a suspended license. After he was securely handcuffed and locked in a patrol car, the officers searched his vehicle, where they found a jacket with crack in a pocket. The five in the majority found the obvious: that the detainee could not have gained access to any gun that might have been in his car, and that the vehicle could not have contained evidence relating to the cause of his arrest, the suspended license.[43]

The usual characters who claim Fourth Amendment violations are not sympathetic types, because their crimes seem clear: They've been caught red-handed with drugs or guns or stolen goods and are seeking to suppress the incriminating evidence. They generate little popular support, unlike Gail Atwater.

She was just a "soccer mom" trying to find a lost toy. Fine, upstanding citizens could identify with her, since she lived within their circle of decency. Yes, she showed a lapse of judgment about safety, but she was no hardened drug dealer armed with deadly weapons. Had her arrest led to a vehicle search that uncovered guns and narcotics, she would have earned condemnation rather than the compassion she won as the mildly careless mother, handcuffed and dragged away in front of her small children.

But the constitutional question would have been the same. When the Bill of Rights is violated, it's usually hard to mobilize public concern, because the most obvious victims are the least admirable—accused criminals whose cases become the means through which courts regulate police behavior by applying the Constitution. And the resulting constitutional interpretations apply to everyone. The system, then, binds together the miscreants and the righteous: The most virtuous among us depend on the most villainous to carry the torch of liberty, for when the courts allow a criminal defendant's rights to be violated, the same rights are diminished for the rest of us. As the bootlegger Carroll, the pistol-packing Terry, the gun-toting Wardlow, the drug-pushing Ross, and the pothead Acevedo lost some of their Fourth Amendment protections, so did we all.

Most citizens who are searched without giving voluntary consent don't go to court for the simple reason that they are entirely innocent. No evidence is found, and so—assuming the police are honest—no charges are brought against them. Yet they have been violated fundamentally. Unless they sue the police for damages, which is extremely rare and more rarely successful, their experiences add up to an invisible record across the United States of countless unconstitutional searches.

Each night, the Power Shift leaves dozens of such victims in its wake. Rushing through blocks and courtyards, the officers consider the entire shift a success if a single gun is found, even when numerous innocents are stopped and frisked, their cars searched, their dignity assaulted, their zones of privacy invaded for naught. If a ballplayer batted with such a low average—one for thirty in this typical shift—he wouldn't be a ballplayer for long. But the officers don't keep track of the fruitless searches, and neither does anyone else. Instead, they reason that "it discourages them from carrying a gun," Neill explained. "If you keep 'em pressured, they won't bring the guns outside," and a gun left home means a few more minutes to cool off before using it. The judicial process, it seems, is only incidental to crime prevention.

On this June night, as Sergeant Neill got ready to take his men into the streets, he sat typing in a bare cubicle at the First District station house.

To guard his privacy, he used his personal laptop instead of a department computer: He didn't want the police department snooping into his files, he explained, or observing when he logged on and off. He wanted to compose his response to a complaint, a Form 119, without being monitored.

Neill was peppered with complaints. He seemed miffed at this one but tried not to let it show much. It was from a driver whom he had pulled over for having tinted windows and a device that made the sound of a police "sirene," as Neill spelled it (pronouncing it "*sireen*"). Neill had to justify frisking the driver, which he did by reporting that the man had seemed nervous enough to make Neill think there might be a gun. There wasn't.

Nothing much seems to result from such complaints. Officers treat them like minor irritants, although when they're introduced into evidence—as judges occasionally allow defense attorneys to do—they can discredit police witnesses, especially among black jurors from poor neighborhoods where they've seen cops in action. Neill had lost some convictions as a result, but he usually reacted with that standard police philosophy: "We'll get him next time."

It was close to 10 p.m. when Neill folded up his laptop, took off the bright red Hawaiian short-sleeved shirt he was wearing, put on a uniform shirt, and walked out to the nearby parking lot, empty at this hour except for three marked cars and six officers hanging around waiting for him. Neill went off to get a squad car of his own, and we began with his favorite starting point, the alley between K and L Streets SW, which ran into a courtyard behind some two-story apartment buildings.

As the officers swept in from two directions, the residents barely reacted, accustomed as they were to the invasions. It was a warm Wednesday, and lots of folks were outside, some sitting in tiny fenced-in patios or yards, a few girls looking pretty high while dancing to music from a boom box. The smell of pot was in the air. Neill frisked one young man, and the rest of the squad spent a few minutes sweeping the ground with the beams of their flashlights. They came up with a small potato chip bag containing marijuana, but no owner. A man so huge he was oozing out of his folding chair caught Neill's eye. "The big fat guy sold me drugs in 1994," he told me, and they nodded politely to each other as the sergeant strode by.

We headed toward Benning Road, and on the way I asked Neill what he thought people felt when he searched them and found nothing. "Relief," he answered. "You're not dealing with people who go to church." But you are dealing with people who may get onto juries, I noted.

On H Street and North Capitol, we came up behind a vehicle that seemed designed to command police attention: a dark sedan with tinted windows and plates that read "RATBABY." Neill radioed the squad car ahead, which stopped and blocked him. Two black men were in the front seats, the driver chatting on a cell phone. Neill quickly had them out of the car and frisked. "I got nothing in there, so you can search it," he later quoted the driver as saying. Nothing was found.

Cruising into an alley off H and Sixth Streets NE, the lead squad car doused its lights. "We call it the stealth mode," said Neill. "We ain't supposed to do that." He pulled up next to a gray sedan that was parked illegally, the driver sitting behind the wheel, which was secured with a locked antitheft bar.

The parking violation gave Neill and his colleagues the legal hook they needed for an encounter, a gaze through the windows, a conversation that they always hoped would get them inside the car. So, a little charade began. The driver, a black man in his thirties, defended himself in tones of sincerity against the grave parking violation that had brought seven officers in four cars swooping down on him, mobilized to stamp out this parking scourge that afflicts back streets. He claimed that the car belonged to his mother, who lived in the row of houses along the alley. (A young black man under the siege of the gun squad often seems to think that he'll inspire sympathy by noting that he has a mother—all the better if he can convince the officers that the little old lady who brought him into the world is actually the owner of the decal-covered SUV he's driving, with beads swinging from the mirror and a woofer that sounds like the muffled thud of distant artillery when the tinted windows are closed.) "We always park right here," the driver declared in a charming confession, as if his record as a serial parking offender would end the surreal scene. But Neill asked the man to get out of the car, frisked him, then teamed up with another officer to search the vehicle. "I used to have a truck, parked it right here," the driver continued, playing along. Then, as if to underscore his naïve ignorance of the momentous crime, he even called his mother on his cell phone so the police could hear his lilt of innocence. "Mama, I'm out back. Police here. They say we can't park out here."

Later, the cops had a laugh about this big man calling his mama. The man may have had his own laugh about disarming the cops with deference. He'd played the game, letting them think they'd fooled him with concern over an infraction they didn't even give him a ticket for. Had the officers gone on to find a weapon, they would surely have written a parking ticket to make the case legitimate.

"Did you say they could search?" I asked him. I hadn't heard him give consent. He looked baffled by the question and didn't answer. "He gave permission," Neill said later. "He was real nervous." Neill seemed to think that unless a black man has guns or drugs, he shouldn't be nervous when surrounded in a dark alley by seven cops, most of them white. But this unreasonably nervous man had no guns or drugs, and I came out doubting that Neill could really tell. The Power Shift's averages in finding guns were probably no better than what would have turned up by doing random stops of males between eighteen and forty-five in these dangerous neighborhoods. Random stops were not constitutional, however; a pretext was required, often of the slimmest sort.

And so it went late into the evening: Three men frisked at G and Seventh Streets NE; "All right, Gee," one said in assent. A lone man frisked in an alley adjacent to a playground. Three men who bolted and ran safely into a house. Another running man, whom Neill tried to catch by climbing nimbly over a locked chain-link fence, but who escaped through a warren of alleys and courtyards. Several guys walking up an alley, stopped and frisked. Three men on a stoop at Twelfth and I Streets NE, frisked while Neill chattered at them: "Wha's up, fellas? Got any guns or drugs? We searchin' for drugs and guns."

"Go ahead," one said.

And then, the first checkpoint of the night, a "pop-up roadblock," as they called it. Prompted by a Cadillac Escalade with no front tags, the squad decided to stop everyone, so Neill parked in the middle of H near Twelfth NE. "Let's get 'em all," he radioed to his men. Straight-faced, they pretended that their checkpoint was aimed at checking licenses and registrations, since the Constitution, as interpreted by the Supreme Court to date, did not permit roadblocks for the Power Shift's purpose of finding guns.

"Get out, man," Neill told a driver, then frisked him. Two cars were being searched at once, then another and another. When Neill couldn't find the lever to open a trunk, the driver, leaning on the trunk in frisk position, gave him a clue: "It's in there. You want me to show you?" Neill answered, "Yeah, come around." And the driver obliged.

The owner of another Cadillac SUV said a search was OK, then got out of the vehicle and was surprised when he was patted down. "Checking me, too?"

"You ain't got a gun, do you?"

"No."

"We don't want anybody gettin' shot up."

After five minutes and a couple of tickets written, the roadblock vanished, the nation's capital having been kept safe from unlicensed drivers. No guns yet tonight.

As we drove into darker, narrower streets, Neill got a radio call. A man was running through an alley. For the first time that night, the sergeant grabbed the shotgun from between our seats, jumped out, and gave chase. Around the corner, cops surrounded a black teenager, tall and lanky with long hair and glasses. A black officer said he'd seen him throw a plastic sack containing ten ziplock bags of weed. "I didn't have anything," the kid insisted.

"I was right there," the cop came back. "You didn't, my ass." When another officer said that he had also witnessed the young man throw the marijuana, the kid's denials dissipated.

"We don't always lock 'em up for ten bags," Neill explained to me. "We're looking for guns. That kind of shit just slows us down."

So, instead of subjecting the youngster to the judicial system, the Power Shift exacted its own kind of justice by confiscating the weed and giving the criminal a hard time. A good defense attorney can often sow the seed of reasonable doubt that the drugs found on the ground actually belonged to the defendant and that the cop is truthful about seeing them tossed. So a trial is not always worth the time and the gamble.

A young white officer took the teenager's license to a squad car with a computer uplinked to the WALES database. "No record," he called out.

"Anything in your house you want to surrender to the police?" asked Neill.

"No."

"We gonna take you home, tell your mama what you been doin'." She was at work at the post office, the kid said. Neill asked for her cell number, got it, and called, but she didn't answer. "Today's your lucky day," the sergeant told the young man. "I see you again, you're goin' to jail."

Another officer chimed in. "You can't be goin' to jail. You like sex, man? They like sex, too. They like somebody fresh like you."

"Yeah, that long hair to hang on to," a third cop added.

Having made the threats, scared the young man, and taken the pot, the Power Shift moved on. They looked through a car where they thought they smelled marijuana—thereby giving them probable cause to search—and found nothing. They had a few bizarre encounters along Benning Road with residents who had been smoking something stronger, it seemed, for they mouthed off incoherently as the squad frisked them and searched their cars. One young woman, babbling noisily, was taken aside gently by an African-American officer who quietly calmed her down. "That's the guy we call the Reverend," said Neill. Every police unit ought to have one.

In Iraq, Neill had learned a technique he brought back to Washington: how to set up roadblocks by staggering boulders in the road to force cars to slow and weave. This he usually did near RFK Stadium in the early morning hours when people drove home from clubs. "This is where the Badlands meet America," he told me.

Tonight, though, the squad used their cars instead of rocks, leaving just enough space along the one-way, three-lane road to allow vehicles to squeeze through. They parked one cruiser facing the wrong way on a ramp, ready to give chase if anybody tried to avoid the checkpoint by backing up. That happened three times on this shift, but only once did two officers race for their car and roar after the offender, who followed normal procedures in this part of town: When you have drugs or guns in your vehicle, and sirens and lights materialize, you do not obediently pull over; you floor it and hope to outrun the cops, which this driver managed to do.

Working efficiently, the Power Shift stopped most cars long enough to go through the act of checking licenses and look over the driver and passengers and decide whether to seek consent for a search. An older man, possibly Latino, was waved through, as were nearly all the women. Only black men from their late teens to their late forties were targeted. Vans or SUVs that seemed fancy, and men with cornrows or braids or baggy clothes were scrutinized closely. Neill said he was looking for people who betrayed nervousness by glancing around inside their car, who answered evasively, who couldn't find their licenses because of the jitters.

Officers engaged in brief conversation, mostly monologues: Got any guns or drugs, man? Mind if we search? Get out of the car, man. Don't want anybody to get hurt. "Got anything in the vehicle I should know about?" one officer asked. "Maybe a little bit of weed?" Then came a quick pat-down, a search of the passenger compartment by two or three officers, who rarely went into trunks, and a wave and a goodnight.

When Neill explained that they were trying to get guns off the street, one driver pulling away cautioned, "Y'all be careful, man." It sounded more like a friendly warning than a threat. Another driver turned out to be a fireman, which reminded Neill of the time they got a gun off a Metro bus driver. A black woman who recognized the sergeant shouted, "Gee! Give me a hug!" and Neill did, through the window. "I love ya, baby!" she yelled gleefully as she drove away, and he smiled sheepishly.

One driver had an open can of beer and a blackjack, its lead cylinder covered in dull black leather. The cops poured the beer onto the ground and confiscated the blackjack. Another had a bag of marijuana in the front seat, seized as well. The squad didn't bother making arrests or writing tickets, though. They were highly focused on their mission.

About a dozen cars were searched thoroughly in forty-five minutes, all after their drivers had given consent.

"Mind if I search?" a white sergeant asked a black driver.

"No."

"I appreciate it," said the sergeant, and then, after he poked his hands around and beneath the front seat only, not the back, he waved the man on with a "Have a good night."

Then a dark sedan came up swiftly, as if trying to slip past the checkpoint. Neill saw the way he was driving and signaled him to a stop. Their conversation was soft, mumbled, and I was too far away to hear it. Neill's reconstruction later was typical. When the driver asked the reason for the stop, Neill answered that they were checking licenses. The driver couldn't find his, and this was interpreted as a sign of acute nervousness. "Can I search?" Neill remembered asking. "Sweat starts dripping off him. He kept looking down." He gave permission, though.

Neill said he'd then got the man out of the car and, when he patted him down, felt a broad belly belt fastened with Velcro, the kind a weight-lifter would use. The belt was stiff and hard and might be expected to conceal a gun. Neill said he'd felt a tip of the handle above the belt, and pulled it out—a nine millimeter Luger. Neill beckoned me closer as the man was handcuffed, and I saw another officer undo the belt. Out fell a magazine clip full of ammunition.

The driver was practically crying, and he flashed that badge of decency, saying, "I got a job at Pepco," the local electric company. He was coming from a workout, trying to lose weight, he said. "I ain't hurt nobody, brother, never in my life." But the computer in one of the squad cars listed him with a prior conviction. Pepco job or not, Neill said to me, this man "can't stop being a thug."

They had gotten their gun for the night. It was 1:45 a.m., Neill had a couple of hours of paperwork to do, and other officers had court appearances the next morning, which meant little sleep and lots of overtime. So we stopped for gas at a Sunoco station, went to a 7-Eleven for some coffee, then cruised back to the First District headquarters.

Hardly any of the searches had been justified by probable cause or even by the lesser standard of reasonable suspicion. The Power Shift had relied almost entirely on citizens' acquiescence. While officers combed through vehicles, I asked drivers who were sitting on curbs or leaning on trunks whether their permission had been requested. Some looked blank, as if they hadn't known that a policeman had to ask and that a citizen could say no.

OBTAINING CONSENT

In 1973, the Supreme Court ruled six to three, in *Schneckloth v. Busta-monte,*[44] that the police did not have to inform people of their Fourth Amendment right to refuse a search, unlike the Miranda warning required before waiving the Fifth Amendment right against self-incrimination. In dissent, Justice Thurgood Marshall accused the majority of allowing "the police to capitalize on the ignorance of citizens so as to accomplish by subterfuge what they could not achieve by relying only on the knowing relinquishment of constitutional rights."

An uninformed public removes a burden from police work, and when a lack of knowledge is combined with a coercive atmosphere, the searches move along rapidly. Even if you know you can say no, you've got to make a quick calculation about whether or not to exercise your right to refuse. When you're a black man surrounded by cops late at night, can your consent really be "freely and voluntarily given," as the case law requires?

It seemed easy to induce the citizens of the nation's capital to relinquish one of the Constitution's key liberties. Those drivers who told me that they had been explicitly asked gave a simple reason for consenting: "I ain't got nothin' in there," as one man said. It was his version of a response typical of a large segment of Americans who don't mind surveillance because they have "nothing to hide."

If I hadn't seen this massive apathy about rights with my own eyes, I might not have credited the claims of another seasoned sergeant, J. J. Brennan, who still, after over thirty-five years on the force, had a slight melody of surprise in his voice as he told of drug couriers letting him search their suitcases—and they certainly had something to hide. It happened in Washington, D.C.'s Union Station, where Brennan had set up a drug interdiction unit of seven detectives in the late 1980s.

With the advice of an Amtrak police officer who had run a similar unit in Dade County, Florida, Brennan developed observation and interview techniques that narrowed the flood of passengers walking through the station to a trickle of potential dealers and couriers. He read the relevant Supreme Court opinions and figured out how to gain consent without being coercive.

Coercion is often in the eye of the beholder, and the Court usually looks through the eyes of the police. As Justice O'Connor recapitulated the case law as of 1991, "The Fourth Amendment permits police officers to approach individuals at random in airport lobbies and other public places to ask them questions and to request consent to search their luggage, so long as a reasonable person would understand that he or she could refuse to cooperate. . . . The encounter will not trigger Fourth Amendment scrutiny unless it loses its consensual nature." She was writing the majority opinion in *Florida v. Bostick,* which extended that police authority to a passenger on a bus that was about to depart. While he couldn't walk away without missing his transport and abandoning any luggage stowed below, the Court found that he could still have rebuffed two officers' request to search a bag, where cocaine was discovered. In other words, as long as a person is free to ignore the police and go about his business, the questioning is just a conversation and not a "seizure" under the Fourth Amendment.

There are few areas of the law where the sterile abstractions of the Supreme Court seem more out of touch with reality. The majority's notion that a passenger could feel perfectly free to say no, while confined in his seat by two armed policemen blocking the aisle during a drug sweep, seemed absurd to Justice Marshall, whose career as a civil rights lawyer had given him plenty of opportunity to understand the dynamics of police bullying. The passenger had only two undesirable options, Marshall noted in his dissenting opinion: to push his way past the policemen and leave the bus, or: "He could have remained seated while obstinately refusing to respond to the officers' questioning. But in light of the intimidating show of authority that the officers made upon boarding the bus, respondent reasonably could have believed that such behavior would only arouse the officers' suspicions and intensify their interrogation. Indeed, officers who carry out bus sweeps like the one at issue here frequently admit that this is the effect of a passenger's refusal to cooperate."[45]

Sergeant Brennan pictured himself as steering well clear of coercion in Union Station. "You're walking on a very thin line," he conceded. But he knew the law cold, and most of his subjects did not, and that gave him an edge as he approached railroad passengers who fit his profiles of likely suspects.

There were indicators of manner and dress. "It was known that females carrying drugs and males carrying drugs would do away with their jewelry," he said. "Jewelry was a big thing—gold chains and bracelets, flashy.

Drug dealers were flashy back then, so they were dressin' down" to look inconspicuous.

His officers ignored passengers who were met by others, since couriers didn't hand off the goods in public. Women who stopped to gaze into store windows were also ruled out. Brennan's attention went instead to any woman who was so focused on getting on her way that she breezed past shops in the station without so much as a glance. "When have you ever known a woman to pass by a clothing store and not take a look?" he asked. It seemed a flimsy clue, a profile that might also fit a corporate lawyer on a tight schedule.

Once someone was chosen for an approach, the detectives tried to be low-key. In plain clothes, they wore no police emblems, no jackets saying POLICE. When they introduced themselves as police officers, "we showed them our identification with our picture on it," Brennan noted. "We thought it was more personable than drawing a badge on them." Then the conversation would begin.

"We'd ask several questions: Where you coming from? You know. Who you going to see? How long you gonna be here? Can I see your train ticket? We'd ask for the ticket, and they'd show us the ticket; we'd look at it. If I held on to that ticket, that means I detained the person," for which he'd have to have probable cause and advise them of their Miranda rights not to answer. "So I'd take a quick look at the ticket, see where the travel was from, New York to Washington, D.C., being round trip, paid for by cash, stuff like that. And I'd give the ticket back."

As Brennan knew, having read the Supreme Court ruling in *Florida v. Royer,* holding the ticket too long, the way narcotics detectives at Miami International Airport had done in 1978, the passenger would have been effectively "seized" without probable cause, and any evidence discovered as a result would have been inadmissible. The Court had thrown out the Florida conviction after detectives had taken a man's ticket and driver's license, had led him to a small room for questioning, and had then obtained reluctant consent (not voluntary, given his unlawful confinement) to open his suitcases, which contained marijuana.[46]

Like Neill in the street, Brennan in the station would watch people's reactions when he asked their names, inquired into their reasons for travel, and the like.

A lot of drug dealers wouldn't look him in the eye, Brennan learned. "They would be talkin' to you but kind of lookin' away from you. Or, they'd be gazing for your backups, you know, trying to look around and see whether or not you had other people with you. Or, possibly, looking for escape routes: If I decide to take off, which way do I go? And then you'd look for the sweating. A lot of times they'd break out in a sweat. Or trembling. You'd see a twitch or you'd see a tremble, or movement of the feet. You know how when you get nervous you can't stand still? And even the breakup of the speech, when they talk. You ask them a certain question, their speech breaks up."

A quasi-scientific school of study, using facial tics as lie detectors, has been promoted by Mark Frank, a former bouncer who came to believe he could tell by looking at people's faces whether they were carrying guns, false IDs, or hot tempers. Now a psychologist at the University of Buffalo, he trains investigators to watch for fleeting "microexpressions" that indicate fear: eyebrows moving up and together, or a muscle that contracts to stretch the mouth, for example. So keen is the Department of Homeland Security to divine emotions this way that it launched an airport security project to detect body language and granted Rutgers university $3.5 million to design computer software that could read faces more reliably than veteran cops like Sergeant Brennan.[47]

But Brennan felt he was pretty good at it, and he found that funny things often happened in Union Station when he asked for identification. "You'd be surprised how often there's no ID, no ID at all," Brennan said, because the passenger had given a false name to begin with and didn't want to produce a contradicting document. "Who travels anywhere on any type of transportation and don't have a driver's license or a wallet with an ID in it? 'Cause you've got your money, your billfold. We got a lot of that.

"So, when I got to a point where I felt comfortable that this whole conversation is a bunch of horseshit, I'd tell him, 'I'm Sergeant Brennan. The reason I'm here at the station is to stop drugs coming into and through the city. Are you carrying any drugs in your bag?' Basically we were focusing on drugs at that time, not weapons. I'd always leave it at drugs. So, 'Are you carrying any drugs in your bag? Are you carrying any drugs on your person?' Always the answer would be no, right? Except for one or two cases, they said yes. But then I'd come right out with the next question: 'Can I search your bag? Can I search you?' I would never say, 'Can I *look* in your bag, can I *check* your bag?' I would use the word *search*. 'Can I search your bag, can I search you?' That's what I wanted to do. I wanted to search. So I wanted to make it clear for the courts that I wasn't asking just to look in the bag, or I wasn't asking to pat this guy down. I wanted to search you. And the answer ninety nine point nine percent of the time would be yes."

Brennan was a streetwise cop steeped in the ambiguities and contradictions of life on the underside, so he was not given to wild, sweeping assertions. Therefore, even if his percentage of 99.9 was exaggerated, his basic point seemed credible. Most people—57.6 percent—who told the Bureau of Justice Statistics that their cars had been searched in 2005 said that they had consented.

If you talk to police officers long enough, many will concede that the crooks they catch are stupid—amazingly stupid—and that the smart ones get away. A prosecutor described his brother, a New York state trooper with a wry sense of humor, dancing his way into probable cause for an automobile search. "I just want to warn you while I'm here," he would say to a driver he'd pulled over for speeding on the Thruway, "it's a criminal offense in the State of New York to carry a loaded gun in a car." More often than you'd expect, the driver would reply innocently, "My gun isn't loaded." Or the trooper might say, "It's a criminal offense to carry more than fourteen grams of cocaine." The driver might protest, "I only have four grams."

In Union Station, any drug courier smart enough to know the law would know that despite Sergeant Brennan's approach, she had the right to keep walking, refuse to answer questions, and not give up her bag for a search.

But some seemed to think they were smarter than they turned out to be. "They'd say, 'Well, it's not really my bag,'" Brennan recalled. "One guy said this: 'I was in the McDonald's, I was sittin' there eatin', and I think I picked up somebody else's bag.' Or, 'I was at the train station, I was sittin' next to a guy, and I picked up another bag.' Those were said several times. So then, when that would happen, I'd get the yes, and the first thing I would do is [search] the person, 'cause if you got a weapon or something like that he's gonna get me with it. . . . Basically it'd be squeezin' the pockets, you know, you can tell when you've got a weapon. Or the crotch, hit the crotch. That's where a lot of drugs were, in the crotch. Then if I found something in the crotch I would just tell him, 'OK, I'm gonna reach inside there and take that out or you can remove it for me. What have you got in your crotch? Most of the time it would be drugs. Well, all the time it would be drugs. When you found an object, it was drugs."

His signal to make the arrest was to say "cigarette," like a magic word. "Boy, I'd like to finish this up and have a cigarette." Or, "I could use a cigarette." And then he and his partner would grab the person and cuff his wrists behind him.

Curious, Brennan started asking those he arrested why on earth they had consented, "and it was just amazing why people told us, 'You can search the bag,'" he said. The answers fell into three categories: First, they thought the police had information on them specifically, which meant, in effect, that they had already been caught. Although informants' tips were often matched to Amtrak passenger lists to guide searches of those still aboard, those who had already left trains were unidentifiable, free and clear until something about them caught Brennan's attention.

Second, they told Brennan that they believed he would search anyway, even if they said no. "'It didn't matter, did it?' he quoted a generic reply. "'If I told you no, you're definitely gonna know I had drugs. So I had no choice but to say yes and try to make some excuse after you found them, if you found them. Or, I was hoping you wouldn't find them.'"

That was the third reason Brennan heard: "They think they have the drugs so well hidden that they won't be found." He once discovered a sixty-gram cookie of crack cocaine disguised as cheese in a sandwich, complete with lettuce and tomato. "You know it's not water soluble, you can't hurt it," he chuckled. "In the shoes, in the socks, in the baby diapers, in the false-bottom cans. One guy on the train had a can of oil. Who in the hell travels from Miami, Florida, to New York City with a can of oil? And you take the bottom off the can, and sure enough, there's a half a kilo of coke in there. Potato-chip bags. That was a big thing, too. Potato-chip bags and cereal boxes. They would take out a portion of the cereal and a portion of the potato chips and reseal the bags. You know, just a dollar-ninety-nine-cent bag of potato chips. They'd remove the potato chips, leave some in there, and put in the cocaine. When you pick up the bag . . . you say, Yeah, I got it. You've never seen a potato-chip bag filled to the top. When they'd take out the chips, they'd fill it all the way up to the top. When you squeeze the top of a potato-chip bag, it's only half full. But this bag is full to the top. And then it weighs about 2.2 pounds—I got a kilo in here. Fantastic."

Ingenious hiding places for both drugs and guns were displayed on the bulletin board of the D.C. police department's Narcotics Branch, where Brennan now headed a unit that included undercover officers. Behind the dashboard of a Chevy Suburban, a void had been fashioned large enough to hold a 135-pound woman, or plenty of drugs. A rifle rack had been concealed in a truck's wide visor. Drugs had been placed in live African snails imported to England, in a car's gas tank that could be reached from the back seat, and in tampons that had been sliced open and resealed.

An entrepreneurial spirit had brought inventive devices to the marketplace. Police had found a Pepsi machine whose front opened to reveal a huge gun locker. A baseball cap contained a pouch, secured by Velcro where the visor met the headband, large enough to conceal a Beretta pistol. And a water bottle had been manufactured with three parts that unscrewed from one another: The top and bottom contained water, but the middle, its contents hidden by the label, could hold drugs.

Brennan liked to illustrate the intersection of police technique and case law by telling the tale of a twenty-one-year-old woman named Robin Nurse, who caught his eye with her purposeful stride through Union Station, off a train from New York at 12:30 a.m. She wore no rings, no necklace, no earrings. She walked past stores, staring straight ahead. Brennan followed her, then approached her, identified himself, and asked where she was going. To visit a friend, she said. And where did the friend live? On 145th Street, the woman answered. Oops, wrong city; there's no 145th Street in D.C.

She averted her gaze, and her answers seemed evasive. She had bought her ticket with cash, which police interpret as an attempt to conceal identity. An ID card she produced could be purchased, he knew, and he later testified that he had "never seen one that was legal." Brennan asked to search her tote bag. She refused. He had no probable cause to arrest her, so he told her that she was free to go but that her interview gave him grounds to detain her bag. She could wait until he got a drug-sniffing dog to check her bag, and if the dog smelled drugs he'd get a warrant to search it, or he'd give her a receipt for it and if it contained no contraband she could return and pick it up.

"She said, 'I'm staying with my bag, and I'm going to sue you.' I said, 'OK, well, that's fine. You have every right to, but I think I have enough from all your answers to have a dog check your bag.' And she had some terrible answers."

When he sent his partner for a dog, she changed her mind. "She decides, 'I'm not staying with my bag, I'm leaving.' I said, 'OK, that's fine. You're free to go.'

"So, a cab driver who was standing nearby says to her, 'Ma'am, did you want a cab?' She says, 'Yes, I do. I want to go to—' and she looked at me right like this, she said, 'I'll tell you when we get in the cab.'" That was enough to establish probable cause, Brennan believed. "I said, 'Now I'm detaining you with your bag. You will stay with the bag because of your statement to the cab driver, "I'll tell you where I'm going when I get in the cab.""

Then, after a dog alerted on the bag and she was arrested, she gave consent to a search without waiting for a warrant, the court record shows; the bag contained two and a half to three kilograms of cocaine. The case was appealed as an unjustified detention, and the federal Court of Appeals for the D.C. Circuit upheld the police, finding that Brennan's initial approach and questioning did not constitute a "seizure."[48] "We got a good ruling," Brennan declared.

"We followed the law so often that we lost cases because we made mistakes," he continued. "But we always fessed up to our mistakes. In other words, if we made a mistake, we learned by our mistake. . . . You held the driver's license too long; you should have gave it back quickly. Or you held the ticket too long. We'd admit it. And that's the best law enforcement. Admit what you do wrong. And you get credibility with the courts. And that's why my group, when I worked with them, was so successful. I had a group of detectives that were fantastic, abided by the law."

CHAPTER THREE

Defending the System

Uncontrolled search and seizure is one of the first and most effective weapons in the arsenal of every arbitrary government.

—Justice Robert H. Jackson

AN INDIFFERENCE TO PERJURY

HERE ARE TWO tales of a city. The first begins during twilight, about 5 p.m. on a December evening in the nation's capital. A twenty-four-year-old black man named Tyshaun Bullock is driving a Mercury Marquis. Three plainclothes "jump-out" officers of the vice squad, specializing in narcotics, happen to be directly behind him in an unmarked, dark green Chevrolet as he runs a red light and turns left at the intersection of Mt. Olivet Road and West Virginia Avenue NE. They activate a siren and a small bubble light on the dash, and he pulls over.

Through his rear window, the officers see Bullock bending down and leaning side to side, as if hiding drugs or a weapon—or reaching for a gun. They have been trained to interpret such movement as suspicious, so one officer approaches the car on each side, while the third hangs back. They order the driver out and ask if he has any guns or drugs. "No, not on me. You can search me," Bullock replies. An officer does a precautionary frisk and finds nothing.

A second officer then asks his permission to search the vehicle. Bullock agrees, and the officers lift the back seat, where they discover twenty-eight grams of crack, nine grams of powder cocaine, and seventy-eight grams of marijuana. They arrest Bullock for the drugs and, in their official report, justify their initial stop by citing him for running the red light. That's the first story, sworn to under oath.

The second narrative begins a little earlier in the day. The Mercury that Bullock bought three months ago has been quitting on him all afternoon. Stalled on Mt. Olivet, he gets a jump start from a truck, leaves the hood up and the engine running, and walks down an alley to urinate beside an abandoned house. He is wearing the uniform of the ghetto:

baggy khakis, a black sweater, a black jacket, black boots, and a ski hat partially covering his dreadlocks.

As he looks over his shoulder, he notices a dark green Chevy stop across from the alley and recognizes the men inside as a jump-out squad. Indeed, as he walks out of the alley while the officers watch, he realizes that he has seen one of them, Vincent Witkowski, at rallies where Bullock has spoken protesting police corruption. "So now in the back of my mind I'm saying I'm going to get messed with," he testifies later. Bullock works in an organization led by his father called Cease Fire: Don't Smoke the Brothers, which teaches street law and preaches against violence and police brutality.

He closes the hood, gets into his car, and is careful to fasten his seat belt, having been stopped once before for not buckling up. Aware of the jump-out squad behind, he drives along Mt. Olivet, enters the intersection on a green light, waits for oncoming traffic to clear, and swings left onto West Virginia as the light turns yellow. The siren sounds. "When I realized that they were stopping me," he later tells the judge, "I was saying, Here we go again."

He does not bend over or move side to side. He follows the procedures he has taught to young people in his program: sit still, put the car in park, turn off the engine, and place your hands on the wheel "where they can see them [because] you don't want to excite the police."

Witkowski, approaching the driver's side, tells him to produce his license and registration. Bullock asks why he's been pulled over. Witkowski repeats his demand for the documents. Bullock asks again, and the officer says he ran a red light. Bullock denies it and gives his version of events in the intersection. As he tries to explain, he senses that "the testosterone level was kind of going up," as he later testifies. Witkowski asks a third time for his license and registration, so Bullock reaches for the glove compartment, where he keeps his registration, but Witkowski stops him with a command: "Get the fuck out of the car."

Walking him to the rear of the vehicle, Witkowski remarks, "I know who the fuck you are, I know who your father [is], I know the work that you do." Another officer then searches him by pulling everything out of his pockets—his extra keys, his cell phone, his money—a far more intrusive search than the external pat-down allowed under *Terry* to check for weapons. Because of his work, Bullock knows this violates the Fourth Amendment, but he doesn't object, because he fears an escalation. He intends to file a complaint later at the Fifth District, a plan disrupted when the officers search his car—without requesting or receiving his consent—and come up with the drugs. That's the second story, also delivered under oath.[1]

Judges rarely choose to believe a defendant's version over a policeman's; someone facing years in prison has a high motivation to lie, after all. Yet the police also encounter tempting opportunities to shade the truth to get convictions and defend their professional behavior. Thanks to the Supreme Court's pro-police permissiveness, cops travel the streets in a legal haze of warrantless searches where small variables can easily be adjusted in the official narrative: furtive movements and suspicious answers, the smell of marijuana, evidence glimpsed through a car window, tips from nameless informants, implicit agreements to search, and myriad traffic violations where no impartial corroboration exists. Sometimes, it takes just a slight revision of a fact to put the police action on the constitutional side of the line. One technique, according to a veteran narcotics cop, is to stop someone, search him, and if anything is found, to justify the stop by reporting that he was carrying an open container of beer.

Officers who work narcotics or guns are not constitutional scholars, but they are trained to understand that if an initial traffic stop is illegitimate, all its results—including even permission for a search—are usually considered "the fruit of a poisonous tree"[2] and cannot be used in evidence. Therefore, dedicated defense attorneys relentlessly scour the record and dispatch investigators to sniff out the scent of a wrongful arrest. And in Bullock's case, his government-provided lawyer, an assistant federal public defender named David Bos, didn't have to hunt for long, because Bullock himself had noticed a way out of his predicament: red-light cameras at Mt. Olivet and West Virginia.

Once the light turned red, any car entering the intersection was automatically photographed, and a ticket was then mailed to the registered owner. When Bos obtained the records, he found no picture of Bullock's car. It had not triggered the camera. So here was an objective, electronic witness contradicting the police report's assertion that Bullock had driven into the intersection "as the traffic signal turned red."

The officers then changed their story by changing the color of the light to yellow—a valiant effort to save their case, but not quite good enough. Not being traffic cops, they didn't know the law and evidently failed to look it up. The statute permitted a driver to go through yellow if he couldn't stop safely.

This was the clincher, Bos thought: His client had committed no traffic violation. But to be on the safe side as he moved to suppress the drug evidence, Bos prepared several other layers of argument, as a skilled defense attorney will do. First, he noted, plainclothes police in unmarked cars were explicitly forbidden by a department regulation from enforcing traffic laws except when "a violation is so grave as to pose an immediate threat to the safety of others." That rule, broken by these officers, made the traffic stop look like a mere pretext for a drug search, Bos contended. But it didn't matter, for as the government correctly countered, pretextual stops were permitted by the Supreme Court under a unanimous 1996 decision, *Whren v. United States.*[3]

Second, Bos argued, the alleged consent to search was involuntary, since Bullock was in custody. Third, even if the judge found voluntary consent, it did not extend to "ripping the back seat out."

Finally, if the case went to trial, Bos was ready to inject reasonable doubt that the drugs actually belonged to Bullock. They might have been inadvertently left concealed when the car was sold to him a few months earlier, the lawyer said, or they could have been planted. A homeless man had told Bos of having seen an officer, with something in his hand, approach the car just before one of the searchers announced the discovery of narcotics. Such testimony might have swayed jurors who distrust the police.

But these allegations never had to be made, because federal District Judge Thomas Penfield Jackson found the officers untruthful. "Not only was their subjective intent at all times to stop and search Bullock and his car," the judge wrote bluntly, "the Court concludes they had no probable cause to stop him for a traffic infraction and they knew it. They cited him for running a *red* light—not a yellow—and would probably have continued to insist that he had done so had it not been discovered that the watchdog camera at the intersection of Mt. Olivet and West Virginia had caught no picture of Bullock entering the intersection on a red light. The officers now recall that it was a *yellow* light Bullock disobeyed, but he clearly did not. The pertinent traffic regulation obliges a driver to stop (if he can do so safely) before reaching the crosswalk; even by the officers' account Bullock was beyond the stop line and moving through the crosswalk into the intersection when the light turned yellow." Jackson also found that Bullock "gave no true permission, much less an invitation, for a search of either his person or his automobile." In other words, the police officers lied under oath. The judge granted Bos's motion to suppress the drug evidence, the government dropped the case, and Bullock went free.

Nothing happened to the cops, though. Despite the rare clarity of this ruling, the officers were not held to account—no perjury charges or suspension without pay, just the typical inaction that prevails even when judges think that policemen have testified falsely. At most, such officers are kept off the witness stand in subsequent cases lest their credibility be assailed by defense attorneys; prosecutors substitute other cops involved in the searches. Those under investigation by the U.S. Attorney's office in Washington are placed on the so-called Lewis List, named after a 1979 case that was thrown out because the prosecutor failed to reveal an officer's transgressions to the defense.[4] Harsher measures are uncommon. "There's an indifference to perjury," said Bos. "The judges who get most upset are the former prosecutors."

Judges themselves cannot always tell when perjury has been committed. The black robe confers no clairvoyance, and the perspective from behind the bench is less incisive than it may seem to laymen who sit in the hard pews of the courtroom. In their quiet chambers, some judges are willing to reflect on their uncertainties. "Most police officers are trying to do the right thing and are trying to do their job properly," federal District Judge Paul L. Friedman said carefully, "but they will push the envelope and try to get as close to the line as they can. There are times one suspects the police are exaggerating and embellishing, but it's very hard to discern."

It's especially hard because "in suppression hearings, it's the rare defendant who will testify," Friedman said. The judge almost never hears directly from the accused; the lawyers mount the arguments. A defendant's insistence that he gave no consent to a search, for example, may seem less credible when conveyed through his attorney. "Unless there's another witness to the search who's not at risk of prosecution, in most suppression hearings all you have is the police testimony. It's uncontested testimony. What do you do with uncontested testimony?" Friedman asked. "It's one person's word against—nothing."

Lawyers don't like to call defendants to the stand for three reasons, according to A. J. Kramer, the Federal Public Defender in Washington: First, judges almost always believe the cops instead of the accused, he said. Second, if the defendant later gives trial testimony, which is more important, it can be undermined if the prosecution finds differences from his statements at an earlier hearing. Third, Kramer said candidly, "Most of our clients are not good witnesses because they get nervous, confused, have bad memories, and tend to say things that don't help them."

The allegation that police lie in court bounces off some judges like water off stone. Astonished, an Alabama judge I talked with could hardly get his mind around the concept. He could see why a policeman might be auto-matically believed, he said, but not why an officer would be automatically doubted. The judge thought it reasonable that defense attorneys tried to exclude potential jurors who said they would probably credit any police testimony, but when prosecutors routinely questioned the jury pool about tendencies to *dis*believe a witness because he was a cop, the judge was unsettled. "Isn't it amazing that that question can even be asked?" he remarked.

It is not amazing, of course, as the judge went on to illustrate with another standard question he heard from prosecutors: "Have any of you folks had an unpleasant experience with a law enforcement officer?" Hands would go up, the judge observed, many of them raised by black citizens. Any predilection either to believe or to doubt a police witness was enough to keep you off a jury, he said.

"We have trouble getting black men on juries because they are asked if they've ever had any bad experiences with the cops," said Mary Petras, an assistant federal public defender in Washington. "I think, Shhh! Don't say anything! Just take your seat on the jury!"

Some prosecutors would rather have middle-aged black jurors from drug-ridden neighborhoods than liberal whites who live insulated from the scourge of gun-toting dealers and junkies. If the evidence is strong, prosecutors say, the fear of crime overcomes the skepticism about the police. Still, in a case relying too heavily on the testimony of one white officer, the defense may stir up enough doubts to get a hung jury or an acquittal. It is hard to find a black man in America who has not been hassled by a cop somewhere, sometime.

How widespread is police perjury? The impression depends on where you sit. "I think it's a common occurrence," said Sheldon Perhacs, a vet-eran defense attorney in Birmingham, Alabama. It's called "testilying," said a New York attorney, Andrew Patel.

"I think that police shade the truth everywhere; I think prosecutors turn a blind eye to it," said Greg Spencer, an assistant federal public defender who worked in Philadelphia and Washington.

The police are driven by careerist pressures, said Tony Axam, an expe-rienced lawyer in Washington's federal public defenders office. "The offi-cers are willing to either lie or buttress or bend the truth because this is their arrest," he contended. "If they find a gun on the street, it's not as good for them . . . if they just take the gun and turn it in to the district and say, 'This is what we found on the street.'" Therefore, he concluded,

"There are five guys standing around the gun, and they arrest one. They don't know whose [it is], but I guarantee by the time they get to court there's going to be some movement by that guy, there's going to be something that distinguishes him from the other four."

"I do not believe that most of our Washington police lie," countered a prosecutor who preferred anonymity. "There's not the need for it," given that the courts have drawn constitutional boundaries to permit officers reasonable latitude. So, I asked, why would so many defense attorneys perceive a pattern of falsehoods? "Most defense attorneys are smart, and they haven't gotten around to the idea that most crooks are dumb," he replied, and then corrected himself: "I can't speak for most crooks. Most crooks *we catch* are dumb." The lawyers think that "nobody could possibly be that dumb, so the police must be lying."

It was an entertaining answer that probably applied to the first few minutes of a defense attorney's practice, when he learns, as Kramer observed, that street crime is usually committed by characters so dim that they can't be trusted to testify in their own behalf.

While criminals are shocking their lawyers, the police are doing the same to prosecutors. So routine was the manipulation of facts by local police in Newark, New Jersey, that seasoned detectives asked Kenneth Ballen, a young assistant U.S. attorney in 1983, what he wanted them to say to make a questionable arrest look legal. "I said, 'We don't do things that way,'" Ballen recalled. "The cops said, 'That's the way we always operate with the prosecutors. We ask them to tell us what they need before we tell them what happened.'"

The detectives had entered a house three hours after an informant had called saying that a fugitive, for whom they had an arrest warrant, was inside with a bank-robbery suspect named Angelo Rivera. They had probable cause on Rivera, who had bought a car using stacks of cash still in the bank's wrappers (brilliant), but they didn't bother to get an arrest warrant; they just grabbed him when they saw him with their fugitive. They claimed consent for a warrantless search of the house, which turned up a gun, but Ballen didn't believe them, so he never planned to introduce the gun into evidence. And he didn't need to: Rivera confessed after his arrest. The question before the judge was whether the arrest was legal.

"They had screwed up, and they wanted guidance," Ballen said. "They fully expected to get it. This was the way they operate. They go out and do their job, and when there are legal problems the job of the prosecutor is to help them along with their testimony to comport with the law. And

I wouldn't do it. They did not like me. It was a very antagonistic relationship. They were very hostile toward the law. They ripped up their subpoenas from defense counsel, so I had to subpoena them."

Ballen put them on the stand with instructions to tell the truth, didn't vouch for them, and argued instead that the warrantless arrest was valid because Rivera was "in plain view," like physical evidence that could be seized. It was a novel application of the concept to a person, but it worked; the judge ruled the arrest legal, the confession stood, and Rivera got twenty years.

"They were incompetent," Ballen said of the police officers. FBI agents never pulled such a stunt with him. If they revised their facts, he never knew, because "the FBI was smart enough that they would never go in to a prosecutor" to collaborate on a fabrication. "They would have changed the story themselves beforehand."

The country has seen egregious examples of police dishonesty. Some three hundred convictions in Philadelphia were overturned in the 1990s after a cell of corrupt cops in the Thirty-ninth District was found to have planted narcotics and rigged confessions; six officers pleaded guilty to federal charges, and the city spent more than $30 million to settle civil lawsuits.[5]

A Los Angeles police unit, Rampart Community Resources Against Street Hoodlums (CRASH), was found in 1999 to have been selling confiscated drugs, shooting unarmed men, and planting narcotics and weapons to get convictions. One of the officers, Rafael Perez, had no remorse. "These guys don't play by the rules; we don't have to play by the rules," he told investigators. "When I planted a case on someone, did I feel bad? Not once. I felt good. I felt, you know, I'm taking this guy off the streets."[6]

After the scandal was exposed, 156 convictions were thrown out, the city paid $75.5 million to settle lawsuits, nine officers were charged, and twenty-three were fired.[7] Several years later, defense attorneys told an investigating panel that problems persisted and cited "compelling examples of erroneous arrests, inaccessibility of evidence needed for fair trials, coercive interview tactics, evidence suppression or planting by officers, alarmingly flawed investigations and police perjury they contend were ignored by judges, prosecutors and LAPD."[8]

Since only a tiny fraction of criminal cases goes to trial, police officers can gamble that they won't be cross-examined. And even in trials, judges often block probing questions by defense attorneys. They did so in ways that prevented the Rampart cops from having to answer for implausible and inconsistent stories. Judges who are elected, as in Los Angeles County, are loath to be seen as soft on crime even when they run unopposed, lest they draw an opponent into the race, which can cost them $100,000 or more in campaign spending.[9]

Such extreme incidents stand at one end of a spectrum of police behavior that runs from abject criminality to pure honesty. In between, in the everyday work of investigations, arrests, and prosecutions, the truth may be shaded more subtly. And sometimes the jurors will see through the deception.

"Our cops are notoriously bad testifiers," said Michelle Peterson, an assistant public defender in Washington. "They do lie. They want to make the story a little bit better." But they can't fool all of the jurors all of the time, especially those from poor neighborhoods where cops don't always behave impeccably. If conservative, middle-class communities contain pro-police jury pools, the nation's capital has a more skeptical mixture, and a lawyer who can drive a small wedge into police credibility finds that "it's very easy to convince the jury that there's reasonable doubt," Peterson observed. A federal judge who spoke with jurors after one acquittal "was shocked when they said that uncorroborated police testimony is not enough."

For attorneys who represent those charged with drug and gun crimes, the precarious grips on the possibility of acquittal are often carved out by police error or misconduct. If the police adhered strictly to the constitutional limits set down by the courts, as permissive as they have become, the lawyers would have little cause to file motions to suppress evidence.

The attorneys tend to see themselves defending not only their clients but the system itself. If they do not monitor, investigate, challenge, and illuminate the transgressions by the police and prosecutors, who will? The courts are passive by design; they can adjudicate only those actions and issues presented to them. Furthermore, the press is evaporating with the declining staffs of newspapers, which once probed and investigated and thereby kept the police in check. After Baltimore police in January 2009 stopped identifying officers who had been involved in shootings, *The Sun*, the largest local paper, did no digging and no effective reporting to uncover the name of the cop who shot an unarmed man a month later.[10] If even police shootings don't merit aggressive reporting, intricate violations of the Fourth Amendment have no chance of emerging from the shadows. Only vigorous defense attorneys are left to prevent those constitutional protections from withering.

DISCREDITING THE POLICE

Ironically, Tyshaun Bullock had tried to dismiss David Bos, figuring—as many poor defendants do—that a public defender would be too over-worked or underqualified to mount an assiduous defense. In this instance he was quite wrong, as Judge Jackson noted in praising Bos while denying Bullock's motion for a new lawyer.

Bos was part of the elite office of federal public defenders in Wash-ington, about twenty talented attorneys who are paid the same govern-ment salaries to defend the accused as assistant United States attorneys are to prosecute them. Nearly all federal districts have such cadres of lawyers to fulfill the government's obligation, under the Sixth Amend-ment's mandate for "the assistance of counsel," to provide a lawyer to any criminal defendant who cannot afford one. By contrast, the individual states' records on fulfilling the requirement vary from adequate to abys-mal, since some rely on private attorneys assigned at low hourly rates to represent indigent clients. So overworked have public defenders become that they refused to take new cases in eleven states as of early 2009.[11] When Georgia's system ran out of money in 2008, a man facing the death penalty for murder, Jamie R. Weis, languished in jail for eight months without steady representation, which meant no defense investigation could be done while witnesses' memories were fresh.[12]

Soaring caseloads provoked a revolt in Miami-Dade County, where fel-ony defenses reached an average of 500 annually per attorney, compared with the 150 maximum recommended by the National Advisory Commis-sion on Criminal Justice Standards and Goals. The average number of jailable misdemeanor cases hit 2,225 per lawyer, more than five times the recommended ceiling of 400.[13]

The backlash by defenders has been getting attention in the courts. An Ohio judge held a public defender in criminal contempt for refusing to take an assignment because of his heavy caseload; an appellate court quickly reversed. Taking the opposite tack, other judges have occasionally threatened to start releasing prisoners who can't get lawyers and can't be granted their right to speedy trials. Chief Justice Pascal F. Calogero, Jr., of Louisiana's Supreme Court, told the state legislature that "unless ade-quate funds are available in a manner authorized by law, upon motion of the defendants the trial judge may halt the prosecution in these cases. . . . The courts, as guardians of a fair and equitable process, must not let the state take a person's liberty without due process."[14]

Some judges have ruled that high caseloads constitute ineffective assistance of counsel. And after defendants filed a class-action lawsuit in Washington State, a superior court judge imposed a settlement requiring Grant County to raise public defenders' trial fees, fund an investigator for every four attorneys, and put a ceiling on each lawyer's work of 150 cases a year.[15]

But the federal system does reasonably well, and the jobs are eagerly sought. Every opening in the Washington office draws applications from hundreds of young lawyers, including law clerks for Supreme Court justices.

Since the District of Columbia is not a state, the U.S. Justice Department prosecutes all crimes, from the momentous to the mundane, and decides whether to try them in federal court or in Washington's Superior Court, which is equivalent to a state system. Drug and gun cases that would be heard in state courts elsewhere are often sent to federal court if the quantity of drugs is large or the defendant's felony record is severe—and the sentences there are usually more severe as well.[16] This puts a lot of street crime on the dockets of D.C.'s federal courts, and on the desks of the federal public defenders.

The defense lawyers occupy the entire floor of a building near the federal courthouse, and their offices throb with the same beat of intense synergy and brilliant bull sessions that can be found among reporters in the top newsrooms. In and out all day, to and from court and jail, the attorneys cross paths with one another in moments of mutual support and consultation, swapping assessments of judges, chewing over ideas for motions, sharing pieces of advice on case law, jury selection, and plea bargains.

They and their five investigators are persistent and relentless in ferreting out the slightest possibility of an unconstitutional stop or search or interrogation, the tiniest inconsistency among police officers' accounts. They pepper the courts with motions for excluding evidence when they think the cops may have stepped over the constitutional line—motions that they rarely win. They are repeatedly frustrated by judges they call "pro-government," usually nominated by conservative presidents.

"If the government can't supply a reason for a warrantless search, the courts will provide it for them," remarked A. J. Kramer, a jolly idealist who leads the team of defenders with a rapier zeal for the truth. "The police will do anything they want," he said, "and the courts will search and try to find a reason."

In these offices, there is a cultural skepticism about the police that spills into distaste and resentment. So often have the lawyers seen manipulated facts that they begin to see them everywhere, making an outsider who tends to trust the police feel gullible. An internal Web site called "Bad Cop. No Donut" carries a shadowy, Darth Vader–type image of a helmeted cop wearing a gas mask and wielding a long baton. It contains press reports of police infractions. There is a lot of impudent humor among these attorneys.

They are not cynics or extremists, though; they have sharp minds and centered judgments. The best of them think as precisely as surgeons, honing their arguments and trying to excise the tumors they see infecting the law. Privately, some federal judges praise them, pronouncing Kramer and his staff "terrific," as Judge Friedman put it. "He's a very good trial lawyer, he's a very good appellate lawyer, he's a very good manager. In most cases he's hired good people and trained them well. He has a lot of credibility with the court."

Since the lawyers attempt to preserve constitutional rights in the course of defending their clients, they must do so not as broad, sweeping campaigns that mobilize the country's conscience, but merely case by obscure case, motion by motion, brief by brief. In the ad hoc system of adjudication, liberty is bolstered by showing the courts where it has been violated. The task is intricately painstaking, threaded with the precedents of arcane legal history, and rarely capped by landmark decisions.

So diligent defense attorneys pore through the backgrounds of police witnesses in a struggle to uncover and introduce evidence of wrongdoing, past and present. Prosecutors are obligated by a 1972 Supreme Court ruling, *Giglio v. United States*,[17] to reveal information impeaching their witnesses, but they don't always do so completely or soon enough for the defense to use it effectively in trial. Therefore, whenever a judge disbelieves a police account, federal public defenders in Washington circulate the officer's name among themselves, filing it away in case the officer surfaces as a witness in future prosecutions.

Even then, however, a judge isn't always willing to let the jury hear about a cop's fabrication in an earlier trial. Kramer ran into this obstacle when the federal District Judge Richard J. Leon denied him permission to cross-examine Officer Efrain Soto, Jr., on precisely that point.

Kramer had the record. In a prosecution three years before, Superior Court Judge Harold L. Cushenberry, Jr., had declared, "I think Officer Soto lied. I think he lied" by giving "palpably incredible" testimony that he had spotted drugs in a defendant's hand.[18] In the new case, Soto claimed to have seen another man, Gerald F. Whitmore, run from the police, hold his right hand to his waist, and then throw a gun into a window well. A second officer saw the sprint and the asymmetrical movement of his arms but not the gun, leaving Soto as the lone witness.[19]

Yet Judge Leon blocked Kramer from using Judge Cushenberry's finding of past dishonesty to question Soto's present veracity. Nor would Leon allow jurors to learn anything else negative about Soto—that he had failed to pay child support and had violated regulations by neglecting to tell superiors that his driver's license had been suspended. Leon ruled that Kramer could neither ask Soto about these matters nor call three witnesses to Soto's untruthful character.

With the judge running interference, the prosecutor was free to call jurors' attention to the absence of any indication that the officer had lied, and the jury, kept ignorant of Soto's background, found Whitmore guilty of the gun charge as well as possession of a small bag of cocaine discovered in his pocket. Leon sentenced him to eighty-three months for the gun and, concurrently, one year for the drugs.

Kramer dug into the jungle of case law, wrote a fifty-five-page brief in appeal, and argued before three judges of the D.C. Circuit that Leon had erred. The appeals court, while finding the character witnesses too remote and biased to be allowed, agreed that Leon should have permitted Soto to be cross-examined on his prior untruthfulness, his license suspension, and his unpaid child support. "Nothing could be more probative of a witness's character for untruthfulness than evidence that the witness has previously lied under oath," the court declared. It overturned the gun conviction and left the drug penalty, which was shorter than the time Whitmore had waited in jail for justice. The government, lacking a sanitized chief witness, didn't bother with a retrial, and he was released.

Two months after the court of appeals opinion, the U.S. Attorney's office decided to keep Soto from testifying as the only officer to see a driver he had stopped drop a bag of cocaine on the ground. The prosecutor tried to introduce Soto's testimony indirectly, through another officer's account, so that Soto couldn't be cross-examined. But Mary Petras put Cushenberry's finding before the judge in the new case, arguing successfully that the stop was unjustified and the evidence inadmissible. The government filed an appeal, then withdrew and dropped the charge.[20]

It shouldn't be so hard for an accused to exercise his Sixth Amendment right "to be confronted with the witnesses against him," which naturally implies the right to confront their foibles as well. In principle, the credibility of any witness, including someone in law enforcement, may be challenged on cross-examination. But there are limits set by the Federal Rules of Evidence, which are promulgated by the Supreme Court and emulated by most states. How a judge applies them can obviously be pivotal to what a jury learns about a cop's prior conduct, and therefore to the outcome of a trial.

The closest you could get to a laboratory test of this variable came in two trials two months apart, with two different results for two men, each of whom Sergeant G. G. Neill claimed to have seen throwing a gun as he ran away. After one judge allowed Neill to be cross-examined about investigations of his conduct, the jury deadlocked; in the other man's trial two months later, different jurors were barred by a different judge from hearing the same information about Neill, and they delivered a guilty verdict.

The rules are aimed at moving a trial along efficiently without creating confusion or prejudice, and they apply equally to prosecution and defense witnesses. But some lawyers find them muddy and contradictory, a blurry labyrinth of obstacles and gateways.

For example, if a judge in an earlier case found that a policeman had done an unconstitutional search, a jury in a later trial could not be told unless the current judge regarded the violation as "evidence of the habit of a person or of the routine practice of an organization," according to Rule 406.[21] That has been practically impossible to demonstrate.

A judge also has discretion under Rule 608 (b) to allow cross-examination about a witness's conduct "if probative of truthfulness or untruthfulness," which means the defense may question the police about past allegations of dishonesty.[22] That was the provision the appeals court found applicable to Officer Soto in the Whitmore case. But the opening is limited by another rule, 404 (b), which bars lawyers from introducing evidence of earlier wrongdoing simply to show that the misconduct is likely to have been repeated in a current situation. The goal is to avoid a detour into an old case, a trial within a trial to resolve disputed facts. So if the vice squad in the *Bullock* red-light arrest made another disputed traffic stop in a later prosecution, a defense attorney probably could not show the jury Judge Jackson's written disbelief of the officers' account in *Bullock*. The lawyer could only ask the cops about it, thereby diluting Jackson's finding with their explanations and denials.

This restriction on evidence of earlier misconduct has two main exceptions: one, if the officer has been convicted of a crime involving dishonesty or a false statement (such as perjury) and punishable by at least a year in jail[23] or, two, if a judge is persuaded that the previous infraction may motivate the witness to do wrong in the current case, such as lie to get a conviction and curry favor with superiors.[24] Only by way of the second route—showing motive to lie currently—could Neill's alleged misdeeds be brought before the juries.

Neill had a reputation among the public defenders. They regarded him as contemptuous of the law on the street and brazen in his storytelling on the witness stand. He navigated along the constitutional boundary with instinctive boldness, or—defense attorneys would say—with reckless disregard and dishonesty. Some lawyers loved to get him in front of a jury. "The art of cross-examination is to take the witness where he doesn't want to go," one private attorney remarked. "If I have G. G. Neill, I've gone head-to-head with him so many times, he thinks I have something on him even if I don't. Ninety percent of what the jury takes in is nonverbal. He twists his body, he makes a face."

Two defense lawyers, Lara Quint and Mary Petras, genuinely doubted Neill's veracity in the case of Marcus Douglas, a twenty-eight-year-old black man he had arrested around midnight as the new year of 2005 arrived.

New Year's Eve is when the guns come out for merriment, and Neill's squad was prowling in a courtyard off Gales Place NE, watching for people getting ready to fire celebratory shots into the air. There was no disagreement between the sergeant and the defendant on the opening scene of their encounter. Douglas was outside drinking a beer with a friend named Shorty, and as midnight approached, the sergeant overheard Shorty say, "Go ahead, they busting off." Douglas replied, "Go get the joint." Neill then saw Douglas touch his waistband, as if he'd read the training manual.

In street slang, "bust off" meant "shoot" and "joint" meant "gun," not a marijuana cigarette, as Quint confessed to thinking. She was a young graduate of Harvard Law School trying her third case, smart in the law but charmingly self-deprecating about her naïveté in the dialect of Washington's tough neighborhoods. That's why she was getting help from Petras, a sassy and savvy zealot of the courtroom wars against the police. Bucking all odds, Petras had compiled a decent record of winning motions for her clients.

When Douglas noticed the police uniforms, he took off running. Neill gave chase, with two police cadets behind. Douglas paused by a bush long enough for Neill to catch him, and as the two bent over, Neill behind Douglas, Neill claimed that Douglas dropped a gun into the shrub. In fact, Neill told me, he was so close that if he had reached out more quickly, the gun would have fallen into his hand.

Douglas, a somber man with liquid eyes, earnestly denied tossing a gun or owning the .38 that Neill found in the bush. His air of sincerity convinced even his lawyers, who were accustomed to a clientele that did not usually radiate innocence. In the police report, signed by both men, Douglas had acknowledged having been told of his rights to silence and a lawyer, but he answered questions anyway. The following exchange appeared:

Q. What do you have to say about this charge?
A. I don't know nothing about the gun. I was running cause I had an open container of beer and I had weed on me.
Q. Do you know whos [sic] print was on the gun?
A. No.
Q. Why was Shorty telling you to bust off?
A. We was talking about busting off something at 1200 and I said go get the joint. It was almost 1200. I was gone drinking. . . . Everyone was talking about busting off.
Q. Why did you stop at the bush where the gun was?
A. I ran to throw the weed. I threw the bag of weed into the bushes. . . .
Q. Why was you fighting?
A. Off the drugs, off the drink.
Q. Is it possible that your prints is on the bullets?
A. No.
Q. Anything else.
A. No I was just trying to get rid of the weed.

The cadets had been too far away to see whether the gun had come out of Douglas's hand, so they would testify unhelpfully, and the case would turn on Neill's testimony alone—and on Neill's credibility. The lawyers found plenty of civilian witnesses, but some were scared of Neill, others had criminal records that would impeach them, and none had seen the conclusion of the chase.

To sow the "reasonable doubt" required for acquittal, then, Quint and Petras needed to introduce Neill's past record. They went through hoops to get it. They wrote the government letters requesting any information that might bear unfavorably on the credibility of the witness, as *Giglio* requires. The government stonewalled. Petras then heard from a private attorney that Neill had faced eight investigations in recent years, so the lawyers wrote again. Finally they had to file motions with the court, which ordered parts of the record turned over.

It included four investigations that were pending on or after the night he arrested Douglas: two complaints by citizens about unlawful automobile searches, one shooting after a struggle with an armed man, and one allegation that Neill had violated the Hatch Act, which prohibits government employees from using "official authority or influence" in a political campaign.[25] He was accused of handing out paper fans promoting a City Council candidate while marching in uniform on July 4, and that was the only investigation still open at the time of the trial. The others had been resolved in Neill's favor. The police department withheld the names of the complainants.

None of the incidents involved untruthfulness as defined by the Rules of Evidence, so the defense had to argue that all four had provided a motive for Neill to lie along the way to curry favor with the prosecution.

This bias theory illustrates how clumsy the law can be when it tries to diagram human behavior. Perhaps a cop under close scrutiny would bend every rule to please superiors with a conviction, or perhaps he would be uncommonly scrupulous. Conduct and testimony could go either way. One prosecutor, familiar with police culture, believed that officers who were investigated repeatedly reacted more typically with resentment toward their commanders, not deference. Nevertheless, logical or illogical, the Rules of Evidence opened only this narrow pathway for the defense, and they took it successfully. Over the assistant U.S. attorneys' objections, Judge Henry H. Kennedy, Jr., ruled that Neill could be questioned about the four complaints that had been in play during the course of the case, but no others.

Wealthy clients with millions to spend on their defense can hire sophisticated jury consultants to work up profiles of citizens likely to convict or acquit. Poor defendants have only the street sense of an experienced public defender, if they're lucky enough to draw one, and Douglas was. As potential jurors were screened in open court, he and his lawyers separately scored them on a scale of one to ten, then used their ten peremptory challenges to exclude people they thought might be too credulous of the police. (The government was granted six such challenges.)[26]

No reason need be given for a peremptory challenge, and lawyers can filter out jurors using any characteristics except race and sex, the Supreme Court has held.[27] But discerning racial and gender discrimination is difficult unless a lawyer acts blatantly to exclude all blacks or all men, for example; it's hard to unravel the prohibited from the permitted rationales.

Methods of weaving race into the selection process were outlined by a senior prosecutor in the Philadelphia district attorney's office, Jack McMahon, in a training video for fellow prosecutors. "In selecting blacks, you don't want the real educated ones," he declared. "Avoid selecting older black women when the defendant is a young black man," he advised. "If you get, like, a white teacher teaching in a black school that's sick of these guys maybe, that may be one you accept," he said. "The only way you're going to do your best is to get jurors that are unfair."[28] The tape, made public as McMahon campaigned for district attorney, contributed to his defeat.

The other method of exclusion, for cause, requires the court's approval and depends wholly on a judge's fair and perceptive appraisal of human shortcomings—a skill not always found on the bench. If a potential juror is the defendant's friend, that's obviously corrupting. If she has ever been the victim of a crime, her bias may be less certain.

During voir dire,[29] as the questioning in jury selection is known, Quint and Petras found that the pool comprised several people who knew the block, a few with relatives in the police force, others with relatives behind bars, some who had been robbed and said they were fed up with crime, and several members of volunteer anticrime patrols.

These categories seemed to cut in various ways. Some said the cops who were relatives never talked about their work. A middle-aged black man with a nephew in jail thought that his sentence was too long, and a white man believed that his brother's was too short. Both got excluded, one by each side. The defense screened out the anticrime patrols. A short, frail man from the neighborhood seemed so nervous that the judge dismissed him, and a woman was excused after she started crying about her niece having been mugged.

Quint and Petras used one challenge for cause to exclude a white man who said that because the police had done a lot of good in his neighborhood, he would tend to believe an officer who testified. They used a peremptory challenge against an elderly black man, formerly an elevator operator, who worked in an after-school program at a recreation center across the street from the spot where Douglas had been arrested. Quint wasn't sure whether he would want to be tough on guns or tough on the police.

"I felt OK about this jury," Quint remarked in the end. Including two alternates, it contained eight African-Americans, five whites, and one Asian. The juror elected foreman was a white man who worked for a pharmaceutical journal.

On the first day of the trial, I was the only observer sitting in the rows of wooden benches. When you're facing prison—and Douglas was facing four to five years—an empty courtroom must be one of the loneliest places in the world. It is a vacuum that engulfs many poor defendants with shattered families and friends who are stressed and busy with overlapping demands of unforgiving work hours, illness, and the desperate search for child care.

Douglas's three-year-old daughter had been brought to court by her mother and her mother's friend during jury selection the previous day. Although they were seated in the very last row, as if trying to be both present and invisible, Petras had quietly asked them to leave. The judge didn't like children in the courtroom, Petras told me later, and she worried that jurors might think it callous to allow the little girl to hear such accusations about her father. So the room now had a sorrowful sense of emptiness.

A federal trial has its costumes. Female lawyers are evidently supposed to dress as if they have come directly from a funeral. Convention assigns males somber suits but permits them flagrant ties. Jurors come in all manner of clothing, from jeans and T-shirts to business attire.

Defendants being held without bail appear in prison uniforms when no jury is present; judges are accustomed to the garb, but it would scream to jurors, "Criminal!" So when juries are seated and trials begin, the accused are outfitted from two racks of variously sized garments in the public defenders' office on the ground floor of the massive federal courthouse. Douglas wore a bright orange jumpsuit to his pretrial motion hearings but for the jurors he dressed more respectably than he generally did as a free man: His lawyers had given the federal marshals who guarded him a pair of dark trousers, a blue shirt, and a dark purple tie to have him put on. He looked splendid.

Neill arrived at the courthouse wearing his police uniform topped off by a pink baseball cap labeled OPERATION IRAQI FREEDOM. He shed the cap before walking into the courtroom and taking his seat on the witness stand.

The opening arguments had sketched the conflicting stories. Douglas was an armed felon "reaching for his thirty-eight-caliber handgun." Douglas was an innocent beer-sipping celebrant who had the "bad judgment" to carry his open can into the courtyard as midnight approached.

Neill tried to be engaging. He lost a little of his ghetto dialect, and as the jurors filed in or out, he faced them and stood with his hands behind his back, as if "at ease" on a military parade ground. "Good morning, Your Honor," he said. "Good morning, jurors." He was a veteran witness, although, a supervisor told me, some of the assistant U.S. attorneys regarded him as a bit of a loose cannon, hard to control on the stand.

One of the prosecutors, Jessie Liu, led him gently through the events. She displayed a huge aerial photo of the courtyard and had him stick orange dots on the spots where he had parked, where he had seen Douglas, where the critical bush was located. With the judge's permission, she had him crouch to demonstrate how he had bent over Douglas. She handed him the gun, in a plastic bag; he removed the weapon and confirmed that it was the same firearm that he had recovered.

After a recess, Mary Petras geared herself up to punch holes in his credibility. She began by introducing the police form on which his questioning had been recorded. Douglas's answers had been blacked out, because his lawyers hadn't yet decided whether to have him testify. The judge had accepted the prosecution's argument that the jury should not see answers on which he might not be cross-examined.

So the questions, not the answers, were Petras's focus—questions she hoped jurors would find unnatural from an officer who had supposedly just seen Douglas toss a gun. "The first question you asked Mr. Douglas was, 'What do you have to say about this charge?' Correct?"

"Yes," Neill answered.

"You don't say, 'I just saw the gun in your hand.'"

"If I say I saw him with the gun, he might get antagonistic," Neill replied, explaining that he always asked open-ended questions in the hope of getting more information.

"You don't say, 'Why did you drop the gun in the bush?' You say, 'Why did you stop at the bush where the gun was?' Correct?"

"Yes."

A seed of doubt had been planted.

She began to ask Neill about two other arrests that night for thrown guns, so close in time that he seemed to be everywhere at once. When she implied that he was picking up guns and linking them to random people, Neill got testy and began speaking rapidly. "If I hadn't seen him with a gun I wouldn't have locked him up. It's easier to get the gun off the street. I don't have to come to court. After twenty-six years I don't like to do it anymore. This is about the truth. You either see it or you don't." (Some cops do like to come to court, though, because it means overtime that can run their pay up above $100,000 a year.)

As Petras proceeded to assemble a timeline suggesting that Neill could not have made such rapid arrests (although he probably could have, based on how fast I saw him move on the streets), Liu objected, and the judge decided after a conference at the bench that the sequence was irrelevant. But another seed of doubt had already been sown.

And then, reconvening after lunch, Petras hit him with the key questions, designed merely to get some facts of his past before the jury. "Sergeant Neill, you are currently the subject of an investigation yourself, correct?"

"Yes, ma'am."

And so it went: A violation of the Hatch Act? A complaint by a citizen that you illegally searched his car? Another complaint that you illegally searched him and his car? A shooting? She deftly avoided asking him to explain any of these incidents, although he jumped in with his excuse for wounding an armed man he had been wrestling to the ground.

"I only shot him when he tried to spin the gun around and said he was gonna shoot me twice," Neill reported. An investigation by the U.S. Attorney's office had been opened and closed, and the Metropolitan Police Department had criticized him for the offense of keeping his ammunition clip only partly full, his method of avoiding excessive pressure on the spring. Also, he added, "MPD wanted to know why I didn't shoot him when I saw the gun in his hand, and I said 'cause he wasn't pointin' it at me."

Now the men and women who would judge Douglas had a slightly more complete picture of the key police witness than jurors usually receive in trials, although it was still rather sketchy. Neill seemed to measure his squad's accomplishments not by the number of arrests or convictions—data he never offered to me—but by the number of guns removed from the streets. "We got a hundred and sixty guns in a year," he once announced as we rode through darkened neighborhoods.

This was not a feature of his professional values that Liu chose to emphasize in her redirect examination; perhaps a jury would speculate that his conviction rate was low, that his police work was shoddy. But she did ask him whether his unit ever found guns without making a charge.

"We've found guns but haven't charged anyone because we didn't see anyone with them," he answered.

And at another point, she aimed the essential question straight at Neill's heart: "Do you have any doubt that you saw the defendant with a gun?"

"No doubt. I have twenty-six years in the force, and I'm close to retirement. I don't want to jeopardize that. I have a top secret clearance in the military." Then he turned to look squarely at the jury. "If you find him not guilty, that's your right." He seemed poised to elaborate but was interrupted by Judge Kennedy, who told him not to go beyond the question. There had been no objection by Douglas's lawyers to Neill's burst of defensiveness; they probably sensed that it would work to his detriment.

After Neill's testimony, the prosecution engaged in some defensiveness of its own. Knowing that no fingerprints had been found on the gun, the government tried to preempt jurors' surprise and doubt by eliciting testimony from a veteran police lab technician about how hard it was to lift useful prints. Either the surface is dusted with black powder, which is then picked up by tape and transferred to a white card, or the gun is placed in a tank where super-glue is heated until it becomes a gas. It adheres to fingerprints, which can be seen using fluorescent chemicals and special light. Only 10 to 15 percent of recovered guns have identifiable prints, the technician testified, because most places that hands touch—the trigger, the handle—are knurled, and prints on flat surfaces are often smeared, especially if the gun is thrown. The explanation, albeit logical, often throws jurors who have watched the fictitious precision of crime-lab work on television.

The prosecution rested, and then the defense had to decide whether to put Douglas on the stand. The problem was, Douglas would have to pay a high price for giving the jury his version: If he testified, the prosecutor would cross-examine him about a prior conviction. It would come down to the word of a young black felon against a veteran white policeman.

In general, a defendant's criminal record remains unknown to the jurors, who are supposed to judge guilt or innocence regardless of prior conduct. But if the accused testifies, the prosecution is free to cross-examine about past convictions involving dishonesty, just as the defense can try to impeach the credibility of testimony by government witnesses.

In this case, however, jurors already knew that Douglas was a felon, because the fact was woven into the federal charge he faced: possession of a firearm by someone "who has been convicted in any court of a crime punishable by imprisonment for a term exceeding one year."[30] It is a highly prejudicial accusation that tarnishes defendants even if they remain silent in their trials.

What the jurors did not know were the details, and his lawyers didn't want them to find out. In 1995, Douglas had been sentenced in Maryland to five years, all but one suspended, for two robberies and a burglary. He had no serious blemishes on his record since, and Petras and Quint hoped that Judge Kennedy would allow him to testify without having that conviction introduced. Petras stayed in jail until midnight prepping him for his possible testimony the next day, but in the morning, Kennedy found the conviction admissible under the Rules of Evidence, which admit priors whose sentences have ended within the previous decade.

Under the circumstances, Quint's more seasoned colleagues advised against putting Douglas on the stand. "They said the details of his priors would come out, and you never know what a defendant will say under cross-examination," she noted. Worse, the Federal Sentencing Guidelines would increase the penalty if he testified and was found guilty: His sentence would be raised by two levels for "obstructing justice," a perverse twist that punishes those who profess their innocence. Just by going to trial and refusing to plead guilty, Douglas had forfeited a sentence reduction of two levels for "acceptance of responsibility." The dice were loaded.

Therefore, the defense didn't really put on a case beyond relying on the holes that Quint and Petras hoped they had poked in Neill's story. After the summations, the jurors filed out to deliberate, and the courtroom was left in heavy silence.

Over the next two days, jurors were confounded and divided. Some had not taken notes, one told me later, so they asked Kennedy twice for transcripts, which they assumed they had a right to see. But the judge refused without telling them why, causing irritation in the jury room; had they known in advance, they would have been writing. Kennedy accepted Quint's argument that excerpts out of the context of body language and inflection would be distorting, and the judge did not want the case retried in bits and pieces of transcript. Quint didn't want Neill's credentials paraded again in print before the jury.

At 3:15 p.m. on the second day of deliberations, the foreman passed Judge Kennedy this note: "Unfortunately, we are at an impasse. We have taken two votes. Please instruct us on how to proceed. We feel we have said all that we have to say." The judge sent them home and brought them in for a third day, when the foreman finally notified him that they were hopelessly deadlocked. Kennedy did what judges hate to do: He declared a mistrial.

The jurors broke down mostly along racial lines, according to one of them, a young white woman. The African-Americans tended to disbelieve Neill, and the whites and Asian man voted for conviction. Some jurors told of friends and boyfriends who carried guns. During voir dire, the young woman added, a number of jurors had concealed their negative experiences with the police, which had created bias, although she obviously had biases of her own. "I'd rather that the cops presumed that something was bad rather than good," she said. "I think the same thing with tapping our phones to catch terrorists. So what? Let the cops presume something and then find nothing." The police, she declared, should have the right to search any car at any time for any reason.

Luckily for Douglas, other jurors were not as credulous, and Quint and Petras had aimed at just the right points of vulnerability. "One gentleman had problems with Neill being under investigation," the juror said. "One gentleman was stuck on the fact that there were not fingerprints, even though statistically only 10 to 15 percent of guns have fingerprints," as the lab technician had testified. Some were bothered by the open-ended questions that Neill had put to Douglas. "I wasn't," the woman remarked. "I'm in marketing, and I ask open-ended questions all the time to get more information."

She found the whole experience frustrating. "There were a couple of people who didn't want to deliberate. They were stuck on the verdict from the beginning. They played paper games, crossword puzzles. I said I could be convinced if somebody could give me reasons why Sergeant Neill would lie. Why would he perjure himself over something as insignificant as this?" But the deliberations moved the other way, she reported, as one black woman who began in support of conviction shifted to not guilty. "Six of us believed Sergeant Neill. He wasn't the most stellar witness. He was very excitable by defense questioning. If he had kept his cool," she said, he would have been more credible. "His demeanor had a huge part" in jurors' reactions to him. So Quint and Petras had been smart to oppose providing the sterile transcript.

Douglas's failure to testify bothered this juror, because "nobody contradicted Sergeant Neill." And there was speculation in the jury room about what Douglas's felony had been. She was surprised to learn from me that his crime was nonviolent and more than a decade old. She had assumed worse, and the new details improved her opinion of him. So, perhaps he would have been helped even further by taking the stand.

An outright acquittal would have set Douglas free, but a hung jury offers the prosecution the option of a retrial, so Kennedy left him locked up pending that decision. A couple of months later, the U.S. Attorney's office offered him a plea bargain, and he took it: guilty of a misdemeanor for possessing a gun and ammunition, twelve months' probation.

In a similar gun-throwing case tried two months later, in March 2006, the same background information about Neill was kept from jurors, who believed his testimony and voted unanimously for conviction.

The arrest had occurred at 1:30 on a cold December morning. As

Franklin Dorn was leaning into a car, Neill's unit approached and asked to search him. "He turned and walked away, which he's allowed to do," said his lawyer, Jonathan Jeffress. "They grabbed him, turned him around, and he ran." He got away by coming out of his coat, which one officer held. Neill said that he saw Dorn throw a gun, and he found cocaine in the coat pocket.

The status of each investigation into Neill's activities was identical to what it had been during the Douglas trial, and Jeffress, an assistant public defender, argued similarly that Neill should be cross-examined about them all. "For at least the past five years," Jeffress wrote in his brief, "Sergeant Neill has been under investigation by the Metropolitan Police Department continuously. . . . Evidence that Sergeant Neill has been investigated—and is being investigated—for conduct related to abuse of authority, excessive force, and violations of the Fourth Amendment makes it more probable that he engaged in such conduct, and/or is biased, in the instant case. In the absence of such evidence, it is less probable that the jury will believe that Sergeant Neill is being dishonest or has a reason to ingratiate himself with the government. . . . The defense should have the opportunity to explore, through cross-examination, whether the range of incidents in Sergeant Neill's history constitute a potential source of bias."[31]

"Logically," the government argued in rebuttal, "a witness accused of misconduct unrelated to the case in which he is testifying, or that allegedly occurred long before the events of the case on trial, or that is being investigated by an entity separate from the agencies handling the trial matter, has little incentive to shade his testimony to favor the prosecutor."[32]

The government's reasoning was accepted by Judge Colleen Kollar-Kotelly, who applied a stricter test than Judge Kennedy had. She found all the incidents too far removed to motivate Neill to lie on the stand. The only pending investigation, into the Hatch Act violation, was being conducted neither by the police department nor the U.S. Attorney's office, she noted, but by the Office of Special Counsel, a federal agency that Neill could not favor by testifying falsely. "From a factual perspective," she wrote, "it is difficult to see how the investigations at issue—all but one of which are presently closed—would prompt biased testimony on the part of Sgt. Neill."[33]

Excluding the allegations against Neill not only kept facts from the jury but also reduced the tension of the cross-examination, which affected Neill's demeanor. He told me later that he thought he had done better in the Dorn trial than against Douglas, and it seemed likely that he had removed one factor that had made the Douglas jurors doubt him: his excitable defensiveness.

Written statutes and regulations and court opinions are too brittle to embrace the supple nuances of human behavior, and so reasonable judges can obviously disagree on how to apply the code to the vagaries of actual conduct. As a general rule, though, investigations exonerating officers have less chance of getting before juries than those that find wrongdoing, and while that seems legitimate, it also provides police officials with additional motivation to whitewash misconduct. If departments justify a citizen's complaint and punish the cop, they may lose a credible police witness.

Dorn was sentenced to twenty-seven years in prison.

Had the investigations of Neill been introduced, "It would have made a difference with some of the jurors," Jeffress speculated. "I don't think we would have gotten an acquittal," but all he needed for a hung jury, of course, was one member who refused to convict.

"Guilty" may be pronounced only unanimously in federal courts, and even as basic rights are battered, this remains a bedrock protection for the tiny fraction of defendants who go for trials rather than plea bargains. The same is true in forty-eight states. (The exceptions, Oregon and Louisiana, require all twelve jurors in first-degree murder and death-penalty cases, respectively, but allow just ten to convict of lesser felonies.) The rule of unanimity annoys the veteran sergeant J. J. Brennan, who thinks that juries should be able to convict by majority vote. "Crooks got enough rights," he told me late one night as he led his narcotics squad on its shift. "They're covered. The right not to give a video statement. The right to this, the right to that. Then the government to convict has to prove it beyond a reasonable doubt." He found it inconvenient.

SOWING REASONABLE DOUBT

Since thrown guns often provide openings for the defense to plant reasonable doubt about police credibility, the police are often tempted— as they write their reports and shape their testimony—to see everything unfold with remarkable clarity.

Formally, they may be taught to document only what they actually witnessed, not what they surmised. "Put down what you saw, not what you *think* you saw," Sergeant Curt Sloan told officers in the Washington,

D.C., training course on finding guns. "If you seen it was a gun, it was a gun," he said. Otherwise, it was "a dark object." Or, he told them, you heard a metallic object hitting the pavement. If you didn't see it in the perpetrator's hand, say so. And write every detail, he instructed, since the case may not come to trial for a year or two, long after your memories will be cluttered by multiple intervening arrests.

Ironically, however, police officers who are precisely honest may lose convictions, because truth invariably contains ambiguities and contrasting perspectives. Reality is rarely neat and orderly, and anyone who investigates it, whether journalist or detective, knows that accuracy includes contradictions and blank spots, which can be spun by a skilled defense attorney into an impression of fabrication. To avoid appearing to have made up a story, then, some officers make up a good one, scrubbed clean of every question mark.

Not so an experienced cop named Wayne, a tall, beefy, talkative officer with a shaved head who was touched when jurors believed him, even though their verdict was not guilty. He had followed three men, hurrying to get away from him, into the hallway of an apartment building, and he could see blurrily through a glass wall as one of them fumbled with his keys. Then he heard a gun drop to the floor.

He had heard a lot of guns drop and knew the sound. When he approached, he saw that the man with the keys had just dumped his pockets on the floor: keys, change, gun, everything. He made the arrest and was honest about saying that he hadn't actually seen the defendant holding the gun. "I could have," he told me. "I could have said I saw the gun. It was a challenge to my integrity."

Jurors told attorneys after the trial that they accepted his account but thought it left reasonable doubt about which man had held the gun. And so, while it was hard to lose the case, Wayne felt proud to be seen as truthful—the lightness in his voice confirmed that this was so.

Another case of a thrown gun illustrated the complicated interaction between honesty and credibility. No dirt on the arresting officers could be found, but the circumstances seemed ambiguous.

About 12:30 one morning, narcotics police observed what they suspected were drug transactions in a parking lot. They saw the dealer get out of a blue Chrysler Pacifica, make what seemed to be sales, and get into a black sedan. The policemen fired several shots to halt the black car, but it rammed a police cruiser and took off.

The cops then stopped the Pacifica, and as it maneuvered in an attempt to flee, they saw the front passenger door open briefly. One officer spotted something silver fly out; another heard a metallic thud and the sound of metal sliding across pavement. Officers found a gun under a nearby parked car and another gun on the driver. Since a thirty-two-year-old man named Antoine Andrews was riding in the front passenger seat, the cops connected him to the tossed pistol. A back-seat passenger was not arrested.

Andrews's lawyer, David Bos, deftly teased out contradictions in the officers' stories. One said the parking lot was brightly lit; another said it was dark. The sketch by a crime-scene technician showed a light blocked by trees. Initially, in a written report and at a preliminary hearing, an officer indicated that the car had come to a halt before the gun flew out but later said that it had been moving. The car's location seemed uncertain.

Andrews had a few convictions behind him, two for drugs and one as an accessory after the fact of murder. But he vehemently denied to me that he'd had a gun and insisted that he'd never owned one. In his version, the cops were shooting at the black car and then stopped his, yanked open the passenger door, pulled him out, threw him on the ground, handcuffed him, and put a foot on his head.

Bos, no stranger to miscreants, thought Andrews was the innocent victim of a drug bust gone wrong. The police, embarrassed that the dealer had escaped, had to file a report after the shooting, Bos surmised, and charged Andrews to lean on him for information about the occupants of the black sedan. When he didn't cooperate, they prosecuted.

Andrews tried to dress up for his trial. He wore a mismatched suit with a dark jacket that was too large, pants of a slightly different color, and a sparkling clean white shirt whose collar was so loose that his tie couldn't be entirely tightened. Jurors were more casual, and some looked like what they were supposed to be: his peers. All were black except for three white men. The foreman was an African-American with his hair in cornrows and his head wrapped in a blue bandanna.

After the jury began deliberations, Easter weekend intervened, and the next Monday morning, Bos carefully placed Andrews on a bench on the main floor of the courthouse, hoping that jurors would see him as they walked by and recognize him as a real person whose life was in their hands. He looked much younger than his thirty-two years and, as a condition of his release pending trial, had been in a halfway house for a year. Bos said that he had never before had a client who actually obeyed all the rules for that long.

At 10:15, the jury sent word that it had reached a verdict. "I'm nervous," Andrews said. His face was contorted with anxiety as he entered the courtroom.

The jurors filed in. The foreman passed a piece of paper to Judge Richard W. Roberts, who read it and then passed it back.

"How do you find the defendant?" Roberts asked.

The foreman answered: "Your honor, we find the defendant not guilty."

Andrews closed his eyes and clasped his hands in front of him, as though praying. Bos put his arm around his shoulder in a brotherly hug. The prosecutor showed no emotion. She had lost cases before.

The judge polled the jurors one by one, thanked them for their service, then adjourned and went back to the jury room to convey my request to talk to any who were willing. Four agreed: the three white men and one black woman.

It turned out that the jurors were not actually unanimous inside their own minds. From the start of deliberations, three of them thought Andrews had thrown the gun out of the car, and all three were sitting before me in the jury room: the African-American woman and two of the white men. The third white man had seen cops misbehave enough to disbelieve them. "I have been around a lot of police officers," he said. "I have a negative feeling about the police. One of the places I go to eat is a Salvadoran restaurant, which is always full of police officers with guns, drinking."

The black woman had changed her mind over the Easter weekend as "reasonable doubt" crept into her thinking while she reflected on Bos's opening statement. "I gave it serious thought," she said. "There was sloppy work on the part of the police department. They could have come in more prepared. . . . There was a lot of confusion going on."

But the two white men did not change their minds, only their votes. "I thought he was guilty," one said.

"He was there," said the other. "The police put him in the passenger seat; the gun didn't fall from heaven."

"He'll be back on the streets, and next time he might kill somebody," the first declared.

So if they still believed in his guilt, why vote to acquit? "Because I knew it wasn't going to go the other way," said the second white man.

"We knew that we weren't gonna sway nine other people," the first explained. "If we had stuck, it would have been a mistrial." He found himself thinking, What if it had been reversed, with himself in the minority for acquittal? In that event, "I would never have changed my vote," he declared, "because I would never want an innocent man to go to jail."

"I would not have, either," said the woman. The second white man agreed. He would never vote guilty if he didn't believe it, he insisted, although he had voted not guilty without believing it.

That was exactly right for a system designed to free a dozen guilty rather than imprison a single innocent. It is an ideal hardly attained, and one seriously eroded in a time of terrorism, but the jurors' adherence to the standard reminded me of an admiring comment I'd heard from a Soviet legal scholar fifteen years before. His own country had no juries, and when he attended trials during visits to England and the United States, he was surprised and moved by watching ordinary people without legal training become attentive, serious jurors who worked hard to be just. They grew into their awesome roles.

Yet the two white men did not feel so noble. "I've never been on a jury before," said the first. "My impressions are not so good, because we let a guilty person go."

"It's not a perfect system," said the second, and it got him thinking. "Out of all the death-penalty cases, how many have this ambiguity?"

THE AIRTIGHT ARREST

Sergeant J. J. Brennan didn't want his drug cases to have any ambiguity at all. When his undercover narcotics officers went out on a "buy-bust" (a purchase and an arrest), the preparations were meticulous, at least when I was present. They xeroxed the fives, tens, and twenties to be paid to a dealer so their serial numbers were recorded. The undercover officer (U.C.) who carried the bills was often wired with a tiny radio transmitter and, if the transaction occurred on the street, videotaped by a plainclothes officer sitting behind the tinted windows of an unmarked car nearby.

If everything went perfectly, the U.C. made the buy with the registered bills, the conversation was recorded, the scene was taped, the U.C. got away safely with the drug evidence, and within minutes the plainclothes officers swooped out of the shadows and down on the seller with the incriminating serial numbers in his wallet—tying it all up for the prosecutors in a neat package of indisputable proof. I watched the unit do this fast-paced sting operation again and again like a well-drilled offensive squad.

It played like any professional team, mostly by the constitutional rules but occasionally with a subtle foul in the hope no referee would notice: a pat-down without suspicion or permission, a quick interrogation without a Miranda warning. Here is where the Fourth and Fifth Amendments met the road—and sometimes got a little bent.

The first time I went out with Brennan's bunch, they were after a bigger dealer than the street sellers who hang around on seedy corners. This one had already sold crack to three U.C.s, and was slated tonight to make a fourth sale of a greater amount, over fifty grams, which would bring a heavier punishment. It's a common police tactic to induce larger and larger sales until the defendant qualifies for a long stay in prison, and sometimes, defense attorneys say, the dealer is duped into borrowing the drugs just to meet a contrived demand that is uncharacteristic of his usual level of business. Usually in vain, the lawyers try to persuade judges that this constitutes entrapment, because the crime—in this case its magnitude—is instigated by the police. Evidence so gathered would be inadmissible.

But few judges put the brakes on the cops. The war on drugs has eroded rights and empowered law enforcement, as the war on alcohol did under Prohibition and the war on terrorism has since 9/11. Rarely do courts find entrapment in any but the most blatant cases. Brennan had no cause for worry tonight.

Unlike the standard buy-bust on the street, the plan here was to do the buy, then to obtain a search warrant for the dealer's home, where a significant stash of drugs and guns might be found, and finally to seek a grand jury indictment.

You would never guess by looking that this was a police unit: a gray-haired black woman wearing a bandanna, a young woman in hot pants, a lithe black man in torn jeans, a beefy white guy wearing a sleeveless shirt and tattoos on his biceps, a short white man with a ponytail and a baseball cap on backwards. He was the lead officer on this case. About twenty members of the squad, dressed down to blend into the neighborhoods, gathered around a table at the Narcotics Branch, a few blocks from Union Station, where "Ponytail" briefed them with sketches, maps, and aerial photos.

There was happy tension in the air, like a football team pumped up in the locker room for a big game. They heard the intelligence about the "target" and his usual patterns: He was five feet five inches tall, two hundred pounds, drove a white Cadillac, and had been watched for a long time. Tonight's buy would be made by a young black female officer, "R,"

who had been introduced to him as the girlfriend of a seasoned confidential informant (C.I.).

The first buy had been here, at the corner of Seventh and P, Ponytail
said, pointing to a grid he had drawn with a black marker, and then the
dealer drove up to this street, across here, down here, and then around,
in a kind of U. "He's very comfortable in this area." The second sale was
made inside a 7-Eleven on the corner here, and then he drove here, down
here, up here. Ponytail expected him to cruise the neighborhood before
meeting R and the C.I. The squad didn't have to be told to park their
unmarked vehicles in quiet alleys or dark lots, and to roll up their tinted
windows so they couldn't be seen.

As practiced as they were, though, they were plainly anxious about R's
safety. They devised a signal for her to indicate danger: two hands clasped
above her head. A sergeant laughed nervously that she shouldn't do any
idle scratching unless she wanted to be rescued. They worried that the
dealer would invite her into his car and make the sale there, out of sight,
without video.

And sure enough. She went to meet the C.I., and the others fanned
out in their unmarked vehicles, found unobtrusive spots to park, listened
to their radios, talked to one another on their cell phones, and waited. R
was in view of the "eyes," a young black officer who watched her from
his car, followed her, monitored the transmissions from her wire, and
gave the squad running commentary. He was one of those people who
marveled that he was actually getting paid for his enjoyment; he loved his
work in narcotics, because it had an exciting element of risk, and he got
to outwit street-smart drug dealers—all on behalf of the Department of
Justice!

Just before the rendezvous, Ponytail reassured R gently on the cell
phone, told her to stay calm and remember that she had plenty of backup.
She linked up with her "boyfriend," the C.I., and when the target came
driving along, not in his white Cadillac but in a burgundy Pontiac, she
did what they'd hoped she would not have to do: She and the informant
got into the car. The tension in Ponytail rippled through him like an electric current; I was sitting behind him, and I could see it in his body. He
gripped a handheld radio in one hand, his cell phone in the other, as the
"eyes" reported that the car was moving, the eyes following and giving
the vehicle's locations as it meandered among the dangerous blocks of the
neighborhood.

The time of sitting and waiting in the darkened car seemed to run on
and on, and finally the crackling voice of the eyes reported her out of the

Pontiac. Ponytail flipped his phone open, its screen glowing in the dark, and made a call to order her picked up. His instructions were relayed by radio, and soon she was safe inside an unmarked police vehicle.

Ponytail hadn't quite relaxed yet. Because the buy hadn't been taped and the C.I. was present, he needed to be sure that it had been done properly. He punched a number on his cell phone, reached R, and asked her whether the drugs and cash had passed directly between the dealer's hand and hers, and not through the informant's. That would have tainted the transaction. "And it went directly from your hand to his hand?" he asked. She must have said yes. "Directly from your hand to his hand?" Again, she must have reassured him. He asked again and again to be sure that it had all been done by the book.

SUBTLE SHORTCUTS

Most members of the squad had been out on the streets long enough to grow calluses against residents' anger and insults, which seemed to slide off harmlessly. But sometimes the officers got annoyed, not just personally but on principle.

A month after the sting against the big dealer in the burgundy Pontiac, we were waiting in the early evening darkness for a buy-bust. The eyes had a woman's voice this time, radioing clear alerts as a U.C. was about to make a buy from a "black male, white T-shirt, gray sweatpants, tan boots, black baseball hat with a brown bill. Stand by."

The sale made, she broadcast, "Good to go!" and gave his location and the direction he was walking. We took off flying in civilian cars with no flashing lights, zooming through streets where people stood gaping at us as if we were completely crazy.

So it went, bust after bust. One nabbed a man older than usual, probably about forty, with a hole in his throat from a tracheotomy, and fitted with a piece of hardware that allowed him to speak when he put a small amplifier up to his larynx.

With his hands cuffed behind him, he couldn't hold the gadget, and the officers confiscated it. "They'll take it away from you" in jail anyway, one politely explained and added that he'd give it to the man's wife, who could deliver it to him tomorrow when he would see his lawyer.

Brennan knew the guy's name: Mr. O. "We've met this man before," he told me. They'd arrested him with drugs and a pistol but didn't prosecute because "he cooperated" by testifying in a murder case. "And he'll cooperate again." Drug charges are routinely used by homicide detectives as leverage to squeeze out information on unsolved murders in the neighborhoods. No matter that such informants and witnesses have high motivation to make up a good story to get themselves off; their unreliability seems more obvious to defense attorneys than to judges.

While Mr. O stood in handcuffs, his family and neighbors poured into the alley to gawk, to object, to plead. A cacophony of chatter and complaint reverberated off the walls. Everyone had something to say except for a sad-faced woman, his wife, who sat silently behind the wheel of an SUV, waiting—waiting, it turned out, to drive their young daughter, about eleven or twelve, to her school graduation. Dressed up neatly in a white blouse and dark skirt, the girl ran out of the house in desperate tears.

Loudly, the dealer's mother protested repeatedly that he had done nothing. His snaggle-toothed sister screamed wildly, "I ain't no crackhead! I ain't no crackhead! You the crackheads!"

Brennan typically tried to strike a balance between vigilance and calm, he told me later. "Somebody could go inside and come out with a pistol," he said, so his men had to be watchful. But if they'd moved too aggressively, say, to arrest the mother and sister for disorderly conduct, which he felt they had cause to do, tempers in the alley would have flared. Only one complaint about his unit had been made in the last eighteen months, he said proudly, and that was for talking in an offensive tone of voice to a man after his arrest.

So Brennan had to cool off a couple of his officers who got into verbal duels with bystanders. "We've arrested him before, and the family always has the same reaction," one told me in disgust. Another grumbled furiously, "How can they be so mad at us? The father is out selling drugs when his daughter's about to go to her graduation! Why aren't they fucking pissed off at him? They ought to dig a deep hole and put dealers like him in it and pile rocks on them!" The police wouldn't mind a little praise from neighborhoods they are trying to protect.

The team searched the SUV and came up with the buy money hidden on the floor under the front passenger's seat, but no drugs. They might have been swallowed by Mr. O—the inside of his mouth was all white—and the cops urged him to spit out the crack, but he kept mouthing the words, "I don't have any." They didn't believe him, told him it was dangerous, and after dispatching him to jail in a paddy wagon, filled out a Form 313 to forward him like a sack of mail to the hospital.

Like reporters and doctors who relieve their own stress after witnessing violence and injury, these narcotics cops indulged in plenty of tasteless gallows humor. One wondered if Mr. O's drugs would pop out of the tracheotomy. Another said maybe they should have gone fishing for them with a spoon through the hole. And the cops often mixed hostility with derisive laughter, as in the case of another dealer they had arrested.

The squad converged on him, wrestled him to the ground, cuffed his wrists behind his back, then jerked him to his feet and frisked him for weapons. Following standard procedures for anyone being locked up, they relieved him of all valuables and any tools that might come in handy for committing suicide: his belt and shoelaces. They took off his watch and emptied his pockets onto the ground, then looked around for a loitering friend or relative whom he might trust with the valuables so they could be spared an inventory. There was nobody for this man.

One possession seemed inseparable from the suspect, who screamed in pain as a beefy officer tried roughly to wrench loose his ring. "You're breaking my fucking finger!" The cop kept twisting, red-faced with frustration, the man kept screaming and begging them to use water, and a gentler officer finally went to his car for a little bottle of lotion and greased the ring loose. Brennan, watching from inside his vehicle, mistakenly thought the guy was holding relentlessly onto some drugs.

The narcotics were discovered as they searched him and pulled a bag of crack from his underwear. "They're not my underpants," the seller protested; they were borrowed, he insisted. The cops got a kick out of this, and to prolong the comic relief made fun of his T-shirt inscribed with drawings of two goats and the inexplicable words GOAT WRESTLER. On the street, you grab a laugh wherever you can find it.

A lot of sellers operate in teams of three: a runner, a juggler, and a holder. The runner makes the connection with the buyer, takes the money, and delivers the cash to the juggler, who gets the drugs from the holder and passes them back through the chain. That way, nobody is actually exchanging drugs for money directly with the U.C. So it seems logical that the less sophisticated operators are the ones who get caught, which raises a question: Has this so-called war on drugs gone about as well as the war in Afghanistan? Supply has increased, driving prices down. Treatment centers are saturated with addicts, with no beds to spare. Drug-related murders continue unabated. And courts whittle away the Fourth Amendment, all in the name of stopping a scourge that won't be stopped.

The cops rationalize their work by speculating that things would be even worse if they weren't there, and that may be. Murder rates do drop when the squad is operating in a neighborhood, Brennan says. But the overall inability to sense significant progress reduces the effort to a series of isolated contests, each of which has to be won individually to cause any satisfaction.

So if the refs aren't looking, you can get away with a foul here and there—and why not? The cops know their man is guilty. They don't need a jury to tell them; he just sold them crack. Besides, it's hard to help crossing the line in the heat of the moment, as it's easy to imagine officers doing when they're less well led than Brennan's bunch and unaccompanied by, say, a civilian writing a book.

I saw a case that skated close to a line and might have fallen apart had it led to an arrest. A U.C. bought drugs from a fellow wearing a Redskins jacket, who then entered an apartment house, exited, and entered again. The narcotics squad swarmed the block of two-story buildings, each with four apartments, two upstairs and two down, but they lost him. Someone on the radio said that he might have left by the back, so we zoomed around into an alley, where a white officer was already questioning a black woman leaning on a fence at the rear of the tiny yard. She was smoking languidly, trying to look casual.

He spoke roughly to her. "I saw you come out of that apartment. I saw you. Open that door." The ground floor apartment he pointed to was dark. She hadn't come from there, she insisted, and took a puff. He then felt the outside of her pockets, looking for keys—an illegal pat-down, since she was not suspected of anything, had done nothing to suggest she was armed, and did not fit the description of the "lookout" the police were trying to find.

The cop went to the back door and pounded on it. No answer. Finally, the door was opened by—another cop! They entered with no warrant, no hot pursuit of anyone with drugs or a gun, and found a vacant flat empty of furniture, under renovation—and no drug dealer. "How do you lose a two-hundred-pound guy?" one officer asked in frustration.

They gave up. They couldn't search further without warrants, and which apartment would they cite to a judge? They hadn't seen the dealer enter a particular one, so they couldn't proceed, despite a tendency by the Supreme Court to give law enforcement more and more latitude for warrantless entry. The Court ruled in 1976 that Philadelphia cops were justified in following a woman into her house after she'd just been paid for heroin by a U.C.[34] In 2006 it exempted police from the warrant requirement if they saw violence inside a private home—in that case, a juvenile punching an adult during a loud party with underage drinking.[35]

But here, the narcotics squad was legally stuck, and they weren't about to search the whole block unconstitutionally, at least not with me along for the ride.

"Cops take shortcuts," said one of Brennan's men, a lean veteran with a shock of gray hair. He didn't do it himself, he said, because he had seen the consequences, like a kid who gets caught cheating in first grade and never does it again. A case many years ago, when he was fairly new to the force, was thrown out because the officer in charge failed to get a warrant. A chambermaid had seen drugs in the room of a prominent basketball player in a Washington hotel. The cop just went into the room, instead of securing it and getting a warrant, and seized the drugs. The judge excluded the evidence.

Since then, the lanky officer told me, he'd been scrupulous about warrants, even to the displeasure of his colleagues on the force, many of whom prefer to just do the search. He remembered once when officers wanted to open two suitcases and he insisted on waiting for a warrant. They were mad at him. But he was right, and they made the case, because inside one they found six kilos of cocaine, and fourteen in the other. "Cops take shortcuts."

CHAPTER FOUR

With Warrants and Without

The Poorest man may in his cottage bid defiance to all the force
of the Crown. It may be frail—its roof may shake—the wind may
blow through it—the storm may enter, the rain may enter—but
the King of England cannot enter—all his force dares not cross
the threshold of the ruined tenement.

—William Pitt

HOME INVASION

POLICE! SEARCH WARRANT!"

The policewoman knocked loudly. She waited about two seconds. She yelled again, "Police! Search warrant!"

In three or four more seconds, too little time for anyone to answer the door, she stepped aside to make way for a brawny officer in civilian clothes. He cradled a cylindrical steel battering ram fitted with handles.

He swung it back and slammed it against the double doors. From inside came a woman's yelp of alarm. Again he swung the ram, the doors burst open, and a dozen armed cops rushed in, big men suddenly filling the house, swarming through the broken entryway and all through the ground floor, up the stairs, fanning out rapidly into every bedroom without a word of explanation to the owner, a black woman of middle age standing with her mouth open, her eyes fixed wide.

She had been in her kitchen talking on the phone. She picked it up again. "They just raided my home," her voice trembled to someone at the other end of the line. Then she hung up. Her personal sanctuary had just been invaded in accordance with the Constitution.

The last bastion of the Fourth Amendment is the home. Honored by history and protected by law, it remains the zone of privacy least vulnerable to the cold pragmatism of judges and legislators who diminish the people's rights in the name of security and efficiency. Unlike automobiles, boats, bank statements, travel records, and even the pockets of a person on the street, the house is mostly—not always, but mostly—impenetrable to police intrusion without a judge's order.

Yet even a legal search feels like a violation. Judicial oversight cannot dilute its brutality. Courteous officers cannot sweeten the insulting upheaval that turns every possession out of the private darkness of drawers and closets into the cruel light of chaos. It is a form of plunder sanctioned by the state, which in the name of order creates disorderly wreckage even when the police observe the strictest requirements of the Constitution.

This was a row house, once elegant, in Northeast Washington, D.C. A confidential informant had told a narcotics officer of buying drugs here, and on the basis of the officer's sworn affidavit as to the C.I.'s reliability, a judge had signed a search warrant.

The squad did not have the dealer's name, but the officers had a briefing in a nearby parking lot by the lead detective, a lanky woman named Lavinia Quigley, an African-American dressed casually in a red shirt and white shorts to blend into the neighborhood. They were a motley bunch of cops, some with long hair and jeans, a few in uniform. "It's a big house," she told them. "He keeps drugs upstairs. The good thing is his toilet don't work. The reservoir don't fill up fast. I ain't seen no dogs, no kids."

The officers were tense and hurried when they entered. As in executing every such warrant, they worried that someone might pull a gun, or at least might flush away the evidence. They left their own guns holstered, but they were as edgy as soldiers going into combat, their hands ready, their eyes watchful. They scattered rapidly through the old house and found nobody else.

They kept the owner, "Wendy," seated in a straight-backed chair in the living room. You have no right to watch a search even in your own home, and it's standard practice to prevent you from wandering around so you can't hassle the cops or hide evidence or grab a gun. This is fine with the Supreme Court, which ruled in 1981 that officers may detain occupants while executing warrants.[1]

The house was already in some disarray when they arrived. Odd pieces of shabby furniture were scattered about; clothing lay on beds, floors, and tables; here and there stood boxes that, when searched, disgorged bits and parts of stereo equipment, CDs, and other random pieces of people's lives. There were no books.

The officers added to the mess many times over. When they confronted a locked bedroom door upstairs, they didn't ask for a key but just busted in the door, afraid somebody armed might be lurking inside. They pulled clothes out of closets, felt quickly along the seams, carefully examined pockets, and threw everything on the floor. They upturned mattresses, emptied drawers onto beds and floors, ransacked storage boxes, and spent a good deal of time admiring the architecture of the house: "I'd love to have this." "This is a gold mine." "This is real construction. This is the way they used to build houses." The hardwood floors of the attic were authentic two-by-sixes, one officer observed, laid at a time when they were actually a full two inches thick and six inches wide, "instead of what you get now at Home Depot." The attic reminded another cop of the one in his childhood home, so big that he used to roller-skate up there.

The unit commander, Sergeant J. J. Brennan, listened to the rhapsodic talk for a minute and said, "I'm glad you guys are finding all this good construction. How 'bout finding some drugs?"

They did not find drugs, however, just some razor blades for cutting and ziplock bags for packaging. In the back bedroom, which was full of men's clothing, they found ammunition—a box of nine-millimeter shells on a shelf in the closet, and a few rounds atop the stereo—illegal at the time in D.C. In the middle bedroom, among the many purses in the closet, an officer opened a black pocketbook, felt something hard inside a pair of black tights, unwrapped it, and shouted, "I got a gun." It was a .38.

In the locked front bedroom, a big cop unpacked a white plastic storage box sitting on the floor, and nestled among the clothes he discovered a small Beretta pistol, fully loaded. He hollered for help, saying he had never seen such a gun and was scared that it might go off if he touched it. Somehow the drill seemed senseless, because once he had gathered others around, he then warned them to step away as he picked it out gently, and safely. Buried further down in the same box, he discovered a sealed letter-size envelope stuffed with cash—the top bill a hundred, the rest singles—which the cops then confiscated as possible drug money.

Downstairs, an officer found a closet locked, asked Wendy for the key, and drew his gun while he opened it. Pawing through the boxes inside, he came across a forgotten Confederate ten-dollar bill carefully preserved in a plastic envelope. He handed it to Wendy, told her it might be valuable, and got a wan smile in return.

"Who do you live here with?" Brennan asked her. He was dressed casually in civvies, his longish hair was slightly disheveled, his voice calm, his low key a relaxed counterpoint to the crisp tempo of the men searching around him.

"My son," Wendy answered, and his girlfriend, she added. He was thirty. Wendy worked at the Department of Homeland Security in a position that had become permanent just a year earlier. "I might as well kiss my job goodbye," she remarked sadly.

Although they had found no drugs and had only an informant's word, Brennan and Quigley had absolutely no doubt that the house was being used to sell narcotics. They figured the son was dealing, and maybe his girlfriend as well, and since he wasn't home they weren't surprised not to have found a stash, which dealers didn't always keep in their houses, especially their mothers' houses.

One after another, as a tag team of cops questioned Wendy, lectured her, warned her, and threatened her, snippets of information came out like the disjointed belongings being strewn about her home.

She played the innocent convincingly. She got up early every morning and went to work and returned at night without knowing what was going on under her roof during the day, she insisted. Quigley asked whether her son had ever been arrested for drugs. Yes, she answered. "Using or selling?" Quigley asked.

Wendy answered in a small voice, "Selling."

"While you out bustin' your butt, you son doin' this stuff," Quigley said disgustedly.

Wendy was sitting, and Detective Quigley stood, bending her tall frame over her and scolding her like a stern mother with a naughty child. "Tell your son he got to get out, do his business elsewhere," she commanded.

The cops were trying to like her. She was not confrontational, she seemed genuinely in shock, and she was cooperating. "Can I have a hug?" Wendy asked at last, and Quigley leaned over and gave her one.

After the Beretta was found in the front bedroom, an officer came down and asked Wendy a few questions without telling her about the gun. Which room was hers? The front bedroom, she said.

The cop had hoped for a different answer. He turned away and made a face of disappointment and regret. Then she was peppered with queries by Quigley and another black officer. They asked about the cash that had been found. She had money hidden all over the house, she said. Where? She was vague, which annoyed them, because they wanted to learn whether she had known of the cash in the white box.

They asked about the girlfriend but couldn't get the last name from her. They asked who had access to the locked front bedroom. She alone, Wendy said. Then, when they told her that they'd found money and a gun in there, she speculated that maybe somebody else could have entered by undoing the chain. But the room had been locked with a key, not a chain. Where did the girlfriend sleep? In the front bedroom with her, Wendy said, not with her son.

The cops were incredulous. A thirty-year-old son who doesn't sleep with his girlfriend? "I don't allow that kind of thing in my house," Wendy said indignantly. The cops didn't laugh.

"You think your son is man enough to step up and own the guns so his mama don't get locked up?" asked Quigley.

"Don't know. Kids nowadays," she answered.

"I'm trying not to lock you up."

"You're treating me like I'm a terrible person," Wendy said. "I get up early in the morning, go to work, come home."

"The government could take your house," Quigley warned, and gave an example of one nearby that had been forfeited as a drug-dealing site.[2] "If I lock you up you could lose your job."

"I haven't seen anything illegal," Wendy declared. "You all did the investigation, you should know I haven't done anything. You should know who the players are. . . . Somebody should come tell the parent that something's going on."

Technically, while Wendy wasn't free to walk around inside her house, she may have been free to walk out of it entirely, so she may not have been in detention, meaning that she may not have been entitled to the Miranda warning about her Fifth Amendment right not to answer questions. But it was a close call, as Brennan conceded later, and one a defense attorney would have made an issue had she incriminated herself by admitting to owning one of the guns. But she did not, and Brennan felt the ownership was too ambiguous to make a case.

"I might as well kiss my job goodbye," Wendy said again.

"I just hope these guns are your son's," Quigley remarked.

This would have been a different conversation had it occurred three years later, after the Supreme Court decided in 2008 that the Second Amendment protected a right to keep a gun at home for self-defense. Wendy's possession would have been legal, provided she had registered the firearms and received a license. But even if she hadn't, the U.S. Attorney's office wouldn't have prosecuted, since the guns were inside her house. Although the D.C. Attorney General's office might still bring criminal charges in such an instance, the Justice Department stopped doing so after *District of Columbia v. Heller*. The department also stopped countersigning search warrants for guns in homes unless connected with drugs or owned by classes of people still barred by federal law from possessing firearms, who included convicted felons, illegal immigrants, and the mentally ill.[3] Outside the home, though, guns were still prohibited, and police gun squads still operated vigorously.

Inside residences, drugs remained a key target of police searches, and this one was finished. Quigley was bending over Wendy and explaining the inventory of items seized (the guns, the ammunition, the money, and photographs to be used to identify her son). A copy was left with her.

At 7:20 p.m., one hour and ten minutes after their arrival, the horde of cops trooped out, leaving mattresses upturned, closet contents heaped on floors, stuff from boxes scattered about, and perhaps a hard lesson imprinted on a mother's life.

As Brennan walked through the doors, left unlockable in a dangerous neighborhood, he teased Quigley about another search, when she had forgotten to look behind the front door and nearly missed a kilo of cocaine. She laughed and checked a bag behind this door. Nothing incriminating.

Without an arrest, the search had yielded only guns and ammunition, no criminals, illustrating the discretion that officers see themselves applying every day to the uncertainties of these neighborhoods. Back in the car, Brennan turned around to me. "People don't realize that the benefit of the doubt is given out here on the street."

The reason, sneered an officer in the passenger seat, was that if a case is to be filed, "the U.S. Attorneys want it on a pillow on a nice little china plate."

Such perfection is not always demanded by judges, however, when they examine applications for search warrants they authorize. The forms often contain sleazy sources of dubious tips that police cite in asserting probable cause to believe that criminal evidence can be found in one house or another. The netherworld of snitches, though not a pretty place, is essential to police work, and it provides constitutional legitimacy.

After the search at Wendy's, on the way back to the Narcotics Branch, Brennan went trolling for informants. He swung into an alley behind deserted buildings that stood like broken derelicts near the railroad yards. He squeezed the patrol car around a sharp bend and pointed to a vacant space, cupped between buildings, where he had seen addicts hang out. Now it contained only shadows, but down at the end of the alley, a young black man in a white T-shirt was walking away.

Brennan and his partner got out and shouted at him, "Come here!" He didn't have to stop, of course, and he didn't have to do what he did—turn around and come ambling back toward the cops. They couldn't seize him, because no probable cause existed to believe that he had committed a crime. In the deepening dusk of a back alley near the railroad tracks, however, the Constitution seemed like a faded idea.

The young man muttered that he was just taking a piss. They asked for his ID. "I ain't got no ID. Somebody took my wallet." They asked his name, he gave one, and they asked if that was his real name. Let's call him Vincent Franklin. Brennan's partner went back to the car's computer and ran it through WALES. No criminal record.

While they had him leaning his hands on the hood of the patrol car, Brennan asked him, "Do you use drugs?"

"Yeah, man. Crack. I'm trying to get off it."

"Where do you get the money for it?"

"Panhandling—one hundred to two hundred dollars a day."

"Did you ever work with the police?" Franklin shook his head. "We need people to go make a buy," Brennan explained. "Then we get a search warrant, and you get paid. A lot of people don't like to do that. They think it's being a snitch. But a lot like it. You get two hundred dollars for a gun, one hundred dollars per person arrested."

Franklin froze in stony silence and looked down at the hood of the car. He did not seem to be thinking, Wow! This is the opportunity of a lifetime!

"In the warrant your name isn't used," Brennan continued in the most reassuring voice he could muster. "You're referred to as 'it.' ' "It" went into the house. "It" bought the drugs.' You don't go to court, you don't testify." The man's face had become a mask without a flicker of interest.

Brennan tried to push another button. "You get these motherfuckers who are selling this crap off the street." I wondered to myself whether Franklin was thinking, But these motherfuckers are my lifeline to pleasure and escape!

"You know something about a shooting," Brennan went on, "we get the guy, you might make twenty-five thousand dollars. There are twenty-five-thousand-dollar rewards." He wasn't getting anywhere with Franklin. "Look, I gotta ask," he said.

A luxury Acela train from New York eased along the tracks toward Union Station, carrying people down from a day of business or in for high-powered work in the nation's capital, passengers oblivious to what they were seeing as they looked out their windows at the tiny figures in the shadows.

Now Franklin was slumping like a frightened dog. He hadn't spoken a word since the offer was made. "You're not gonna turn yourself around unless you do something about it," Brennan said. Hearing no answer, Brennan told him that the branch was just down the street, on Third, and that he could stop by anytime. We got into the car and picked our way slowly out of the alley.

Sometimes, Brennan told me, such a man turns up a couple of weeks afterward at the unmarked, light gray one-story building that houses the Narcotics Branch. "After they do a couple of cases with us, they like it," he said, adding that he protects them when they make buys, with as many backup cops as an undercover officer receives. A C.I. got beaten up recently in the Fifth District, Brennan said, but one of his had never been killed.

In practice, then, "the right of the people to be secure in their persons, houses, papers, and effects" can be overcome by the anonymous assertions of a questionable character who is motivated by cash from the police or leniency from the prosecutor. On the basis of a furtive phone call about a gun someone has supposedly seen or a bag of crack he's bought, a home can be invaded. The officer signs a sworn affidavit reporting the tip, which is often hearsay, thereby establishing probable cause, and a judge issues the search warrant. As far as is known, judges seldom refuse, although statistics on rejections are not collected.

Ironically, this thin justification for turning someone's house inside out is actually the gold standard of constitutional protection under the Fourth Amendment. The search warrant is the strictest procedure that we possess to preserve that right, and so it is hailed by outspoken defenders of civil liberties as a bastion against the groping hands of the state. As flawed as it has become, it remains the model, the benchmark for measuring deviations. Searches that are done without it—of pedestrians and vehicles openly, of computer files and library records secretly, of e-mail and phone and bedroom conversations among suspected terrorists—are dangerous departures from the paradigm, the imperfect paradigm.

The warrant requirement has a noble history as a rebuff to the British writs of assistance, which allowed whole villages to be searched for contraband in Colonial times. "A man's house is his castle; and whilst he is quiet, he is as well guarded as a prince in his castle," argued James Otis on behalf of Boston merchants in 1761. "This writ, if it should be declared legal, would totally annihilate this privilege. Custom-house officers may enter our houses when they please; we are commanded to permit their entry. Their menial servants may enter, may break locks, bars, and everything in their way; and whether they break through malice or revenge, no man, no court may inquire."[4]

The answer, in the Fourth Amendment, provides for the checks and balances that limit governmental power: The warrant is requested by the executive and issued by the judicial branch. It requires a threshold of evidence that is designed to prevent fishing expeditions and harassment. And unlike the British writs of assistance, it is limited by specificity as to time, place, and items of evidence sought.

These characteristics create obstacles to outright police fabrication, although it sometimes happens. A single officer cannot easily invent probable cause, as he can during a traffic stop. At least a measure of proof is required, not beyond the reasonable doubt that must be exceeded for a jury to convict, but enough to ensure that the search occurs after, not before, some investigation has begun. A logical progression is thereby prescribed: Only as the facts grow more certain may the inquiry grow more intrusive—and more regulated.

Furthermore, the accused ultimately has the right to challenge the basis of the warrant in court, which cannot happen when information is obtained secretly through methods expanded since September 11, 2001. These methods include the administrative subpoena known as a National Security Letter and the clandestine warrant issued by the Foreign Intelligence Surveillance Court. Both devices were broadened by the Patriot Act.

Finally, the warrant alerts police to the potential of a challenge, which makes them careful, as Brennan's squad demonstrated.

Before going out on another search, the unit's dozen officers, all dressed down in casual civilian clothes, gathered in the conference room at the Narcotics Branch. The policeman with the long ponytail described the location: 1914 I Street NE, Apartment 3—marked by a white door bearing the number 3—where a black male had reputedly sold a C.I. ten zips, as the small ziplock bags used to package drugs are called. "He is heavily watching out the window. Once the back-door containment is in place, we'll go in the front. The back door is the fourth from the alley, but unmarked. A huge tree covers the steps with overgrowth." The squad was shown pictures of the area.

The front door was "a lockout," he said, meaning that a key or a code was needed to get into the building. This was a complication, because the cops didn't want to bust down the outside door and give the occupant enough warning to flush the drugs or grab a gun. "Could we go in the back?" one asked, and a few others picked up on the idea, because the back door led directly to the apartment. But Ponytail was hesitant because the door had no number, and bursting into the wrong place would ruin everyone's day.

Brennan drew a diagram and gave the assignments, and we set off in three cars, one unmarked, with everyone except me wearing dark blue bulletproof vests emblazoned with white letters spelling POLICE. Brennan wore a blue shirt with a Narcotics Division logo; his badge hung on a string around his neck.

We drove into a parking lot a few blocks away and waited out a fierce thunderstorm. Quigley was not with us. She was undercover in the neighborhood, hoping to get into the building's vestibule so that the cops could avoid using the battering ram. She waited on the stoop until somebody came out, then slipped through the open door and radioed to Brennan that she was inside.

The squad drove up, the cops jumped out and rushed the building, jamming into the narrow hallway and up the stairs to the apartment on the left, on the second floor.

There they stopped cold. The numeral nailed to the apartment door was 2, not 3. Even though a uniformed officer had confirmed the number as 3 a few days earlier, drug dealers sometimes switch digits to foil cops. And here it worked, because the warrant said number 3, and Brennan and the others knew this was just the kind of detail that a good defense attorney could use to have the search declared illegal and its fruits excluded.

A television police show would surely picture this as an absurd technicality, but it was a protection, and the cops seemed to accept it as part of the game; they weren't grumbling. Either they would ask the judge to change the warrant to read "upper left apartment," Brennan explained, or they would have the C.I. do another buy and get a whole new warrant. Hopefully the dealer hadn't been frightened off by the commotion.

Through the crowd of cops came a boy down the stairs. "Where do you live?" one asked him. He was so scared he was practically speechless. He pointed and said something about living down the street. The cops demanded the address of his house. Paralyzed, he didn't answer. They got gruff. "What's the number? You don't know the number? How old are you?" Fifteen, he said, and finally gave them a location a couple of houses away.

"You have any guns?" asked Brennan. He patted the teenager down perfunctorily, violating his rights under a Constitution whose defining authority a moment earlier now suddenly receded. *Terry* required reasonable suspicion to believe that someone was armed.

Then the narcotics squad performed a bit of street theater for the benefit of the boy in case he spread word around about the police invasion.

"We had a call that there was someone with guns in the hallway here," Brennan lied.

"I ain't seen no guns," answered the youngster.

Detective Quigley, in her red shirt and white shorts (and no police vest), joined the production. "Can I go?" she asked Brennan as if they had never met before.

"Yeah," said Brennan. "What are you doin' in the hallway anyway?"

"It was rainin'," said the consummate detective-actress, and she was out the door in a flash.

DETERRING THE POLICE

If we drew a rough trajectory of the Fourth Amendment's power to protect individual privacy, the line would begin low in the left-hand corner of the chart during the country's early decades and then rise during the first two-thirds of the twentieth century (jumping upward in 1914, with the exclusion of illegally obtained evidence from federal trials, and soaring again in 1961 as the Supreme Court applied the Fourth Amendment to the states). The line would describe something of a plateau, and then begin a downward course through the end of the twentieth century and into the beginning of the twenty-first.

We find ourselves now on the declining slope, heading toward the lower ground last occupied more than half a century ago. Even the search warrant, designed by the framers as the bedrock guarantee of the Fourth Amendment, has been eroded by the trickle of pro-police rulings from the courts. These have worn away the definition of probable cause, making it easier for cops to get a warrant on the basis of flimsy hearsay.

A 2003 case in Washington illustrated the point. A federal agent's affidavit requesting a warrant contained only one substantive sentence justifying probable cause, a reference to a confidential informant designated as CI-1, who had worked with the police for only two months, on just four other warrants. "Within the last 72 hours," the affidavit stated, "your affiant was contacted by CI-1 regarding a handgun that it observed within 5320 2nd Street NW, Washington, D.C., the residence of an individual CI-1 knows as 'Jimmy.'"[5]

That was all. There was nothing more. "The affidavit was insufficient to support a probable cause finding," argued the appeals lawyer, Neil Jaffee. There was no date on which the gun had supposedly been seen (only when the informant had reported), raising the possibility that the information was stale enough to violate guidelines established in a 1932 Supreme Court case.[6] There was nothing about the gun's make or description or location in the house, no allegation of drugs or violent activity at the address, no explanation of the informant's presence or relationship with Jimmy, nothing on who else resided there, and no statement that law enforcement officials had observed criminal behavior at the building. The affidavit also exaggerated Jimmy's criminal record by stating that he had three convictions for carrying a pistol without a license; in fact, Jaffee learned, he had only one, nearly twenty years earlier.

It shouldn't have mattered, but it surely did, that the search turned up heroin, two guns, and nearly $10,000 in cash. The trouble with challenging search warrants, as with warrantless searches, is that only those producing incriminating evidence make their way to court. However defective the means, the end is almost always graphic proof of the party's guilt, and judges don't like to let such people walk. So a judge does not throw out a search warrant—issued by a colleague on the bench, after all—without finding an egregious constitutional affront.

If there was a violation here, it was not dramatic. The case was in a gray area, where reasonable lawyers and judges could disagree on whether this affidavit supported this warrant. Without a hearing, federal District Judge Ellen S. Huvelle denied the motion to reject the search warrant and suppress the evidence. The defendant, James Gaston, got five years, and the circuit court refused to consider his appeal.

The case was ordinary, and that marked its significance. Sometimes legal lessons are learned by examining the outrageous, the sensational, the landmarks, yet often they are taught more accurately by the run-of-the-mill. Here was a decision that would never be analyzed in law journals, but which spoke to how insubstantial an unnamed informant's tip could be to justify a legal invasion of a person's home.

The judges were bound by a twenty-year-old precedent in *Illinois v. Gates*,[7] a six-to-three ruling by the Burger Court that relaxed the standard for establishing probable cause. Previously, under a pair of earlier decisions by the Warren Court,[8] a two-pronged test had been required: first, that a warrant application demonstrate the informant's "basis of knowledge" (showing that he could know what he was talking about) and second, that either the informant's "veracity" or the information's "reliability" be shown by sufficient facts.

Gates swept aside that test and substituted a less demanding and more flexible criterion known as "the totality of the circumstances." The two prongs were no longer to be satisfied independently but were reduced to "relevant considerations" in "a balanced assessment of the relative weights of all the various indicia of reliability (and unreliability) attending an informant's tip," as William Rehnquist wrote for the majority before he became Chief Justice.

The strength of one characteristic could overcome weakness in another, Rehnquist held. For example, he said, if an informant has proved reliable in the past, his failure this time "to thoroughly set forth the basis of his knowledge surely should not serve as an absolute bar to a finding of probable cause based on his tip. . . . Conversely, even if we entertain some doubt as to an informant's motives, his explicit and detailed description of alleged wrongdoing, along with a statement that the event was observed firsthand, entitles his tip to greater weight than might otherwise be the case."

Oddly, the basis of the warrant in *Gates* was weaker than either of Rehnquist's criteria. The case began not with a reliable informant, or even with an identifiable source whose motives inspired "some doubt," but with nothing more than an anonymous letter. The police department of Bloomingdale, Illinois, had no clue about its author, who claimed that a married couple, Lance and Susan Gates, were storing more than $100,000 worth of drugs in their basement, and were planning to transport more from Florida. Susan was to drive down on May 3, 1978, leave the car, and fly back, the letter predicted. Then Lance would fly down, pick up the car loaded with drugs, and return.

The police confirmed that Lance had a reservation to fly to Florida on May 5. The Drug Enforcement Administration (DEA) saw him take the flight and followed him to a motel in West Palm Beach, where he stayed with his wife overnight, contrary to the letter's forecast. They left together the next morning for the twenty-two-hour drive home to Illinois. So there was partial police corroboration of the tipster's projections of their movements, but not of their alleged drug possession. An Illinois judge issued a search warrant for the house and car, and marijuana was found.

Rehnquist wrote in a spirit of pragmatism. He did not want to discourage anonymous tips. He also sought to avoid such close scrutiny of police affidavits that "police might well resort to warrantless searches, with the hope of relying on consent or some other exception to the Warrant Clause." He declared: "Probable cause is a fluid concept—turning on the assessment of probabilities in particular factual contexts—not readily, or even usefully, reduced to a neat set of legal rules."

Yet the anonymous letter alone would not have justified the warrant, Rehnquist noted; some substantiation was required to support probable cause. He thought the police surveillance had provided as much.

Justice John Paul Stevens disagreed, noting in dissent the tipster's important mistake: that Susan would fly home before Lance left for Florida. With both of them absent, he said, their supposed $100,000 stash of drugs was left unguarded, undermining the letter's thesis and leaving only lawful behavior as the basis for the warrant. "The mere facts that Sue was in West Palm Beach with the car, that she was joined by her husband at the Holiday Inn on Friday, and that the couple drove north together the next morning," Stevens wrote, "are neither unusual nor probative of criminal activity."

As in many warrant applications, all the seemingly innocent actions were colored by the anonymous tip; without the letter, the police had nothing but a sequence of insignificant events. Reasoning backwards, then, the Court's opinion seemed like common sense: Marijuana was found after the couple had made an oddly arranged journey to Florida, which the tipster had known about in almost precise detail, portraying it as a drug run.

But another scenario could have been constructed from the same set of facts, before the ultimate discovery of marijuana: A disgruntled neighbor, relative, or employee knew enough details of a quick, innocent trip to twist them into a criminal conspiracy, subjecting the couple to a police assault on their privacy. When seen through a malevolent lens, the most ordinary features of life can take on sinister shapes, as they have in some erroneous terrorism prosecutions.

This is the danger of relaxing the standards for searches, wiretapping, and various forms of surveillance: Unchallenged assertions, innuendo, rumor, and fragments of fact can be used to pry open people's private worlds. It is wise to remember that in the days after 9/11, unnamed callers with unsavory motives sent FBI agents scurrying in frenetic searches for hundreds of "suspicious" Arab-looking men who were rounded up, searched, jailed in brutal conditions mostly for immigration violations, and never found to have any links to terrorism. The results were both inhumane for the victims and dangerously distracting for a law enforcement agency with a serious, urgent job to do.

That was panicked policing, lasting for a moment of history. A more durable defect in the constitutional structure has been created by courts that imagine the anonymous tip to be a pillar of probable cause. The notion undermines the integrity of the search warrant.

Law enforcement agencies adjust to a judicial subculture. They tend to learn by trial and error what they need in a warrant application, which may vary from one state to another, from one county to another, from one magistrate to another. We don't know how often they get it wrong. Unless a victim dies or chooses to sue the police—rare events—fruitless search warrants remain as invisible as the frisks and car searches that turn up nothing. How often do police break down a door, rush into every room, dump the contents of drawers and closets onto beds and floors, and find no evidence of a crime?

"It happens every day in this business," said Captain Art Binder of the Cumberland County Sheriff's Department in North Carolina.[9] But the public doesn't learn about the everyday errors, only those tragic enough to break through the wall of police silence.

Here are a few examples:

- Armed with a "no-knock" warrant, thirteen members of a narcotics SWAT team burst unannounced into the Boston apartment of a retired seventy-five-year-old minister, Accelynne Williams. He ran to the bedroom, officers broke in the bedroom door, he struggled, they handcuffed him, and minutes later he died of a heart attack. No drugs were found, because the cops had made a slight mistake. Their informant had not given them an apartment number, only a diagram; the apartment he had meant for them to search was one floor above.[10]

- On the other side of the country, in the affluent Southern California town of Poway, federal agents were staking out the house of a forty-one-year-old computer executive named Donald Carlson when he drove into his garage about 10:30 p.m. A tipster had told them that the house was unoccupied, the garage full of cocaine, and the premises protected by four armed Mexicans. So they also obtained a "no-knock" warrant, an instrument issued with growing frequency by judges who are persuaded that police need the element of surprise to forestall violence against them or the destruction of evidence.

  The light went on whenever the garage door opened, Carlson later told congressional investigators, so "anybody observing the garage can easily see inside. The garage was mostly empty."[11] Nevertheless, around midnight, after Carlson had gone to bed, the agents broke into the house. The commotion woke him with the terrifying thought that he was being assaulted by burglars, so he did what any red-blooded Westerner would have done: He pulled out his gun. He fired twice at the front door, he said later, and was shot three times by police; it took him four months to recover enough from his wounds to get back to work full-time. No narcotics were found in his house.

- Donald Scott, a wealthy recluse, grabbed a gun as well. Again, the events began with hearsay. His wife was supposedly flashing hundred-dollar bills and tipping generously. Thousands of marijuana plants were supposedly growing on Scott's two-hundred-acre ranch in Malibu. The

DEA couldn't spot them from the ground, or during two flyovers, but on a third pass at 1,000 feet, an agent without binoculars imagined that he could recognize marijuana's shade of green. He took no photographs.

Despite the weakness of these indicators, a judge found probable cause and issued a search warrant, setting in motion a disastrous chain reaction. A force of thirty was mobilized from the DEA, the Los Angeles Sheriff's Department, the California Bureau of Narcotic Enforcement, the U.S. Forest Service, the National Park Service, the Los Angeles Police Department K-9 Unit, and the National Guard.

Their interest in the valuable ranch went beyond the alleged marijuana cultivation. An investigation later by the Ventura County district attorney concluded that the sheriff's department in particular "was motivated, at least in part, by a desire to seize and forfeit the ranch for the government." The officers were evidently betting on a bountiful result, for they were briefed before the raid on the possibility of forfeiture and were given documents containing an appraisal of the place. Law enforcement agencies usually receive the proceeds of confiscated property used in a crime.

Scott had been drinking and taking Valium until about 2 a.m., according to press reports, and was still intoxicated and asleep with his wife when the agents moved onto the ranch in the early morning, some surrounding the garage and barn, others taking positions behind their vehicles, and five more stationed at the house. A sheriff's deputy knocked and announced that they had a search warrant.

His wife got up first, but before she could get to the door, the police broke it in with a battering ram and rushed inside, guns drawn. Scott, sixty-one, groggy from sleep and drink, must have thought that thugs and thieves were overrunning his house and attacking his wife. He grabbed a revolver and ran into the living room. When the police identified themselves, he held the gun over his head; a deputy ordered him to drop it, and as he lowered it slowly, officers thought that the barrel pointed in their direction, so they fired, hitting him twice in the chest and killing him. No marijuana plants were found growing on the ranch, and no other drugs were discovered.[12]

- In late 2006, Atlanta police arrested a low-level marijuana dealer on the street. As the story was pieced together by a team of reporters at the *Atlanta Journal-Constitution,* the dealer tried to wriggle into the cops' favor by pointing out a small brick house nearby as a center of drug sales. The narcotics squad, under pressure to make busts, immediately applied for a search warrant by swearing falsely in an affidavit that they had sent in an informant who bought fifty dollars' worth of crack cocaine from somebody named Sam. On that basis, a magistrate issued a "no-knock" warrant the same day, and that evening, the police pried open a set of burglar bars, smashed through the door, and were met by gunfire from Kathryn Johnston, who was ninety-two.

She lived alone and was armed with a rusty revolver that had been given to her by a relative just in case a gang tried to break in. She managed to fire one shot, grazing one of the officers, but the cops, wearing bulletproof vests, answered with thirty-nine rounds, hit her five or six times, and killed her. No cocaine was found in the house, so they planted some marijuana in the basement.

Since Johnston was black and the cops were white, the shooting inflamed racial tensions in Atlanta and prompted criminal investigations by the FBI and the district attorney. Three white officers pleaded guilty in federal court, and two of them in state court, drawing prison terms ranging from five to ten years. A sergeant in the narcotics squad was sentenced to eighteen months for entering another apartment without a warrant.

The incident threw a spotlight on patterns of falsehood in search-warrant applications. A long-time informant told investigators that the narcotics officers, to make their affidavit look true after the fact, had pressed him to state untruthfully that he had bought crack in the house. To meet monthly quotas, one of the officers testified, detectives routinely lied under oath to judges by swearing that they had performed a procedure critical to the validity of evidence: that before sending informants in on buys, they had searched them to make sure they weren't carrying drugs—a way of proving that any narcotics the informants had when they emerged were actually obtained inside. In fact, they had not taken this precaution. The U.S. Attorney in Atlanta denounced these "routine violations of the Fourth Amendment."[13]

Many other cases of mistaken search warrants surface in the press, usually as local stories in scattered towns and cities around the country, but we do not know the overall error rate. The libertarian Cato Institute catalogued hundreds in a 2006 report.[14] Bill Torpy of the *Journal-Constitution* reported that four hundred warrants for drug searches were executed in 2006 by Atlanta police, but he couldn't determine how many had actually yielded narcotics. "A lot of the affidavits and warrants have no return sheets of what evidence was seized," he noted. "A lot of them list minuscule amounts of drugs. Also, we've seen returns where nothing much was mentioned, but a police report of that same incident shows drugs or other evidence that was not listed on the warrant return."[15]

Similarly, we cannot be sure how readily judges are satisfied that probable cause has been demonstrated. We cannot tell how often, or why, judges find policemen's warrant affidavits lacking. Rejections are not announced, reapplications are not disclosed, and no overall records are kept. Even the most experienced defense attorneys concede that they have no good feel for the situation. And this is where law enforcement is most accountable, as contrasted with the secret, uncontestable warrants issued clandestinely against suspected terrorists and spies by the Foreign Intelligence Surveillance Court.

Now and then, courts have overturned ordinary criminal warrants based on Rehnquist's admonition in *Gates* about the inadequacy of anonymous tips alone without something more to corroborate the unsourced allegations. How much more is a question that different judges answer differently, as a divided panel of the Ninth Circuit demonstrated in ruling on a 2006 appeal from Thai Tung Luong in Los Angeles.

Luong came to the DEA's attention during surveillance of a Taiwanese citizen, Chun-Ying Jao, who had been identified to the DEA's Hong Kong office as a "chemist" traveling to the United States to set up a laboratory to make methamphetamine. Federal agents and local police followed Jao from the Los Angeles airport to a hotel, where Luong picked him up the next day and drove him to lunch and then to his house.

According to a Monterey Park police officer's affidavit in the warrant application, the two men walked back and forth between the front door and the backyard several times. They were seen taking a red high-pressure hose to Home Depot, where they asked a clerk to help them find an adapter, bought the fitting, and then returned to the house. Such hoses, the officer said, were used with vacuum pumps in meth labs, which are sometimes located in garages behind houses.

On that basis, a search warrant was issued, and laboratory equipment was discovered along with documents for a rented storage unit. A second warrant, obtained for the storage locker, turned up sixty-eight pounds of methamphetamine. A federal district judge ruled, and the appeals court agreed by two to one, that the warrant lacked sufficient indicators of probable cause. The evidence was suppressed.[16]

To decide for the defendant in such a case, judges have to rewind the tape, ignore the ultimate discovery of drugs, and imagine the observed behavior without any taint from the anonymous allegation. This takes a certain discipline of mind. When you strip away the DEA's unsourced

Hong Kong report, the events witnessed by the police look pretty innocuous: A man picks another man up at his hotel, takes him to lunch, takes him home, walks around his yard, drives with him to Home Depot, and buys a fitting for a hose. Or, without the anonymous letter in *Gates,* a woman drives to Florida, her husband flies to meet her and stays overnight with her in a motel, and they then drive home.

It's hard to see much difference between the cases, yet they were decided differently. That the Supreme Court's opinion upholding the *Gates* warrant did not prevent a lower court from overturning the search in *United States v. Luong* illustrates how amorphous the concept of probable cause has become, how dependent it is on which judges are randomly assigned to trials and appeals. If one additional judge on Luong's appeals panel had gone against him, the majority would have shifted and Luong would have faced a trial, probable conviction, and a long term in prison.

Any investigation of drug-dealing, terrorism, and other crime has to start somewhere, and that place is often beyond the reach of the Bill of Rights. A tip, a hunch, or a guess can legally trigger a tail and a stakeout; it can send FBI agents onto Web sites and into open meetings of mosques and peace groups. It can induce local police to sit outside gatherings and write down the license plate numbers of those who attend. But it cannot—or should not—justify a search. There is no constitutional right to invisibility in a public place, but when the state seeks to reach into your privacy, especially behind the walls of your home, the Fourth Amendment is supposed to kick in.

So it was for Martedis McPhearson, the subject of an arrest warrant for simple assault.[17] When two policemen knocked on his door in Jackson, Tennessee, on December 12, 2003, McPhearson answered, confirmed his identity, and was arrested on his front porch. Since everyone taken into custody can be legally frisked, an officer patted McPhearson down and discovered nearly seven grams of crack in his pocket.

It was too little for McPhearson to be considered a dealer. Nevertheless, on the basis of that small amount, the police swore out an affidavit surmising that evidence of drug trafficking would be discovered in his house. They got a judge to sign a search warrant, and, indeed, found "distribution quantities of crack cocaine and firearms" inside.

The federal trial judge, and two of the three judges on a Sixth Circuit appeals panel, overturned the warrant, ruling that the "totality of circumstances" test formulated by Rehnquist in *Gates* had not been met. "The affidavit did not allege that McPhearson was involved in drug dealing," the majority wrote, "that hallmarks of drug dealing had been witnessed at his home, such as heavy traffic to and from the residence, or that the investigating officers' experience in narcotics investigation suggested to them that 6.9 grams of crack cocaine was a quantity for resale. Nor did the affidavit allege anything else tying McPhearson or his home to any criminal activity other than personal possession of crack cocaine (and the simple assault for which he was arrested)."

A dissenting judge argued that McPhearson's possession of crack as he emerged from his house provided probable cause, since "it is a reasonable inference that at least some people who carry crack cocaine around with them in their homes would leave some of the contraband, which they could divide into smaller amounts, elsewhere in their homes." Besides, he added, even if probable cause had not been established, the police thought it had, and that was enough to admit the evidence under the loophole devised by the Supreme Court called the "good-faith exception."

That came from a pernicious ruling in 1984, *United States v. Leon*,[18] holding that a judge's error in approving a search should not result in the exclusion of evidence when the police, in good faith, have relied on the warrant. The case was a complex narcotics investigation involving multiple defendants, residences, and automobiles.

All three levels of the federal judiciary—a district court judge, a Ninth Circuit appeals panel, and the Supreme Court—agreed that a warrant to search for drugs in Alberto Leon's house in Burbank, California, was flawed because it was based on an unreliable informant with stale information, five months old, which the police had failed to corroborate. Following precedent, the two lower courts suppressed the pound of cocaine that was discovered.

But a six-to-three majority of the Burger Court used the opportunity to carve out an exception to the exclusionary rule, noting that "the Fourth Amendment contains no provision expressly precluding the use of evidence obtained in violation of its commands." The opinion, by Justice Byron White, concluded that "the exclusionary rule is designed to deter police misconduct rather than to punish the errors of judges and magistrates."

So, if officers honestly believe they have probable cause, if the issuing judge agrees, and even if a court later finds probable cause lacking, the evidence is still admissible. The reasoning has a whiff of Lewis Carroll: A police officer executes a sworn affidavit that forms the sole basis for a judge's issuance of a warrant, but then it's all the judge's fault, not the officer's, when the affidavit is found to fall short of probable cause. And since the judge is in error, it is pointless to deter the police with the exclusionary rule, and so the defendant is punished. One can almost hear the Queen declaring to the accused: "The judge was wrong, so off with your head!"

White inserted caveats into his opinion. Evidence can still be excluded if the police mistake is "substantial and deliberate," such as the "knowing or reckless falsity of the affidavit," or if the affidavit fails to provide "substantial basis for determining the existence of probable cause." To get evidence suppressed, then, the police error must be egregious. Anything short of that extreme, some attorneys have noticed, now induces courts to skip past their essential role of judging probable cause, concentrating instead on whether the police acted in good faith.

"If subjective good faith alone were the test," the retired justice Potter Stewart remarked a year before *Leon,* "the protections of the Fourth Amendment would evaporate, and the people would be 'secure in their persons, houses, papers, and effects,' only in the discretion of the police."[19]

UNDOING THE EXCLUSIONARY RULE

What prevents the police from violating the Fourth Amendment, and what is the remedy if they do?

America's unique answer has been the exclusionary rule, but it was assembled haphazardly and is now being similarly dismantled. "Looking back," said Stewart in 1983, "the exclusionary rule seems a bit jerrybuilt—like a roller coaster track constructed while the roller coaster sped along. Each new piece of track was attached hastily and imperfectly to the one before it, just in time to prevent the roller coaster from crashing, but without the opportunity to measure the curves and dips preceding it or to contemplate the twists and turns that inevitably lay ahead."[20]

It has never sat as comfortably in the criminal justice system when applied to the Fourth Amendment, as when it enforces the Fifth. There is a practical reason. A confession coerced in violation of the Fifth Amendment can easily be false, given only to stop the abuse; so even a defendant who confesses can be innocent. Excluding the confession forces the police to prove the case.

But physical evidence is tangible and real, confirmation of guilt in most prosecutions. Its suppression often sets criminals free. Consequently, no country but the United States has such a mandatory exclusionary rule, and many have none at all, including China, England, Germany, Israel, and Italy. Russia has one on paper only, and in keeping with Russia's long history of legal-looking charades, it is rarely observed in practice.[21]

The exclusionary rule did not exist in English common law, the uncodified tradition that forms the basis of law in almost all American states.[22] It is not mentioned in the Constitution (but neither is any remedy for any violation of fundamental rights), and it was not required as a corrective mechanism in federal courts for the first 123 years after the Bill of Rights was ratified, and not in state courts for another 47 years after that. An illegal search "is no good reason for excluding the papers seized in evidence," ruled a Massachusetts court in 1841. "When papers are offered in evidence, the court can take no notice how they were obtained, whether lawfully or unlawfully."[23]

Not until 1914, in the landmark case of *Weeks v. United States*,[24] did the Supreme Court decide that evidence illegally seized was inadmissible at trial. The opinion applied to federal courts only and, despite its ringing language, left ambiguous the supposed origins of the cure. Was it embedded implicitly in the bedrock of the Constitution, or was it a judicial invention, merely a new rule of evidence? The uncertainty carries into the present and fuels ongoing controversy about the rule's merits.

The circumstances of the case were clear, however. While Fremont Weeks was being questioned by police at his job, other officers—without a warrant—twice searched his room in Kansas City, Missouri, found envelopes with illegal lottery tickets, and arrested him for transporting gambling materials by mail. He petitioned unsuccessfully for a return of his papers, whose seizure, he argued, violated not only the Fourth Amendment but also the Fifth, which bars both compulsory self-incrimination and the deprivation of property without due process. The Supreme Court addressed only the Fourth Amendment issues.

"If letters and private documents can thus be seized and held and used in evidence against a citizen accused of an offense," the Court declared, "the protection of the 4th Amendment, declaring his right to be secure against such searches and seizures, is of no value, and . . . might as well be stricken from the Constitution. The efforts of the courts and their officials to bring the guilty to punishment, praiseworthy as they are, are not to be aided by the sacrifice of those great principles established by years of endeavor and suffering which have resulted in their embodiment in the fundamental law of the land."[25]

The Court did not apply *Weeks* to the states, however, and explicitly refused to do so in the 1949 case *Wolf v. People of the State of Colorado*,[26] leaving police and prosecutors with creative detours around the Fourth Amendment. State and federal officials collaborated in the "silver platter" technique in which state agents with illegally obtained evidence would turn it over, as if on a silver platter, to federal officials for prosecution. As long as the Fourth Amendment violation had not been committed by federal agents, the evidence was admitted in federal courts.[27]

Local police in states with no exclusionary rules of their own were free to seize evidence with scant regard for individual rights. "When the exclusionary rule was not in effect in the state of Ohio, for example, the Cincinnati police force rarely applied for search warrants," writes Timothy Lynch of the Cato Institute. "In 1958 the police obtained three warrants. In 1959 the police obtained none."[28] The same was true in New York City, where policies were abruptly changed by the Warren Court's reversal of *Wolf.* It came in a landmark 1961 case, *Mapp v. Ohio,*[29] which imposed the rule on the states.

Dollree Mapp was visited on May 23, 1957, by three Cleveland police officers who demanded that she allow them into the top-floor apartment of the two-family house where she lived with her young daughter. The cops claimed to have information that someone wanted for questioning in a bombing was hiding inside, and that papers relating to an illegal numbers game would be found. With the police at the door, Mapp consulted with her attorney by phone and then denied them permission to enter without a search warrant.

Three hours later, the three policemen, joined by four more, again knocked on the door and quickly forced it open. The Court's majority opinion recounted the events: "Miss Mapp was halfway down the stairs from the upper floor to the front door when the officers, in this high-handed manner, broke into the hall. She demanded to see the search warrant. A paper, claimed to be a warrant, was held up by one of the officers. She grabbed the 'warrant' and placed it in her bosom. A struggle ensued in which the officers recovered the piece of paper."

A policeman twisted her hand, handcuffed her, and forced her "upstairs to her bedroom where the officers searched a dresser, a chest of drawers, a closet, and some suitcases," the Court said. "They also looked into a photo album and through personal papers belonging to the appellant. The search spread to the rest of the second floor including the child's bedroom, the living room, the kitchen, and a dinette. The basement of the building and a trunk found therein were also searched." When her lawyer arrived, the officers barred him from the house and would not let him talk to her.

They discovered no bomber and no gambling receipts but charged Mapp for possessing "lewd and lascivious books, pictures, and photographs." She appealed on the grounds of the First Amendment, but it was the Fourth that got her off, as applied through the Fourteenth Amendment's due process clause (". . . nor shall any State deprive any person of life, liberty, or property, without due process of law . . .").

"There is no war between the Constitution and common sense," the majority declared. "This Court has not hesitated to enforce as strictly against the States as it does against the Federal Government the rights of free speech and of a free press, the rights to notice and to a fair, public trial . . . the right not to be convicted by use of a coerced confession. . . . Why should not the same rule apply to what is tantamount to coerced testimony by way of unconstitutional seizure of goods, papers, effects, documents, etc.?" The vote was six to three.

"The *Mapp* case was a shock to us," New York's Deputy Police Commissioner Leonard Reisman told *The New York Times* in 1965. "We had to reorganize our thinking, frankly. Before this nobody bothered to take out search warrants. Although the Constitution requires warrants in most cases, the Supreme Court had ruled that evidence obtained without a warrant—illegally, if you will—was admissible in state courts. So the feeling was, why bother? Well, once that rule was changed we knew we had better start teaching about it."[30]

Since then, to a layman who knows a little of the law, the suppression of illegally seized evidence has seemed integral to criminal procedure, an invincible shield against unconstitutional behavior by law enforcement. It has ensured that illegal searches yield nothing of value to prosecutions; it has reinforced judicial oversight; it has forced many police officers on the front lines to learn the law and temper their abuses against the Constitution. Yet the rule has been under assault by some conservative legislators and judges—not libertarian conservatives, to be sure, but those in the political right's dominant mainstream.

In 1995, soon after Republicans gained a majority in Congress, they made a failed attempt to legislate the exclusionary rule out of existence, and they succeeded for certain terrorism cases in 2006, during the waning days of their majority, prohibiting military commissions from suppressing evidence seized without a warrant, even inside the United States. This was narrowed in 2009, by the Democratic-led Congress and administration, to bar the exclusion of such evidence collected only outside the country.[31]

Over the years, the increasingly conservative Courts of Warren Burger, William Rehnquist, and John G. Roberts, Jr., have whittled away the rule on several fronts by deciding that illegally obtained evidence can be used in grand jury questioning (1974),[32] civil trials (1976),[33] the cross-examination of an accomplice testifying for the defense (1980),[34] and circumstances where it would be inevitably discovered through legal means (1984).[35] The Court in 1976 denied prisoners federal review after state appeals courts rejected claims that evidence was illegally seized.[36] The progression of these decisions was characterized by Justice William J. Brennan, Jr., in his *Leon* dissent, as "the Court's gradual but determined strangulation of the rule."[37]

Leon's good-faith exception in 1984 was expanded in 1995 to include erroneous computer records. A driver whose outstanding arrest warrant had been revoked but not removed from the database was stopped and arrested, his car searched, and marijuana found. Without the arrest warrant, the arrest was illegal, and therefore so was the search, but the Court, finding that the police had relied on the computer in good faith, allowed the marijuana into evidence.[38]

Similarly, the Court ruled five to four in 2009 that a man erroneously arrested on a warrant that had been withdrawn but left in a computer system could still be charged for possessing a gun and methamphetamine discovered when he was frisked after being taken into custody. "When police mistakes leading to an unlawful search are the result of isolated negligence attenuated from the search, rather than systemic error or reckless disregard of constitutional requirements, the exclusionary rule does not apply," wrote Chief Justice Roberts. "To trigger the exclusionary rule, police conduct must be sufficiently deliberate that exclusion can meaningfully deter it, and sufficiently culpable that such deterrence is worth the price paid by the justice system" in "letting guilty and possibly dangerous defendants go free."[39] The ruling may have raised the bar for the exclusion of evidence, since defense attorneys may find it hard, in individual instances, to show "systemic error" or "reckless disregard," a vague standard giving pro-police judges wider latitude to indulge their predilections.

Another exception, devised in 2006, released police from pausing before breaking down doors after knocking and announcing themselves. Previously, evidence could be suppressed if cops executing a warrant waited less than ten or twenty seconds, provided they faced no imminent violence. Just three years earlier, the Court had calculated the reasonable delay in a drug search as fifteen to twenty seconds so the narcotics couldn't be flushed.[40]

That meant that in 2005, the five or six seconds that Sergeant Brennan's crew gave Wendy before ramming her doors might have made the guns they found inadmissible had there been a trial—and had a judge believed a defendant, rather than the police, about how little time had passed.

But in 2006 the rules were changed by the Supreme Court in *Hudson v. Michigan*. Detroit police had waited three to five seconds before entering through Booker T. Hudson, Jr.'s unlocked door. They found a gun and drugs. The Michigan Supreme Court had already decided in earlier cases that a violation of the "knock-and-announce" rule should not result in suppression, and now a newly constituted Supreme Court, with Sandra Day O'Connor replaced by Samuel A. Alito, Jr., agreed five to four.[41]

"The common-law principle that law enforcement officers must announce their presence and provide residents an opportunity to open the door is an ancient one," Justice Antonin Scalia conceded as he wrote for the majority. The doctrine is encoded in a federal law that specifies no timetable,[42] he noted, and he listed the rule's several justifications: to avoid provoking violence by a surprised citizen, to minimize property damage, and to preserve privacy and dignity.

But the connection between the method of entry and the discovery of evidence was too attenuated to support exclusion, Scalia reasoned. Criminals would go free or "officers would be inclined to wait longer than the law requires—producing preventable violence against officers in some cases, and the destruction of evidence in many others."

If the police crash in too soon, then, the appropriate remedy would be not the suppression of evidence but rather, in Scalia's view, civil lawsuits by aggrieved citizens against the offending officers, an option expanded since *Mapp* in 1961 by court decisions, public-interest law firms, and federal civil rights statutes.[43] Where he thought victims would get the money to hire lawyers for such a long shot he did not say; the government is not obligated to pay poor people for attorneys in civil suits, only in criminal cases. The dissenters found nothing persuasive in Scalia's approach, noting that he had "failed to cite a single reported case in which a plaintiff has collected more than nominal damages solely as a result of a knock-and-announce violation."

I called Sergeant Brennan to ask how he thought the ruling would play on the street. "The decision is great, because we don't have to count," he remarked. "Some judges would say you should wait fifteen to twenty seconds, others would say less," so it was hard to know. "The good thing is we're not on a time frame anymore. It makes our job easier."

It may also reduce the temptation to lie. He remembered once hearing an officer testify that he had stood in front of a door waiting for twenty-five seconds, and Brennan's silent, sardonic reaction was, "Yeah, right."

When you've shouted and knocked and stood there thinking there might be somebody inside with a gun, "that's a very long time," he said.

Still, "We'd rather knock on the door and yell, 'Police!' If the guy is sitting watching television and playing with his gun, which is not unlikely, we'd rather have him hide the gun. If we just ram that door and knock it down without making a sound [first], he might shoot." So the police were now freed to march to their own cadence, just a few beats longer than unannounced shock and considerably more rapid than the slower tempo previously prescribed.

And what about Scalia's point that citizens could sue? It would have no effect, Brennan said dismissively. "Everything we do on the street is a potential civil suit. We have so many people making things up." If Justice Scalia honestly believed that lawsuits would be a deterrent, it seemed, the distance between his desk and Sergeant Brennan's, a mile or so away, was a chasm.

Coleen Rowley developed a different view as an agent and legal adviser with the FBI.[44] "Civil liability has a much greater effect on law enforcement officers than the exclusionary rule," she countered. She and her colleagues took the suppression of evidence with a shrug, she said. "OK, you lost a case. It hurts your feelings, it hurts your pride. But it ain't like being civilly liable," when you couldn't count on the Department of Justice to defend you. "If you did something and all of a sudden the media viewpoint swung the other way, DOJ would be very tempted to go the other way: 'Let's just let this guy shoulder this on his own. He's been a bad agent to begin with.'

"We all had malpractice insurance," she continued. "A couple of hundred dollars a year, and it protects you up to $1 million. You're almost paying it for nothing, because they also have a lot of small print: They won't defend you if you're outside the realm of employment, blah, blah, blah. Civil liability has a pretty good chilling effect. Exclusion of evidence is a very indirect thing."

Characterizing the exclusionary rule as a deterrent, not a constitutional mandate, makes it easier to undermine. Judges who can't stand throwing away incriminating evidence love to find reasons that the rule doesn't deter, deters this when it should deter that, or deters what it shouldn't deter at all. The Supreme Court made the distinction explicit in 1974, declaring in *United States v. Calandra,* "The rule is a judicially created remedy designed to safeguard Fourth Amendment rights generally through its deterrent effect rather than a personal constitutional right of the party aggrieved."[45]

Once defined as a remedy and not a right, the suppression of evidence is conveniently reduced to part of a legal superstructure that can be remodeled or torn down. Were it a constitutional pillar as well, then it would stand impervious to the shifting winds of pragmatism. A core principle, unlike a practice, cannot be carved, divided, diluted, adjusted, and ultimately obliterated by Congress and the courts. It cannot be evaluated opportunistically. It is subject to constitutional analysis, not sociological research, and cannot be made victim to the kind of empirical appraisal that the exclusionary rule has suffered.

But the line of cases since *Calandra* has indulged in a brand of pinched micro-logic in which the Court manipulates the exclusionary rule as if it were a mechanism of personnel management. So in *Leon*, the majority decided that the rule was aimed at cops, not judges, and therefore wouldn't deter cops who were imbued with "good faith" in the warrant they managed to obtain without showing probable cause. In *Arizona v. Evans*, the Court decided that suppressing evidence wouldn't deter cops because a police database was at fault. And what, then, is to deter those who create and operate the expanding, intrusive databases?

Oddly, rightward-leaning justices have come to see the suppression of evidence as a method of punishment, not protection, a measure to curb particular officers' misconduct, not to preserve defendants' rights. Justice White made this cramped argument in *Leon*, saying, "Penalizing the officer for the magistrate's error, rather than his own, cannot logically contribute to the deterrence of Fourth Amendment violations." But the officer didn't have probable cause to get a warrant in the first place; why should he be absolved? And what is to deter the sloppy magistrate? When the judge is *also* wrong, couldn't he use a little correction? The Court's solution is to punish the violated citizen for the judge's error.

The illegal search and the admission of the illegal evidence are parts of a whole, seamlessly coupled, wrote Justice Brennan. "Police and the courts cannot be regarded as constitutional strangers to each other," he said in his *Leon* dissent. "Because the evidence-gathering role of the police is directly linked to the evidence-admitting function of the courts, an individual's Fourth Amendment rights may be undermined as completely by one as by the other."

Brennan tried to elevate his gaze beyond the intricate question of how to deter police errors. He noted that the original *Weeks* opinion establishing the exclusionary rule was not aimed at punishing individual officers, but at safeguarding rights by encouraging broad institutional procedures in law enforcement. Nor did he believe the deterrent effect could be accurately assessed; such attempts led the Court into guesswork. He predicted that the majority's decision in *Leon,* allowing an officer to escape penalty if he does not know he is acting unconstitutionally, "will tend to put a premium on police ignorance of the law."

Brennan also worried about damaging the constitutional structure by marginalizing the judiciary. He accused the majority of drawing "an artificial line between the constitutional rights and responsibilities that are engaged by actions of the police and those that are engaged when a defendant appears before the courts," a decision that "rests ultimately on an impoverished understanding of judicial responsibility in our constitutional scheme." The Fourth Amendment "restrains the power of the government as a whole; it does not specify only a particular agency and exempt all others," Brennan wrote. "The judiciary is responsible, no less than the executive, for ensuring that constitutional rights are respected."

He bolstered his point with a quote from James Madison's address to the First Congress on June 8, 1789:

> If [these rights] are incorporated into the Constitution, independent tribunals of justice will consider themselves in a peculiar manner the guardians of those rights; they will be an impenetrable bulwark against every assumption of power in the Legislative or Executive; they will be naturally led to resist every encroachment upon rights expressly stipulated for in the Constitution by the declaration of rights.[46]

Indeed, the strongest constitutional case for the exclusionary rule may lie in the separation of powers, the Constitution's ingenious division of authority among the executive, legislative, and judicial branches. Without the judiciary's tool of suppressing evidence, the foundation of the Constitution is undermined, argues the libertarian conservative Timothy Lynch. "When agents of the executive branch (the police) disregard the terms of search warrants, or attempt to bypass the warrant-issuing process altogether, the judicial branch can and should respond by 'checking' such misbehavior," Lynch writes. "The most opportune time to check such unconstitutional behavior is when prosecutors attempt to introduce illegally seized evidence in court." He believes that the legislature cannot constitutionally alter the exclusionary rule, because it is a judicial function integral to the judiciary's warrant-issuing power.[47]

But judges have been stripping themselves of the power, often by weighing the benefit of suppressing evidence against the risk of releasing people who are presumed guilty. "Some guilty defendants may go free or receive reduced sentences as a result of favorable plea bargains," White wrote for the majority in *Leon*. "The magnitude of the benefit conferred on such guilty defendants offends basic concepts of the criminal justice system." He referred to studies showing that suppressed evidence freed 0.6 to 7.1 percent of felony defendants.

Brennan replied derisively:

> The language of deterrence and of cost/benefit analysis, if used indis-criminately, can have a narcotic effect. It creates an illusion of techni-cal precision and ineluctability. It suggests that not only constitutional principle but also empirical data support the majority's result. When the Court's analysis is examined carefully, however, it is clear that we have not been treated to an honest assessment of the merits of the exclusionary rule, but have instead been drawn into a curious world where the "costs" of excluding illegally obtained evidence loom to exaggerated heights and where the "benefits" of such exclusion are made to disappear with a mere wave of the hand.

Rights and risks coexist in a complex tension that was reduced to a simplistic observation by Judge Benjamin N. Cardozo: "The criminal is to go free because the constable has blundered," he declared sardonically as he refused to adopt the exclusionary rule for New York State in 1926.[48]

His line is often quoted by opponents of exclusion, but it was a "mis-leading epigram," in Justice Brennan's view. Evidence is suppressed not because the constable has blundered, "but rather because official com-pliance with Fourth Amendment requirements makes it more difficult to catch criminals. Understood in this way, the Amendment directly con-templates that some reliable and incriminating evidence will be lost to the government; therefore, it is not the exclusionary rule, but the Amend-ment itself that has imposed this cost." So, we are back to the risks of freedom.

The same argument found support from the retired justice Potter Stewart. "Much of the criticism leveled at the exclusionary rule is mis-directed; it is more properly directed at the Fourth Amendment itself," he wrote in the *Columbia Law Review*. "The exclusionary rule places no limitations on the actions of the police. The Fourth Amendment does. . . . Police officers who obey its strictures will catch fewer criminals. . . . That is the price the framers anticipated and were willing to pay to ensure the sanctity of the person, the home, and property against unrestrained governmental power."[49]

But is it a price that we are willing to pay in a time of terrorism? Justice Brennan offered a warning: "The task of combating crime and convicting the guilty will in every era seem of such critical and pressing concern that we may be lured by the temptations of expediency into forsaking our commitment to protecting individual liberty and privacy."

SUSPICIONLESS SEARCHES

The lure is almost irresistible, especially in this era. Forsaking privacy to law enforcement seems to offer sanctuary from terror in many forms, not only the terror brought by the suicidal ideologue but by the lone school shooter, the child rapist and pornographer, the purveyor of narcotics.

It was the terror of narcotics that propelled a divided Supreme Court into a rash of rulings that allowed suspicionless, warrantless drug and alcohol testing in various settings. In 1989, the tests were precisely targeted, at U.S. Customs employees[50] and railroad workers,[51] because of the risks those personnel might pose to others. Then that legitimate opening was widened step by step. "Following those rulings, more than forty federal agencies began conducting drug tests under an executive order for a drug-free federal workplace," the constitutional scholar David M. O'Brien observes.[52] A Justice Department attorney who challenged this dragnet practice lost in the D.C. Circuit in 1992, and the Supreme Court denied review, sweeping away a measure of privacy for government workers by allowing tests of all federal employees, even those not in positions to threaten public safety or enforce narcotics laws.[53] The quaint notion that individualized suspicion was necessary for a search to be "reasonable" had disappeared, and the Fourth Amendment seemed to be evaporating from the landscape like a shallow pool of water in a hot sun.

When the Court forces a constitutional right into retreat, government officials across the country advance to occupy the new ground: They regulate, investigate, intrude, outlaw, and prosecute until they meet the limits the Court decides to draw. The justices finally penciled in some lines on drug testing. A Georgia law requiring a test of any candidate who wished to run for office was struck down eight to one.[54] The practice in Charleston, South Carolina, of testing pregnant women for cocaine and referring positive results to the police for prosecution, was overruled six to three.[55]

Public school students fared less well. In 1995, the Court approved testing all athletes in Vernonia, Oregon, reasoning that children on drugs could injure themselves and others playing sports, and that athletes were models whose narcotics use led other children astray, undermining school antidrug policies. In addition, "Fourth Amendment rights . . . are different in public schools than elsewhere," the majority held. "The 'reasonableness' inquiry cannot disregard the schools' custodial and tutelary responsibility for children."[56]

Thus emboldened, school officials in Tecumseh, Oklahoma, responded to parents whose parenting had failed. "The mother of a football player caught her son and some of his friends using drugs in her home," recalled Lindsay Earls, then a sophomore at Tecumseh High School, "so she went to the school board and said, 'I don't have control over my son. Is there any way you guys can help me with my son's drug problem?' I guess there were a few other parents of kids who were at that party and said, 'Our kids are out of control. You fix this for us.'"

Inviting an arm of the state to monitor your children should have appalled true conservatives touting restrictions on government and the preeminence of family. But no. Parents who distrusted their own teenagers prevailed, and the school board decided to stretch suspicionless drug testing beyond the athletes authorized by the Supreme Court in the *Vernonia* case to all students who participated in virtually all extracurricular organizations that involved travel or competition. That included the choir, the color guard, and the quiz bowl team—the three that Lindsay Earls belonged to.

She was something of the perfect teenager: an excellent student admired by teachers, a responsible youngster who never did drugs, a "Goody Two-shoes," as she described herself. Practically alone in her school, she also had that internal gyroscope that kept her on course when individual liberty was challenged.

When the policy was announced, she thought it a joke at first. Tecumseh didn't have much of a drug problem, and most kids didn't care about the testing, she said, figuring that since they didn't use drugs, it wasn't a big deal. Those wanting to continue extracurricular activities willingly brought a parental permission slip and a four-dollar lab fee, and submitted to random urine tests throughout the year. She guessed that kids who did drugs probably thought they'd get lucky—or they just avoided extracurricular activities that might have given them something fun to do besides smoke pot. One girl, who refused to be tested because her mother objected, was kicked out of the choir.

Lindsay objected, too, but took a different tack. While the tests were random and suspicionless, they were not seen that way in the high school's culture. The arrival of an office assistant in a classroom to summon a few students by name aroused a buzz of suspicion. "There was no other reason for us to be called out of class," Lindsay said. "It was supposed to be this hush-hush thing, but everyone knew."

It also carried a dose of humiliation. The students were led immediately to a bathroom by a staff member who waited outside the closed stall to "listen for the normal sounds of urination in order to guard against tampered specimens and to insure an accurate chain of custody," according to court papers from the school board.

A positive test required drug counseling in an effort to help, not just punish, and the results would be turned over to the parents but not to the police. Nevertheless, Lindsay had read the Fourth Amendment, was familiar with the principles, and saw this as an unreasonable invasion. Her mother and father regarded their children's behavior outside of school as a purely parental responsibility, and this suspicionless, warrantless intrusion into the zone of individual and family privacy violated their sense of the spirit of American freedom. "Dad's always been pretty strong in telling us to be sure you know your rights," Lindsay said, a teaching reinforced by his position as a social worker dealing with teenagers, many of them in trouble with the police.

Lindsay's father contacted the American Civil Liberties Union (ACLU), which found Lindsay's exemplary record ideal for her to be the lead plaintiff in a constitutional challenge (it always helps if your client is "squeaky clean," as she put it). So the lawsuit was filed, working its way through the lower courts as Lindsay and her younger sister, Lacey, worked their way through a maze of hostility in their hometown.

Despite her family's sterling reputation, "a lot of people began speculating on my drug problems and my family's drug-use problems," Lindsay said a few years later, when she could smile faintly at their fantasies. "People who didn't know my family were talking about how the only people who would care are kids who are druggies, that we were complainers, just wanted to cause a fuss." Lacey was targeted by students who parroted their parents' unfounded accusations that her sister or father used drugs. Lindsay was derided for her frequent appearances in newspapers and on television, as if she were trying to get publicity rather than preserve her rights—their rights. "One kid sent an e-mail saying, What you're doing is not a Christian thing to do and blah, blah, blah. He didn't have very good reasoning as to why this wasn't a Christian thing to do, and I didn't respond to the e-mail, and I pretty much stopped seeing him." Her close friends stuck with her.

Outside of school, the verbal attacks got so bad that "I wasn't allowed to listen to any talk-radio stations, because they were saying such mean things about me especially," Lindsay recalled. "My parents wouldn't let me read a lot of letters to the editors of the papers. My parents were very protective about all the terrible things that were being said."

So were some teachers, who tried to stop the harassment and offered to take Lindsay and Lacey home if it got out of hand. What they did not do, Lindsay said, was use the opportunity to teach about the Fourth Amendment or to open classes to discussions of the case and its significance, to examine the country's ebb and flow of relations between the individual and the state. They were afraid of being fired, she thought, although it would have been easy enough to consider the issues even-handedly, without taking sides. And so a rare educational opportunity got lost, as it usually does when schools do searches and restrict speech and thereby teach their students all the wrong lessons. The Bill of Rights, studied as an archaic document in history courses, did not seem to have much vitality in America's heartland.

"It didn't surprise me a whole lot," Lindsay said. "Since I've been there my whole life, I know what these people find important, and civil liberties hasn't been shown to be one of those things." The scary problem of drugs and kids "clouds people's perceptions."

The tensions ground on her, but she had wise adult counsel, from her ACLU lawyer, Graham Boyd, who reassured her that she was free to quit, and from her father. "When I was getting fed up," she recalled, "I was like, 'Dad, do I really have to keep doing this?' He was like, 'You don't have to, but if it's something that you really care about, you'll want to.'" And it was. Softly amazed by her fame, teary when telling parts of her story, she was no militant firebrand, just resolute. When she applied to Dartmouth, she wrote of the lawsuit in her essay, which surely helped her get accepted. "I think it made me stick out a bit more than if I'd written about hiking."

The case was headed for the Supreme Court when Lindsay graduated from Tecumseh High and walked across the stage, on her way to the Ivy League. As she picked up her diploma before an audience of classmates and their families, her guidance counselor shook her hand and said quietly, "I'm really glad that you brought that case. I'm glad I can finally say this to you, but I'm really glad you did what you did."

Lindsay's voice broke as she remembered the moment. The counselor had always been friendly to her, but this was his first indication of support. "I was crying so hard when I walked across the stage," she said.

She had lost in the federal district court, won in the circuit court, and headed down to Washington during spring break of her freshman year at Dartmouth, in March 2002, for oral arguments in the Supreme Court. It was an intense, dizzying experience. "I was sitting between my parents, and I remember my dad kept having to pinch my leg because I was moving around and talking under my breath, and he said, 'If you don't be quiet you're going to have to leave. They're going to ask you to leave. You have to be still.'"

At one point, Justice Anthony Kennedy, his face red as he questioned her attorney, committed a breach of judicial protocol. "Most surprising was Justice Kennedy's implied slur on the plaintiffs in the case," wrote Linda Greenhouse for *The New York Times*. "He had posed to Mr. Boyd the hypothetical question of whether a district could have two schools, one a 'druggie school' and one with drug testing. As for the first, Justice Kennedy said, 'no parent would send a child to that school, except maybe your client.'"[57]

"And I just started laughing," Lindsay remembered. "I laughed out loud. It was so ridiculous to me that he said that. And a lot of people in the courtroom, people couldn't believe he could say that. There was kind of a silence, except for my little chuckle, and my dad pinched me and said, 'Shut up.'"

She laughed, but what did she feel? "I was shocked and hurt. It hurt me because he didn't know anything about me. Everything he knew about me was in those briefs, and everything that he'd seen about me—nothing spoke to the fact that I had ever used drugs, that I'd had a drug problem; it spoke to the fact that I was an outstanding, good high school kid, typical, normal high school kid that wasn't using drugs. So how could he say that? It blew my mind. It was kind of painful. It made my parents really angry, too. My dad, I remember him fuming for days about that."

On a Thursday morning that June, Boyd called her in her dorm with the result: The Supreme Court had narrowly ruled, five to four, that such drug testing was constitutional. She cried for a while before passing the bad news on to her parents. "It was really upsetting. I was really disappointed."

Unsurprisingly, Kennedy was in the majority, but so was Justice Stephen G. Breyer, who is often on the liberal side. When he visited Dartmouth to lecture during Lindsay's junior year, she sat next to him at a breakfast and used the occasion to ask if Supreme Court justices ever recognized that they had made a mistake. Yes, he said, "but not in your case."

The majority opinion, written by Justice Clarence Thomas, emphasized the school's custodial responsibilities and argued that competitive extracurricular activities, governed by state rules, carry a diminished expectation of privacy. The penalty for refusal to be tested or a positive result was minimal—dismissal from activities—without either academic or legal consequences. (He didn't mention that the lack of extracurricular involvement damages the chance of getting into a good college.) "Given the minimally intrusive nature of the sample collection and the limited uses to which the test results are put," Thomas declared, "we conclude that the invasion of students' privacy is not significant."[50]

The school's policy didn't pass the laugh test for Justice Ruth Bader Ginsburg. In *Vernonia* she had voted for testing athletes, accepting the argument that those on drugs might hurt themselves or others. But she couldn't take seriously the Tecumseh school board's lawyer as he made a valiant attempt to highlight the dangers of band members wielding musical instruments, Future Farmers of America controlling 1,500-pound steers, and Future Homemakers of America with access to knives.

"Notwithstanding nightmarish images of out-of-control flatware, livestock run amok, and colliding tubas disturbing the peace and quiet of Tecumseh," she wrote in dissent, "the great majority of students the School District seeks to test in truth are engaged in activities that are not safety sensitive to an unusual degree." She found the testing program "capricious, even perverse" in targeting only those active in school organizations—just the students least likely to use narcotics.

Principals and police took great license amid the antidrug frenzy. In the South Carolina bedroom town of Goose Creek, officials apparently thought that the students most likely to use drugs were black, because African-Americans made up two-thirds of the nearly one hundred fifty who were searched roughly by police with drawn guns during a raid at Stratford High School. The cops had been invited by the principal, George C. McCrackin, who'd had a tip that drugs were being sold early each morning after the first buses arrived. So at 6:45 a.m. on November 5, 2003, police officers hid in stairwells and closets and on McCrackin's signal exploded into the hallways, pistols in hand, a drug-sniffing dog on a leash. Watching a video, you might have thought that a SWAT team was assaulting a crack house loaded with weapons. Cops were waving guns around and yelling, "Get down! Hands behind your head!" They forced teenagers to kneel facing walls, frisked them, and rummaged through whichever backpacks caught the dog's interest.

But no drugs were found. Settling a lawsuit, the city, the police department, and the school district paid $1.6 million and, more significantly, signed a consent decree barring police action in the school without warrants, probable cause in an emergency, or voluntary consent by those to be searched.[59]

Again the following year, a zealous principal named Gordon Sampson in rural Chestertown, Maryland, requested a police team, which invaded the high school and swept a dozen classrooms with a canine unit. The dogs erroneously alerted on eighteen book bags, which were searched and their owners patted down. Two teenage girls were pulled aside and put into a room where a school official watched while a female deputy, Marcellene Beck, ordered Lacey Fernwalt, sixteen, to remove her pants, and then checked inside the girl's bra. Heather Gore, fifteen, was told to take off her skirt; Beck pulled up her tank top to expose her breasts, asked Gore to spread her legs, and tugged at her underpants. "I was crying and hyperventilating," the girl told a *Washington Post* reporter. "I sat there in disbelief." No drugs were discovered, and the girls won $285,000 and apologies from the school system and the Kent County Sheriff's Department.[60]

Had the case not been settled before trial, however, the courts might have found the searches constitutional, given the probable cause signaled by the dogs. Judges had a mixed record on protecting schoolchildren from humiliating examinations of their bodies, and had left students—along with parolees and welfare recipients—with their Fourth Amendment rights seriously diluted.

So confused and unclear was the case law on strip searches in schools that the Supreme Court in 2009 felt compelled to grant "qualified immunity" to an assistant principal, a secretary, and a school nurse in Safford, Arizona, who had ordered and carried out invasive inspections beneath the underwear of two young girls. One of them, thirteen-year-old Savana Redding, sued. She won the constitutional challenge but lost the right to damages.

Strict school policy in Safford banned all medicines, even those sold over the counter, without authorization from parents or doctors. So when a girl was found with prescription-strength tablets of the anti-inflammatory drug ibuprofen, she was called in, searched beneath her bra and panties, and asked where she'd obtained the pills. She named Redding, who denied it but consented to a superficial pat-down and search of her back-pack, which turned up nothing. With no more "evidence" than the other girl's claim, and with no indication that pills might be hidden beneath Redding's clothes, the assistant principal, Kerry Wilson, sent her off with instructions to the school nurse and a female counselor to perform a more intrusive search. They told her to strip to her underwear, made her pull out her bra and shake it, and do the same with the elastic on her panties while spreading her legs, "exposing her breasts and pelvic area to some degree," as the justices stated. No pills were found.

The Court, ruling that the search violated the Fourth Amendment, set a low standard for school searches—"a moderate chance of finding evidence of wrongdoing"—but decided that "here, the content of the suspicion failed to match the degree of intrusion." There was "reason to question the clarity with which the [student's] right was established" before the incident, however, so the justices granted "qualified immunity" to the school employees, since government officials cannot be held liable unless they act outside well-defined legal limits.[61]

After the humiliating search, Savana Redding said she developed stomach ulcers and a distrustful wariness. She couldn't bear to return to school, "never wanted to see the secretary or the nurse ever again," and studied at home for months until she transferred elsewhere. Studying at Eastern Arizona College to become a counselor, she told a *New York Times* reporter that if she were ever ordered to strip-search a student, she would refuse. "Why would I want to do that to a little girl and ruin her life like that?"[62]

Even while imposing restraints on government here and there, the Supreme Court has continued to narrow the scope of the Fourth Amendment. Legislatures and executive branches across the country have carved out exceptions by targeting citizens at the margins of society, those with whom the majority couldn't identify. In 2006, the Court upheld, six to three, a California law permitting warrantless searches without cause of parolees, who were required to sign away their rights as a condition of completing their sentences outside of prison.[63]

In 2007, it denied a writ of certiorari—an order accepting a case on appeal—and let stand a practice in San Diego of doing unannounced, warrantless searches of welfare recipients' homes by criminal investigators looking for signs of fraud: men's underwear in drawers, for example, as evidence that a supposedly single mother actually had a man in the house. Consent for the search was required from the recipient, but a refusal could provoke a cutoff in payments.

Seven dissenting judges in the Ninth Circuit called this "an assault on the poor" and declared: "There can be no true consent here. Applicants are not given notice of when the visit will occur; they are not informed of their right to withhold consent; they are told the visit is mandatory; and they are aware of the severe consequences of refusing the search. San Diego's program requires destitute, often disabled, persons and their families to forfeit all rights to privacy to qualify for welfare." The dissenters noted that farmers receiving subsidies were not subjected to such invasions.[64]

By refusing to hear the appeal, the Supreme Court was allowing Fourth Amendment protection to be scaled back in a serious way. In 1971, in *Wyman v. James,* it had ruled that social workers could do warrantless home searches, but the consequences were limited to a termination of benefits.[65] Now the consequences could be criminal charges as the search authority was extended to the district attorney's office—and not just for welfare fraud, because if investigators happened to see evidence of other crime "in plain view," such as drugs, for example, they could prosecute. As *The New York Times* editorialized, "It would be a mistake . . . to take consolation in the fact that only poor people's privacy rights were at stake. When the government is allowed to show up unannounced without a warrant and search people's homes, it is bad news for all of us."[66]

And this bad news was what we could see in the open sunlight. There were deep shadows, too.

CHAPTER FIVE

Patriotic Acts

*Do I want the government breaking down my doors to interrogate
me? Of course not. Something in the middle, however, is not outrageous for our protection. I wouldn't mind if they peeked into my
life as long as I don't notice them there.*

—Lauren Olson, student at Stetson University

SNEAK AND PEEK

SOMEBODY HAD BEEN in the house again. The top bolt was locked,
something the Mayfields never bothered to do. A fairly new carpet,
freshly vacuumed, was indented with footprints shaped like shoes, which
the Muslim family didn't wear inside. In the teenage son's bedroom,
the louvers of a blind overlooking the driveway were cracked open at a
height above the boy's eye level, as if a tall intruder had peered out to see
whether anyone was coming.

Mona Mayfield called her husband at his law office. "Brandon, I'm at
the house," he remembered her saying. "The thing's bolted; I didn't leave
it bolted." He questioned her: Was she certain? She passed the phone to
their son Shane, with instructions: "Tell your dad this is bolted." He did,
and Brandon Mayfield said, "OK, it's not burglars."

He had worried about burglars, even arsonists, since there had been
some fires set in the neighborhood. More than once during that spring
of 2004, the unused bolt above the main lock had been thrown. Digital
clocks and VCR lights had been blinking, as if the power had been turned
off and then on again. A creepy feeling had led him to call the police, who
offered to send someone. But since nothing had been stolen except the
family's sense of security, he declined and waited to see if it happened
again.

It did. Telltale signs of invasion appeared weekly, on a Tuesday or a
Thursday. Computer hard drives in his law office crashed. As he walked
and drove, he was chilled by the uneasy sensation of being watched and
followed. Occasionally he noticed someone tailing him from his office.
He began to look for unfamiliar vehicles parked on his street.

Then one day, Shane, age fifteen, stayed home sick alone after Mona and Brandon and the two youngest children had left in a van and a car. "It might have appeared to anybody doing surveillance that everybody had gone," Brandon surmised. "They probably assumed that nobody was home that day, and it might have been pretty quiet."

Shane slept late in his room above the garage, then got up and went to the kitchen to eat. Suddenly, through a window, he saw a man walking deliberately toward the house. He heard noises. "He was scared that it could be unsavory characters coming through the door," Brandon said. There seemed to be more than one. "They didn't knock. They immediately went for the door, they were messing around with the door. He was getting nervous. They were not knocking and announcing, they were trying to break in. He went upstairs to my daughter's room, and he took it a step further and went inside the attic. He was hiding in a crawl space in the attic, just there, scared." With his cell phone, Shane tried to call his parents but couldn't reach them, so he phoned his aunt half a continent away in Kansas City.

Then, just as suddenly, Brandon reported, "Whoever it was must have realized he was there. We speculate they were monitoring calls. They left." And they left behind a boy who "was pretty shaken up," his father said.

The Mayfields were being subjected to secret searches, clumsily executed but clandestinely approved by an unnamed judge based on a confidential affidavit submitted by the FBI citing classified information—erroneous, it turned out—that Brandon Mayfield was an agent of a foreign power involved in terrorism. It was based on a fingerprint, from train bombings in Madrid, that the vaunted FBI laboratory had misidentified as his.

If all had gone as the FBI had planned, he would never have learned that his phones were being tapped; that his intimate and professional conversations at home and work were monitored with hidden microphones; that his private papers and his clients' privileged files had been copied; and that he and his family were followed to work, to school, and to the mosque where they worshipped. He would not have known that agents copied three computer hard drives and one external drive, took ten DNA samples on cotton swabs, collected six cigarette butts to compare the DNA with that found in a van used by the terrorists, and took 335 digital photographs of his house and office.[1] This occurred legally in the United States—in a suburb of Portland, Oregon.

The law authorizing such secret snooping, the Foreign Intelligence Surveillance Act (FISA),[2] was passed in 1978 as a check on an FBI that had run rampant in the 1960s and 1970s by monitoring not only foreign spies but domestic antiwar and civil rights groups through its COINTEL program. When congressional hearings exposed the extent of abuse, in which J. Edgar Hoover's agency had bugged and wiretapped Martin Luther King, Jr., and other American dissidents, the backlash took a creative turn. The most doctrinaire civil liberties advocates rejected any wiretapping as equivalent to a general search that violated the Fourth Amendment's particularity requirement, because it collected all information passed on a particular phone line, not just that related to the crime under investigation. Pragmatic liberals, however, led by Senator Edward Kennedy, recognized that "if you opposed a statute saying you had to have a warrant, you'd be left with warrantless wiretapping," recalled Jerry Berman, who was chief legislative counsel of the ACLU. Believing that the FBI had to be reined in but that clandestine methods were necessary to counterespionage, Congress then enacted FISA to regulate the surveillance by constructing a layer of judicial oversight far less demanding than for traditional criminal warrants.

The result, a parallel system of shadow warrants, functioned appropriately when limited to intelligence gathering in the dusky world of spies, where a Soviet agent would not be prosecuted but simply expelled from the country. "It was a remarkable experiment, saying we can legally regulate the way intelligence is gathered," noted Stewart Baker, general counsel for the National Security Agency and later an assistant secretary of Homeland Security. "There was never a country that tried this."

But the experiment began to fail during the Clinton and Bush administrations. Initially limited to electronic surveillance, the law was expanded in 1994 to permit physical searches,[3] and has since spread beyond the bounds of intelligence into ordinary criminal investigations, disrupting the equilibrium calibrated so carefully by the Bill of Rights.

The differences between FISA orders and criminal search warrants are monumental. While the target of an ordinary warrant is notified of the search, at least eventually, the target of a FISA warrant has no such right to know.[4] The police affidavit supporting an ordinary warrant is later made public so that it can be challenged, but the affidavit for a FISA warrant is not. Nor is the name of the judge who signs the FISA order, one of eleven federal judges appointed to the Foreign Intelligence Surveillance Court by the chief justice of the Supreme Court to consider such applications in secret. The specifics of the FISA order may remain sealed, and therefore unchallengeable, even if they become the basis of an ordinary search or wiretap warrant under Title III of the U.S. Code. The law permits judges to keep the rationale for the FISA order secret from the defense in a suppression hearing unless they find disclosure essential, which they virtually never do.

If FISA material is used as evidence, it must be turned over to the defense, but before the defendant can see it, it must be declassified. If the government wants it to remain classified, the defense attorney and any translator have to get security clearances to pore through it, and the defendants themselves may never be allowed to know its contents.[5]

A heavier handicap is imposed if the material collected under FISA isn't used in trial. Then, it never has to be revealed to the accused and their attorneys unless it contains exculpatory evidence—and the government is empowered to decide unilaterally what's exculpatory. This burdens the fact-finding process. The e-mails, Web searches, conversations, and documents collected through FISA may have been used to focus and further the investigation, but the defense will probably never know of their existence. When a body of evidence is rendered invisible, there is no way to put statements in context, rebut assumptions, or contest fragmented facts that shape the government's theory of the crime.

Secrecy invariably permits abuse, as documented by the Foreign Intelligence Surveillance Court's disclosure that in 2000 "the government came forward to confess error in some 75 FISA applications related to major terrorist attacks directed against the United States. The errors related to misstatements and omissions of material facts," the court said. As a result, "The Court decided not to accept inaccurate affidavits from FBI agents whether or not intentionally false. One FBI agent was barred from appearing before the Court as a FISA affiant."[6] But if the executive branch itself had not revealed these "errors" to the court, nobody would have known, because FISA permits no adversary proceeding.

In other ways, too, the looser standards depart from the Fourth Amendment's language of protection. While an ordinary warrant is supposed to meet the requirement for particularity ("particularly describing the place to be searched, and the persons or things to be seized"), a FISA warrant does not have to specify the "things to be seized" and thereby becomes a fishing expedition. The requirement to name places or individuals in the FISA application was eliminated, by amendments in 2008, when a target overseas is not a "United States person," even where one end of the communication is inside the United States.[7]

Nor does there have to be a crime to justify the snooping. As outlined in the Justice Department's report on the Mayfield case, "To obtain authority for FISA surveillance of a particular telephone line, the government must show probable cause to believe that the target is an agent of a foreign power and that the target uses that telephone line to communicate.[8] In contrast, in a criminal case the government must show that there is probable cause to believe that an individual is committing, has committed, or is about to commit a particular criminal offense specified by statute, and that particular communications about that offense will be obtained through the interception."[9]

In other words, while an ordinary search warrant demands that the police show probable cause to believe that criminal evidence will be found, a FISA warrant mandates probable cause only that a target is somehow in coordination with a foreign entity that can include a government or a terrorist organization.[10] This lower threshold, reduced further by amendments to FISA following 9/11, has permitted wide scale surveillance of people without substantial evidence of criminal behavior.

In addition, a criminal wiretap order requires agents to restrict interception to communications involving the alleged crime, whereas FISA practices allow constant monitoring and only later, when tapes are played and transcripts made, is the intercepted material narrowed by indexing and logging. These are called "minimization procedures," designed to diminish intrusion into private lives, but they kick in only after the intrusion has occurred.

FISA also contains a more relaxed requirement for timeliness: To get a criminal wiretap order, for example, police have to show probable cause (known in the vernacular as "P.C.") that a phone line has been used for a crime within the last forty-eight to seventy-two hours, and if they can't do so, a judge will often tell them to "freshen up the P.C." FISA surveillance invites more flexibility, according to Michael E. Rolince, who headed the FBI's International Terrorism Operations Section on 9/11: "You can say, 'The Soviets used this safe house on Bleecker Street three years ago; let's see if it's been reactivated.'" Rolince's reading may take liberties with the law, which actually requires that "each of the facilities or places at which the electronic surveillance is directed is being used, or is about to be used, by a foreign power or an agent of a foreign power."[11] But nobody can get into a Foreign Intelligence Surveillance Court hearing to contest an FBI interpretation.

Because FISA warrants are secret and sweeping—authorizing bugging, wiretapping, and clandestine searches more typical of dictatorships than democracies—Congress initially required that "the purpose" be to gather foreign intelligence rather than criminal evidence for prosecution. Over the years, federal courts and the Justice Department translated this into "the primary purpose," which prevented FISA from becoming a substitute for the ordinary criminal search warrant or wiretap order. The aim was to mandate that the secret FISA tool be used only where prosecution was incidental to intelligence gathering and thereby preclude law enforcement from evading the Fourth Amendment.

Furthermore, to guard against judges throwing out evidence, administrative walls were erected in the mid-1990s under Attorney General Janet Reno to prevent intelligence officers, whether in the FBI, the CIA, or other agencies, from sharing information with criminal investigators who were digging up evidence for trials.[12] These barriers were designed to reinforce the limits on FISA by blocking criminal investigators from expropriating FISA as their tool of research—to prevent cops from relying on spies to do end runs around the Constitution's stringent warrant requirements. But they also created what officials came to see as absurdities.

"In terrorism cases, this became so complex and convoluted that in some FBI field offices, FBI agents perceived walls where none actually existed," said Rolince. "In fact, one New York supervisor commented that 'so many walls had created a maze,' which made it very difficult for the criminal investigators."[13] The confusion impeded information-sharing that might have instigated a search for one of the nineteen September 11 hijackers, Khalid al-Mihdhar. Among many communications failures in his case was a mistaken belief by CIA and FBI intelligence analysts that the wall barred them from conveying reports to agents who were doing a criminal investigation of his role in the USS *Cole* attack.[14] Jealousy over jurisdictions may have played a role as well: When an FBI agent working in the CIA's bin-Laden office learned that Mihdhar had a multiple-entry U.S. visa in his passport, his message to FBI headquarters was blocked by a senior CIA official.[15]

"You were moving bricks in the wall," Rolince told me. "If I'm doing a wire on you because I think you're doing espionage, and get something on money laundering, I had to go through hoops to walk down the hall and tell the agents investigating money laundering." The hoops included approval from the attorney general or another top official, and as a result, Rolince claimed, "dozens of cases were not pursued." Aside from the Mihdhar catastrophe, he couldn't come up with any examples, and few others have come to light. Other hijackers were missed because of turf battles, poor intelligence gathering, and miscommunication, not because of the wall.

There were examples of the opposite—of the FBI breaking the rules—as disclosed in 2002 by the Foreign Intelligence Surveillance Court, whose judges had themselves acted as the "wall." They cited "an alarming number of instances" in which the information barrier—and the court—had been evaded by the FBI in New York alone, before the Patriot Act amendments. The bureau had given unauthorized FISA information to federal prosecutors in four or five cases, the judges said. In field offices where separate intelligence and criminal squads were supposed to be operating, "all of the FBI agents were on the same squad and all of the screening was done by the one supervisor overseeing both investigations."[16] As a result, the commission that investigated 9/11 reported, "the court began designating itself as the gatekeeper for the sharing of intelligence information."[17]

Now agents can legally walk down the hall.[18] Six weeks after September 11, Congress hastily removed the wall and downgraded foreign intelligence from "the purpose" of a FISA warrant to "a significant purpose."[19] This allowed criminal investigation to become the leading motive for acquiring secret and sweeping surveillance powers. With that change, the secret warrants have been used in ordinary criminal investigations unrelated to intelligence gathering or terrorism, including narcotics, white-collar crime, child pornography, money laundering, and blackmail.[20]

Those revisions, and many other amendments to various statutes, were contained in the law entitled the Uniting and Strengthening America by Providing Appropriate Tools Required to Intercept and Obstruct Terrorism Act of 2001, a mouthful designed for translation into a stirring acronym: The USA PATRIOT Act. Although it undermined some key constitutional protections, it passed with little debate by votes of 357–66 in the House and 98–1 in the Senate.[21] Congress renewed most of it unchanged five years later, and extended it again in 2010.[22]

A decade or so before Brandon Mayfield's life was upended by the Patriot Act, he served in the army as a platoon leader on a Patriot antimissile battery. The word "patriot" kept sailing through his world like a wind-blown poster. His youth could have been a patriotic painting by Norman Rockwell, as he described it, rooted in the black earth of Kansas where he helped his father, a combine driver, follow the harvest from farm to farm. "I had a wonderful childhood," Brandon remembered, "jumping off of rope swings on the Arkansas River, putting pennies on the railroad tracks."

It was a different Kansas then. "I know what's wrong with Kansas," he said in a sardonic take-off on the best-seller.[23] "It's gone from a populist place to a conservative place. My family was pretty liberal and always looked on the government with a certain suspicion, as did a lot of local farm families, didn't want to look to the government for a handout. I always had this idea that we should be more free rather than less free. Let's be very free and open, and I was always critical of new government rules, regulations, programs. And therefore it seemed odd to join the military . . . nobody in my family had ever been in the military."

As he drew a sketch of himself, he might have been any decent, directionless middle-American kid in the 1980s, setting off without much of a compass. His parents were split up. He tried community college for a year, and "didn't do so hot; I just wasn't into my studies." He loved his hometown of Halstead, which "is called the biggest little city in Kansas," he said, "but it wasn't big enough for my dreams." So he enlisted "mainly because I wanted to see the world," to fulfill the recruitment slogan's promise. Maybe that's why so many enlistees come from small towns.

The world he got to see was one of discipline and structure, which appealed to him. It contained people from all over the country. It was largely a Republican world: "You know if you vote Republican you're likely to get more funding for the branch that feeds your family." It extended from Fort Lewis in Washington and Fort Bliss in Texas all the way to Fort Gordon in Georgia and bases in Germany and South Korea. It took him in and out of the army three times. He finished his B.A. at Portland State, in Oregon, was commissioned as a second lieutenant, and served as a military intelligence specialist, of all things.

Indirectly, the army gave him his wife and his religion, for it was while he was stationed at Fort Lewis that he found both. "I was somewhat an agnostic," he recalled, "unconvinced that there was anything to organized religion." But after meeting Mona, whose family had brought her from Egypt when she was five, he felt gradually drawn to Islam. "I was trying to figure out, answer the bigger questions of who we are and why we're here." And the Koran tied up loose ends, patched up the holes in his understanding. "There's a saying in Islam that if you take one step to Allah, he'll take two to you or come running to you." Mayfield came to see in Islam the concept that free will and destiny could coexist. There is a divine plan, "but you are still accountable for your own actions."

Having family and religion to organize his life, he now sought the professional pillar and found it in the law. The year he left the army, 1995, he picked up Mortimer J. Adler's *We Hold These Truths,* and was taken by its discussion of the Constitution's principles on the relationship between the people and their government. "The book talked about the notion of ordered liberty," Mayfield recalled. "I liked that, looking at it that way." He was intrigued by the prospect of learning more, and so he was drawn into learning the law.

For a constitutional history course at Washburn University School of Law in Topeka, he wrote a twenty-page paper entitled "Liberty" that documented "the erosion of our rights," as he recalled, and the danger that government would "become a bloated bureaucracy and would give rise naturally to a police state. There is a tendency naturally to overpolice the citizens. We're not subjects of the government, but more and more we tend to be seen that way."

Such concerns drive some young attorneys into civil liberties work, but Mayfield settled for a tamer route as a sole practitioner on divorce, child custody, and immigration. These specialties seemed benign until one client's name jumped out to FBI agents investigating Mayfield and reinforced their ill-founded suspicions: Jeffrey Battle, a black Muslim now doing eighteen years after pleading guilty as part of the Portland Seven group that tried to go fight with the Taliban in Afghanistan. Mayfield represented him in a child custody case: "I was just trying to get his son into the care of a responsible adult after he was arrested."

JUNK FORENSICS

Eleven backpacks stuffed with explosives, fitted with copper detonators and set with cell-phone triggers, were strategically positioned on Madrid's commuter trains during the morning rush hour of March 11, 2004. When ten of them blew up on four trains jammed with passengers, the concussions and shrapnel killed 191, wounded more than 1,400, and provoked a chain reaction of intrusive bungling by the FBI.

As rescue workers raced frantically to identify the living among the shattered bodies, the Spanish National Police sifted through the debris of glass and bones and twisted metal. They quickly discovered the eleventh bomb and disarmed it. Near a station, inside a stolen van, they found a blue plastic bag containing seven detonators like the one in the unexploded device.

The bag was covered with fingerprints, most of them partial or smeared. But two seemed clear enough to be useful, so they were photographed and sent as digital files on March 13 to Interpol, whose Washington office e-mailed them to the FBI laboratory in Quantico, Virginia.

The lab had a checkered reputation. For three decades, into the early 2000s, the FBI used junk science that purported to match bullet fragments at crime scenes with suspects' boxes of ammunition on the theory that each batch was manufactured with lead containing unique proportions of trace elements. At first, bombarding the bullets with neutron beams, the lab measured antimony, arsenic, and copper; in later years, using spectroscopy, it added bismuth, cadmium, tin, and silver.

The measurements were accurate, but the theory was false, as the FBI itself discovered in 1991. Some bullets made fifteen months apart had identical contents, and variations could exist even within a single box. Yet the bureau continued doing the tests and introducing the results as evidence. When differences appeared within a lot, the lab simply relaxed its standards by increasing the range of tolerable variation to produce phony matches. FBI examiners testified in at least 250 state and local trials throughout the country, misleading jurors into believing in the precision of the matches, and helping put behind bars untold numbers of innocents who remain in prison today. Not until 2005, a year after the National Academy of Sciences produced a study debunking the entire theory, did the FBI finally stop dispatching its "experts" to court to tout the results of bullet-lead analysis. It failed to inform the defendants or their lawyers about the testing flaws, however, and has even opposed new trials.[24] Many state and federal courts resisted defense requests to confront the crime-lab technicians themselves, until the Supreme Court ruled narrowly in 2009 that the examiners could be summoned to be cross-examined in trials.[25]

Various techniques of forensic analysis have proved unreliable. In the mid-1990s, personnel in the FBI lab's Explosives Unit, Materials Analysis Unit, and Chemistry-Toxicology Unit were accused by a colleague of fabricating evidence and committing perjury in hundreds of instances, including high-profile terrorist cases. The whistle-blower, Frederic Whitehurst, a forensic analyst with a Ph.D. in chemistry, provoked a lengthy investigation by the Justice Department's inspector general, Michael R. Bromwich, which confirmed only a minority of his allegations but found "significant instances of testimonial errors, substandard analytical work, and deficient practices." Invariably, the "errors" were made in favor of the prosecution. They included alterations of Whitehurst's reports by superiors, "inaccurate testimony" (a euphemism for perjury), incompetent examiners who were never relieved or reprimanded, analysts lacking "requisite scientific qualifications," and examiners making categorical assertions beyond their expertise—usually to enhance the impression of a defendant's guilt.

When Mohammed A. Salameh and others were tried for the February 26, 1993, bombing of the World Trade Center, for example, an analyst of explosives residue, David Williams, "gave inaccurate and incomplete testimony and testified to invalid opinions that appeared tailored to the most incriminating result," the inspector general's report declared. Undaunted by the fact that FBI chemists "did not find any residue identifying the explosive at the World Trade Center," Williams testified that urea nitrate was used in an amount—about 1,200 pounds—that conveniently happened to fit the quantity he estimated defendants were capable of manufacturing. The report found his assertions "deeply flawed" and concluded, "His testimony about the defendants' capacity exceeded his expertise, was unscientific and speculative, was based on improper non-scientific grounds, and appeared to be tailored to correspond with his estimate of the amount of explosive used in the bombing."

He performed the same backwards reasoning in the Oklahoma City bombing case, where he "did not draw a valid scientific conclusion" when identifying the explosive used in the attack as ammonium nitrate fuel oil (ANFO), the investigation found. He relied not on forensic evidence from the scene "but rather speculated from the fact that one of the defendants purchased ANFO components." So, because a defendant had bought the ingredients of ANFO, ANFO must have been used in the bombing. "His estimate of the weight of the main charge was too specific, and again was based in part on the improper, non-scientific ground of what a defendant had allegedly purchased. In other respects as well, his work was flawed and lacked a scientific foundation. The errors he made were all tilted in such a way as to incriminate the defendants."

The lab seemed incapable of rigorous analysis. Another examiner, Richard Hahn, was found to have jumped to an unwarranted conclusion about the type of explosive that brought down an Avianca plane in Colombia in 1989. "We concluded that Hahn's correlation of the pitting and cratering to a high velocity explosive within a narrow range of velocity of detonation was scientifically unsound and not justified by his experience," the investigators declared.

And so on through multiple cases. The individuals who usually suffered from examiners' mistakes were defendants, not the examiners themselves. But even when sloppy work resulted in an acquittal—and in one case, criticism of the examiner by a federal prosecutor—no self-correcting impulse was stirred. It took the lab six years to investigate the offending analyst, and then his supervisor coupled a verbal reprimand with a $500 check as an incentive bonus.[26]

While forensic evidence was not pivotal in every conviction, Bromwich thought that his voluminous investigation should have reopened some prosecutions. "Much to my shock, no cases were reversed or retried," he told me. The FBI and the Justice Department insisted that the outcomes would not have been affected. Nor had defendants mounted sufficient challenges to the respected FBI lab in the first place. "The FBI had done such a good job of embellishing its myth that defense lawyers got weak in the knees," Bromwich observed.

His report should have punctured the myth. The lab was infused with "a pro-prosecution bias, which is intangible," he told me. "It's not anything you find on paper. It's not in documents; it's almost in the air, so it was more a sense of things, when you talked to people and reviewed everything with a large lens." He noted "an absence of a true scientific culture in the lab. These were agents, self-taught with inadequate training, with totally inadequate scientific peer review."

Into that culture came the fingerprints from the plastic bag in Madrid. The high-priority case brought a unit chief, Michael Wieners, into the lab on a Saturday, and he summoned one of his most experienced supervisors, Terry Green. They quickly realized that the prints' resolution was inadequate, so they requested better images from Spain. When they received them on Sunday, they got down to work.[27]

Since 1999, the FBI has used a computerized tool known as the Integrated Automated Fingerprint Identification System (IAFIS), which compares a crime-scene print against those of 47 million people held in digital files and then spits out ten to twenty possibilities. But it takes a specialist to use the system, because it's not as simple as just feeding in a print and getting a match. First, a real human being like Green has to "encode" the print on a screen by electronically marking some, but not all, of the points at which ridges either end or split into bifurcations; he also draws lines to show the directions of ridges. Like every computer system, this one is governed by the doctrine "garbage in, garbage out."

IAFIS does not do well where the number of ridges between marked points is uncertain, so to help it along, examiners tend to label only points in the clearest area of the print, where the ridges can be counted precisely. They also avoid flagging points in clusters that are separated by gaps, a pattern that seems to baffle the system. Green's later analysis confused ridge endings and bifurcations, although on balance his initial encoding seemed "competent," according to an investigation by the Justice Department's current inspector general, Glenn A. Fine.

The computer won't find you unless you're in one of three databases of digitalized prints: a Special Latent Cognizant File of suspected terrorists, a Civil File of people fingerprinted for immigration purposes and for military and other occupations, and a Criminal Master File of anyone who has been arrested. Green searched all three databases, and the IAFIS nominated twenty candidates as possible matches to Latent Fingerprint 17. One of them, to which the computer gave a high score, belonged to Brandon Mayfield, who would have been spared all the ensuing misery if not for a fateful flat tire late on a cold night two decades before.

Mayfield's prints were not in the Civil File, since the FBI had begun entering prints of military personnel only after he had left the army. He had never been suspected of terrorism, so they were not in the Special Latent Cognizant File either.

But in 1984, as a teenager just out of high school, he and some friends had had a blowout in a car without a jack. "It was late at night, far from home, and well below freezing with no nearby help," he told me. "We tried to contact others in a sparsely populated neighborhood without any luck." So he eyed another car, imagining the jack within. "I weighed the option of freezing or taking the jack, and decided to take the jack," he said. "I contacted the owner of the car, paid for damages, and the charges were later dropped."

When he was charged, however, he was also fingerprinted. That slender thread of circumstance put his prints in the Criminal Master File and placed him twenty years later in the path of a relentless federal juggernaut.

Once the IAFIS had generated possible matches, Green was supposed to do a finely focused analysis of every attribute at three levels of detail. "The human brain is the best tool available for image processing and comparison," said an FBI report on the fiasco.[28] But the human brain can also be influenced subjectively. Under pressure to identify the print in such a dramatic terrorist attack, Green and other examiners suffered from what the FBI later called "context bias." They were pushed—and pushed themselves—so hard for a definitive conclusion that they ignored contradictory evidence. That predisposition came to infect the entire investigation, including agents in the field.

The lab identified the print as Mayfield's on March 19, and he was put under twenty-four-hour-a-day surveillance by the FBI's Portland office.

The prints displayed unusual similarity, and Green found fifteen points in common; later, other investigators found ten. But he misinterpreted distortions in the latent print as minute features known as Level 3 details, such as pores and dots between ridges, and he erroneously identified them as identical to Mayfield's. Wieners confirmed the match, as did a retired FBI examiner who was called in as a consultant despite having been reprimanded three times for misidentifications.[29] An expert appointed by the court at Mayfield's request also agreed with the identification.

But none of the examiners came untainted to the task. None approached it as a fresh problem, because all knew that a match had already been made by a respected specialist. Furthermore, two examinations raising doubts were dismissed as "incomplete and inaccurate," said an internal FBI review. "To disagree was not an expected response."[30] (The FBI insists that it now insulates examiners from each other's conclusions, but it refuses to say whether it combats "context bias" by preventing them from knowing the nature of the case.)[31]

As in the first bombing attack on the World Trade Center, circular reasoning also contaminated the work in this case, the inspector general reported. "Having found as many as ten points of unusual similarity, the FBI examiners began to 'find' additional features in LFP 17 that were not really there, but rather were suggested to the examiners by features in the Mayfield prints."

Even more startling, the examiners knew that the prints didn't fully match but rationalized away the disparities. Contrary to the lab's "one discrepancy rule," which is supposed to defeat an identification if a single difference exists, Green and the others reached very far to discount a major dissimilarity between Mayfield's print and the upper-left-hand portion of LFP 17. The examiners explained it as coming from a separate touch by a different finger, even though "the ridge flow was consistent" with the rest of the print, the inspector general found, and "deposition pressure was consistent in both parts of the print, indicating that both areas were part of a single print."

Furthermore, when the identification was sent to Madrid, the Spanish National Police (SNP) disagreed and issued a "*Negativo*" report. They saw no match at all. The FBI tried hard to interpret "negative" as "maybe," and flew agents and examiners repeatedly to Madrid in a vain effort to persuade Spanish officials that the print was Mayfield's.

"It seemed as though they had something against him," Carlos Corrales, a commissioner of the Spanish National Police's science division, told a *New York Times* reporter, "and they wanted to involve us." The FBI "called us constantly," he said. "They kept pressing us."[32]

A major reason must have been Mayfield's conversion to Islam, judging by FBI affidavits, which cited his religion. But that factor probably entered the equation after the lab made its initial identification. Although he and his attorneys argued in a lawsuit that religion was the reason his print was chosen in the first place, religion is not indicated on the inked fingerprint cards that examiners pull after the computer generates candidates, according to the inspector general, and nothing in Mayfield's name gave a clue.

Once the investigation was launched, though, the FBI's Portland office quickly learned that Mayfield was Muslim, had married a woman born in Egypt, had represented Jeffrey Battle of the Portland Seven, and attended the Bilal Mosque where other members of the conspiracy had worshipped. "One of the examiners candidly admitted that if the person identified had been someone without these characteristics, like the 'Maytag Repairman,' the laboratory might have revisited the identification with more skepticism and caught the error," the inspector general reported. "A Portland Assistant United States Attorney called Mayfield's religious beliefs a 'mildly corroborating factor.'"

SECRET SURVEILLANCE AND SELF-DECEPTION

The inspector general's book-length report is heavily censored—"redacted" is the official euphemism—with black strips and blocks obliterating much of the text regarding the secret FISA searches. Nevertheless, because Mayfield sued the government, many details were pried out into the open, and we know more about the use of FISA in this case than in practically any other investigation thus far.

Having the erroneous fingerprint identification and the sketchy profile of Mayfield, the FBI worried that he might be part of a second-wave attack inside the United States. The concern was so urgent that agents invoked a FISA provision allowing secret searches to begin without a court order—and therefore with scant justification—provided a judge is notified within seventy-two hours. The investigation was then propelled into its own orbit with little gravitational pull from the facts on the ground.

The FBI used FISA, not ordinary criminal warrants that would have authorized wiretapping, because it was convinced that it could not show a criminal violation by Mayfield. A senior attorney in the Justice Department disagreed, "stating that given the gravity of the Madrid bombings and the fingerprint identification of Mayfield, he believed the government could have obtained a criminal wiretap."

Furthermore, the FBI claimed that its initial interest in Mayfield focused on gathering intelligence, not preparing a criminal case against him, and that therefore the Patriot Act amendment to FISA, downgrading foreign intelligence from "the purpose" to "a significant purpose," was not essential; Fine's office accepted this official spin and concluded that even before the Patriot Act, FISA warrants could have been obtained, since investigators were not aiming at a criminal prosecution.

But this convenient interpretation after the fact, possibly devised to protect the Patriot Act from political assault, was belied by statements at the time from agents who told Mayfield and his family "that he was being held as a primary suspect on offenses punishable by death," meaning for a potential criminal charge, not for an intelligence purpose.[33] Technically, he was arrested not for a capital crime but as a "material witness" under a statute designed to hold someone deemed likely to flee before testifying. It is a pernicious law now widely used as a form of preventive detention while criminal evidence is gathered. Together with FISA, it builds a legal labyrinth through which the FBI and the Justice Department adroitly evade protections enshrined in the Bill of Rights.

With Mayfield profiled as a Muslim involved in the Madrid bombings, the scattered bits and fragments of information that the FBI secretly collected were spliced neatly into a gathering fantasy. It was a thought process demonstrating the danger of clandestine spying, for when the target never has a chance to respond, the thinnest string can be spun into a shroud of suspicion. And thanks to the Patriot Act's destruction of the wall between intelligence and criminal investigations, the "evidence" assembled was widely dispersed among at least eight federal agencies.[34]

Mayfield had once taken flying lessons, for example: very suspicious. If you're Muslim, the last thing you want to do in America is learn to fly. A home computer had been used to research flights to Spain, rental housing there, and Spanish railroad schedules: doubly suspicious, especially since the agents didn't realize that it was his twelve-year-old daughter's school assignment to plan a fictitious vacation. A note they thought was Mayfield's—actually an entry in her journal—displayed political heresy in criticizing the U.S. bombing of Afghanistan, declaring: "Who is America to bomb the Taliban because they don't like Afghanistan's law? All I say [is] that Americans should think twice about the example you are setting on the rest of the countries."[35] A phone number in Spain was found written down: the clincher! Except that it was merely the number of an exchange program Mona had been considering for Shane.[36]

Even a lack of evidence was used to bolster suspicion. When the inventive investigators couldn't find any hint of foreign travel, they twisted two inconvenient facts into a sinister supposition. First, Brandon's and Mona's passports had expired, and second, there was no record that he'd left the country since his army service in 1994. The absence of such documentation led FBI Special Agent Richard Werder to make up this scenario and swear to it under oath, in an affidavit applying for an arrest warrant:

"Since no record of travel or travel documents have been found in the name of BRANDON BIERI MAYFIELD, it is believed that MAYFIELD may have traveled under a false or fictitious name, with false or fictitious documents."

Werder then made an enormous leap that took his affidavit close to perjury: "I believe that based upon the *likelihood* [emphasis added] of false travel documents in existence, and the serious nature of the potential charges, Mayfield may attempt to flee the country if served with a subpoena to appear before the federal grand jury."[37]

So much for the argument that if you've done nothing wrong, you shouldn't mind the government spying on you.

Agent Werder also mixed religion and association into the grounds for suspicion. He noted that Mayfield attended a mosque and advertised in "Jerusalem Enterprises," which was known as the "Muslim Yellow Pages" (and where, he neglected to mention, Avis, Best Western, and United Airlines also advertised).[38]

Mayfield's attorneys called these "false and misleading affidavits" that were fabricated to justify the searches and arrest. "The concocted affidavits," the lawyers noted, "falsely claimed that the SNP 'felt satisfied with the FBI laboratory's identification'" and omitted the negative finding by the Spanish National Police, which was issued April 13 as the FBI was snooping into Mayfield's life.[39] Inspector General Fine used milder language, concluding that the affidavits "contained several inaccuracies" that were "troubling in several respects."

After a month following him around, sneaking into his house and office, going through files covered by attorney-client privilege, monitoring his conversations, looking over his finances, and even doing a "trash pull" of garbage discarded from his law office, the FBI had "no additional evidence linking Mayfield to the bombings," according to one internal memo. Quoting a lead case agent, the document said: "If he is guilty, he is one cool customer."

And that was the preferable theory, not the possibility that Mayfield was actually innocent. So the agile minds of the investigators created two possible scenarios to keep the presumption of Mayfield's guilt alive. As recorded in a summary of the investigation approved by leading agents in Portland, they went like this:

> Either Mayfield himself traveled to Spain and had contact with the bag there, perhaps while knowingly participating in the bombings; or Mayfield came into physical contact with the bag while it was in the United States, after which he or some other individual shipped the bag to Spain or some other individual traveled with it to Spain. To date, investigation suggests it is extremely unlikely Mayfield traveled under his own name to Spain, although the possibility exists that he has an alias that has not yet come to light. Given the character and known terrorism ties of several of his associates, it appears possible that someone else in the community is the link between Mayfield and the Madrid bombings.[40]

As erroneous as it was, the fingerprint identification became indisputable fact in the agents' minds, the fulcrum of their analysis. Everything pivoted on that error. The overwhelming lack of evidence from the extensive surveillance and searches seemed to carry no weight—and for understandable reason, according to Mayfield's lawyers. The lab had already bet its reputation on the supposed match, insisting after repeated queries that it was a "100% identification."

Not only professionals' careers but future confidence in the fingerprinting technique itself were at stake. So by the climax of the case, his lawyers wrote in a brief, "The FBI was willing to subject Mr. Mayfield and his family to his public branding as a mass murderer, and an international terrorist, and subject Mr. Mayfield to the ultimate penalty of death, in order to save their own jobs, the reputation of the FBI, and in order to secure the admissibility of the alleged science of fingerprint [analysis] in the courts."[41] In the end, he was just barely saved by the solid competence and expertise of the Spanish National Police. It is frightening to think what might have happened to him if there had been no other law enforcement agency to contradict the FBI.

FISA warrants have time limits of ninety days, and although judges can extend them, they cannot be used indefinitely. The FBI figured that by the end of May it would turn off the surveillance, analyze the results thoroughly, and then attempt to interview Mayfield in June to see what he knew about the Madrid bombings. Somewhere along the line, though, Mayfield stopped being a "cool customer" and started getting suspicious.

He had no inkling of the fantastic web of conjecture being spun by the FBI, of course, but he started checking to see if he was being followed. He "began an attempt to make surveillance, as apparent from his driving," one FBI document reported. "He engaged in pulling into driveways and cul-de-sacs, only to quickly turn around. He would drive into parking lots, sit for a few moments, and then pull out. He circled his residence several times and drove slowly. When he eventually pulled into the driveway, he sat in the car for an extended period."[42] Mayfield confirmed this for me, saying that he "sometimes took various routes to verify the presence of the surveillance and watched for unusual vehicles out front or across the street from our house."

The FBI began to get nervous that he might flee or destroy some imagined evidence. The anxiety was compounded when leaks, possibly from Interpol, started appearing in the press that an American's fingerprint had been discovered in the Madrid case.

The timetable was then accelerated. The FBI applied for ordinary criminal search warrants of Mayfield's home and office, and, because there was "not enough evidence to arrest him on a criminal charge," an FBI official in Portland conceded,[43] a warrant was issued to seize him as a "material witness."

Intending to interview him, agents went to his office May 6 armed with the arrest warrant in case he wouldn't cooperate. And he would not. When they knocked on the door, he told them that he had privileged client information inside, that he wanted them to leave, and that he would consider answering any written questions they cared to submit. Without telling him what their visit was about, they then handcuffed him, took him away, and searched his office. At the same time, the FBI detained Mona at home, executed an ordinary search warrant on the house, froze his financial accounts, and sent agents elsewhere in the country to question his mother, father, brother, and stepfather.

To disguise their tactics and protect their "witness," the agents booked Mayfield under the pseudonym Randy Taylor, and the FBI refused for a time to tell Mona where he was being held. It was in a county jail full of inmates, some dangerous, who wouldn't be expected to greet a suspected terrorist with high-fives. Mayfield feared that they might learn the reason he was there.

"The guards would sometimes call me Brandon, sometimes Randy," he said, "and it would make me nervous because I was worried I was getting closer to being exposed. I didn't want any vigilante justice."

Mostly he was alone in a cell. But there were moments of risk. "You have people jailed next to you who are maybe innocent like myself," he observed, "but some are hardened. I was in a lockdown situation the first week with people who are most dangerous," and in that week "I had an hour a day to walk the floor. Usually you'd walk with one or two other people on the floor. Some of them I was OK walking with, others I was very uncomfortable walking with."

Little news penetrated the cellblock walls, fortunately. The television set in the middle of the common room was usually tuned to a country music station or to Black Entertainment Television, "and I was OK with that," Mayfield said, but "occasionally somebody would go to a news channel, and I just prayed they didn't have anything about me."

Then one day as he sat on an upside-down trash can watching, with another prisoner behind him, there suddenly appeared "a short clip about me," he said. "So this one guy, I could tell he had made the connection. He got up and went to his cell and his complete demeanor changed, and I figured it was just a matter of time until word got around."

Mayfield's most acute vulnerability came during transfers to and from court, when federal marshals "would put me in a jail cell for extended periods of time without any supervision, sometimes with one or two, sometimes with eight or nine." Yet he was never attacked by prisoners, just "manhandled a little bit" by FBI agents and marshals.

"I had manacles on my feet, chains on my arms, and chains around my abdomen when I was transported from place to place," he noted, and the chain between his legs once caught on the lip of a van's door as he got out. "I tripped," he said, "and barely caught myself before I broke my nose on the pavement. I sprained my wrist and hurt my shoulder," and "this grumpy little marshal," as Mayfield described him, "just stood there with a smirk and a smile, doesn't help me get up."

He endured insults from guards but no beatings. "I think the jailers for the most part were professionals," he conceded. But "the toilets wouldn't flush, you were sleeping there with your own feces," and "some female jailer said when I complained about the toilet not flushing, 'He's just a crybaby.'" It got worse, but in ways that he labeled "too personal" to recount. "I felt the whole thing was an abusive, humiliating experience. . . . I was subject to strip searches: I couldn't see my family without a strip search. You wouldn't have a face-to-face—even with my attorney— without a strip search."

During Mayfield's two weeks inside, the FBI stood by its fingerprint match and the Spanish police stood by their denial, and the FBI would not be convinced of its error until a fragile trail of evidence in Madrid led the Spanish authorities to the man who had actually left the prints on the bag.

On April 3, when the Spanish police raided a suburban apartment to arrest alleged bombers, the suspects blew themselves up, leaving in the debris documents bearing the name Ouhnane Daoud, an Algerian whose fingerprints happened to be on file because of an immigration violation. Six weeks later, checking his prints against those on the bag, Spanish examiners made two matches: Daoud's right middle finger had left LFP 17, they concluded, and his right thumb had made the other legible print. It was May 15, and Mayfield was in jail. On May 19 the police arrested Daoud, and the next day Mayfield was released to home detention while the FBI, trying to wipe egg off its face, pondered the Daoud, Mayfield, and latent prints.

On May 22, two FBI examiners arrived in Madrid, on yet another taxpayer funded trip, this time to collect copies of Daoud's ten-print cards, which they took to Quantico on May 23. An all-night reexamination was conducted by a team at the lab, which concluded that LFP 17 was of "no value," a reluctant and partial retreat. Only in late June did the FBI finally concede that the prints on the bag were Daoud's.

Could this happen again? The lab at Quantico may work more accurately now. It agreed to implement over one hundred recommendations for improving various technical and administrative procedures suggested by eight internal review teams.[44] In response to my inquiries, however, the FBI declined to offer any evidence that it had taken any action against the agents and analysts who had cost an American his good name and his sense of security, and the taxpayers millions. Nor was the bureau willing to say that it had made good on its public pledge to review death-penalty convictions that had relied on fingerprints; officials were content to leave the impression that neither of these steps had been taken.[45]

More striking was the FBI's statement the day a lawsuit by Mayfield and his family was settled by the Justice Department for $2 million and a formal apology. There could have been no more complete admission of guilt by the government, yet the head of the Portland FBI office, Robert Jordan, declared: "If a similar investigation was being conducted, and we were provided a fingerprint identification, we would do exactly what we did in the case of Mr. Mayfield. Of course we regret what happened to Mr. Mayfield, but again, we are proud of what we did here."[46] Proud?

Mayfield was cleared, but he was not released from the sleeplessness, the "mental distractions," as he called them, the diffuse haze of anxiety. "I'm not as focused as I was before," he said nearly three years later. "I'm not quite sure why. I was more driven, I was more into my work." He now functioned less efficiently, he felt. "Once this has happened, you're always wondering, is this going to happen again? Am I really safe now? Are they going to come knock in my door again? Is my family going to be thrown upside down in their lives? I try not to think about those things. You try to get on with your life."

I asked if he had sought counseling, whether he might suffer from post-traumatic stress disorder. "PTSD?" he answered. "I don't want to use that term. It would belittle the experience of others. I had sleep disorders for a long time. You'd awake in the middle of the night and think there was someone there. . . . It's pretty traumatic, what happened, what you go through physically and emotionally. It's probably hard for people to appreciate how it affects someone." Nevertheless, he added, "I was the fortunate one, in jail for two weeks in shackles and chains, and under house arrest for a week. There are people for whom that goes on for months or years."

But something was still going on, for the experience had planted insidious seeds of wariness. "I was suspicious of people I know. Were they informants? People I maybe trusted and maybe I shouldn't have trusted them? They weren't who they appeared to be?" He didn't get the support that he needed from fellow Muslims, because many who had rallied behind the Portland Seven had felt shocked and betrayed by their guilty pleas after they'd tried to fight in Afghanistan. The same people could not shake misgivings about Mayfield, and he paraphrased their thinking: "Even though we think he's innocent, how do we know?"

His practice suffered. "I lost clients at the time I was arrested," he said, including a personal-injury case he was working on that day. "I had retainers I had to give back. I had to seek help from other attorneys. . . . I lost money immediately. The practice had to shut down. My wife helps as a part-time paralegal, but there was no way she could keep the office open."

Even after his two weeks in jail, business didn't exactly spring back to normal, in part because clients were afraid that he was still under surveillance. "When you practice in the area of immigration, it's not unusual to have somebody come to you and say, 'My spouse slipped across the border without documentation,'" Mayfield noted. "Sometimes people will tell you things that they will only say in confidence to an attorney or a priest.

"After I was arrested, I had a guy come to the office. He knew what had happened to me. He started to tell me a little bit about his case, he stopped and looked at me and said, 'Before I go on, is your place bugged?' I smiled and said, 'I don't know. I can't say it isn't.' He said, 'I'm pretty sure it is.' We had to remove ourselves and go to a coffee shop and continue our initial client interview. I've had other people say they're not comfortable because they think my office is bugged. There are lots of attorneys in the phone book."

Some clients have less specific apprehensions. After a woman hired Mayfield to file a personal-injury lawsuit, she told him that a friend had advised: "'You might not want to stick with Brandon because of all the baggage tied to him; it may affect the kind of settlement you can get.' That client, to her credit, did stick with me, and I got a good result." But he lost others.

Surreptitious surveillance never quite ends, at least inside your fears. The FBI "never told us," Mayfield said, "where they placed the electronic bugging or cameras and recorders. To this date they haven't told us where they put it, so we're thinking that we're still kind of violated, that they were listening to our most intimate conversations and watching our most intimate moves." Even after being cleared, "I couldn't help feeling I was being bugged and watched. I didn't feel comfortable after coming home from jail talking to my wife in my living room. It took me a year to feel comfortable."

Hiring a private contractor "to do what they call a military sweep" would cost $30,000, he learned, with no guarantee that all the bugs would be discovered, because "you cannot find evidence of a certain type of electronic bugging equipment if it's there and not activated." With their house having been invaded, he said, "We're thinking of moving." And they did.

As part of his financial settlement with the government, Mayfield retained the right to pursue a lawsuit challenging the constitutionality of the Patriot Act, and in 2007 won a ringing declaration from federal district court judge Ann Aiken that Section 218 of the statute, changing "the purpose" to "a significant purpose," violated the Fourth Amendment by permitting search orders from the secret Foreign Intelligence Surveillance Court, without probable cause, that aimed not just at foreign intelligence but primarily at domestic criminal activity—just the kind of law enforcement the framers envisioned as requiring ordinary search warrants. "Now, for the first time in our Nation's history," she wrote, "the government can conduct surveillance to gather evidence for use in a criminal case without a traditional warrant, as long as it presents a non-reviewable assertion that it also has a significant interest in the targeted person for foreign intelligence purposes."

Under the law, she noted, that assertion cannot be rejected by judges of the Foreign Intelligence Surveillance Court (FISC) unless it is "clearly erroneous,"[47] a threshold so high that it's virtually impossible to cross without hearing arguments from the target, who is completely unaware that he has become so interesting. Congress had cleverly constructed a closed circle of executive power.

Mayfield's case was a textbook example of its abuse. "Here," Judge Aiken wrote, "the government chose to go to the FISC, despite the following evidence: Mayfield did not have a current passport; he had not been out of the country since completing his military duty as a U.S. Army lieutenant in Germany during the early 1990s; the fingerprint identification had been determined to be 'negative' by the SNP; the SNP believed the bombings were conducted by persons from northern Africa; and there was no evidence linking Mayfield with Spain or North Africa. The government nevertheless made the requisite showing to the FISC that Mayfield was an 'agent of a foreign power.' That representation, which by law the FISC could not ignore unless clearly erroneous, provided the government with sufficient justification to compel the FISC to authorize covert searches and electronic surveillance in support of a criminal investigation."

The judge summed up the impact of the law as amended by the Patriot Act. "In place of the Fourth Amendment, the people are expected to defer to the Executive Branch and its representation that it will authorize such surveillance only when appropriate," she wrote. "The defendant here [the government] is asking this court to, in essence, amend the Bill of Rights, by giving it an interpretation that would deprive it of any real meaning. This court declines to do so."[48]

However, a three-judge appeals panel in the Ninth Circuit vacated Aiken's decision, ruling that Mayfield had no standing to pursue his claim that his Fourth Amendment rights had been violated, "because his injuries have already been substantially redressed by the settlement agreement." The judges did not address Mayfield's central point: the unconstitutionality of the Patriot Act's amendments to FISA.[49]

THE INVESTIGATOR'S TOOLBOX

If the means of surveillance exist, an investigator will use them: That is the axiom of the law. Liberty cannot rely on the restraint of individual officials, depend on their discretion, or presume that powers will be exercised judiciously. At the very least, whatever the law allows will be done, and done enthusiastically, as it was in monitoring Jeffrey Battle and the other Portland residents after they tried to join the wrong side in Afghanistan. The case illustrates how usefully the traditional tools of criminal investigation can be enhanced by FISA.

On September 29, 2001, a group of Oregon men, most of them African-American Muslims dressed in robes and turbans, drove to a private gravel pit in Washington State to practice shooting an assortment of shotguns, pistols, and rifles. They were interrupted by a deputy sheriff who had been called by a neighbor after hearing the shots. Despite their appearance, their arsenal, and the nation's high state of anxiety, the deputy did not detain them or check the legality of the firearms, which included a fully automatic Chinese SKS 7.62 assault rifle, banned by federal law. This was gun country, after all. He merely took their names and told them that because they were on private property, they had to leave.

They did, although Battle, running his mouth later, bragged that "we was gonna pop him" and left him alive only because "the cop was cool . . . a gun guy."[50]

Toward the end of October, several weeks after the American invasion of Afghanistan, the men flew to China, where one of them, Patrice Lumumba Ford, had studied Mandarin for two years in a Johns Hopkins postgraduate program. Intending to cross into Pakistan and then Afghanistan, they made their way to western China's Xinjiang Uygur area, but with warfare raging on the Afghan side of the border, Chinese patrols and checkpoints had multiplied, and the main highway toward the mountainous frontier had been closed for the coming winter to all but returning Pakistanis.

The "muscular men," doing chin ups from a hotel lobby's rafters and practicing martial arts in the courtyard in Kashgar, seemed like "uniformed goofballs" to an American journalist, Ron Gluckman, who was there reporting a story on Chinese Muslims. They dissembled, he said, giving various versions of their travels. "Ford told me directly that he had never been to China before, then spoke Mandarin on the phone." They seemed out of their element. "You meet all kinds on the road," Gluckman observed, "but you sometimes worry about lost souls." And worry more than suspicion propelled him to notify the American embassy back in Beijing, "not to get them in any trouble, really just for their own good," to "at least let someone in authority know there was a bunch of guys that might wind up in trouble out there."[51]

They hired a driver, but he backed out because of Chinese security on the road. Then they tried a bus, but the driver wouldn't let them board.[52] Retreating to Beijing, they applied at the Pakistani embassy for visas, were turned down, and then split up, two returning to the United States immediately, others traveling to Malaysia, Indonesia, and Bangladesh, apparently searching for a Muslim struggle to support, before going home. One was arrested in Malaysia, and another—a Jordanian, Habis al-Saoub—managed to get to Pakistan, where he was reportedly killed.

Otherwise, they never reached the battlefield, never fired a shot, and never even made contact with al-Qaeda or the Taliban. Instead, they were caught in the snare of their own delusions.

"I don't think their purposes were well defined," said Kristen L. Winemiller, who represented Battle. The victim of a violent home, he had meandered from one faith to another during his twenties, she said, ending as a convert to Islam after seeing the film *Malcolm X*. Funny, dramatic, with a bent for wild talk, he seemed entirely unsuited for combat. "My client had enlisted in the U.S. Army and washed out because he was not physically fit," she noted. "He was overweight and not a very good soldier. I can't imagine the Taliban would have looked at him and said he'd make a good soldier."

Ford's mother, Sandra, remembered his saying that "he was going to try to lend assistance to women and children." Her voice was still laden with sad disbelief. "He didn't question enough the reasons other people were going, and he didn't explain enough his reasons for going. I believe he was truly going for humanitarian reasons. He got raised that way. All his siblings have the same sense of charitableness and caring for other people. He's a cerebral person, a thinking person."

And a bit too trusting, added his father, Kent, who founded Portland's Black Panther chapter in 1969 and became a target of surveillance, secret searches, harassment, and arrest during the years of the FBI's counterintelligence program COINTELPRO. The experiences had taught him lessons that he regretfully neglected to impart to his son. "You shelter your kids, and he was just a baby, and he didn't know the extent they would go to entrap you," said Kent. "I wish I had talked to him about this. I never did say much unless he asked. He did not ask very much." And if the conversations had occurred, would his son have behaved differently? "I don't know," Kent answered. "He's the kind of person where he trusted everybody." Including an informant, as it turned out.

Federal authorities paid no attention to the men until well after most of them had returned from their abortive adventure. One day, a vigilant landlord arrived at an FBI office carrying a bag of trash containing items that looked suspicious: an expired Jordanian passport (al-Saoub's), writings in Arabic, and a martyr's will about dying in Afghanistan. The investigation began in earnest.

Khalid Mostafa, an FBI informant, was inserted by the government into the Muslim community, where he attended services at a mosque and befriended Ford and Battle, recording conversations that he "repeatedly steered . . . to topics involving illegal arms purchases and violence," according to the defense.[53] It is possible, but has never been confirmed, that warrantless surveillance by the National Security Agency was used. What is known is that both FISA warrants and ordinary Title III criminal warrants were combined in a potent system of monitoring.

According to Charles Gorder, the assistant U.S. attorney who prosecuted the case, FISA was used to tap telephones and to place a bug in Battle's apartment, which his lawyer told the court captured "highly personal" family conversations unrelated to the investigation.[54] Other information came by traditional means: Travel records were obtained through grand jury subpoenas, Gorder said, and "e-mails were obtained through criminal search warrants after the fact." The e-mail addresses were found when Battle naïvely gave his computer to Mostafa for safekeeping, and Mostafa turned it over to the FBI.

This interaction among various methods, and especially the flexible intelligence-gathering mechanisms of FISA, reduced one significant source of tension that often runs through such cases: While the FBI was gathering enough evidence to prosecute, the suspects were on the loose, possibly poised to attack. Battle had been recorded by the informant as toying with the notion of assaulting a synagogue or a Jewish school to retaliate for Israeli attacks on Palestinians. "If every time [the Israelis] hurt or harm a Muslim over there," Battle said, "you go into that synagogue and hurt one over here, OK, they're gonna say, Wait a minute, we gotta stop, we're seeing a connection here."[55]

So the government wanted close monitoring, and FISA was the instrument, used "to keep investigators apprised of what these guys were doing," Gorder explained. "There was a point where we had enough evidence to arrest Battle," said the prosecutor, "but we didn't have enough evidence to arrest" the others, who would "undoubtedly scatter or attempt to cover up their crimes" once Battle was seized. "It was important to keep track of Battle so we could be comfortable in waiting to arrest him. . . . If he had gotten the word to start some domestic attack, we would have had a good chance of knowing about it in advance."[56]

But why use FISA? There was "no reason why this case could not have been investigated like any other criminal case," wrote Kristen Winemiller in a motion seeking to have the FISA recordings suppressed and FISA struck down as unconstitutional. Using FISA was "the simplest way to circumvent safeguards the United States Constitution provides its citizens," she argued.[57]

That made FISA a handy tool. Without it, the surveillance of Battle and Ford would have been less comprehensive. To get an ordinary wiretap warrant under Title III of the criminal code, Gorder explained, "you have to show probable cause that a telephone line is being used for criminal activity." For example, "In a traditional narcotics wiretap, you normally have to show that drug dealers have discussed their business over that particular phone line in the recent past."

Even if that had been possible in the Portland case, investigators didn't want to be restricted to a particular phone. They might have obtained roving wiretaps, which have been legal since the mid-1980s to monitor any phone that a suspect is using, but those "require showing that the guy is changing phones to evade detection," Gorder said. With Title III warrants, "it might have been possible to cover some of the facilities being used by these guys, but not all." By facilities, he evidently included Battle's apartment.

A FISA warrant has a looser standard—or, as Gorder preferred to say, "a different standard." To monitor a U.S. person—a citizen or resident alien—you need "probable cause to believe the subject is an agent of a foreign power, and he's committing some crime as part of being an agent of a foreign power. Then you can get an order to surveil all specific facilities that he's using. You don't have to tie it to a particular phone." That was convenient, but it was not clear what "foreign power" the Portland group represented, since they never contacted the Taliban, al-Qaeda, or any other such entity. The basis for the FISA order remained classified.

Information collected under FISA typically stays in the shadows, serving as a kind of electronic tipster, a lead to other facts that can be gathered through conventional warrants and subpoenas. That has been facilitated by the Patriot Act's removal of the wall between those gathering intelligence and those investigating crime. "The FBI could have done FISA on

Battle or Ford pre–Patriot Act," Gorder said, "but what they were finding out they could not have shared with us, when we were in the middle of conducting a criminal investigation."[58]

Then prosecutors had to decide whether to keep the FISA phone and apartment recordings secret or use them in a trial. "Most evidence was developed through more traditional investigative techniques," he said. "Although we probably would have used some of the phone calls that were intercepted through FISA, it was more important in terms of intelligence." Introducing FISA "intelligence" material into evidence means declassifying it, often a trade-off between strengthening a prosecution and disclosing surveillance methods. It requires a high-level decision, and "we got the attorney general's approval in the Portland Seven case," Gorder said.

Had they gone to trial, the defendants' lawyers would have argued that they intended merely to render humanitarian assistance during the war. But on the eve of oral arguments on the suppression motion challenging the constitutionality of FISA, the government offered a deal, probably to avoid that litigation. Ford's parents were divided on whether he should take it. "I wanted them to go to trial, but I got overruled by his mother," said Kent.

"He wanted to go to trial," Sandra said of her son. "His lawyer did a poll of the jury pool in the tri-county area, and the majority believed that if you're Muslim you're a terrorist, and the government was asking for life in prison. We pressured him to plead guilty. We're poor. He's a young black man."

Other families had similar reactions, so the men pleaded guilty to conspiring to levy war against the United States, a law dusted off from the Civil War.[59] The sentences ranged from seven to eighteen years.

Gorder was satisfied with the exercise in prevention. "What were they going to do next?" he asked. "Whether Battle was blowing smoke or not, he was talking about blowing up synagogues and Jewish schools. Do you let him wander around the streets of Portland?"

CHAPTER SIX

The Law Falls Silent

For laws are silent when arms are raised, and do not expect them-
selves to be waited for, when he who waits will have to suffer an
undeserved penalty before he can exact a merited punishment.

—Cicero

THE CONTINUUM OF INTRUSION

GEORGE CHRISTIAN found himself very far from the Constitution, in a black hole of liberty where no judge presided, and where all three branches of government had allowed the rule of law, the Bill of Rights especially, to stand silently aside.[1]

It was July 13, 2005. Christian looked at the piece of paper served by an agent—a simple, one-page document on FBI stationery, known as a National Security Letter—and knew instinctively that he had to fight it. Unlike most of his fellow citizens, he displayed a red-blooded American revulsion when the government trespassed outside the Constitution. Practically alone among other Americans who had received nearly 150,000 orders through such letters since 9/11, he resisted.

What he held in his hands was neither an ordinary warrant signed by a judge nor a subpoena issued by a grand jury but merely an administrative demand from the head of the FBI's New Haven office. The document required "any and all subscriber information, billing information and access logs of any person or entity related" to a computer carrying the Internet Protocol (IP) address 216.47.180.118 between 4 and 4:45 p.m. on the previous February 15. Moreover, he was prohibited "from disclosing to any person that the FBI has sought or obtained access to information or records under these provisions."[2]

Christian was executive director of Library Connection, a consortium of twenty-seven public libraries in the Hartford area, and he was well prepared. Because librarians had been braced for some kind of intrusion since the Patriot Act, his staff had been told that only he could release information. And since the FBI had alerted an employee by phone that the letter was coming, he'd had a chance to contact an attorney at the University of Connecticut School of Law, who had assigned a law student to do some research.

"I'd never heard the term 'National Security Letter,'" Christian remarked, and added wryly, "Sounds pretty important." Indeed it was, but as the student quickly learned, the device had already been struck down as unconstitutional by federal district court judge Victor Marrero in New York, who ruled in favor of an unnamed Internet provider's challenge; the government was appealing.[3] Christian also knew that Connecticut was one of forty-eight states with laws requiring libraries to protect clients' privacy,[4] a mission he embraced passionately. "Free public libraries exist in this country to promote democracy by allowing the public to inform itself on the issues of the day," he declared later, when he regained his freedom to speak.

Furthermore, he was convinced that the gag order violated the right to free speech under the First Amendment, as Judge Marrero had found. And so he decided to fight.

The FBI had been led to Christian's door by an anonymous e-mail warning of a terrorist threat, according to the U.S. Attorney for Connecticut, Kevin J. O'Connor. The authorities wanted to know who had sent it. They first contacted the company that had sold the IP address, and that firm referred them to the purchaser, Kenneth Sutton, the technical chief at Library Connection, which provides the libraries with Internet access. Sutton sent the agents to Christian, the only one authorized to release records.

Since the FBI was looking for the name of a person, probably a library patron who had walked in off the street, the search would have to probe many names. The IP address cited by the NSL could not be narrowed down to one computer, only to the router of a certain library, serving multiple computers. "There was no way of identifying a specific computer at the library," Christian explained. To discover the e-mailer, then, the FBI "would be forced to go to the library and find out who was using every machine that day," he noted. That would sweep a lot of innocent people onto the government's radar.

An FBI request for information to help catch terrorists, and possibly foil a plot, would not strike most Americans as anything out of line, and certainly not something to litigate ponderously through the courts while the culprits might be preparing an attack. Such "exigent circumstances," as they're called by laws permitting shortcuts, excuse warrantless interventions in the face of imminent danger. The National Security Letter is such a tool, quickly and easily issued by the head agent of any FBI field office.

But the FBI seemed in no hurry here. A full five months had passed since the suspicious e-mail had been sent. The National Security Letter addressed to Sutton was dated May 19, nearly two months before the FBI had gotten around to calling him. And not until ten days after that conversation had agents finally bothered to serve the letter on Christian. This was hardly being treated as an emergency, Christian observed, "so we weren't worried that we were aiding and abetting some terrorist plot" by contesting the demand.

His chief worry was the gag order.[5] Until the Patriot Act was revised the following year to permit consultation with an attorney, it wasn't clear whether someone served could even call a lawyer, much less notify supervisors or colleagues. This imposed a paralysis that distorted the normal practices of good governance, which obligated Christian to inform the entire board of his intention to fight. On the one hand, he couldn't make such a momentous decision alone; on the other, telling the board might expose him to prosecution. So, he sought sanctuary in middle ground. "I decided, if we're going to take on the attorney general of the United States, I had to consult with the three other members of the executive committee, which has the power to take action."[6]

It was a gamble. Unlike most gag orders, which are issued by judges against lawyers during trials and can be appealed, this broke an American tradition by taking the form of a lifelong, blanket prohibition framed in absolute language, with no court involvement. It was modified by a later revision to the Patriot Act, which gave with one hand and took away with the other; it permitted a court challenge to the letter itself, and to the gag order once a year, but required a judge to defer to the government's determination that disclosure would endanger national security, diplomatic relations, an ongoing investigation, or personal safety—thereby eliminating judicial discretion, fact-finding, and analysis. Moreover, where no penalty had existed in the original statute, the revision added a fine and five years in prison for violating the gag order, and contempt of court for failing to provide the information demanded.[7]

At the time, Christian couldn't be sure what punishment he might face if he spoke out, but he thought he was taking a chance even by consulting the executive committee, which approved the lawsuit and agreed to be represented by the American Civil Liberties Union.

Christian still felt professionally compromised. "My job is to manage a corporation owned and entirely funded by its participating member libraries," he said. "I need to maintain their confidence and trust." Although the small executive committee gave him full support, it went against his grain to keep secret the fact that an NSL had been served, that the organization was resisting, and "that we were committing the corporation to a lawsuit against the attorney general of the United States. These were all issues that should have been discussed and voted on by the full board." The gag order "impacted my personal and professional relationships by placing me in uncomfortable circumstances where I couldn't be completely open and honest." That is how intrusively government can reach into private institutions.

To avoid revealing Library Connection as the plaintiff, the government barred Christian and his three colleagues from the federal courthouse in Bridgeport where the first hearing on their lawsuit was held. Instead, they were escorted through two security levels to a locked and guarded room in a federal building sixty miles away in Hartford, where they watched on closed-circuit television. "We were plaintiffs, but we were treated like criminals," remarked one of the members, Barbara Bailey, a library director in Glastonbury.

Happily for democracy, censors are rarely perfect, and thanks to a chance episode of government sloppiness, more has been learned about this National Security Letter than any other. When papers were filed in the lawsuit, the plaintiff was disguised with the pseudonym "John Doe," but when a list of pending cases was posted on the court's Web site, the real name accidentally appeared, there to be found by an alert *New York Times* reporter as *"Library Connection Inc. v. Attorney General."*[8] Alone among the multitudes of National Security Letters served secretly on individuals and companies, therefore, this one jumped into view from the shadows of post-9/11 surveillance.

Three months after the NSL was issued, federal judge Janet C. Hall rejected the government's speculation that releasing the recipient's name would harm national security investigations in the case. She found the law's blanket secrecy provision "overbroad," in failing to require "any showing that each piece of information, if disclosed, would adversely affect national security." The law was not tailored narrowly to protect an investigation, she ruled, but rather gagged "a citizen complaining about governmental action." Silencing recipients of NSLs, she observed pointedly, "creates a unique situation in which the only people who possess non-speculative facts about the reach of broad, federal investigatory authority are barred from discussing their experience with the public. . . . The potential for abuse is written into the statute."[9]

Her warning was prescient, for the Bush administration used the gag provision to censor the librarians during critical congressional deliberation. Since a district court judge has the first word but not the last, Judge Hall followed customary procedure by temporarily staying her order pending appeal, leaving the gag on as long as the Justice Department pursued the case. And the Justice Department pursued the case as long as it wanted the librarians quiet. As a result, the FBI continued to issue the letters and silence their recipients. Neither the judge's ruling nor the disclosure of Library Connection's name released Christian or his colleagues to speak, creating painful zones of secrecy within their own families and blank spots in the public debate.

When Peter Chase, a librarian from Plainville, drove home one day, his college-age son "came up to the car, and he looked a little worried like something was wrong. 'Dad, you just got a call from the Associated Press. They said something about the FBI. Is the FBI after you, Dad? What is going on?' And really, all I could say was that I was involved in a case, it was a secret case, we're not supposed to discuss it, he shouldn't tell anyone about this, and I wasn't going to say anything either." Then Chase chuckled. "I never did ask him what he thought was going on. I should ask him what he thought I was up to!"[10]

More gravely, the four librarians' political speech was suppressed. They could not enter the growing debate over National Security Letters, which was coming to a head as Congress considered reauthorizing sections of the Patriot Act that were set to expire. They could not use their experience to rebut Attorney General John Ashcroft's condescending dismissal in 2003 of librarians' civil liberties concerns as "breathless reports and baseless hysteria,"[11] which Christian neatly characterized as "a defamatory thing to say against a profession dominated by women."

Muzzled by law, Christian and the others had to turn down speaking requests while the government was free to explain and defend its position. This especially rankled Peter Chase, because he was the chairman of the Connecticut Library Association's Intellectual Freedom Committee.

"It was galling for me to see the government's attorney in Connecticut, Kevin O'Connor, travel around the state telling people that their library records were safe, while at the same time he was enforcing a gag order preventing me from telling people that their library records were not safe," Chase declared when he was finally free to talk. "On one occasion, we were both invited to speak at the same event in Hartford, sponsored by the Women's League of Voters [sic].[12] Mr. O'Connor accepted his invitation, but I had to refuse mine because of the gag order."

It was on Capitol Hill in the winter of 2006 that the censorship acquired its rawest political purpose. As congressional hearings on extending the Patriot Act convened in early 2006, Christian and others were eager to testify, but they couldn't as long as the Justice Department continued to defend the stay and pursue an appeal. The bizarre result—that people known publicly to have received an NSL couldn't discuss it—suited no national security objective. A political goal was achieved, however: While misinformation circulated that libraries had been spared such searches,[13] Congress might have been enlightened by librarians who had, in fact, been subjected to secret orders to produce records on readers and Internet users. "I very much wanted to focus public attention and the attention of Congress on my concerns," Christian said. "As the recipient of a National Security Letter, I felt I had an important perspective to offer."

The Justice Department evidently felt the same way. To spare lawmakers his "important perspective," it waited until after Congress had renewed a slightly amended Patriot Act to decide that the nation would not be endangered by knowing Christian's views on the NSL he had received. Only in April 2006, after President Bush had signed the extension into law, did the government drop its appeal on the gag order, thereby allowing the librarians to enter an expired debate. A month later the administration abandoned its pursuit of the information it had secretly sought to save the country from an episode of terrorism. "I can only conclude that the intent of the delay was to keep me from speaking to Congress while the renewal of the Patriot Act was being debated," Christian declared.

Had the initial demand for information come in the form of a grand jury subpoena or a court order, Christian said later, he would have consulted a lawyer and then complied.

But neither would have been obtainable in a case of that kind, said U.S. Attorney O'Connor. "You cannot get a court order under these circumstances," he conceded. "There's no crime that has been committed yet. You need probable cause to believe a crime has been committed to go in to a federal judge. And you need a prosecutor. Now remember, a National Security Letter is issued by intelligence agents, not for the purpose of putting people in jail. Search warrants, court warrants are in the criminal system. That's when the U.S. Attorney goes to a federal judge

and says, 'I believe there's probable cause. I want to search this library.'"
Since September 11, 2001, "the public doesn't expect us to ignore anything," O'Connor added. "It's an incredibly burdensome task."

It was true. Officials now stood to be criticized more vigorously for
failing to protect Americans' security than for failing to protect their civil
liberties. Consequently, FBI agents—striving to prevent attacks rather
than prosecute them afterward—worked under standing orders from
their director, Robert S. Mueller III, to check out every single tip. "We've
said no lead goes uncovered," explained Michael Rolince when he was
special agent-in-charge of the Washington, D.C., field office. He had
previously been head of counterterrorism. "It's an incredible, at times,
waste of manpower. Yet you don't have the option. So you've taken the
discretion away from the manager, the supervisor." That didn't seem very
sensible, I said, and he replied: "There would be a lot of people in the FBI
who would agree with you, and I would be one of them."

Yet that was the practice that governed the issuance of the National
Security Letter to Library Connection. Of the thousands of tips that pour
in, said O'Connor the prosecutor, "I'll be honest with you, ninety-nine
percent of them are hoaxes. I don't necessarily know if they're intentional or mentally ill people. But people write us every day and send us
messages saying this is going to happen, this is going to happen. In the
old days, pre-9/11, I think we ignored most of them and just rightfully
assumed that these people were mentally unstable. We can't do that anymore. The public expects us to run these down." An alternative—a grand
jury subpoena—cannot be justified unless a crime is being investigated.
"But the reality is I'm not trying to investigate a crime," he said. "So if we
do not use an NSL under that situation, you do not get the information.
That's the simple fact."

Not getting the information in such a nebulous circumstance as a
vague, anonymous tip might seem exactly right to someone concerned
with walling off government from libraries and other zones of personal
freedom. Indeed, if the tipster had wanted the FBI to know her identity,
she would presumably have put it in the e-mail. And if people realize
that anonymous alerts will be tracked back to them, tips are likely to dry
up. But officials trying to head off terrorist attacks see the world through
a different lens. A lead landing on a desk or popping up on a computer
screen becomes a puzzle to be solved, sometimes urgently.

"The purpose of this [National Security] Letter is to allow intelligence
people to quickly ascertain whether or not there is a threat," O'Connor
explained. "And they have to prioritize, and it may take them a month

because the nature of the communication may not be an imminent one, but they can't ignore it, either. So they eventually get around to having to address it, and then the question is, how do we figure out if this is a hoax or not? How do we do that? The only way you do that is to find out as much as you can about who sent it. If it's somebody you have reason to believe is capable or may have knowledge of something, then obviously that gets front-burnered. If it's somebody who has a history of mental illness and writes to the federal government, the president, the mayor every day with conspiracy theories, then obviously you can de-prioritize that. And that's the reality we're in.

"Look, if we could get court orders for some of these things, we would. We simply cannot. So the choice is not get a court order or use an NSL. The choice is use an NSL or don't pursue the lead at all. And by the way, that's not my decision. That's for Congress." As a solution, Congress could revise the statutes to make NSLs more difficult to issue, in part by requiring judicial oversight. But the Obama administration has moved in the opposite direction, to ease the use of NSLs to acquire people's Web-browsing histories.

Getting judges involved would not please federal investigators, who already chafe at bureaucratic obstacles. Even now, "an NSL is not something you can whip off in an afternoon," O'Connor remarked, because it calls for three levels of FBI approval. "I guarantee you if there were a case where an NSL were not issued and God forbid an act happened, the first thing you would hear is, 'Why is the FBI so incompetent? It can't get one of these things out without three layers of review?'"[14]

DATA: DESTROY OR DISSEMINATE

The public doesn't have to depend on the government to protect private information. Librarians have learned what Mike German, a former undercover FBI agent, has understood for a long time: The best way to avoid turning files over to law enforcement is to retain no files. "I'm just as upset at the library's keeping the records as at the government's keeping the records," German remarked a month before Christian was served with the NSL. The same could be said about phone companies, Internet providers, and a host of other private entities whose records are exposed to government snooping.

"If you keep it, they will come," said Alan Davidson, senior policy counsel for Google. "Just like in *Field of Dreams:* If you build it, they will come." If it's available, investigators and intelligence agents will want to look at it. So Google, which used to keep all records indefinitely to help evaluate and improve its mammoth search engine, imposed an eighteen-month limit, then shortened it to nine months and may go lower on files linking computer IP addresses to Web-page searches on the Internet.[15] The company has debated internally how to weigh the preservation of privacy—from government, commercial, and criminal intruders—against the business's needs to polish its performance. Destroying records has become a competitive feature of Internet service providers, which jockey for customers who want retention to be as brief as possible.

Librarians have had similar discussions. If a loaned book is not returned, the library wants the name of the borrower to track her down. But once the book is back, there's no need to know who she is. So after the NSL was served, those in the Connecticut consortium stopped keeping files on who borrowed what books and who used which computers. Some libraries had previously maintained paper lists, others had retained the information electronically. Some had kept computer records for a day and erased them every evening, others for two weeks, some forever. Now, Christian reported, "Everyone's decided not to keep records. In terms of sign-up sheets [for computers], libraries have stopped."

Purging book-lending files is more complicated, because librarians watch circulation patterns to know what books to order and to keep on shelves. "Many of these systems were never designed to prevent against intrusion, because nobody ever imagined that the government could be looking," Christian observed. "Now people developing software are scrambling to keep records but erase the linkage between the volume and the patron" so that once books are returned, libraries can see only what books are borrowed, not who borrows them.

Concealing patrons' reading and Internet habits was raised to a policy objective by the American Library Association, which enacted a resolution in June 2006 urging members to "limit the degree to which personally identifiable information is collected, monitored, disclosed, and distributed; and avoid creating unnecessary records; and . . . dispose of library usage records containing personally identifiable information unless they are needed for the efficient and lawful operation of the library." The association also called on libraries to resist any subpoenas until "good cause" had been shown in court, which implied that National Security Letters—which do not require court approval—would be automatically challenged.[16]

The trouble is, the government can push back and enact legal requirements for record keeping. There is a precedent of sorts, in the form of the

1994 Communications Assistance for Law Enforcement Act (CALEA), requiring telecommunications carriers to make their systems wiretap-friendly for government agencies. Part of the statute reads:

> A telecommunications carrier shall ensure that its equipment, facilities, or services that provide a customer or subscriber with the ability to originate, terminate, or direct communications are capable of—
> (1) expeditiously isolating and enabling the government, pursuant to a court order or other lawful authorization, to intercept, to the exclusion of any other communications, all wire and electronic communications carried by the carrier within a service area to or from equipment, facilities, or services of a subscriber of such carrier concurrently with their transmission to or from the subscriber's equipment, facility, or service, or at such later time as may be acceptable to the government.[17]

This law, designed to keep pace with the transition from copper-wire to digital technology, was passed by a Democratic Congress and signed by a Democratic president, once again demonstrating the bipartisan tilt toward policing powers over individual rights. It was written largely by Jim Dempsey, then assistant counsel to the House subcommittee dealing with wiretap legislation, now policy director for the Center for Democracy and Technology, which defends the Internet's openness and advocates restraints on government's technological intrusions into privacy.

Thanks to the advancement of the computer systems that handle communications, Dempsey noted, the statute gives law enforcement access to a wealth of information that was previously inaccessible: for example, the destination of a call-forwarding order, the translation of a one-digit speed-dialing command into a seven-digit number, perpetually unblocked caller ID so that every incoming number is instantly visible, the tower location used by every cell phone, the identification of every party who joins and leaves a conference call.

Dempsey opposed the bill's concept, "but at a certain point it was made clear to me that President Clinton would support the FBI's request for this kind of legislative mandate." And since a number of Democratic senators favored it as well, "it was going to happen." So he built in checks and balances, assigning regulatory authority not to the Justice Department, as the FBI wanted, but to the Federal Communications Commission. "I said a law enforcement agency should not be regulating the telephone industry," he recalled. "The FCC is the regulating authority and should be considering privacy. Everything I wanted to see get into it got into it. My ideas just weren't good enough." Far from defending the public's privacy, the FCC rolled over for the FBI, and in 2005 even extended the law's application to broadband e-mail and voice Internet providers, which had not been explicitly covered in the legislation. The expansion was challenged but was upheld by the U.S. Court of Appeals for the D.C. Circuit.[18] An additional expansion, proposed by the Obama Justice Department, is aimed at empowering government to intervene in the very design of Internet technology, whose lightning advances have impaired companies' ability to comply with surveillance warrants, sometimes for weeks or months. CALEA might be revised to require FBI or FCC approval before services were updated or launched.

Furthermore, backstage, the Justice Department and some members of Congress have considered legislation that would require the Internet, phone companies, and certain others to retain data for certain periods, as required of financial institutions under the Bank Secrecy Act of 1970.[19] That would strip from companies the option to protect customers by destroying records.

The legislative branch might be able to fashion statutes nuanced enough to facilitate law enforcement while defending liberties. The language of laws can govern investigators' behavior more precisely than the brittle opinions of the courts, which lurch from case to case by chipping away and patching statutes, creating exceptions, and constructing guidelines that can be confusing to agents in the field. Congress has done well at times only to unravel its good work in moments of fear or intellectual corruption.[20]

National Security Letters are a disheartening illustration. They became civil liberties problems after they were expanded by the Patriot Act. Before that, they were calibrated tools designed to spy on spies, like narrow peepholes drilled through three different walls of privacy that Congress had erected to guard Americans' personal information.

Much of that privacy legislation had come in reaction to the government's secret, illegal surveillance of civil rights and antiwar activists from the 1950s into the 1970s, an assault on privacy that in 1972 Justice William O. Douglas called "an important phase in the campaign of the police and intelligence agencies to obtain exemptions from the Warrant Clause of the Fourth Amendment."

Citing "national security," the executive branch had bypassed the courts and placed warrantless wiretaps on phones of allegedly violent protesters. The wiretaps were struck down unanimously by the eight

Supreme Court justices participating in a key case, and in his concurring opinion, Douglas sounded this warning:

"If the Warrant Clause were held inapplicable here, then the federal intelligence machine would literally enjoy unchecked discretion. Here, federal agents wish to rummage for months on end through every conversation, no matter how intimate or personal, carried over selected telephone lines, simply to seize those few utterances which may add to their sense of the pulse of a domestic underground."

Removing judges from the process produced warrantless wiretaps lasting much longer—78 to 209 days—than the average of 13 days under court order, indicating that thousands of citizens were monitored for extended periods without judicial oversight. "Even the most innocent and random caller who uses or telephones into a tapped line can become a flagged number in the Government's data bank," Douglas declared. "More than our privacy is implicated. Also at stake is the reach of the Government's power to intimidate its critics."[21]

Nevertheless, by 1975, with the cooperation of communications companies, the National Security Agency was intercepting most of the millions of private cables that Americans sent, picking out 100,000 a month to analyze.[22]

Congress acted. Three new laws barred private firms from revealing the personal data they had on file—credit reports, bank and brokerage statements, telephone records, and, later, video-rental and Internet activity—unless served with a warrant, a subpoena, or a court order. Before disclosure, the individual had to be notified and given a chance to mount a challenge. Anyone wronged could sue the company in federal court.

The laws acknowledged reality—that you can't live normally in an electronic age without placing personal information in the hands of third parties, usually corporations that have little interest in fighting the government to protect your privacy.

Meanwhile, the Supreme Court was moving the other way by ruling that you lose your Fourth Amendment protection as soon as you provide records to banks, phone companies, and the like. In 1976, it reversed a circuit court decision to suppress the evidence of microfilmed canceled checks and deposit slips subpoenaed from two banks, finding in *United States v. Miller* no "expectation of privacy" in such commercial documents voluntarily conveyed to a financial institution. "The depositor takes the risk, in revealing his affairs to another, that the information will be conveyed by that person to the government. This Court has held repeatedly that the Fourth Amendment does not prohibit the obtaining of information revealed to a third party and conveyed by him to government authorities, even if the information is revealed on the assumption that it will be used only for a limited purpose and the confidence placed in the third party will not be betrayed." Consequently, the warrant contemplated by the Fourth Amendment was not required; a subpoena—or, by implication, nothing more than a polite request to the bank—was sufficient to get your records.[23]

Three years later, the Court subtracted phone records from Fourth Amendment protection, finding in *Smith v. Maryland* that a customer has no "legitimate expectation of privacy" over what numbers he calls from his home telephone. A pen register, an electronic device placed by the company at police request to record outgoing phone numbers, is not a "search" because it keeps track of only the calling destinations, not the conversations' contents. "Since the pen register was installed on telephone company property at the telephone company's central offices, petitioner obviously cannot claim that his 'property' was invaded or that police intruded into a 'constitutionally protected area,' the Court ruled. "We doubt that people in general entertain any actual expectation of privacy in the numbers they dial. All telephone users realize that they must 'convey' phone numbers to the telephone company, since it is through telephone company switching equipment that their calls are completed. All subscribers realize, moreover, that the phone company has facilities for making permanent records of the numbers they dial, for they see a list of their long-distance (toll) calls on their monthly bills."[24]

Maybe I don't fall into the category of "people in general," but I don't think that my bank and the phone company are the same as the FBI. In my mind, there is a difference between the private sector and the state. When I push buttons on my phone, I recognize that the phone company's switching equipment has to work for me, but I don't *expect* the numbers I call to show up on the computer screens of government agencies. When I give my banker and broker personal financial information, I don't *expect* cops to be looking over their shoulders. My *expectation of privacy* does not disappear when I share information with trusted service providers, because I am not placing it in the public square. My personal information should be treated like my personal property, inaccessible without my permission.

The Supreme Court has ruled otherwise, and its sophistry is a curse on the Bill of Rights. It goes like this: Because your personal information is collected by companies, you cannot expect it to remain private, and therefore government may acquire it. Since the government can get it, you have no expectation of privacy in such records, which allows the government to act as if there were no privacy.

In other words, obtaining the information is possible, so it is also permissible, for if you have no "expectation of privacy," a "search" is not actually occurring under the Fourth Amendment. Your entire financial, travel, communications, purchasing, Web-browsing, and library-book-borrowing activities may be collected by law enforcement, but these are not "searches." The logic is relentless: Citing Supreme Court opinions, "several senior FBI attorneys" told Justice Department investigators that National Security Letters for phone records "do not implicate privacy interests under the Fourth Amendment."[25] To protect information, you have to keep it solely in your home or office or wallet.

In a technological age, when few details of a person's life remain in her desk drawer alone, this circular argument diminishing the "expectation of privacy" creates a whirlpool that sucks down a critical constitutional principle: that the state must be held at bay to preserve individual liberty. It's a bit like the old Soviet Union arguing that since Russians obviously had no expectation of privacy on their phones, the KGB was perfectly entitled to listen in.

That interpretation leaves only the law, not the Constitution, to restrict third parties from revealing data. Read the little privacy brochures your bank, broker, and Internet provider send periodically and you'll notice that they invariably begin with high-sounding promises: "We are honored that you have entrusted us with your financial affairs, and we are committed to safeguarding the privacy of information we maintain about you," says Charles Schwab's "Commitment to Your Privacy." It sounds good until you get to page three, which notes the big exceptions: "We provide access to information about you to outside companies and other third parties in certain limited circumstances, including . . . when we believe that disclosure is required or permitted under law. For example, we may be required to disclose personal information to cooperate with regulatory or law enforcement authorities, to resolve consumer disputes, to perform credit/authentication checks, or for risk control."[26]

In the 1970s and '80s, as the boundaries of privacy were being redrawn by the courts, the Congress, and the executive branch's law enforcement and intelligence agencies, the limits were made fluid by crosscurrents of invasion and protection. Into the ebb and flow came the three federal privacy statutes designed to defend Americans from government snooping by prohibiting companies from releasing information without overt, challengeable orders. And then each was diluted by the provision authorizing secret National Security Letters.

The Fair Credit Reporting Act of 1970 required firms to keep your credit reports private and, even if properly subpoenaed, to reveal only your name, addresses, and places of employment. It was watered down with an NSL section in 1996.[27]

The Right to Financial Privacy Act, passed in 1978, concealed your check-writing, investing, travel, and other such records. It was weakened by an NSL exception in 1986.[28]

Your telephone and Internet browsing records and e-mails were made inaccessible under the Electronic Communications Privacy Act, which took effect in 1986 only to be breached by expanded NSL authorizations in 1993 and 1996.[29] A fourth law, the National Security Act of 1947, was amended in 1994 after the arrest of the CIA spy Aldrich Ames, to permit NSLs against government employees suspected of disclosing classified information.[30]

Even in its early form, the investigative tool of the NSL circumvented judicial oversight, carried the automatic gag order, and provided the target with neither notification nor appeal. Yet it generated little opposition. Its limitation to counterintelligence, plus the six to twelve months it took to get a letter issued, made it relatively unpopular in the FBI. So it lurked in legal shadows until the rush of panic that produced the Patriot Act after September 11, 2001. Then the number of annual requests for information via NSLs soared, from about 8,500 in 2000 to 56,000 in 2004 (decreasing somewhat to 47,000 in 2005), according to incomplete FBI records. (An internal sampling of files found the actual number to be 17 percent higher than these official figures.)[31]

Furthermore, the Defense Department secretly issued about five hundred NSLs for contractors' and employees' financial and credit card records between September 11, 2001, and 2007, according to an internal review, thereby breaching the traditional barrier designed to prevent military involvement in domestic intelligence and law enforcement. The letters, made public in an ACLU Freedom of Information suit, sometimes asked for all credit card charges or bank account records over as much as a five-year period, indicating that investigators were looking for purchases and deposits beyond a person's means, perhaps from extraordinary payments for espionage.

In the hands of the Pentagon, the tool was a request, not a requirement, legally less powerful than the FBI's version. The air force letters that were released contained a standard warning not to disclose the request "regardless of whether you provide this information," suggesting that compliance was optional. But one letter also called itself a "subpoena" and was stamped "This Subpoena contains a: NON-DISCLOSURE ORDER. Do Not Notify Customer. Do Not Charge Account." In the face of such a document stating that it was part of "an official foreign counterintelligence investigation," very few institutions refused, the records showed. To add muscle, the FBI was sometimes asked to use its more draconian variant to get information the Pentagon wanted for investigations of alleged spying, terrorism, or other supposed threats against the military. The ACLU believed the targets included antiwar activists.[32]

MISSION CREEP

This history of the National Security Letter is a cautionary tale of metamorphosis, illustrating how an intrusion that seems reasonable and tightly focused can evolve into a menace. In all three privacy statutes, the limited NSL loopholes that had been added in the 1980s and 1990s were broadened by the Patriot Act. No longer did the letters require "specific and articulable facts giving reason to believe" that the records sought belonged to "a foreign power or agent of a foreign power," but now could be gathered if "relevant to an authorized investigation to protect against international terrorism or clandestine intelligence activities."[33]

It was a powerful sentence. Adding antiterrorism to counterintelligence, removing the foreign-agent criterion, and making the information merely "relevant" eliminated the concept of individualized suspicion that is central to the Fourth Amendment. It opened the NSL for use against more than the suspect in an investigation by permitting information collection on relatives, friends—indeed, anyone the suspect may have contacted, including innocent people whose data are now floating around in numerous agencies' computers. How many non-suspects have been targeted is unknown, since the FBI did not keep track before 2006.

The amendment in the Patriot Act also invited the use of the NSL in criminal cases. If a foreign spy has diplomatic immunity from prosecution—as most probably do—agencies might just want to monitor him or expel him from the country, the customary remedy. Americans and nondiplomats can be arrested, of course, but those instances come along infrequently. By contrast, a suspected terrorist on U.S. soil is usually put into the criminal justice system: arrested, indicted, tried—certainly not expelled. So the NSL, a device conceived for intelligence gathering, was transformed into an evidence-gathering tool, raising constitutional implications.

The Patriot Act expanded the number of people who could issue a letter, from ten high-ranking officials in FBI headquarters to the heads of all fifty-six FBI field offices plus numerous managers in various divisions based in Washington.[34] This made authorization quite easy. Furthermore, a new form of NSL was added to the Fair Credit Reporting Act permitting authorities to demand from credit companies any information on individuals, including full credit reports.

The amendments allowed a continuous hailstorm of NSLs to pepper Internet providers, telephone companies, banks, libraries, and other institutions holding private records of millions of people. The nature of the targets also shifted. Before the Patriot Act, about 39 percent were "U.S. persons," a term defined in law as citizens and legal immigrants who are permanent residents.[35] From 2003 through 2005, U.S. persons jumped to 53 percent in the FBI's official tallies, and a sample survey by the Justice Department's inspector general showed the figure as 12 percent higher, or about 65 percent overall.[36] Terrorism investigations accounted for about 73 percent of the NSLs, intelligence cases for just 26 percent, and foreign computer intrusions for the remaining 1 percent, according to the inspector general's study. The National Security Letter had been entirely transformed.

But even the loose standards weren't loose enough for agents who violated them frequently. Two official studies found the FBI files on NSLs laced with evidence of bureaucratic confusion and shortcuts, ignorance of the law, and outright dishonesty.

Part of the fault lies with a Congress skilled in writing complexities into statutes. Hapless FBI agents, few of whom are lawyers, cannot always be blamed for mistakes as they journey through bewildering loopholes and labyrinths. "We found confusion about the authorities available under the various NSL statutes," the first study reported blandly in 2007. It did not go on to suggest the remedy: either judicial oversight or a straightforward prohibition against administrative government access to private records. Instead, we have protective laws riddled with exceptions.

The confused legal terrain allows officials to wander unbridled as they issue NSLs. The inspector general found "no clear guidance" to FBI agents, for example, on how to reconcile "the expansive authorities in the NSL statutes" with a long-standing presidential executive order mandating "the least intrusive collection techniques feasible."[37]

The FBI's carelessness in drawing up National Security Letters rivaled its laboratory's imprecision in analyzing evidence. Its official statistics understated the number of NSLs actually in the files, the inspector general found, and forty-eight violations were discovered in a relatively small sample of 293 NSLs. Despite the Patriot Act's vague requirement that the information be "relevant to an authorized investigation," many letters were issued where no investigation had been launched. In three of the four divisions surveyed, signed copies were not kept, so investigators could not check on whether they had been approved by an official authorized to issue them. A cavalier approach prevailed.

Mistyped phone numbers and e-mail addresses produced personal information about the wrong people. Communications companies turned over more than was requested or allowed. Nine NSLs were illegally used to obtain full credit reports for counterintelligence, although the law authorized them only for counterterrorism.[38] Two NSLs illegally sought content information from e-mails, beyond the addresses and subject lines the law permitted. Time limits were violated as phone records were obtained for periods thirty to eighty-one days longer than prescribed by the NSLs. One agent, using a bank customer's PIN obtained through a FISA warrant, got illegal access to the person's account without an NSL.

Thanks to press reports, the inspector general learned that a North Carolina university was served with an NSL going far beyond its legal authority by demanding "applications for admission, housing information, emergency contacts, and campus health records," as the FBI investigated a student's possible involvement in the 2005 bus and subway bombings in London. Oddly, a grand jury subpoena for the records, already in process, was later served, and the university complied. Agents seemed to see the NSL as a shortcut.

"In most cases," the report concluded, "the FBI was seeking to obtain information that it could have obtained properly if it had followed applicable statutes, guidelines, and internal policies." But the broadened NSL became the administrative path of least resistance where even the thinnest checks and balances were missing. This led some agents to cheat the law and lie to each other, as well as to telecommunications firms.

The FBI entered into contracts with three unnamed phone companies to provide information on thousands of numbers, often through pen registers, which record the destinations of outgoing calls, and through trap-and-trace devices, which capture incoming numbers. (The names are anachronistic, dating from an era of copper wires and electromechanical switches; their functions are now performed by computers.)

The inspector general, Glenn A. Fine, blasted the FBI in 2010 for the "casual culture" that had grown up between agents and telecom firms. Instead of using NSLs or other legal means, "FBI personnel sought and received telephone records based on informal requests made by e-mail, by telephone, face-to-face, and even on post-it notes," he reported. At least 3,500 phone numbers were monitored in this informal manner, facilitated by three phone companies stationing employees in the FBI's Communications Analysis Unit, which "blurred the line between the FBI and the service providers" and "contributed to the serious abuses." In a practice called sneak peeks, the company representatives "would check their records and provide a preview of the available information for a targeted phone number, without documentation of the fact of the request. At times, the service providers' employees simply invited FBI personnel to view the telephone records on their computer screens. Notably, virtually none of these FBI requests for telephone records—either the exigent letters or the other informal requests—was accompanied by documentation explaining the authority for the requests." Agents obtained phone records on news reporters without the required authorization by the attorney general.

The FBI also "made inaccurate statements to the [secret] FISA Court," Fine discovered. "In several instances, the FBI submitted affidavits to the Court that information in FISA applications was obtained through NSLs or a grand jury subpoena, when in fact the information was obtained by other means, such as exigent letters."

Evading even the relaxed procedures for obtaining National Security Letters, agents in the Counterterrorism Division who were not authorized to sign NSLs issued 739 of these so-called exigent letters requesting data on about 3,000 phone numbers from March 2003 to December 2005. They were trying to invert a Patriot Act provision allowing telecom firms that see something suspicious to tell the government without risking a lawsuit by the customer. But here, the FBI was initiating the request, and agents lied to the phone companies, and sometimes to other FBI officials, that NSLs or grand jury subpoenas had been applied for and would soon follow, and that the situations were emergencies.

In fact, the inspector general found, not a single subpoena had been requested, most of the letters were issued in nonemergency situations, and "there sometimes were no open or pending national security investigations tied to the request." The FBI didn't even keep track of whether NSLs were ultimately issued after the exigent letters were sent, relying on the phone company to maintain such records. And when attorneys in the Justice Department's National Security Law Branch learned of the practice and tried to stop it, the Counterterrorism Division's Communications Analysis Unit went through the motions of applying for National Security Letters after the fact, without telling the lawyers that the phone information had already been received.

The same thing happened on a smaller scale when nineteen "certificate letters," instead of NSLs, were sent to a federal reserve bank in search of federal wire transfers by 244 people. Prompted by the Justice Department's investigation, Federal Reserve attorneys conceded that the records should not have been provided on the basis of the certificate letters.

Even where proper procedures were followed, the justification for issuing National Security Letters could be flimsy, as in a request stating merely, "The subject is in contact with the subjects of other international terrorism investigations. These subscriber and toll billing records are being requested to determine the identity of others with whom the subject communicates."[39] The chief division counsel who received this sparse application for an NSL turned it down but circulated the text among twenty-two other FBI chief division counsels to collect their views. Thirteen agreed that it should be rejected, but nine said they would approve it. One of those who would have turned it down told investigators that nothing had caused more friction in his twenty years with the FBI than the questions he had raised about NSL requests.

The criteria were so loosely constructed that the National Security Law Branch felt it necessary to post this sardonic guidance on its Web site in March 2006, after the Patriot Act was reauthorized: "A perfunctory recitation that (1) the subject is the target of the investigation, (2) he has a telephone, and (3) therefore, it follows that an NSL for his telephone records is relevant to the authorized investigation will not suffice. Otherwise, any target with a telephone or a bank account is subject to an NSL. And that is not the standard for issuance of an NSL."[40]

A BIGGER HAYSTACK

Following the revelations in the 1970s about FBI snooping, the agency reportedly stopped amassing huge files on people who were not part of criminal or counterintelligence investigations. In the first place, everything was on paper, one former agent noted, and warehouse space was limited. But it doesn't take warehouses to store data in a computer age, and since 9/11, law enforcement and intelligence officers have understood one very bold lesson: They risk more criticism from Congress and the public by missing an attack than by violating privacy.

So, they collect. "As a criminal investigator, my goal is to gather evidence necessary to prosecute a bad guy," to get "one step closer to putting that guy in handcuffs and going to court," said Mike German, the former undercover agent who infiltrated domestic militia groups for the FBI. "As an intelligence investigator, your goal is to collect. The evaluation of a criminal investigator is based on actual success. But a collector, they're measured by how fat their file is. And if you collect every day in and day out, you're going to have a fat file—and particularly if it's all classified, you don't have anybody looking over your shoulder. And if you're mindful of protecting civil liberties and are judicious, your files are not going to be so fat."

Computer systems obviously make it easier to share intelligence information. Unsourced records obtained from NSLs—including those on innocent people not being investigated—are uploaded into databases accessible by 34,000 officials throughout government in U.S. Attorneys' offices, the Drug Enforcement Administration, the Federal Bureau of Prisons, Homeland Security, and the CIA, as well as state and local law enforcement agencies that are part of joint terrorism task forces throughout the country.

The FBI and other collectors claim to have enhanced their capacity to analyze the burgeoning mass of information, but German has his doubts. "That was the lesson of 9/11," he said, "and unfortunately people didn't catch that." Some fifty or sixty officials in the CIA and the NSA had known that two of the nineteen hijackers had arrived in the United States, but nobody told the FBI.[41] Since then, impediments to sharing may have been reduced, but the inundation of information has remained overwhelming, producing few significant prosecutions, German noted. "Is that really an efficient use of all those agents and all that money?"

It's hard to make a case that the extensive collection and sharing of data have made agencies smarter and more agile. They failed to search multiple databases and consolidate scattered intelligence reports on a Nigerian student, Umar Farouk Abdulmutallab, whose radicalization had prompted his father to visit the U.S. Embassy and warn the CIA. The young man's multiple-entry U.S. visa wasn't withdrawn, he wasn't placed on the no-fly list, and he wasn't even given extra screening in Amsterdam before he boarded a Northwest flight to Detroit on Christmas Day of 2009, explosives hidden in his underwear. A blast that would have brought down the plane over Michigan was narrowly averted when the bomb fizzled and passengers subdued him. A preliminary investigation into the intelligence failure hinted at the burdens created by over-collecting. "The information that was available to analysts, as is usually the case, was fragmentary and embedded in a large volume of other data," said the report. President Obama instructed officials to examine "how to meet the challenge associated with exploiting the ever-increasing volume of information available to the Intelligence Community."[42]

One example of wasted resources was witnessed by Lawrence Wright, author of a book on al-Qaeda, when he was visited at home by FBI agents inquiring about calls he'd made to Egypt. One of the conversations, with a relative of Ayman al-Zawahiri, Osama bin Laden's deputy, was summarized in an intelligence database, he was told by an official. "I was surprised, because the FISA law stated that my part of the conversation should have been 'minimized'—redacted or rendered anonymous— because I am an American citizen," the author wrote.

Wright had done a profile of Zawahiri for *The New Yorker* and was contacted by the relative, an architect in Cairo, to ask "if I could learn whether all of Zawahiri's children were dead." The FBI told him erroneously that they were, Wright passed the misinformation to the relative, and the call was monitored and filed. "He's a terrorist, or he's associated with terrorists," said Mike McConnell, director of national intelligence, when Wright told him the story. "Now, if I'm targeting, I'm looking at his number. If he places a call, I listen. If he gets called, I listen. I don't know who is going to call him, but once I got it, I gotta deal with it. Turns out it is Larry Wright. You would have been reported as 'U.S. Person 1.' You would never have been identified, except if the FBI learns that this unidentified U.S. person is talking to a known terrorist. Then the FBI would go in and request the identity of U.S. 1. The NSA would have to go through a process to determine if the request was legitimate. So here's what I think—I'm guessing. You called a bad guy, the system listened, tried to sort it out, and they did an intel report because it had foreign-intelligence value. That's our mission."[43]

The same was true of the domestic surveillance against civil rights activists, the Black Panthers, the Weathermen, and various antiwar organizers decades ago, recalled Jerry Berman, who worked for the American Civil Liberties Union. "They didn't prevent zilch," he said. "And the reason they didn't prevent zilch is the FBI had records on everybody, and they didn't know what was important."

Captain Jeffery Herold, head of intelligence for the Washington, D.C., police department's Office of Homeland Security and Counterterrorism, told me the same thing when I asked if too much information was coming through. "Oh, my God. Turn it off. I'll get three hundred e-mails a day," so many that his unit does nothing about most of them. "We have to hire analysts to analyze it. If you get too much, which threat are you going to follow?" He wouldn't say how they decide, except, "You look at what's possible. Do those capabilities exist? Can they really fly airplanes into the World Trade Center?"

The ACLU has a favorite metaphor to describe the absurdity of trying to catch a terrorist through the insatiable collection of personal information on vast numbers of people: You don't find a needle in a haystack by increasing the size of the haystack.

In its study of National Security Letters, the Office of the Inspector General attempted valiantly to portray their usefulness. They were called "indispensable" and "our bread and butter" by unnamed FBI officials who claimed that the information on phone, Internet, and financial records could connect groups and individuals with one another by following money and communications. Leads were generated for joint terrorism task forces and foreign governments, information was used to induce cooperation by suspects, and targets of investigations were exonerated by agents who closed cases more confidently after using NSLs to eliminate concerns.

Most examples supporting such claims, given by the Justice Department and the FBI, have been less than definitive. The inspector general found that twenty-seven of the forty-six FBI divisions studied had used NSL evidence to refer counterterrorism targets for prosecution, but because the FBI's records were in disarray, it was impossible to document how effective the NSLs had been in those cases. Information in criminal files was not tagged as deriving from NSLs, and most charges labeled "terrorism" were actually for fraud, immigration offenses, and money laundering.

If those don't sound like grave threats to national security, consider this: The median sentence under the "terrorism" rubric was twenty-eight days during the first two years after 9/11, dropping to twenty days through May 31, 2006. Furthermore, Justice Department attorneys declined to prosecute 67 percent of the "terrorism" cases brought to them by the FBI during the five years through 2008, an unusually high percentage that rose over time.[44]

Rachel Brand, a young right-wing ideologue who served as assistant attorney general in the Bush administration, made sweeping public statements about the usefulness of FISA orders and NSLs in heading off terrorist attacks, promised me examples, and never delivered. Her spokeswoman, Kimberly A. Smith, was repeatedly waved off by superiors as she rummaged around in the thicket of the Justice Department for more than a year, and came up with nothing beyond press-release platitudes—no level of detail sufficient to permit true evaluations. Nor was an FBI spokeswoman, Angela Bell, able to find a good case after eight months of searching—at least not one the FBI was willing to cite as an example of FISA orders and NSLs that had prevented violence. (After she gave up trying, FISA surveillance led to the arrest of an Afghan immigrant, Najibullah Zazi, accused of buying chemicals to manufacture bombs; he pleaded guilty.)[45]

The dearth of obvious cases doesn't necessarily mean that NSLs are ineffective, perhaps just that nobody in the FBI really knows how valuable they have been. The inspector general reported that National Security Letters were employed as an initial step in gathering skeletal evidence before applying for a secret FISA warrant from a judge. An investigation has to start somewhere, after all, and the NSL is a relatively easy instrument to use at the outset.

A more traditional tool, the grand jury subpoena, carries pluses and minuses from the FBI's perspective. It can be issued quickly, but it requires enough cause for a grand jury to be convened. It is more likely to be obeyed promptly, the study found, but it can be leaked to the press and the public. And if a judge turns down a criminal warrant or subpoena, agents fear, courts may look askance if the FBI later seeks a FISA warrant or issues a National Security Letter. The judicial branch is evidently less offended if its oversight is evaded beforehand.

NSLs have been most useful in tracing finances. The FBI used them to get the bank records of convenience stores that were conduits for funds through the informal *hawaladar* transfer system to the Middle East, and allegedly on to al-Qaeda, the inspector general reported. The government opened fire with a broad battery of charges against storekeepers who had sent two individuals millions of dollars. Prosecutors replayed an old strategy: If you can't get the Mafia boss on a murder charge, get him for tax evasion. The storekeepers were accused of "money laundering, sale of untaxed cigarettes, check cashing fraud, illegal sale of pseudoephedrine (the precursor ingredient used to manufacture methamphetamine), unemployment insurance fraud, welfare fraud, immigration fraud, income tax violations, and sale of counterfeit merchandise."

Looking at credit reports, the FBI was also able to track the address changes of subjects in a terrorism investigation who were uprooted by Hurricane Katrina. And financial records established a connection between a prisoner in Guantánamo and the target of another investigation, who was then convicted of providing material support to terrorists.

Two successful financing cases were made by sharing information between intelligence and law enforcement on Mohammed Ali Hassan Al-Moayad, convicted in March 2005 and sentenced to seventy-five years for funneling millions to Hamas and al-Qaeda, and Enaam Arnaout, the executive director of the Illinois-based Benevolence International Foundation, who pleaded guilty to sending money to help rebels in Bosnia and Chechnya buy military supplies.[46] But the Justice Department never offered persuasive details on how essential FISA orders or NSLs were in bringing these prosecutions, so the question remained whether ordinary criminal warrants and wiretaps, consistent with the Bill of Rights, would have been sufficient.

FISA orders and intelligence sharing were touted by the Justice Department as essential tools in a few dubious prosecutions. A Florida computer science professor, Sami al-Arian, was charged along with three co-defendants with supporting Palestine Islamic Jihad, which had killed more than one hundred people in Israel, including a young American woman. Sections 218 and 504 of the Patriot Act "enabled prosecutors to consider all evidence against al-Arian and his co-conspirators, including evidence obtained pursuant to FISA that provided the necessary factual support for the criminal case," the Justice Department boasted.[47] The evidence was so questionable, however, that a jury failed to convict any of the four, unanimously acquitting al-Arian on nine counts and voting ten to two to acquit on the remaining eight.

Federal prosecutors weren't deterred. While al-Arian languished in prison, where he had spent more than three years, they threatened to retry him on those eight counts. To get out of jail and to get out of the country, he pleaded guilty to a lesser charge—conspiring to help people associated with the terrorist group—and accepted deportation (he was a Palestinian born in Kuwait). But when he appeared in court expecting to be released, a federal judge condemned him as a terrorist (as the jury had refused to do) and gave him the maximum sentence, which sent him back behind bars for an additional nineteen months, making fifty-seven all together.

Then, to turn the screws a bit more, federal prosecutors in Virginia summoned him before a grand jury to testify in another investigation, and when he refused (in the belief that his plea bargain had not required his cooperation) he was cited for contempt of court and given another six months.

CONTEMPT OF COURT

At the opaque end of the spectrum most distant from the Fourth Amendment, where searches and surveillance escape review by the judicial branch, the Bush administration stepped far outside the law—even the most permissive law—to enlist the National Security Agency in broad sweeps of electronic communications. There were no established legal ways to do so: no wiretap warrants, no National Security Letters, no classified orders under the Foreign Intelligence Surveillance Act.

In the panic following September 11, 2001, the White House—understandably eager to learn everything possible about future plots of terrorism—had the CIA director, George Tenet, ask the NSA director, Michael V. Hayden, what more interception and surveillance the NSA could do. Nothing more within existing authority, Hayden replied. And if he had more authority? Hayden answered by assembling a description of the NSA's "operationally useful and technologically feasible" capabilities, which became the basis of Bush's secret plan.[48] The program was not designed to fit within the law; instead, the law was interpreted—and then ultimately revised—to accommodate the program.

Under instructions from Vice President Dick Cheney's office, a zealous young lawyer in the Justice Department, John Yoo, concocted arguments that were later derided by some who saw his classified memo—a "legal mess" in the words of Jack Goldsmith, who found the sloppy work when he took over the Justice Department's Office of Legal Counsel.[49] Yoo had contended that the president's constitutional powers as commander in chief conferred the authority, bolstered by the congressional authorization of force following 9/11, to ignore the FISA statute and eavesdrop without applying first to the FISA court. As self-serving as the reasoning was, the program's chief architect, Cheney's counsel David Addington, refused to let NSA officials see the legal opinion supposedly justifying their activities—a bizarre turn even for that White House.[50]

Convinced that the impediments of FISA and its court put the country at risk, Addington told Goldsmith during a contentious meeting in February 2004, "We're one bomb away from getting rid of that obnoxious court." Goldsmith, a conservative himself, seemed stunned by Addington's contempt for the law. "He and the vice president had abhorred FISA's intrusion on presidential power ever since its enactment in 1978," Goldsmith wrote. "After 9/11 they and other top officials in the administration dealt with FISA the way they dealt with other laws they didn't like: They blew through them in secret based on flimsy legal opinions that they guarded closely so no one could question the legal basis for the operations."[51]

The NSA, so secret it's sometimes called "No Such Agency," was created in 1952 primarily as a cryptographic enterprise to invent and break codes. Only a tiny facet can be seen by the public, at its museum of cryptography adjacent to its headquarters in Fort Meade, Maryland, halfway between Washington and Baltimore. A glass case in the museum's entrance holds a large, jagged chunk of the Pentagon where it was struck on 9/11 but nothing else from the current era. It has displays of outdated code machines from the two world wars, the Korean War, and the Vietnam War, but that's where history ends, as if the recent past is itself a secret. From the roadway to the museum, you can see the agency's bunker-like concrete buildings and the two newest structures, block shaped, which look as if they are made of blue-green glass. They appear deceptively transparent.

When Bush visited the NSA in September 2007, reporters noted a tough-minded sign on a wall: "We Won't Back Down. We Never Have. We Never Will."[52] Evidently not. Led by a military officer, the agency was designed to spy on communications overseas but was secretly driven off course by one president after another to monitor domestic antiwar activists, civil rights organizers, Black Panthers, and other dissident Americans during COINTELPRO and other surveillance programs of the 1950s, 1960s, and 1970s. NSA officials were uncomfortable with those assignments, recalled Jerry Berman, who worked to end warrantless wiretapping as chief legislative counsel for the ACLU when the Foreign Intelligence Surveillance Act was passed. "Of all the agencies that wanted to get this right," he said, "NSA was the leader at the time. The culture of the Justice Department was [J. Edgar] Hoover. NSA was created on a different front, less ideological, more interested in real espionage, and I think they felt burned by having been asked to participate in this program."

Once FISA was enacted, the NSA on its own was not supposed to eavesdrop on communications involving anyone inside the United States. If one party to an international phone or Internet exchange turned out to be on American soil, a warrant was sought from a FISA judge. Say someone in Yemen, suspected of links to al-Qaeda, phoned or e-mailed someone in Los Angeles. Communications within Yemen or between

Yemen and another foreign country lay outside FISA's jurisdiction and could be monitored by the NSA at will. But as soon as the traffic entered the United States, FISA kicked in, requiring a secret warrant. That wasn't hard to get if there was enough contact for the government to show probable cause that the L.A. party was a foreign agent. If speed was essential, FISA's emergency provision authorized monitoring first—an approval often issued in minutes—and then an application to a judge within three days.

But Bush changed the rules by fiat, with a secret sleight of hand. Even while pressing quickly after September 11 for the Patriot Act amendments broadening FISA, he stealthily evaded FISA itself by signing a classified executive order mobilizing the NSA's global arrays of antennas and computers to monitor e-mail and telephone traffic into and out of the United States—without the required FISA warrants. Shift managers chose their own targets without approval from the White House or the Justice Department, much less a court, according to James Risen and Eric Lichtblau, who disclosed the surveillance in *The New York Times*. In addition, communications wholly within the United States were often captured—by accident, officials told them—because the location of a cell phone or an Internet user wasn't always obvious.[53]

Although 9/11 was the excuse, the concept of comprehensive intercepts predated the attacks, according to Risen and Lichtblau. In 2000, they discovered, NSA officials "wrote a transition report to the incoming Bush administration, saying the agency must become a 'powerful, permanent presence' on the commercial communications network," whose executives were sounded out by the NSA soon after the inauguration.[54] When communications relied on microwave or satellites, the NSA could eavesdrop using its own equipment, but the growth of fiber-optic cables for transmission had thrown the agency into a dependence on communications companies.

Most big firms cooperated and thereby violated the Electronic Communications Privacy Act, inviting customer lawsuits. The companies allowed the government to tap into fiber-optic cables where they entered the United States at coastal landing stations, and to install such filters as the Narus STA 6400, a splitter box, to copy, slow down, and sift through huge volumes of data. An AT&T technician, Mark Kline, who learned that the device had been placed in a secret room at AT&T's switch center on Folsom Street in San Francisco, told the author James Bamford that the location, a nexus for domestic as well as foreign traffic, suggested an interest in eavesdropping inside the United States. "The NSA was spreading an electronic drift net across cyberspace," Bamford concluded.[55]

The clandestine surveillance created a farcical illusion in the post-9/11 debate over civil liberties. While the ACLU and others believed that the Patriot Act made FISA too loose, the Bush administration saw FISA as too restrictive. While those concerned with Americans' privacy regarded FISA as an end run around the Fourth Amendment, the administration was secretly making an end run around FISA. Rights advocates thought they were challenging the government's most intrusive tools, but in fact the public arguments merely skated along the surface of intrusions whose depths remained unseen.

Unnamed officials who thought the program illegal and unconstitutional told Risen and Lichtblau that it had been launched after the seizure of cell phones, computers, and address books from al-Qaeda operatives taken prisoner in Afghanistan. Phone numbers and e-mail addresses found in those records, some of them for people inside the United States, were given to the NSA to monitor, forgoing the well-established legal procedures.

Beyond spying on particular phone lines and e-mail accounts, the NSA's program of broad data-mining and computer sweeps sifted many quadrillions of bytes for words or phrases that would trigger detailed examination. That may have explained why officials circumvented FISA. At the time, even a FISA warrant required some specificity: a particular number or person or place, something narrower than a vast net to scoop up huge volumes of phone and e-mail communications indiscriminately.

A former manager in an unnamed communications firm explained the government's objectives in the *Times* article. "If they get content, that's useful to them too, but the real plum is going to be the transaction data and the traffic analysis," he told the reporters. "Massive amounts of traffic analysis information—who is calling whom, who is in Osama bin Laden's circle of family and friends—is used to identify lines of communication that are then given closer scrutiny."[56]

AT&T and Verizon both cooperated, the *Times* reported, as the NSA reached far beyond counterterrorism into the common crime of drug trafficking. Without court orders, the companies allowed the NSA to install equipment that collected records on "thousands of Americans and others inside the United States who call people in Latin America" and other narcotics-producing regions. Only Qwest refused an NSA request to monitor local switches carrying mainly domestic calls. But that didn't matter, Bamford reported, since Qwest's cables came through AT&T and were routed through the Narus splitter.[57]

Since the technology allows particular phone numbers and e-mail addresses to be programmed for monitoring, it can also exclude them from surveillance. But the NSA has deliberately eavesdropped on journalists and humanitarian organizations overseas, even on their private communications with relatives back home, regarding them as useful sources of information, "eyes on the ground," Bamford was told by an agency linguist, Adrienne J. Kinne. On a scale of one to eight, they were assigned priorities of five to seven, she said.[58]

Inside the country, the phone records of "tens of millions of Americans" were being handed over to the NSA by AT&T, Verizon, and BellSouth, officials told *USA Today*. Numbers called and received—not the content of conversations—were being compiled to create a national database of all calls to and from businesses, friends, family members, colleagues, and the like, through which "the NSA has gained a secret window into the communications habits of millions of Americans."[59]

Under the more focused, targeted program, Risen and Lichtblau reported, about five hundred people in the United States were being monitored at any one time, and five thousand to seven thousand overseas. Yet the surveillance apparently uncovered few terrorist plots, and officials seemed hardly ecstatic about its results. It received only middling marks in 2009, after an unprecedented investigation by the five inspectors general of the CIA, the NSA, the Justice Department, the Defense Department, and the Director of National Intelligence. While the secret program "had value in some counterterrorism investigations, it generally played a limited role in the FBI's overall counterterrorism efforts," they reported. The NSA bragged about its having helped disrupt al-Qaeda operatives, but no examples were made public, so the claim could neither be refuted nor verified by the investigators. Most officials interviewed for the report "had difficulty citing specific instances" where the surveillance "directly contributed to counterterrorism successes." A senior CIA official said that the monitoring "was rarely the sole basis for an intelligence success, but that it frequently played a supporting role," and served as "an additional resource to enhance the CIA's understanding of terrorist networks." However, the information was discounted by other CIA officials as "vague or without context."[60]

One exception cited by officials was a plot to bomb pubs and railroad stations in Britain. Another was an Ohio truck driver named Iyman Faris, who pleaded guilty in 2003 to what seemed a rather unlikely fantasy: a scheme to use blowtorches to bring down the Brooklyn Bridge. At least he wasn't accused of trying to sell it first.[61]

It is worth repeating that prevention provided the motive for the surveillance, which was described in a Justice Department paper as "an early warning system to detect and prevent another catastrophic terrorist attack on the United States."[62] Bush shrewdly entitled it the Terrorist Surveillance Program following its disclosure. In the minds of officials charged with keeping the country secure, the attacks of September 11 redefined the relationship between crime and law enforcement. No longer did the time-honored sequence of criminal procedure—first the crime, then the punishment—seem relevant. No penalty could be levied on the nineteen hijackers after that clear September morning; terrorists whose mission includes suicide leave behind no opportunity for justice. So the traditional approach of investigating, gathering evidence, arresting a suspect, and proving a case seems about as sensible as sealing the leak after the ship has sunk.

"You want to catch a terrorist with his hands on the check instead of his hands on the bomb," said Deputy Attorney General James B. Comey, testifying before Congress in 2005. "You want to be many steps ahead of the devastating event. The way we do that is through preventive and disruptive measures, by using investigative tools to learn as much as we can as quickly as we can and then incapacitating a target at the right moment. Tools such as enhanced information sharing mechanisms, roving surveillance, pen registers, requests for the production of business records, and delayed notification search warrants allow us to do just that."[63]

This sounded like a persuasive rationale, yet two years later Comey revealed to Congress that in 2004 he had refused to sign an extension of the surveillance operation because "I could not, after a whole lot of hard work, find an adequate legal basis for the program."[64] He was reportedly concerned less with the NSA activities than with other, unspecified intelligence methods that had not been accurately described in Yoo's memos, according to the five inspectors general. Comey's resistance set the stage for a dramatic, high-level confrontation at the hospital bedside of a critically ill Attorney General John Ashcroft.

Bush had launched the surveillance by executive order but had required its renewal every forty-five days, a reauthorization that relied on the Justice Department to certify its legality. A green light had been given for at least two years by Jay S. Bybee and his assistant John Yoo, but this time, the new head of the department's Office of Legal Counsel, Jack Goldsmith, had completed "a very intensive reevaluation" and found "no legal basis," Comey testified. Such a determination is usually binding on the entire executive branch.

The inadequate descriptions in Yoo's memos had left the attorney general unaware of what he had been certifying as legal, according to the five inspectors general.[65] So Comey held an hour's discussion with Ashcroft, and the two decided together that to conform with the law, the program had to be changed—in what manner Comey would not say publicly. This put them on a collision course with the White House, which was keen to continue the spying.

Just hours after the meeting, Ashcroft fell gravely ill, was rushed to George Washington University Hospital for emergency surgery to remove his gallbladder, and was placed in intensive care suffering from pancreatitis. Comey became acting attorney general and told the White House and other agencies that "I would not certify the program as to its legality and explained our reasoning in detail." He made his views clear at a March 9 White House meeting that included Cheney and David Addington, now Cheney's chief of staff, who pushed hard during his tenure for expansive executive power.[66] This set in motion an extraordinary attempt by the White House to circumvent the Justice Department.

As Comey was being driven home by his security detail along Constitution Avenue about 8 p.m. on March 10, 2004, the night before the periodic authorization expired, a call came from Ashcroft's chief of staff, David Ayres. He had been phoned from the hospital by Ashcroft's wife, Janet, who was also a lawyer, to say that she had fielded a call to her husband from President Bush and White House Chief of Staff Andrew Card. "She had banned all visitors and all phone calls," Comey noted, but the president was dispatching Card and White House Counsel Alberto Gonzales to see Ashcroft.

Comey ordered his security detail to rush him to the hospital, where he and his men ran up the stairs and into Ashcroft's darkened room. Card and Gonzales had not yet arrived, so Comey called the FBI director, Robert Mueller, who was also on his way, to make a precautionary request: that he order an FBI detail guarding Ashcroft to prevent the White House officials from removing Comey from the room during the coming confrontation. Comey was joined at the hospital by Goldsmith, whose doubts about the program's legality had provoked the review, and another staff member, Patrick Philbin, an archconservative who had helped in the assessment.

When Card and Gonzales entered, carrying the authorization they wanted signed, Ashcroft rallied long enough to rebuff them. "He lifted his head off the pillow," said Comey, "and in very strong terms expressed his view of the matter, rich in both substance and fact, which stunned me—drawn from the hour-long meeting we'd had a week earlier—and in very strong terms expressed himself, and then laid his head back down on the pillow, seemed spent, and said to them, 'But that doesn't matter, because I'm not the attorney general. . . . There is the attorney general,' and he pointed to me, and I was just to his left."

Card and Gonzales "did not acknowledge me," Comey said. "They turned and walked from the room." Then summoned to a late-night White House meeting, Comey told Card and Gonzales that there was no legal basis for the surveillance. Yet the next day, Bush extended the program over the Justice Department's disapproval, triggering threats from Ashcroft, Comey, and other senior officials to resign en masse.[67] Mueller, the FBI director, drafted a letter saying he was ready to "withdraw the FBI from participation in the program" and resign.[68] The rule of law was being tested at the highest level.

Faced with such a high-profile protest, Bush then called Comey aside after a routine counterterrorism briefing on March 12, spoke with him alone for fifteen minutes for "a very full exchange" of views, then met alone with Mueller, who "carried to me the president's direction that we do what the Department of Justice wanted done to put this on a sound legal footing," Comey said. "And then we set about—I don't remember exactly how long it was—over the next few weeks making changes so that it accorded with our judgment about what could be certified as to legality."

Intelligence officials told Eric Lichtblau vaguely that the NSA was ordered to shut down certain unspecified techniques using "data-mining to trace communications patterns across U.S. borders," and that a twenty-item checklist was developed to assess whether a person could legitimately be designated for eavesdropping.[69] Whatever these mysterious changes, they satisfied Comey enough to get his signature on the reauthorization, and he remained in office nearly a year and a half longer. However, Cheney blocked Philbin's promotion to deputy solicitor general,[70] despite Philbin's extremely conservative credentials: He had clerked for the right-wing federal appeals court judge Laurence Silberman and had written two legal opinions later overturned by the Supreme Court, one supporting the president's "inherent authority" to establish military commissions without congressional statute, the other arguing that Guantánamo Bay prisoners had no habeas corpus rights in federal courts.[71]

How was the surveillance revised? Speculation within Washington legal circles took two paths: Either Comey was a stickler for detail and had drawn some internal procedural line that previously had been crossed, or the monitoring had been aimed at purely domestic communications, probably wholesale interception of e-mails inside the United States as well as those involving at least one party overseas.

In any event, the change that erased Comey's objections did not satisfy one of the FISA judges, James Robertson, who quietly resigned from his FISA responsibilities more than a year later, after the *Times* broke the story about the surveillance. Only the two judges who had presided over the Foreign Intelligence Surveillance Court during the period had been briefed by administration officials on the spying; most of the others hadn't known a thing about it.[72]

Robertson, a federal district court judge in Washington, D.C., pointed to two concerns: First, he did not want to be part of a system in which the executive branch could either choose or reject judicial oversight according to the president's fancy; the Constitution did not make going to court optional. Second, Robertson felt he could not intelligently decide whether FISA warrant applications had sufficient probable cause if he didn't know the source or the reliability of the information; he and other judges were afraid that some applications might be tainted by having originated in the warrantless NSA monitoring. The presiding judge in 2004, Colleen Kollar-Kotelly, complained about just that, according to the *Times,* worrying that in using information collected secretly by the NSA, the government may have misled the court about its sources in warrant requests. The administration had even concealed the NSA as the origin of intelligence information distributed to the CIA and the FBI, James Risen reported.[73]

Judge Robertson, whom Clinton had appointed in 1994, had joined the FISA court as a dubious volunteer. "I was skeptical of the whole FISA process. I wanted to see how it went on," he said. And until the disclosure of the NSA surveillance, "I thought the FISA process had a lot of integrity. People took it very seriously." The Justice Department "had careful, dedicated, patriotic people. I felt good about the process. It had a lot of integrity."

But it also had a lot of paperwork, he conceded, which may have made it an undesirable route for investigators, especially those in a hurry. "I think there's some merit in that argument that FISA warrants have become too cumbersome," he said. "The procedure could be leaner." That was the view of senior intelligence officials, who regarded the process as "too cumbersome and time consuming to address the current threat," according to the report by the five agencies' inspectors general. "CIA officials stated that FISA required extensive paperwork and high-level reviews and approvals," and complained that the FISA court "did not always approve FISA applications in a timely manner."[74]

This seemed a product of the court's reluctance to turn down requests—official records show hardly any rejections: Only 2 of 13,102 applications were modified in the first twenty-two years of the secret court's existence; more were later, but still just 179 of 5,645 in 2003 and 2004, with at least 6 rejected. Subsequent years showed similar patterns: 86 of 2,370 applications modified in 2007, for example, but just 3 denied, and in 2008 just 1 rejection out of 2,095.[75] Instead, judges apparently increased demands on applicants. "Over twenty, thirty years, as the court wasn't comfortable with something, instead of saying no, they asked for more information," said Stewart Baker, assistant secretary for policy at the Department of Homeland Security. Each application grew from a couple of pages until the thickness of "the paperwork required to get a FISA order now measures in inches."

But that seemed sensible to Royce Lamberth, presiding judge of the FISA court from 1995 to 2002. "The judges have been approving these surveillances because, really, they're so well scrubbed by the time the court sees them," he told the American Library Association in 2007. "They are the kinds of things we ought to be doing for the good of our nation. They are the kinds of surveillances that are needed. You would expect if the government is doing its job right, we should be approving what they're doing. . . . I have not seen any proposal for a better way of doing it. I have seen a worse way, and that's what the president has been doing with the NSA program."

The courts should have oversight, he argued. "There's nothing wrong with letting the judges take a peek," he said. "We're only taking a peek, but we're making sure there's not some political shenanigans going on or some improper motive for the surveillance, but some valid purpose for it. Whether we're approving ninety-nine percent or not, the fact they have to submit them to us makes them honest."[76]

The approval system doesn't have to move slowly, as Lamberth's experience demonstrated. Even before the urgency following 9/11, Lamberth got calls in the middle of the night to sign orders. First a Justice Department lawyer and an agent—usually from the FBI but sometimes from the NSA or the CIA—would stop by the attorney general's house to get a signature, then proceed to Lamberth's home, where gaps that the judge might discern could be filled. "The agent's before me," Lamberth noted. "I can question the agent. I can read their tone. I can ask any question I want to ask, can modify anything, swear the agent first so they're under oath. Then I rule. Almost always if I wanted more information, the agent had it."

When two American embassies were bombed in Africa, Lamberth recalled, "We were pretty sure it was bin Laden from the beginning. We had five targets the FBI wanted to go up on that night. They reached my house at three o'clock in the morning, I signed the warrants for those applications. Those five wiretaps turned out to be very productive. One of them was bin Laden's secretary, who was a car tire dealer in Texas—Arlington, Texas. He later went to trial in New York and was tried and convicted."[77]

An emergency order was sought in 1999, when a would-be terrorist, Ahmed Ressam, was stopped by Customs as he drove from Canada into Washington State with a plan to attack the Los Angeles airport at the beginning of the new millennium. In his wallet agents found a scrap of paper with a phone number. "The FBI came to me the same night for a warrant for that number," Lamberth said. "I gave it to them. It led to an apartment in New York, and a tap on that apartment led to a cell in Montreal. . . . That's the kind of little thing that can lead to a real intelligence coup, and that was a real intelligence coup."

Knowing that flurries of e-mail typically follow an attack, intelligence officials have to move quickly to pick up the traffic. That's what they did on September 11, 2001.

Lamberth was driving that morning from the dentist to the federal courthouse to preside over an ongoing murder trial. He was near the Pentagon when the plane hit, enveloping his car in smoke. He couldn't move. Federal marshals couldn't reach him. But he had his cell phone, and he and other judges "started approving FISA coverages on everybody we could dream up who might know anything," he said. "By the time the FBI got to me in my car, I had already approved five FISA coverages that morning. It was quite a day. By the time I went home that night, we had every hijacker identified." And that was done according to law through the FISA court, before the new powers of the Patriot Act. "The courts can respond in times of emergency," Lamberth declared, "and we did, we have."

Yet the Bush administration thought otherwise and stretched quite far to reach legal justifications for using NSA surveillance to evade FISA judges. Perhaps mirroring John Yoo's classified memo, administration lawyers fell back, first, on an old constitutional argument used prior to FISA's enactment: that Article II, Section 2, designating the president as commander in chief, gave him "inherent authority," in the Justice Department's words, "to conduct warrantless surveillance of enemy forces for intelligence purposes to detect and disrupt armed attacks on the United States."[78] The concept was endorsed almost verbatim by the three-judge Foreign Intelligence Surveillance Court of Review, which had never sat until November 2002, when its initial ruling cited "the president's inherent constitutional authority to conduct warrantless foreign intelligence surveillance."

Second, the administration relied on the Authorization for Use of Military Force, passed by Congress one week after 9/11, which permitted the president to "use all necessary and appropriate force against those nations, organizations, or persons he determines planned, authorized, committed or aided the terrorist attacks."[79] Officials observed that electronic intercepts, known in the business as "signals intelligence," were fundamental to conducting any war.

The Justice Department claimed that this combination of constitutional and congressional authorities put the president at "the zenith of his powers" according to the formula devised by Justice Robert Jackson in 1952. But it seemed a perverse argument, since Jackson was going the opposite way, against expansive presidential authority. He was concurring in the Supreme Court's rejection of President Truman's attempt during the Korean War to seize the nation's steel mills on the eve of a planned strike.[80] No congressional authorization existed for such seizure, Jackson found, only three statutes on taking private property that were not cited by Truman and contradicted his actions. "When the President takes measures incompatible with the expressed or implied will of Congress," Jackson wrote, "his power is at its lowest ebb, for then he can rely only upon his own constitutional powers minus any constitutional powers of Congress over the matter."

And those were the precise circumstances of the NSA surveillance, argued fourteen eminent constitutional scholars—"circumstances," quoting Jackson's words, "which leave presidential power most vulnerable to attack and in the least favorable of possible constitutional postures." Far from authorizing warrantless domestic eavesdropping, the scholars said in an open letter, Congress had explicitly banned it when passing FISA in 1978.[81] "In the years before FISA was enacted," they wrote,

> the federal law involving wiretapping specifically provided that "nothing contained in this chapter or in section 605 of the Communications Act of 1934 shall limit the constitutional power of the President . . . to obtain foreign intelligence information deemed essential to the security of the United States."[82] But FISA specifically repealed that provision and replaced it with language dictating that FISA and the criminal code are the "exclusive means" of conducting electronic surveillance.[83] In doing so, Congress did not deny that the President has constitutional power to conduct electronic surveillance for national security purposes; rather, Congress properly concluded that "even if the President has the inherent authority in the absence of legislation to authorize warrantless electronic surveillance for foreign intelligence purposes, Congress has the power to regulate the conduct of such surveillance by legislating a reasonable procedure, which then becomes the exclusive means by which such surveillance may be conducted." . . . [Since 1967] the Supreme Court has never upheld warrantless wiretapping within the United States.

As a general principle, the scholars noted, constitutional authority can be regulated by Congress, as it had done in FISA, which "specifically allows for warrantless wartime domestic electronic surveillance—but only for the first fifteen days of a war."[84]

Bush sought neither judicial review nor a change in the law until the secret surveillance program was exposed by the *Times*. Then, in January 2007, faced with the possibility of congressional action, he volunteered to get blanket authorizations from the FISA court for the NSA eavesdropping. How that worked—whether the court required particular and targeted surveillance or permitted broad sweeps for long periods—was kept secret. But Attorney General Alberto Gonzales indicated that a general authorization was provided, writing that "on January 10, 2007, a Judge of the Foreign Intelligence Surveillance Court issued orders authorizing the Government to target for collection international communications into or out of the United States where there is probable cause to believe that one of the communicants is a member or agent of al Qaeda or an associated terrorist organization."[85] The court reportedly narrowed its authorization that spring.

That dissatisfied intelligence gatherers, who wanted carte blanche to avoid the FISA court when both parties were abroad, even if their conversations or messages passed through the United States. The issue arose because of a change in technology. A great deal of the global communications traffic among foreign countries is relayed by equipment in the United States, where FISA applies.

Mike McConnell, the director of national intelligence, stood at a map and demonstrated the problem for Lawrence Wright of *The New Yorker*:

> "Terrorist on a cell phone, right here"—he pointed at Iraq—"talking to a tower, happens all the time, no warrant. Tower goes up to a microwave tower, no warrant. Goes up to a satellite, back to the ground station, no warrant. Now, let us suppose that it goes up to a satellite, and in the process it does this"—his finger darted to the U.S. before angling back to Pakistan. "Gotta have a warrant! So it was crazy."[86]

So, the White House proposed revising FISA to legalize its own evasion—and essentially won. First it got the Protect America Act to remove protections by sanctioning the warrantless surveillance from August 2007 to February 2008.[87] Then the shock and outrage that had erupted in Congress over the program evaporated in the hot political summer of 2008, when most candidates (Barack Obama included) were unwilling to be demonized as soft on terrorism, and few Americans agitated on behalf of personal privacy. The Democratic-led Congress severely undermined FISA by passing amendments containing the thinnest possible oversight by the FISA court. Bush was understandably delighted, declaring at the signing ceremony, "The bill will allow our intelligence professionals to quickly and effectively monitor the communications of terrorists abroad while respecting the liberties of Americans here at home."[88] The law had no requirement that the monitoring be limited to terrorists, however, and Americans at home had a good deal to worry about.

Public discussion was fixated on a provision immunizing the telecommunications companies retroactively from lawsuits for violating customers' privacy. The firms' only legal motive to guard personal information is now gone. But far more significant is the virtual free hand given the government to collect and monitor communications that appear international (but might be domestic) without individualized warrants meeting any of the Fourth Amendment's key requirements. As long as the targets are "reasonably believed" to be outside the country and not "United

States persons" (American citizens and "aliens lawfully admitted for permanent residence"), the FISA court is required to approve eavesdropping applications containing minimal information. No particular individuals, groups, phone numbers, e-mail addresses, or other limiting details have to be specified, and no probable cause has to be shown that the targets are foreign agents, criminal suspects, or associates of terrorist organizations. The rationale for monitoring is broad and vague, merely "to acquire foreign intelligence information," which can include not just classified military matters but anything that might interest journalists, scholars, or human rights advocates about a country's political, economic, legal, and cultural issues.

Taken together, all of the loose requirements allow "mass acquisition orders" that can sweep up communications, albeit inadvertently, from Americans inside and outside the United States. The law says only that the government "may not intentionally target" such parties. If it accidentally does so, or if the parties on U.S. soil are not the true targets but only ancillary to the focus of the surveillance, no more demanding FISA warrant is required. And the FISA court has a role only at the outset, with no continuing oversight to make sure the surveillance ceases, as the law requires, if a U.S. person or anyone inside the country turns up in the communications.

The court's power is further undermined by a provision allowing emergency eavesdropping without a court order for up to seven days before going to the judges; if it's denied on procedural or even constitutional grounds, or in the unlikely event that a telecom company appeals, the surveillance "may continue" until the appeal is exhausted, which could take years. (The target does not know that he's being monitored, of course, so has no opportunity to file a challenge.) Nor does the law authorize the court to enforce the statute's so-called minimization procedures, which are vague restrictions on the dissemination of information and could lead to the storage of vast databases for later use against law-abiding people whose communications happen to be swept up in the net.[89]

Indeed, it's hard to see how any of the mild limitations are truly enforceable, given that nobody can seriously watch what the NSA and other agencies are doing. Congress has given them the power to snoop pretty much as they see fit. The five inspectors general concluded that the 2008 law "gave the government even broader authority to intercept international communications" than the "Terrorist Surveillance Program" that Bush had secretly launched in 2001.[90]

If lawmakers had intended to be satirical, they couldn't have done better than the provision that the surveillance "shall be conducted in a manner consistent with the Fourth Amendment to the Constitution of the United States."[91] There is practically nothing in the statute consistent with the Fourth Amendment's requirements for probable cause, particularity, and individualized warrants.

Secret government behavior is like black ice: You can't see it, and it's hard to get enough traction to fight it. It's impossible to find anyone who knows he's being monitored. Therefore, while a group of organizations, scholars, and writers who communicate frequently overseas won in federal district court against the warrantless surveillance program before it was codified in law,[92] a panel of the Sixth Circuit ruled two to one that they had no standing to sue, because they couldn't prove that they were targets of eavesdropping.[93] You don't get to file a lawsuit unless you've been harmed, and if the government prevents you from knowing that you've been injured, too bad.

Undaunted, however, a collection of lawyers, writers, and human rights organizations represented by the ACLU challenged the 2008 FISA amendment, arguing that they could not effectively gather information from persecuted dissidents, abused women, tortured inmates, and others overseas who would assume and fear that their e-mails were being read, that their phone calls were being heard, and that they could suffer as a result. Human Rights Watch, Amnesty International, and others predicted that the law would require employees "to travel long distances to collect information . . . and in some circumstances to forgo particularly sensitive communications altogether." A federal judge dismissed it on the same grounds—no standing, since they couldn't show that they'd been under surveillance.[94]

At least Bush found something to laugh about. "Half the time they say I'm isolated and don't listen," he remarked. "Then when I do listen, they say I need a warrant."[95]

A bumper sticker countered:

**BUSH IS LISTENING
USE BIG WORDS.**

CHAPTER SEVEN

The Right to Be Let Alone

I have here in my hand a list . . .

—Senator Joseph McCarthy

THE POETRY OF PRIVACY

NOBODY KNOWS WHERE we are. Our sailboat is anchored near the shore of a Maine island, in a quiet cove disconnected from the technological world. Our cell phones pick up no signal here, so their location cannot be traced. I can write on this computer, but the Internet is inaccessible, so I can't be monitored sending e-mails or visiting Web sites. Our ATM and credit cards are useless in this pristine place, so they generate no "transactional data," in the jargon of police intelligence. No security cameras survey this rough coast of granite and spruce. My wife, Debby, and I are happily invisible.

We aren't trying to hide, just basking in our natural privacy. Here, we are the sole owners of our seclusion and our freedom, setting our courses and choosing our harbors subject only to our whim and the wind. Nobody can watch us.

As pure and genuine as this feels, it is uncommon to the twenty-first century. We have vanished from the screen, leaving no electronic trails—but only in the present and just for a while. Our past has been intricately recorded, and the moment we reenter the ordinary world—the moment we make a call, send an e-mail, pay a bill, withdraw some cash, book a plane ticket, drive through a toll booth, enter a hotel room with a key card, even walk into certain buildings—we are back in view, and the government can see us if it wishes.

The Supreme Court seems to think that we have a choice about this reentry, that living a normal life is optional, that whenever we punch in a phone number or send a check or use a piece of plastic in our wallets, we give bits of personal data away willingly, not by necessity. In doing so, by the justices' reasoning, we voluntarily relinquish our Fourth Amendment right to keep information about ourselves secure. The contents of domestic communications by e-mail and phone still require warrants to obtain, but the addressees and subject lines of e-mails, and the numbers we call, are easily accessible without judicial oversight. In other words, the Court has ruled that phoning, traveling, banking, and other everyday activities are purely elective, for which we freely discard a constitutional protection.

The Court has always been slow to catch up with technology. Not until 1967, more than half a century after the first transcontinental telephone line was strung, did the justices protect phone conversations by finding warrantless wiretaps unconstitutional. Their ruling reversed an antediluvian opinion that had stood since 1928, when the Court decided in *Olmstead v. United States* that it was OK for agents to tap bootleggers' phones without warrants, because their voices were transmitted outdoors where no search or seizure could occur, and therefore no violation of the Fourth Amendment could be committed. "The language of the amendment cannot be extended and expanded to include telephone wires, reaching to the whole world from the defendant's house or office," the majority wrote. "The intervening wires are not part of his house or office, any more than are the highways along which they are stretched."[1] This was known as the trespass theory of the Fourth Amendment, which saw no infringement unless agents entered private property uninvited.

That old-fashioned view wasn't erased until *Katz v. United States* in 1967, when the Court devised a new test to determine the Fourth Amendment's jurisdiction—"first that a person have exhibited an actual (subjective) expectation of privacy and, second, that the expectation be one that society is prepared to recognize as 'reasonable.'"[2]

Our expectation of privacy has now plummeted. Especially since September 11, 2001, we have submitted our personal space to routine invasions. We have grown so numb to the indignities of airport searches that we shamelessly whip off our belts and jackets and shoes, allow strangers to pat our bodies and paw through our toiletries, flash picture IDs at the least provocation, and even parade through a growing number of scanners that render us naked on-screen. Protests by angry travelers have fizzled; helplessness prevails. "I'm thinking of starting my own airline, which would be called: Naked Air," the columnist Thomas L. Friedman wrote in December 2001. "Its motto would be: 'Everybody flies naked and nobody worries.' Or 'Naked Air—where the only thing you wear is a seat belt.'"[3]

As a real-life alternative, more than 260,000 travelers eagerly acquiesced to government background checks, fingerprinting, and iris scans (and paid about $200 a year) just to get into express lanes and save a few minutes at airport security with the Clear card from Verified Identity Pass—before the company suddenly went out of business.[4]

Where the Fourth Amendment still applies—as in personal searches—authorities extract preemptive consent in exchange for entry, not only at airports and courthouses but even on Maine State ferries, which have been adorned with signs reading, "Boarding This Vessel Is Deemed Valid Consent to Screening or Inspection" and "All Persons and Vehicles Aboard This Vessel Are Subject to Electronic Monitoring/Surveillance." Searches are not actually done on the ferries, but closed-circuit television cameras, known as CCTV, sweep the little island terminals, which are now garishly lit at night like shopping malls before Christmas. On board, cameras give the captain and crew in the wheelhouse views of the passenger cabins below—a bizarre convenience one winter's day on the boat between Swan's Island and Bass Harbor. With the heat in a cabin too low, shivering high school students held a handwritten complaint up to the camera. The engineer soon appeared; he couldn't read the writing on the screen and wondered what it said. We're cold! the kids declared, and so they got some warmth. Being watched is sometimes useful.

Americans (and not only Americans, of course) are induced constantly to expose themselves to monitoring. They welcome "cookies" into their computers for the convenience of being recognized and catalogued by marketers, they reveal their mothers' maiden names and their Social Security numbers to anonymous customer-service agents in Bangalore, and they seem entirely comfortable in the ubiquitous lenses of camera phones and security cameras. In a kind of mass exhibitionism, many put intimate videos and information on YouTube and Facebook and MySpace for the world to see, place webcams in their bedrooms for streaming online, and tweet constantly on Twitter about the mundane things they're doing.

At some level, the violation of privacy is a thrill—gee, they know what I want to buy and eat and see and read! Outside attention seems akin to fame, and it appeals to a lot of people, whether the noble cause is consumerism or national security. After all, if they're watching a good guy like me, they're surely watching the bad guys, too. I *feel* safer. "To keep our national defense up," wrote William Safire, "we have let our personal defenses down."

So irresistible are banking and shopping online, so enticing is the ease of e-mail, that hardly anyone now is careful to keep personal and sensitive information out of the digital universe, where it can be hacked and read and saved indefinitely. Incautious embezzlers, fraudsters, and inside traders send and retain self-incriminating e-mails, oblivious to their ready accessibility by government agencies trolling for evidence.

Yet against this nonchalance runs a current of discomfort. Government snooping draws complaints in blogs and chat rooms and dining rooms. Some citizens begin to act as if someone is listening or looking in, and they take precautions. Reporters use disposable cell phones to avoid exposing anonymous sources in case calling records are secretly obtained. A producer doing a television documentary on circumcision hesitates to type the word into Google because it links to pictures of naked children, "and that can be misconstrued," he tells *The New York Times*. A telecommunications engineer worries that her interest in Palestinian issues will spark interest from "someone in my government [who] would someday see my name on a list of people who went to 'terrorist' web sites."[5] A scientist friend of mine uses euphemisms in e-mails to colleagues and avoids words he imagines might trigger a data-mining program.

And a fog of fear creeps into the lives of some who feel especially vulnerable. Following a minor car accident a few years after 9/11, a naturalized U.S. citizen who had been raised in Pakistan pleaded desperately with his American-born wife not to make an insurance claim, lest he end up in some database with vague, unwelcome consequences. Some Americans now think twice before donating to Muslim charities.

Employees would be also advised to think twice when sending text messages from their workplace pagers, even when they work for government agencies, which are subject to the Fourth Amendment. A California police officer, Jeff Quon, was disciplined after sexually explicit texts were discovered in his account. He sued, challenging his employer's right to read his messages. The police department, which had a contract with a private firm setting a ceiling on the number of characters per month, was doing an audit to see whether pagers that exceeded the limit were being used for professional or personal messages. In 2010, the Supreme Court, in *City of Ontario v. Quon,* found the search "reasonable" under the Fourth Amendment, since it was not investigatory but done for a work-related purpose, and "was not excessive in scope."[6]

The concept of privacy may or may not be in the Constitution. The word is never mentioned, as conservatives accurately observe, the principle never explicitly articulated. Yet liberal and moderate judges see privacy woven implicitly into the First Amendment's guarantee of the rights to worship, speak, and assemble, and into the Fourth Amendment's defense of "per-

sons, houses, papers, and effects against unreasonable searches and seizures." What do these limits defend, if not the private zone of individual
life and action? *Griswold v. Connecticut,* which struck down bans on con-
traception, and *Roe v. Wade,* which overturned prohibitions on abortion,
found that privacy was mixed into the mortar of the Constitution.[7]

In 1928, when the Court approved the warrantless tapping of telephones in *Olmstead v. United States,* Justice Louis Brandeis coined a
famous phrase in his dissent. "The makers of our Constitution undertook
to secure conditions favorable to the pursuit of happiness," he wrote.

> They recognized the significance of man's spiritual nature, of his feel-
> ings, and of his intellect. They knew that only a part of the pain, plea-
> sure and satisfactions of life are to be found in material things. They
> sought to protect Americans in their beliefs, their thoughts, their emo-
> tions and their sensations. They conferred, as against the government,
> *the right to be let alone*—the most comprehensive of rights and the
> right most valued by civilized men. To protect that right, every unjusti-
> fiable intrusion by the government upon the privacy of the individual,
> whatever the means employed, must be deemed a violation of the
> Fourth Amendment.[8]

The right to be let alone has intrinsic worth, difficult to define and
explain and justify in a policy debate, especially today in a time of terrorism. Its virtue cannot be measured by pragmatic rationales, its purpose
cannot be calculated with any precision. Privacy is like a poem, a painting, a piece of music. It is precious in itself.

Government snooping destroys the inherent poetry of privacy, leaving
in its absence the artless potential for oppression. At the least, if the collected information is merely filed away for safekeeping, a weapon is placed
in the hands of the state. If it is utilized, acute consequences may damage
personal lives. Even where government is benign and well-meaning—a
novelty that neither James Madison nor Tom Paine imagined—the use
of everyday information about someone's past to predict his behavior can
lead to obtrusive mistakes known in the jargon as "false positives." Worse,
the power of surveillance tempts the executive branch to aim at political opponents or "others" who seem "unpatriotic." This is especially so
when courts and legislatures retreat and fail to check and balance, for the
vacuum they leave will be filled by expanding executive authority.

Those who trust the state make this standard argument: If you're
doing nothing wrong, you have no reason to worry about being bugged. "I

love comments like this," wrote "Andrew" in an online posting about an ABC story on tapping cell phones. "What happens when they decide the websites you view are 'wrong' or the books you read are 'wrong'?" Or, in states with laws against certain sexual activity, another reader suggested, why not accept a policeman in your bedroom, since you're not doing anything "wrong"?[9]

If you think you're being constantly watched, you may behave differently, for better or worse—better if you hesitate to shoplift because you're on camera, worse if the spying steals your political fearlessness.

Yet the deterrent effect is not always dramatic. England, which tried to curtail Irish terrorism by saturating itself with CCTV during the 1990s, saw crime fall only slightly in some areas, 2 to 6 percent,[10] a drop possibly caused by other variables, including declining unemployment and shifting police tactics. Ever-hopeful officials think the statistics may be improved by cameras with loudspeakers so operators who spot wrongdoing can scold miscreants at high volume. Meanwhile, some misdeeds merely move out of view, as prostitution did in Hull, England, when twenty-seven cameras were installed at a housing project. Prostitutes actually felt safer, the legal writer Jeffrey Rosen reports, but their clients were scared off, "especially after the police recorded their license numbers, banged on their doors, and threatened to publish their names in the newspapers." The hookers went inside or moved to the city's red-light district.[11]

It's boring to gaze perpetually at routine street scenes, so CCTV operators relieve the monotony with voyeurism. Rosen watched the watchers in Hull for three hours and noticed that they zoomed in on good-looking women or spied on couples making out in cars. "'She had her legs wrapped around his waist a minute ago,' one of the operators said appreciatively as we watched two teenagers go at it."[12] Privacy advocates in the United States have proposed that CCTV recordings be made available to law enforcement only with a search warrant.

In the eternal confidence that technology will outperform humans, software developers are coming up with programs to recognize both certain behavior and certain faces. The Modular Integrated Pedestrian Surveillance Architecture System sets off alarms if a camera detects unusual motion as in people fighting, someone loitering, a person repeatedly walking past the same spot, or a bag left unattended—in which case the file can be rewound to see who put it there.

FaceIt matches a face on camera with one in a database, often erroneously at this stage of technological skill. It was used on tens of thousands of fans entering the 2001 Super Bowl in Tampa and spotted nineteen people who supposedly resembled those with outstanding warrants, but for only minor offenses. The accuracy was never checked, because officers couldn't find any of the nineteen after they melted into the crowds. The police then installed the network in Tampa's nightlife district, Ybor City, where it was defended as a more efficient version of a cop standing on a corner with a mug shot. For two years, it spit out false positives, mixed up men and women, and failed to lead to a single arrest, so it was finally abandoned. There's nothing quite like a cop holding a mug shot after all.[13]

Not only sights but also sounds are being fed into police computers, with more accurate results. ShotSpotter, a system installed in a few American cities, can determine a gunshot's location within ten to twenty feet by triangulating the noise received by sensors the size of coffee cans, which are concealed atop buildings in high-crime areas. (Gang members get it: They fired at technicians placing microphones in Los Angeles and Oakland.)[14]

At Washington, D.C.'s Joint Operations Command, a darkened room on the fifth floor of police headquarters, walls covered with huge screens depict jerky scenes from major streets and Metro stations, maps, TV news channels, and lists of recent crimes constantly updated. Here, in comfortable swivel chairs at computer consoles, officers monitor neighborhoods whose residents hear so much gunplay that they're too jaded to bother calling 911—or, if they do, can't pinpoint the location. Originally designed to monitor earthquakes, the acoustic software can distinguish between a car backfiring and a gun firing, says the center's commander, Captain Victor Brito, who insists that the microphones are designed to pick up only loud bangs, not conversations. The explosive noise rings out in the command center, a location flashes onto the map, and a street address appears on the computer screen. In several instances, police have been dispatched without a 911 call, or long before, to arrive quickly enough to find the gun or to arrest a fleeing suspect, as officers were able to do in the murder of a landscaper in October 2006. The FBI is paying for the system.

Better yet, while the police watch the public, the public watches them. In Gadsden, Alabama, cops were beating prisoners in an elevator that took them from courtrooms to jail cells, City Councilman Robert Avery told me, until he got closed-circuit cameras installed in the elevator and cellblock. The abuse rate plummeted.

In Washington, D.C., one Friday afternoon, as the men and women of a narcotics squad began a briefing on search warrants they were about to execute, Sergeant J. J. Brennan warned them about monitoring.

Businesses' video and audio surveillance are widespread, he cautioned: Officers in the Fifth District had just been suspended after videotapes showed their brutality against a man they'd chased into a liquor store. "Stores have cameras, some have cameras outside," Brennan said as his squad sat around a long table. "I'd hate to see one of you guys spend a year or two in noncontact status. You got to be stern, but be careful how stern you are." He reminded them that comments they made to each other could seem, in a recording, to have been made to a civilian, and a joke may not sound funny on tape. The men and women of his unit, who had been joking around with one another as usual, fell silent.

THE TYRANNY OF TECHNOLOGY

For several years, the Bush administration's Department of Homeland Security used images of American territory from the Pentagon's spy satellites for domestic security and law enforcement. President Obama ended the practice,[15] but it could be resumed in a flash, and the near future promises other ways to peer into citizens' backyards. Defense Department researchers are miniaturizing aerial drones, reportedly getting them down to the size of a bird. After antiwar protesters got suspicious about oversized dragonflies hovering around street demonstrations, *The Washington Post* dug up information on Pentagon-funded experiments aimed at implanting electronics in live moths to control their flight and turn them into perfectly camouflaged surveillance machines.[16]

It might seem paranoid to imagine dragonflies photographing your demonstrations, but since we live with one foot in the realm of science fiction, what seems far-fetched today can be routine next month. A private company has announced the development of an infrared sensor that can detect human skin, to be directed at cars in H.O.V. lanes to make sure they have the requisite number of passengers. A Massachusetts firm manufactures backscatter X-ray units, so-called "naked scanners," mounted in vans to cruise streets and ports to locate explosives and humans inside buildings and containers. Georgia Tech has developed flashlight-sized radar that can detect heartbeats at a distance and human respiration through walls to help police locate fugitives in closets and people in hostage situations.[17] Similarly, to select passengers for secondary screening at airports, the Future Attribute Screening Technology (FAST) is being designed to do remote measurements of stress indicators: respiration, eye movement, heart rate, skin temperature, body language, and voice quality.[18] From the sound of this, if you're nervous about being late for your flight, be prepared to miss it as you get pulled off for additional scrutiny.

RFIDs, or radio-frequency identification devices, are growing in use—in passports, in E-ZPass transponders, on cartons of goods—so that a radio wave beamed at one triggers a unique signature identifying the owner. Unfortunately, hackers can also skim personal data as they pass by. GPS receivers, employing the Pentagon's Global Positioning System of navigation satellites, are now ubiquitous—in cell phones, planes, boats, and cars. Using microchips to compute minuscule time delays from satellite signals, GPS calculates your latitude and longitude within a few yards, and if coupled with transmitters, can send your position to the watchers. Distrustful parents track their children around town by watching blips on computer maps, receiving text messages if kids venture outside an invisible boundary. Emergency operators pinpoint your location when you call 911 with a properly fitted cell phone. Company executives watch you travel in a company car. For a monthly fee, General Motors offers the OnStar system to find your vehicle if it's stolen and find you if you break down. And if I want to be found on my boat—if I'm in danger—I can press a red button on my VHF radio, which is wired to my GPS, and transmit my position and identification to the Coast Guard.

If I don't want to be found, though, I'd better turn off my cell phone. Without a showing of probable cause, federal magistrate judges have approved numerous government applications for orders to track cell-phone locations in real time, which can fix a person's whereabouts within thirty feet if his phone has GPS, or if not, within larger areas based on which cell tower his phone is using. Even when a call is not being made, a cell phone scans for the best reception every seven seconds, and wireless companies can tell which aspect of which tower faces the phone, triangulating the position if multiple towers are being used, as is common in urban areas. The accuracy is improving, because under the FCC's Enhanced 911 order of 1997, companies must be able to locate 95 percent of cell phones within three hundred meters.[19]

To get these approvals, the government has persuaded a lot of judges—but not all—that something less than probable cause is adequate. Since location is not content, which requires an ordinary warrant, most judges have accepted the argument that a lesser standard is allowed: "reasonable grounds to believe" that the information is "relevant and material to an ongoing criminal investigation."[20] The language comes from the Stored Communications Act, which allows the release of "information pertaining to a subscriber" but makes no mention of cell-phone locations. Nor does another law the government cites as its authority, the Pen/Trap Statute, which permits the installation of devices to register the phone numbers of outgoing and incoming calls.[21]

Beginning in 2005, magistrate judges, who usually decide on issuing federal search warrants, began rejecting the applications, noting that Congress had not explicitly legislated on tracking cell phones, and that while past locations might be accessible under the Stored Communications Act, real-time movements were not. "Surely if these various statutory provisions were intended to give birth to a new breed of electronic surveillance, one would expect Congress to have openly acknowledged paternity somewhere along the way," wrote Magistrate Judge Stephen Wm. Smith.[22] Some judges differentiate between tracking in public places, where the Fourth Amendment is not implicated, and inside private homes, where it applies. But of course, "the government cannot guarantee the cell phone and its possessor will remain in a public place," noted a federal judge in Maryland,[23] one of at least seventeen judges who had denied the requests through 2007.[24]

The Justice Department doesn't usually bother to appeal these rejections. It either submits an affidavit asserting probable cause and gets the order, as it did after the Maryland judge turned down the initial request, or it simply proceeds with other applications before other judges in other cases, and usually it succeeds.

In New York, where it lost an attempt before one judge, it later won a ruling by another, Magistrate Judge Gabriel W. Gorenstein, that looked a lot like the Supreme Court's reasoning in exempting, from Fourth Amendment protection, checks written, phone numbers dialed, and other data "voluntarily" provided to third parties. "The individual has chosen to carry a device and to permit transmission of its information to a third party, the carrier," Gorenstein declared.[25]

But what if you don't know that you're being tracked? Police who have secretly installed GPS devices underneath suspects' cars, providing people's locations every minute for weeks or months, have faced mixed reactions in the courts. Some federal judges have seen nothing different in this technique from using old-fashioned tails, in which cops follow in vehicles or on foot—and do not need a warrant to do so. The Fourth Amendment "cannot sensibly be read to mean that police shall be no more efficient in the 21st century than they were in the 18th," wrote Judge Richard Posner in a 2007 case. Other judges have taken note of the constancy of the GPS device, however, worrying that the nonstop recording of a person's movements creates a picture much more comprehensive than the fragmentary snapshots available from other methods. Therefore, police should have to show probable cause and obtain a search warrant. In throwing out a drug conviction in D.C., an appeals court panel found in 2010 that the sheer quantity of the GPS surveillance transformed it. "A person who knows all of another's travels," the judges declared, "can deduce whether he is a weekly churchgoer, a heavy drinker, a regular at the gym, an unfaithful husband, an outpatient receiving medical treatment, an associate of particular individuals or political groups—and not just one such fact about a person, but all such facts."[26]

The immense power that technology gives to those who possess it—whether government, industry, or ordinary individuals—has been a sword for good or ill, protecting and invading simultaneously, expanding the public square for debate while shrinking the landscape of privacy.

In domestic disputes, for example, cyber-stalking by spurned lovers has become so widespread that it's now a concern of domestic-violence counselors. One Virginia man infected his former wife's computer with software that could read her e-mail; when he let her know the personal information he had learned, he terrified her with a sense of violation and vulnerability as profound as if he had been inside her home. "When the stalking comes from someplace, anyplace, it makes you wonder what he's really capable of . . . what he was going to do next," she told *The Washington Post*. "He could have been anywhere at any time looking into my life and getting to me. He could have seen anything, like legal documents I was forwarding; or where I was going to be. That's what I never knew."[27]

Magnified by Internet technology, the casual cruelty of pranksters and voyeurs is no longer limited to backyards and dorm rooms. In September 2010, after a Rutgers freshman asked to have his room to himself until midnight, his roommate activated a Web camera remotely, saw Tyler Clementi romantically entwined with another man, and streamed the video online. Three days later, Clementi, a promising violinist, jumped to his death from the George Washington Bridge. What George Orwell portrayed as the menace of Big Brother in *1984* has now become what the writer Walter Kirn labels as Little Brother, a small-time, grassroots, Peeping Tom intruding through a multitude of lenses.

It's so easy to cull vast records, one CEO told me, that her midsized company runs every job applicant's name through databases and rejects anyone who has ever sued an employer for discrimination or sexual harassment, whether or not the suits were justified. The firm might as well hang up a sign: LITIGIOUS WORKERS NOT WANTED.

One catch is that mistakes are made interpreting the flood of digital files. Whether the surveillance and search are done by government or a private firm, the collected information spans a spectrum from definitive to ambiguous, and where it is misread, it can make innocent people's lives quite miserable. It is one thing to search an airline passenger, who either possesses something dangerous or does not. It is quite another for government to arrange scattered shards of data about individuals into caricatures that are not subject to testing or rebuttal, to forecast some deed that cannot be proven in advance. Law enforcement has enough difficulty finding who committed a crime in the past, much less predicting who will commit one in the future.

In an odd way, "the metal detector is a perfect privacy tool," says Jim Dempsey, policy director of the Center for Democracy and Technology: Everybody is screened equally, there is an immediate alarm audible to the screener and the screened, the problem can be resolved just by emptying pockets, and no records are kept to prejudice the situation the next time you fly. It is a model whose characteristics of transparency, immediate resolution, and zero data collection might well suit other security measures and information gathering, Dempsey believes. The same might be said of the millimeter-wave devices that make people appear practically naked.

But constructing profiles and making predictions are now central tasks of intelligence and law enforcement agencies, which are charged with countering suicidal terrorists who cannot be punished afterward. Undeterred reverence for the wizardry of computers has fueled law enforcement's growing infatuation with the vast reservoirs of digitally stored data that describe the buying, traveling, reading, viewing, renting, and possibly political habits of millions who live in the United States. If only the data could be mined and sifted and sorted into patterns that fit profiles, officials imagine, perhaps the occasional nugget of warning would lead to the cell or the plot or the threat, and disaster could be intercepted. "Connect the dots" has become the mantra in reaction to the government's failure to assemble all the bits and pieces of information about the nineteen 9/11 hijackers' travel, rentals, and flight lessons, which were scattered throughout databases. That lack of coordination was a theme of the 9/11 Commission's exhaustive study of the attack.

The commission paid practically no attention to the stress on an open society caused by extensive surveillance. "When we say we are fighting for an open society, we don't mean a transparent society," Jeffrey Rosen writes. "We mean a society open to the possibility that people can redefine and reinvent themselves every day; a society in which people can travel from place to place without showing their papers and being encumbered by their past; a society that respects privacy and constantly reshuffles social hierarchy. One ideal of America insists that your opportunities shouldn't be limited by your profile in a database."[28]

Go to GangNET's Web site and watch the demonstration to see how easily a patrol officer, with no gang-unit training, can click a mouse and enter a person's name in a database labeling him a gang member. Based mostly on "field interviews"—stops and interrogations without probable cause—the gang databases require no proof and allow no challenge to the assertion that someone is affiliated with a gang. The police listed more than 66 percent of all the black males in Denver between ages twelve and twenty-four, and 47 percent in Los Angeles. During a sweep of a school in Union City, California, sixty Asian and Hispanic students were plucked from the cafeteria for interviews, then added to the database.

Being listed has several disadvantages. It is taken as fact by judges, juries, and prosecutors, even though it may have been done at the whim of a single cop, without even the slightest internal review. A court can cite the listing in ordering you, without charge or conviction, to avoid certain people, locations, and clothing. If you're charged with a crime, the prosecutor can use the listing to press you to plead guilty. If you don't, your supposed gang membership can be presented to the jury as your motive for the crime, and in California and elsewhere, it enhances your sentence. It can deny you employment, and getting off the list is difficult, because most departments don't update or purge their records.[29]

Whether you're in a gang database or another digital place, you cannot escape from an electronically frozen profile. Its errors cannot be easily erased. Unflattering fragments can pierce a job application or a security clearance like shrapnel, shredding a college acceptance, a promotion, an election campaign years later. If compiled by watchers with both power and political motive, the dossier becomes a threat waiting in the background, inducing a quiet inhibition among the citizenry. Those who are careful to keep their files clean—who decide not to speak, not to assemble, not to step into what they fear might be a zone of government concern—take an invisible path away from civil society. Their choices are silent and hard to discern, especially against the noisy background of acerbic political irreverence and free-wheeling debate that America still enjoys.

"The price of lawful public dissent must not be a dread of subjection to an unchecked surveillance power," the Supreme Court declared in 1972 as it unanimously ruled against warrantless wiretaps of violent protesters. "Nor must the fear of unauthorized official eavesdropping deter vigorous citizen dissent and discussion of Government action in private conversation. For private dissent, no less than open public discourse, is essential to our free society."[30] Otherwise, the justices understood, something can gradually happen inside people's minds.

I saw it in the Soviet Union. Russians who were aware of living in a surveillance society were wary of contact with American correspondents, which could get them into unspecified trouble. But those who were oblivious to being watched, who had never bumped up against the limits of expression and association, sometimes displayed such naïve (and refreshing) boldness that I felt obligated to warn them. This I did for a young law student I met at a restaurant in the city of Dushanbe. We spent a few evenings in interesting conversation, and he said he'd like to get together again when he visited Moscow. Fine, I said, and gave him my address and phone number but told him that my phone was probably tapped, that KGB guards screened people entering my apartment house, and that his visit to me would be noted. "Outrageous!" he said indignantly. He never called.

The chilling sensation of being watched can generate internal censorship and self-policing, as described by a Pentagon committee on privacy and technology, headed by Newton Minow, a former chairman of the Federal Communications Commission:

> It is this principle that was at the heart of Jeremy Bentham's concept of the Panopticon—a model prison consisting of a central tower surrounded by a ring of prison cells. One-way windows would allow a person in the tower to see into the prison cells, but prevent the prisoners from seeing into the tower. Bentham posited that a single inspector in the tower could control the behavior of all of the prisoners through "the illusion of constant surveillance." According to philosopher and historian Michel Foucault, "modern society increasingly functions like a super Panopticon," in which government constrains individual behavior by the threat of surveillance. . . . Knowledge that the government is observing data we generate through thousands of ordinary activities can alter the way we live our lives and interact with others. Knowledge of that power can cause people to change their behavior to be more consistent with a perceived social norm, to mask their behavior, and/or to reduce their activities or participation in society to avoid the surveillance.[31]

My behavior changed when I lived in Moscow. According to my ethics as a correspondent, I was doing nothing "wrong" by going to see political dissidents or taking them books that were banned by Soviet authorities. But to protect them, Debby and I kept a Magic Slate handy in our bugged apartment. Whatever we wished to discuss without the KGB hearing—mostly plans to visit one or another dissident—we wrote with a stylus, then erased by lifting the slate's plastic sheet. Or we used hand signals to make the first letters of our dissident friends' names. We were circumspect on the phone, received our mail through the U.S. Embassy's diplomatic pouch (a privilege granted to journalists even though we weren't diplomats), and spoke most freely while outside in Moscow's expansive parks. We did not quite realize how thoroughly the anxiety over surveillance had filtered into us during our four years there until we left and it began to drain away. It took a year or more before I lost all hesitation about speaking openly at home—as long as it took Brandon Mayfield, the Portland lawyer whose house was secretly searched and bugged by the FBI.

Technology was relatively primitive during my Moscow days in the late 1970s. The KGB was rumored to be bombarding the embassy with microwaves to eavesdrop on conversations by picking up vibrations from window glass, and it could reportedly monitor electric typewriters by remotely detecting which keys were pressed. Compared to today, however, those were the Dark Ages.

Agents followed people around (often clumsily), penetrated campuses and workplaces with informers, tapped phones, opened mail, and drew conclusions about citizens from fragmented reports by party loyalists. In this low-tech police state, the information was "stored on millions of yellowing pieces of paper, typed or handwritten," *The Economist* observed in 2007. "These days, data about people's whereabouts, purchases, behavior, and personal lives are gathered, stored, and shared on a scale that no dictator of the old school ever thought possible." The magazine published a photograph that seemed positively nostalgic: an East German clerk standing in a narrow aisle between towering shelves, filing stacks of folders bulging with dossiers—on paper.[32]

There is no telling whether the paper files were more or less accurate than their electronic descendants, but today's caricatures are more easily disseminated, and some are plainly erroneous, fingering the wrong people and missing the right ones. That happens when digital data are collected on a whim without showing grounds for suspicion, and when government abandons the rigorous discipline imposed by the strictures of probable cause, adversary proceedings, and the dispersal of authority, all of which are designed to enhance the truth-finding process. The immense force of the state to prosecute and imprison individuals, confiscate their property, or merely keep them off airplanes is easily misused unless it is checked and balanced.

What has been colloquially called the no-fly list, for example, is designed to flag dangerous passengers for either close searches and questioning or outright denial of permission to board. But the errors that have occurred, the infliction of penalty without due process or appeal, and the dangerous characters it misses, have made the list a laughingstock. Trying to fix it, the government has been floundering around for years.

CAPPS, the Computer-Assisted Passenger Profiling System (later changed to ". . . Prescreening System"), relied on private commercial-data providers. A ticket purchaser's name, address, phone number, and date of birth would be transmitted to the company to confirm her identity, and the company would send back a score on her risk level: green would get normal security checks, yellow would get closer screening, red would be denied boarding and referred to law enforcement. How these scores were determined was an obscure secret, and CAPPS was so flawed that it was later replaced by a supposedly improved system, CAPPS II.

When CAPPS II failed to meet congressionally imposed standards, though, it was supplanted in 2004 by a system called Secure Flight, whose similar flaws led to its suspension in 2006. By 2010 it was being revised and revived. Government operatives seemed less skilled at administering than at naming; they masterfully composed titles that invoked fear or patriotism. Whenever a program provoked protests, you could be sure it would get a new name containing "terrorism," "prescreening," "secure," or another trigger word to soothe or scare you into giving up freedoms to the state as noble guardian of safety.

Luckily, enough Americans still bridled at the privacy invasions that class-action lawsuits were directed against airlines, which—like communications companies—became enablers of government surveillance. JetBlue, it was disclosed, provided personal information on 1.5 million passengers to a defense contractor, Torch Concepts, which was researching data-mining techniques for the army. American Airlines sent private data on 1.2 million customers to four firms competing for a contract with the Transportation Security Administration.

The most potent argument against CAPPS was that it was so often wrong. On five occasions, Senator Edward "Ted" Kennedy was initially rejected for flights because "T. Kennedy" turned up on the list as a pseudonym used by a suspected would-be terrorist. The real Kennedy described this encounter with a ticket agent: "He said, 'We can't give it to you. You can't buy a ticket to go on the airline to Boston.' I said, 'Well, why not?' He said, 'We can't tell you.'" A supervisor finally intervened and let him board, the senator told a Judiciary Committee hearing.

"Tried to get on a plane back to Washington," he continued. "'You can't get on the plane.' I went up to the desk and said, 'I've been getting on this plane, you know, for forty-two years. Why can't I get on the plane?'"[33]

Again, a supervisor recognized the veteran legislator and overruled the computerized list, which had been alerting authorities to many other sinister figures. They included Representative Jim Davis, a Florida Democrat; two San Francisco peace activists, Jan Adams and Rebecca Gordon; and numerous Americans named David Nelson, who were put through the wringer whenever they checked in. The real David Nelson on the list was reportedly a white Irishman, but the database flagged a black David Nelson, a Milwaukee Brewers coach, who had to spend at least forty-five minutes before every flight under questioning by local police and FBI agents. A business consultant named David Nelson was pulled off a plane to be interrogated on the ramp. Another David Nelson, a graduate student, got a quizzical look from every ticket agent whose screen flashed some secret message that she could not reveal to him. She invariably made a flurry of phone calls, then the police appeared, intrusive questions were posed, and Nelson may or may not have made his flight. The actor David Nelson from *Ozzie and Harriet* was stopped a few times, as was a nine-year-old David Nelson from Alaska. Feel safer?

An ACLU lawsuit on behalf of Adams and Gordon dislodged about three hundred pages of government documents, including the admission that names were placed on the list using "necessarily subjective" criteria and "not hard and fast rules." The number of people on the list rose from just 16 on September 11, 2001, to more than 400 the next day, 594 by that December, about 1,000 a year later and, the ACLU estimated, tens of thousands by 2006. "In November of 2005, the TSA"—the Transportation Security Administration—"indicated that 30,000 people in the last year alone had contacted the agency because their names had been mistakenly matched to a name on the federal government's watch lists," the ACLU reported.[34]

In addition, a database maintained by the Terrorist Screening Center, which alerts local police, border patrol agents, and U.S. consulates when somebody's name matches one on watch lists, went from about 170,000 individuals in July 2004 to 300,000 by April 2007.[35] By the time Umar

Farouk Abdulmutallab tried to blow up that Northwest flight to Detroit on Christmas Day 2009, the list contained an unwieldy 550,000 names, with subgroups of 14,000 listed for secondary screening and 4,000 truly designated as "no-fly."

After the bombing attempt, concern naturally focused on oversights in placing potentially dangerous people on the lists, and top intelligence officials expressed regret over giving in to "pressure" by imposing curbs on adding names.[36] The comments seemed to forecast a rapid growth in the no-fly list, but it hadn't grown quite enough by the following May, when a Pakistani-American named Faisal Shahzad nearly succeeded in flying from Kennedy Airport after parking an inexpertly assembled car bomb that fizzled in Times Square. His name was added to the list only a few hours before Emirates airline personnel, doing their screenings from an earlier version, ignored an electronic notification to check for an update and allowed him onto Flight 202, bound for Dubai. At the last minute, officials spotted him on the passenger manifest that airlines send routinely to Customs and Border Protection just before departure. The plane was still at the gate. Agents boarded and arrested him.

A more widespread problem has been the inclusion of innocents. At least nine U.S. citizens, three of them military veterans, were stranded overseas in 2010 after being placed on the no-fly list while traveling or studying abroad—in Colombia, the United Kingdom, the Virgin Islands, Germany, Egypt, Yemen, and Saudi Arabia. They could not enter the United States by air. One of them, Stephen Durga Persaud, eventually made it by ship from the Virgin Islands to Miami, according to their complaint filed in federal court, then by train to Los Angeles in time to join his wife there for the birth of their second child. Another, Steven William Washburn, spent fifty hours flying from Dublin to Mexico City via Germany, Brazil, and Peru, then hours more being interrogated by Mexican officials before finally crossing by land to the United States, the country of his birth. But others, more distant or without extensive funds, remained stuck abroad until months after they sued the Obama administration.

The government then agreed to a one-time waiver for each of them, said Ben Wizner of the ACLU, which handled their case. Facing a court challenge, officials seemed willing to defend the no-fly list but not the exclusion of Americans from their homeland. They would be allowed to fly back. But they would not be told if they remained on a watch list that could bar them from leaving, entering, or traveling inside the United States by air. While the litigation continued, those who had not managed to get home by land or sea took the deal and returned, except for two students who chose to avoid the risk. They were halfway through a two-year Arabic course at a Saudi university and could not get the U.S. government to tell them whether they would be permitted to fly back to Saudi Arabia to complete their studies. What had led to listing them and the others—whether error or superficial profiling or unverified intelligence— the government would not reveal, but at least into late 2010, none of the nine had been charged with a crime. They were punished nonetheless, for the ban on flying shackled their lives, and it came without accusation, proof, or the semblance of due process. The men had no idea how to respond to invisible allegations embedded in government databases.

Zealous to deny terrorists enough information to foil this "system," the federal government denies citizens the basic information to judge its effectiveness or repair its shortcomings. With no scrutiny of how someone gets onto a list, what information contributes to the labeling of people as nefarious characters, and what procedure can be used to correct the record, there are no brakes to impede innocent error, political targeting, and the disruption of lives based on ethnic or religious identity. Without a chance to see the collected information and what agents conclude from it, neither the Congress nor the courts nor the public can tell whether innocents are being pursued, whether the precious resources of law enforcement are chasing around fruitlessly. After investigating itself, the Department of Homeland Security found its procedures to remove names listed incorrectly to be wholly inadequate.

A healthy correction by the judicial branch stopped the executive branch in 2007 from using a severely flawed database to ferret out illegal immigrants. The plan required employers to submit Social Security numbers provided by their employees for verification against a government master file. It seemed straightforward enough. The government would issue "no-match letters" when workers provided phony numbers, and employers would be required to fire them within ninety days or face prosecution. But the database was a mess. Sampling showed that false alerts would have been generated on many legal residents and U.S. citizens, for the 435 million individual records held by the Social Security Administration contained 17.8 million with errors, according to the agency's own inspector general, including 12.7 million for native-born Americans. The Bush administration's program, which would have sacrificed the well-being of law-abiding citizens as collateral damage to detect undocumented aliens, was halted by a federal judge. President Obama's administration dropped the no-match rule after he took office.[37]

In response to concerns about innocents being wrongly targeted, one might argue that it's the partial picture that leads to mistakes and that *more* intrusive surveillance would provide more complete profiles and reduce the error rate. Technology is bound to improve, mining data more reliably, connecting dots more accurately. It's an alluring prospect—that the pieces of ordinary life can be "aggregated," as intelligence types say, into revealing mosaics. But having accurate raw data solves only the first of three basic problems that concern Jim Dempsey of the Center for Democracy and Technology. There can also be false inference. "You can have perfect data," he says, "but perfect data plus false inference equals bad outcome." Finally, there can be intentional abuse and political monitoring: "He opposes the war in Iraq, he must be a security threat." This has certainly been the mentality of law enforcement when monitoring peace groups and policing demonstrations.

So the mosaics still have to be interpreted, and interpretations of such material have been notoriously bizarre. When intelligence files are eventually released—as were those kept on George Orwell during a dozen years of surveillance by England's Special Branch—their portraits look more like Picassos than photographs, with body parts rearranged unrecognizably. A sergeant in Scotland Yard, reporting that Orwell "dressed in a Bohemian fashion both at his office and in his leisure hours," labeled him "a man of advanced communist views" just three years before the writer deftly skewered communism in his parable, *Animal Farm*. This "old and forbidding dance, the one between the watchers and the watched," *The New York Times* observed, produces dossiers that are "nearly always perspicacious—not about the subjects being watched but about the fears of the watchers. This is something Orwell understood perfectly well, how fear enhances perception, but also corrupts it."[38]

The fears of the watchers thrive in an institutional police-and-intelligence culture that rewards suspicion as smart, derides innocent explanations as naïve, and views much of the public as criminal. This is the culture that could see a fantasy Spain vacation, researched online by Brandon Mayfield's middle-school daughter, as evidence of his involvement in the Madrid train bombings. This is the culture that could interpret a deranged tenant's mad scribblings as diagrams of an airbase and a military hospital slated for attack, and could prosecute as a "sleeper cell" the men in Detroit who had the misfortune, two years later, to rent the same apartment where the drawings had been left. We need cops, spies, and intelligence analysts, but we don't need to give them excessive power. When they jump to conclusions, they jump on people's heads, which is especially easy in a digital age.

THE SURVEILLANCE-INDUSTRIAL COMPLEX

If technology were perfect, surveillance comprehensive, and error eliminated, arguments other than inaccuracy would be needed to protect zones of privacy from electronic snooping. Or, if information cannot be kept private in this digital age, at least its use needs to be controlled. "Privacy advocates can no longer rely on inefficiency for their privacy," Dempsey says. "We need a set of laws and policies that create a web of protections."

But how to make the case? We have no Soviet system any longer as a totalitarian model to avoid, no Orwell to chill us with ironic fantasies. Most of us are constitutionally illiterate and complacent about our liberties. We have few jurists eloquent enough to tap that deepest well of patriotism: the resonant devotion to founding principles.

On nearly every issue, we have to reach back decades for inspiring admonitions. Most judges don't write well, it's sad to say, and more significantly, as one judge told me, Reagan and the two Bushes appointed men and women to the bench who "don't believe that the primary function of federal courts is to protect individual rights." Rarely now do we hear thundering reminders of basic truths equivalent to the warning Justice Jackson delivered in 1949, writing in a dissent, that the Fourth Amendment's provisions "are not mere second-class rights but belong in the catalog of indispensable freedoms. . . . But the right to be secure against searches and seizures is one of the most difficult to protect. Since the officers are themselves the chief invaders, there is no enforcement outside of court."[39]

And so, there is virtually no enforcement at all, not in vast areas of modern life. Most personal electronic information is in private hands, and savvy entrepreneurs manage it for profit by selling the data to retailers of all stripes. The government can buy it, too, and since 9/11 various proposals for using it have generated a blizzard of collection programs. Total Information Awareness, for instance, was to be a Pentagon sweep of credit-card and other information in an effort to detect significant patterns. It had a creepy motto, *"Scientia est potentia"* (Knowledge is power), and a logo depicting the globe overlooked by the all-seeing eye of God atop a pyramid (from the Great Seal of the United States). Trying to save both its initials and its purpose, its backers changed its Big Brotherish name to Terrorism Information Awareness. It crossed a line, generated an outcry, and was suspended.

With less fanfare, however, the FBI continues to amass vast amounts of data on people who are not suspected of any wrongdoing, according to official documents obtained by *Wired* magazine under a Freedom of Information Act request. These include 1.5 billion records from government and corporate databases—Avis car rentals, Wyndham Worldwide hotels, casinos, airlines, and financial institutions, for example—adding up to a Total Information Awareness program under a less scary name: the National Security Analysis Center.[40]

What the ACLU calls the surveillance-industrial complex is run by retailers, communications firms, financial institutions, and other companies that collect information to process your transactions, evaluate your credit, enable screening by your potential employers, and analyze your buying preferences to target you for marketing. This creates a rich reservoir of data, which one blue-ribbon panel of experts saw as indispensable to police and intelligence agencies.

"Today, the private sector is on the frontline of the homeland security effort," wrote the panel, assembled by the Markle Foundation of New York in 2003. "Its members are holders of data that may prove crucial to identifying and locating terrorists or thwarting terrorist attacks, and stewards of critical infrastructure and dangerous materials that must be protected. Thus, the private sector is the source of information that is essential to counterterrorism."

The panel, which included the future attorney general, Eric Holder, and a scattering of civil libertarians, struggled to find mechanisms that would simultaneously provide and deny information to government investigators. On the one hand, it recommended that private firms institute voluntary data-retention programs for government's benefit—the opposite of the American Library Association's suggestion that data be erased to protect privacy. On the other, it urged that records be left in private hands and not transferred in bulk to state agencies, noting that information in government possession can be spread through agency databases and evade legal restrictions that apply to evidence in criminal prosecutions. Furthermore, government agencies keep what they gather.

For example, "The FBI acquired all passenger name records from all airlines for 2001—a quarter of a billion," said David Sobel, senior legal counsel of the Electronic Frontier Foundation, who learned of this through a Freedom of Information Act request. "They still retain it. They said it's not of any current usefulness" but could be tapped to see if someone happened to be on the same flight with someone under scrutiny. Guilt by association is bad enough; suspicion by contact can taint a person's life and send law enforcement on distracting detours. That this data can be demanded under the law's loose standard that it be "relevant" to an "investigation" is a major part of the problem.

"Their definition of what the appropriate scope of 'investigation' is, is just incredibly broad," Sobel said. He and others from the "privacy community," as they call themselves, have been told by FBI officials that investigators want to construct networks of contacts. "They say a person of interest is calling a, b, c, and d; what is the problem with our knowing who b, c, and d are calling?" He added, "It's a complete redefinition of what an investigation is. We want to anticipate things that haven't happened yet, and we want to look at the largest amount of information we can collect and analyze."

Innocent facts gathered for one purpose can be used for another, less legitimate purpose, as the Pentagon's committee on privacy observed: Looking at a passenger's request for a special meal, officials might jump to a conclusion about her religion.[41] Using false inferences, that might lead to an assumption about a political affinity and support of violence in its name.

The Markle panel urged that the government "not have routine access to personally identifiable information even if that information is widely available to the public." The reason is clear: The hardships in the private sector resulting from the spread of such information, "such as loss of job opportunities, credit worthiness, or public embarrassment," are less severe than the government's power to exact a "loss of liberty and encroachment on the constitutionally rooted right of privacy." The Fourth Amendment "is designed to protect citizens from intrusions by government, not neighbors or credit bureaus."[42]

But the transfer of privately held data to government is barely restrained by current law. As we have seen, federal privacy acts have been shot full of holes, and where obstacles remain in the communications field, for example, they have been secretly evaded by big companies and the National Security Agency. Congress in 2008 immunized the companies from customer lawsuits.

Now that huge warehouses aren't necessary for storing vast amounts of information on paper, and computer processors can swiftly sort through myriad indicators of private lives, such firms as ChoicePoint and Acxiom gather everything from real estate transactions to purchases of ice cream. Facebook tells each member's friends what he's buying online through its shopping portal, and breaches have allowed unauthorized access to private information, including chats.[43] At least forty private firms operate Web sites that offer individuals' wireless and landline calling records and other personal information, including the identities of people who use screen names at America Online and other Internet sites. They even trade in rumor, connecting data points to construct a montage of a person's behavior that may be greater—and less accurate—than the sum of its parts. At abika.com, for example, you can get a criminal background check on someone for $30, a determination of sexual orientation for $90, a report on an individual's "unconventional behavior" for $110, and a "psychological profile" for $200.[44] These may be drawn from unverified bits of innuendo.

Personally identifiable information exists roughly at three levels of availability: government records in the public domain, nonpublic data for sale, and private information accessible only with an individual's approval.

Collecting public records used to require tedious travel to far-flung courthouses, city halls, and county offices. Now, subject to some limitations by various states' laws, you can pay to download much of this data from aggregating companies: marriage, divorce, and death records; business licenses, corporate-officer lists, and company filings with the Securities and Exchange Commission; political contributions, bankruptcies, evictions, criminal convictions, civil suits, property deeds, and liens on houses; and licenses for hunting, fishing, driving, trucking, carrying guns, flying, instructing pilots, and transporting hazardous materials.

A good deal of nonpublic information is also for sale: your e-mail addresses, newspaper and magazine subscriptions, annual income, whether there are children in your home, products you've bought and warranties you've activated, school and college records, memberships in trade associations, your attendance at conferences, and your inclusion on lists of executives and professionals.

The third level—private information—is the most restricted, but intelligence and law-enforcement agencies have little difficulty weaving their way through the complex labyrinth of laws. All they need these days is a subpoena, a National Security Letter, or—in the case of suspected terrorism—voluntary cooperation by a private entity to get a person's records on cable-TV viewing, video rentals, book purchases and borrowing, numbers called on phones and calling cards, cell-phone locations, text messages, Internet chat-room dialogues, instant-messaging transcripts, e-mail content, online file downloads and purchases, Web site search histories, express-mail forms, credit-card applications and transactions, fraud-protection registrations, loan applications and issuance, insurance policies and claims, frequent-flyer and loyalty-card records, air-travel itineraries, taxi pick-up requests, car rentals, buses and trains taken, hotel and cruise ship reservations, automatic-toll payments, drug prescriptions, laboratory results, infectious-disease records, drug-test results, memberships in labor unions and political organizations, post-office box numbers, job applications, and employment history.[45]

Provisions of the Patriot Act exempt communications firms from lawsuits if they suspect dangerous activity and voluntarily give the government customers' information. And financial institutions are required to alert law enforcement to suspicions of money-laundering, which creates "every incentive to over-report," according to Timothy Lynch of the libertarian Cato Institute. There is scant evidence that the reporting of such suspicions has unraveled major terrorist plots, but it has generated mountains of specious alerts sending agents chasing phantom perpetrators of nonexistent crimes.[46]

It also caught New York's Governor Eliot Spitzer patronizing a high-priced prostitution ring, which forced his resignation. Two banks, North Fork and HSBC, which had been forced by Spitzer as state attorney general to repay illegal fees they had charged homeowners, had watched his transactions closely and had filed "suspicious activity reports" with the Treasury Department after his cash transfers broke from usual patterns and included payments to shell companies. Spitzer, who had pressed banks to be more aggressive about monitoring the movement of money, was hoist with his own petard.[47]

The thirst for instantaneous information led the Markle panel to call for sophisticated computer networks that would enable the government to obtain a suspect's financial records and a list of his known associates within thirty seconds, and do real-time checks of someone's identity as she opens a bank account, applies for a job, makes a travel reservation, shows a pilot's license, and the like. "This necessitates, for example, checking identities against death records for individuals (usually children who have died young enough to avoid acquiring a Social Security number) whose identities might be used to generate a false identity and flagging improbable identities, such as that of a thirty-five-year-old with unusually few public records (for example, no phone book records, no credit-header files, no driver's license)," the panel wrote.[48]

The targeted individuals usually don't know that personal information is being turned over to the government. Private firms rarely give notice and hardly ever contest the government's demands in court, taking refuge behind the glaring caveat in their "privacy policies," that "we may be required to disclose personal information to cooperate with regulatory or law enforcement authorities."[49] This is precisely the loophole that should worry citizens the most.

Firms have adopted a wide variety of practices. In the Markle survey, a major (unnamed) telecommunications company said that it always required a subpoena to provide information on its customers, and a court order for a wiretap. An Internet service provider said it would demand a subpoena to identify a member and his accounts, and a court order to probe his online activities or name his interlocutors. There is reason to doubt this claim. If true, it would mean defying a National Security Letter, which is issued by the executive branch alone without judicial imprimatur. Through mid-2010, there had been only one known instance of an ISP resisting an NSL.

The huge exception in this company's policy was this: It would voluntarily turn over data if the government asserted "exigent circumstances," such as lives in danger. The FBI has asserted such circumstances even when no emergency existed.[50] Other firms—in the chemical and consumer-service fields—would willingly release information on terrorism matters but would insist on subpoenas in normal criminal investigations. An insurance firm and a financial-services company voluntarily turn over information from their brokers and dealers in terrorism investigations but require subpoenas for credit-card transactions.

Beyond these disparate guidelines, however, corporate security officers admitted that their own security personnel, many of whom had been police officers, informally gave information to law enforcement, bypassing company restrictions.[51]

Since it's difficult to find real cases where the influx of data has contributed to a counterterrorism success, the Markle study invented hypothetical examples, the most compelling of which was this one:

> The NSA issued a report in late June that sensitive intercepted communications among known Al Qaeda leaders abroad indicate that final preparations are being made for terrorist operations against targets in the U.S. Speakers have mentioned "malls," or perhaps "The Mall," and have referred to "the other city." In one conversation they also mentioned "movie theaters."
>
> Earlier, the FBI's Chicago field office picked up some information from an informant claiming that terrorist cells in the U.S. were discussing various methods for attacks, including general aviation, scuba divers, crop dusters, and skydivers. The Urgent Report from the Chicago field office to FBI headquarters, dated March 30, 2003, indicates

that the [Strategic Air Command] thinks this is pretty low-level intelligence but is "leaning forward" on reporting.

In early August, the NSA picked up a communication in which a presumed Al Qaeda figure mentioned skydivers. The speaker has been identified, and it is known that he has visited Texas twice. Now, five individuals with names of apparent Middle Eastern origin/ethnicity have enrolled in skydiving classes in five divergent areas of the country (Texas, Pennsylvania, Rhode Island, Illinois, and Florida). All have used student identification from nearby universities.

Interest is converging on Texas, however, where one of the skydivers is asking to rent a Cessna 182 (commonly used by skydivers). Another individual, possibly with a similar ethnic origin, is trying to rent another Cessna 182 at another airfield in Texas. Both individuals want to rent the planes during Thanksgiving weekend—a big shopping weekend, and therefore a possible "mall" connection.

The skydiver in Texas is also showing an interest in explosives. He has visited a relevant website and has ordered a how-to book, using his VISA card.[52]

This fictitious case illustrates the creative blend of targeted searches and data-mining that can make up a counterterrorism investigation. The al-Qaeda intercepts would be targeted searches; that is, they zero in on particular individuals and groups. The skydiving and Cessna rental information would be the result of data-mining, a survey of large electronic files with no identifiable person in mind. Here, lists of skydiving students and Cessna renters would be scanned for Middle Eastern names.

The federal government has obviously been secretive about how much data-mining occurs, but it certainly continues, largely unseen, across a range of government agencies. Although Congress cut off funding for Terrorism Information Awareness (TIA) in 2003, for example, it also enacted a classified annex permitting the Pentagon's Defense Advanced Research Project Agency to sweep databases "for counterterrorism foreign intelligence," either outside the United States "or wholly against non-United States citizens." The program's documents, posted and then removed from its Web site, described an effort to detect patterns in transactions "related to potential terrorist planning," by surveying huge electronic files in the areas of communications, finance, education, travel, medicine, housing, critical resources, and government.[53]

In addition, the Defense Department conducts data-mining in search of people who may threaten American military forces overseas. The NSA runs both its controversial warrantless surveillance program and the Advanced Research and Development Activity center, which designs methods of "extracting intelligence from, and providing security for, information transmitted or manipulated by electronic means."[54] It reportedly signed contracts with the three largest telecommunications companies, AT&T, Verizon, and BellSouth, to provide domestic calling records aimed at doing "social network analysis" on relationships among people. Firms rarely want to antagonize the federal government, a source of carrots (huge contracts) and sticks (regulatory powers).

To gather "open-source intelligence," the CIA provides funds through its investment arm, In-Q-Tel, to the private firm Visible Technologies, which monitors "social media conversations" on Twitter, YouTube, Flickr, blogs, and online forums on about 500,000 Web sites a day. Such corporations as Microsoft, Dell, AT&T, and Verizon have hired Visible to track what is said about them. The CIA is reportedly keen to watch posts in foreign languages.[55]

Data on Americans are also searched by the Treasury Department's Financial Crimes Enforcement Network; Secure Flight, the passenger-screening system; the Multistate Anti-Terrorism Information Exchange (MATRIX), which connects private and government databases using ethnicity as one of its components; ATS, the Automated Targeting System, which screens incoming passengers as well as cargo; STAR, the System to Assess Risk, which rates potential terrorists; a database on identity theft; another containing health-care insurance claims to combat fraud; car-accident claim files; public records on real estate transactions to identify fraudulent housing purchases; and presumably other agency programs.[56] "TIA was not the tip of the iceberg," Minow's Pentagon report declared, "but rather one small specimen in a sea of icebergs."[57]

A major problem for intelligence agencies is this: the more information accumulated, the more complex the analysis. The NSA noted that "some intelligence sources grow at a rate of four petabytes (one petabyte = one quadrillion bytes) per month now, and the rate of growth is increasing." A study by the Congressional Research Service reported, "Whereas some observers once predicted that the NSA was in danger of becoming proverbially deaf due to the spreading use of encrypted communications, it appears that NSA may now be at greater risk of being 'drowned' in information."[58]

Data-mining may or may not be useful. On the one hand, terrorist attacks are so few in number, and each one has such particular characteristics, that the precursors of travel, transactions, or other behavior may not organize themselves into predictive patterns. It's not like foreseeing credit-card default, a more common phenomenon. On the other hand, the more experience the watchers accumulate, the more skilled they may become in picking out indicators. The public simply cannot know the effectiveness of data-mining without the government's willingness to open the process to some scrutiny, at least.

What we do know, however, is that broad sweeps through databases create less and less "expectation of privacy," and therefore less and less constitutional protection for our personal information. According to the Supreme Court's circular logic, when we don't expect privacy, we have no right to it, so the Founding Fathers—inadvertently, no doubt—left us exposed to whatever third parties know about us. And since the Fourth Amendment does not apply to such information, the only way to build walls around it is by statutes enacted by the legislative branch. Current protections are fragmented, and as we have seen, Congress is easily spooked into drilling holes through whatever walls it erects.

The United States is less free in this regard than most European countries, where laws restricting the collection and sharing of personal data apply to the private sector as well as to government. Privacy International classifies the United States as an "extensive surveillance society," ranking ninth from the bottom of forty-seven countries, including the twenty-five in the European Union—barely better than Russia, China, Singapore, Malaysia, and the United Kingdom. The main American weakness is not in the Constitution, but in the courts' flawed application of its principles, and in the loose laws, which have allowed extensive communication surveillance and workplace monitoring.[59] In large measure, this results from the American aversion to a tightly regulated private sector: Data-mining is so useful to industry in detecting fraud, assessing risk, and targeting advertising that legislators are ideologically reluctant to impede such activity, even in the interest of individual privacy.

Congress could stiffen protections, according to David Sobel, by closing an escape clause that now allows federal agencies to declare their databases exempt from the 1974 Privacy Act by merely publishing a rules notice in the Federal Register. It could grant citizens access to information that is collected about them and create a special judicial procedure to allow individuals to challenge inaccurate government dossiers. Information could be kept in anonymous form through encryption. European-style privacy laws could impose restrictions on private firms' ability to collect and keep personal data, and enable customers to correct or expunge information on themselves held privately. In sum, the law could use a good deal of updating and polishing.

THE PRIVATIZATION OF SEARCHES

The jumbled legal landscape in the United States has created many oddities, one of which is this: Without a proper warrant signed by a judge, law enforcement can get your Web-browsing history from your Internet service provider but not from your personal computer. Even from a distance, using "Trojan Horse" software that downloads data from your hard drive, the government needs a search warrant.

If a private individual who is not a government agent takes it from your computer, however, and then turns the information over to the police, that's just fine. The Bill of Rights restricts what government may do, not what private entities may do. So the Fourth Amendment does not prevent an individual or a private institution, such as a company or a college, from searching an employee's desk, a student's room, or anyone's personal computer. Any restrictions must rely on laws passed by legislatures, not on the Constitution as interpreted by the courts.

Private colleges—not state universities—have exploited this constitutional loophole to send campus police on dormitory searches for drugs, which local police then subpoena and use in criminal prosecutions. This happened to a Dartmouth College student named Adam Nemser, who took his case all the way to the New Hampshire Supreme Court and lost.

In their police-style uniforms, Dartmouth's unarmed campus security officers could be mistaken for officers of the law. Their patrol area has no visible boundaries, for the campus has no walls or gates but spills across the village streets of Hanover, New Hampshire, into charming neighborhoods where students mingle with townspeople.

There are more campus cops than town cops, and they coordinate with each other. The campus cops check fraternity basements to enforce the college's alcohol rules, take drunken students to the infirmary, and investigate burglaries and sexual assaults. Only occasionally do they enter students' rooms without consent to search for drugs. But they don't have arrest powers and usually destroy small amounts of narcotics, referring minor cases for college disciplinary action and only those involving large quantities or trafficking to the police for criminal prosecution.[60]

The campus cops can search without warrants because they don't act on behalf of government. Dartmouth is a private college, its security officers are not agents of the police, and their searches are therefore not "searches" within the meaning of the Fourth Amendment.

This Adam Nemser learned to his distress. Officers of Dartmouth Safety and Security (DSS) entered and searched his room, found marijuana, confiscated it, placed it in the security department's safe, and notified the Hanover police. DSS then insisted on being served with a search warrant before turning the pot over to the police, who obtained the warrant, got the drugs from the safe, and charged Nemser with possession.

The student's lawyers argued that this little charade violated the Fourth Amendment, since the campus security officers were acting essentially as agents of the state. It is well established in case law that if an "agency relationship" exists, the private actor is governed by the same constitutional rules as a police officer. The trial judge saw such agency here and granted Nemser's motion to suppress the marijuana evidence. The police and DSS had an "implicit understanding," observed Judge Albert J. Cirone, Jr. "The College's agents conduct private area searches of drugs, not necessarily in plain view or with consent." When they seize narcotics, the campus cops don't get prosecuted for drug possession themselves, he noted. The warrant directed at DSS is designed "to 'legalize' the process by cloaking the search with judicial approval."

The prosecutor appealed successfully to the New Hampshire Supreme Court. Without proof that a private party's search was induced by prior "affirmative action by a governmental official," it said, no agency relationship could be shown. The court found multiple facts establishing the independence of the college security officers: They were not asked by the police to do the search; they received no equipment, information, or assistance in the case; and they neither trained with, took instructions from, nor formulated policies jointly with the police. The marijuana was admitted into evidence.[61]

State universities operate under stricter rules, since their security officers are state agents in fact. They have at their disposal all the exceptions to the Fourth Amendment's requirements that have been carved out by the courts, plus two: Searches can be made if students have signed a general consent as part of a housing agreement, provided the main purpose is not a criminal investigation,[62] and "administrative searches" can be made for health and safety reasons with an easy-to-get warrant that doesn't have a probable-cause requirement.[63] In either case, if drugs are seen "in plain view," they can be used as evidence.

· · ·

"If a burglar brings us documents he stole from someone's house," said a federal prosecutor in California, "the law is clear that we can use that information. There's no Fourth Amendment violation, as long as we didn't instigate the burglary."

So, the private, high-tech burglar has flourished in the computer age like a digital bounty hunter. Immune from the Fourth Amendment, a hacker with a moral cause can burrow into people's online crimes for the sheer satisfaction of seeing the criminals put away. Even if he violates anti-hacking laws, he hardly risks arrest by police who are grateful for his tips and files of electronic evidence. Even if he routinely helps law enforcement, the private nature of his activity is usually accepted by the courts unless there is clear proof that the police in a particular case knew of his upcoming search, acquiesced, or gave him guidance.

But the relationships between these computer vigilantes and the cops are often muddy, contradictory, and open to competing interpretations, as Ronald Kline discovered.

He was in his late fifties, a California State Superior Court judge in Orange County, when in May of 2000 he sat at his home computer and clicked on what appeared as a picture file. Instantly, a stealthy program known as a Trojan Horse was downloaded, making his computer accessible to Bradley Willman, a nineteen-year-old operating from his parents' basement 1,300 miles away in Langley, British Columbia.

Willman had planted the malware (short for "malicious software") on pornographic sites to catch people in possession of sexual images of children, a federal and state crime. Motivated by unspecified "incidents in his past that he had 'very bad dreams' about," according to a Justice Department brief,[64] the young man could sit comfortably in Canada and—committing a crime himself—search through the hard drive of every computer that downloaded his Trojan Horse. He could read personal files and e-mail, track Internet activity, and even monitor each keystroke. He believed that he had infected about three thousand computers.

It took him a while to get around to looking through Judge Kline's files, but when he did, he struck gold. Along with some pictures, he found an electronic diary that "detailed defendant's sexual interest in young boys," the brief reported,

> specifically identifying young boys in the Little League games defendant umpired, as well as young boys defendant met while naked in

the spa at an athletic club. For example, defendant wrote that taking a specific boy to a baseball game was "like I was getting ready for a date. Well, I was, really." Defendant also recounted instances in which he surreptitiously touched and rubbed some of these boys. Defendant described in detail the private areas of these prepubescent boys and his careful plots to befriend boys without arousing suspicion. For example, defendant wrote, "I gave a lot of thought today about this business of approaching these kids too fast. . . . You have to make them come to you or it doesn't work." With regard to one boy, defendant was "trying to arrange a 'sleep over' if I can, and I'm trying to play it right."[65]

Willman didn't give the diary directly to police. Using the pseudonym Omnipotent, he sent it anonymously to PedoWatch, an organization devoted to nabbing pedophiles; PedoWatch transmitted the diary to California authorities who notified the police in Irvine, where Kline lived. To make sure the diary was authentic, Detective Ronald Carr matched dates and details with Kline's docket of court hearings, found that he belonged to the athletic club he mentioned, and verified that boys he named had played in games he had umpired.

It was harder to identify the tipster. Omnipotent told PedoWatch by e-mail that he had no further information. The e-mail account he'd used was registered under a false name and address, he didn't answer Carr's e-mails, and a subpoena for records of a site he had given PedoWatch as a storage place for files turned up a pseudonym as well.

The breakthrough came when PedoWatch gave Carr a Web site the tipster maintained, and the subpoenaed records revealed a false name but a real address. A Vancouver detective visited the house, found that Willman was living there, asked around, and heard that he had been in touch with a member of the Royal Canadian Mounted Police, George Barnett. Carr called Barnett, "who knew Willman because Willman had provided a March 2000 tip about a man who had offered over the Internet to provide his eight-year-old daughter for sex," the Justice Department reported; Willman was a "predator hunter" who infected the computers of child pornography suspects, Barnett told the California detective. Carr and a U.S. Customs agent went to Vancouver to interview the young man.[66]

Like most private informants, Willman had traveled in a swampy landscape, breaking laws ostensibly to help law enforcement, and twice becoming a suspect himself. In 1998, a cooperating witness in a federal case had downloaded pornography received from Willman, prompting "a Customs agent to alert his counterpart in Canada that Willman could be a criminal," according to the government's brief. The following year, U.S. Customs issued a "lookout report" at the borders based on speculation that he might try to enter the country to meet with a thirteen-year-old boy in Arkansas. Detective Carr also became suspicious after interviewing him and checking him out—suspicious enough to send e-mails suggesting that Willman "was likely a child pornography trafficker who Carr hoped Canadian law enforcement would prosecute."

The Justice Department made a point of these incidents to argue that Willman was never a government informant subject to the Fourth Amendment. "He was completely unknown to the particular state and federal agents that used the fruits of his search here," the government brief argued. "In fact, the agents had to conduct an investigation even to identify and locate him. A tipster can hardly be said to be working for government agents under these circumstances." Had he been someone a government agency "either knew or should have known" was searching people's computers, according to an earlier Ninth Circuit decision, his role might have made his search unconstitutional and the subsequent evidence inadmissible.[67] But the government portrayed Willman's association with law enforcement as "scattered and haphazard."

Judge Kline's lawyers saw more of a pattern. Willman had told investigators that he had given information to police in Canada, Kentucky, Arkansas, New York, northern California, and Texas, some before the Kline search, some after. "Law enforcement provided a number of benefits to Willman for his work for them," Kline's appeals brief noted: He was spared prosecution for possessing child pornography, the illegal materials were never confiscated, "nor did law enforcement ask him to return the money he made from his sales." Furthermore, in the midst of ongoing cooperation, the trial judge found, law enforcement asked Willman for more information: Customs had requested his help investigating a Russian pornography ring.[68]

Indeed, despite the government's attempt to dissociate itself from Willman's searches, Detective Carr, in applying for a search warrant of Kline's home, cited Willman as a source who had proved "reliable" in prior relationships with law enforcement.[69]

When the police confiscated Kline's home computer, an investigator opened a video file depicting "two minor boys engaged in oral copulation." The local district attorney's office then turned the case over to Customs, which got federal warrants for the judge's home and office computers.

The home hard drive contained the diary and more than 1,500 pictures of boys, including 100 pornographic images. "The court computer contained more images of naked boys," the government reported, "diary entries discussing defendant's sexual interest in particular boys, and records of defendant using his court computer to access websites that appeared to cater to pedophiles."[70]

When Kline moved to suppress all this evidence as the fruit of an unconstitutional search by Willman, the trial judge agreed, finding that Willman was in effect an agent of the state. On appeal, government attorneys worried that the intermediary PedoWatch, which worked closely with law enforcement, might be considered a quasi-government agency. But Kline's lawyers didn't make that argument, and a three-judge panel of the Ninth Circuit saw no agency relationship.[71] With the evidence reinstated, Kline pleaded guilty, and when the trial judge in February 2007 sentenced him to twenty-seven months in prison, he collapsed into the arms of his lawyer.[72] He was placed in the Federal Medical Center at the Butner federal prison in North Carolina, evidently for treatment of his pedophilia.

"The Internet is a lawless country," wrote a blogger. "Without those willing to establish justice, chaos will always ensue. Brad Willman should be handed a badge and a $100k salary."[73]

Ah, but then he would need search warrants.

CHAPTER EIGHT

Life, Liberty, and the Pursuit of Terrorists

*I have no faith in these prosecutions. The government has no idea
what they're doing. They have no idea where the terrorists are or
who the terrorists are. They're just running around showing off, or
pretending to show off. America's at such risk from these people.*

—William Swor, defense attorney

RORSCHACH TESTS

IF THE WORLD'S major intelligence agencies could be so thoroughly
mistaken in their consensus that Iraq under Saddam Hussein possessed
chemical and biological weapons in 2003, if all the espionage and surveillance powers of the United States, Britain, Russia, and others could
combine themselves into such a colossal error, then how can mid-level
operatives reliably conclude that someone is a terrorist? You might think
that after providing the false rationale for launching a long, brutal, and
unnecessary war, failed intelligence methods would be greeted with skepticism, especially when aimed at identifying dangerous individuals. But
no, intelligence remains central to counterterrorism. Disjointed eavesdropping, unchecked hearsay, and maps of people's contacts are assembled into caricatures—some accurate, some not.

It is well known that fragments of unverified intelligence, from
searches and surveillance conducted outside the rigorous requirements
of the Fourth Amendment, overwhelm analysts and send investigators
on wild forays of speculation. Sometimes clear-thinking officials stitch
together disparate scraps to produce legitimate prosecutions. But an initial thread of information can also be spun into a hunch and then a theory
and then an elaborate scenario that weaves a tale of partial distortions
and imaginary facts. That is what happened in the first major terrorism
case after September 11, illustrating how the evasion of constitutional
demands can corrupt an investigation. It began with a shard of misleading intelligence and continued in violation of rules that have matured in
accordance with the Constitution—procedures that would have offered

a better chance of testing the government's allegations and getting at the truth.

At the center of the case stood Karim Koubriti of Fez, Morocco, who had the misfortune to win a United States immigration visa in the annual State Department lottery. He had never dreamed that going to America would be possible, and had never imagined that being in America would be a nightmare.

Koubriti seemed an affable man. Six feet tall with a shaved head and a very short goatee, he smiled a lot and laughed easily at absurdities, although it was often a bitter laugh. His dark eyes looked wounded. On a strap around his right ankle, he wore a black box, about two inches square, that sent a signal through his phone when he was home near Detroit, as he was required to be at certain times of day.

His sister in Fez had heard about the lottery first. Every year, among millions of applications throughout the world, the State Department randomly chooses 50,000 for "diversity visas" from countries with low immigration rates to the United States. "She asked me if I wanted her to fill it [out] for me," and he still remembered his sarcastic reply: "'Yeah, right, I'm lucky.' She was like, 'I'm gonna fill it anyway.'" And she did: for him, for herself, for their cousin, all sitting in Morocco hoping to win. Koubriti's number came up, and he alone got a coveted green card, certification of legal residence. "So why not?" he asked himself. "I have the green card! This is America!"

Just twenty, he had dropped out of college after two years of courses on French law. "I got tired of studying," he admitted, "so my father opened a coffee shop for me. It was enough for me as a single man," but not enough for the "better future" he thought America would offer. Like many, he was charmed by the promise. "That's why everybody comes to the United States: make more money, allow you to get married and have children and have comfortable life."

Never out of Morocco before getting on a plane to New York, "I just flew. I don't know nobody. I don't know where I'm going, just take the plane." It was October 2000, when America still stood on the better side of the dividing line drawn by September 11, 2001.

Koubriti traveled on the hard, familiar ground walked by legions of immigrants before him: a room in Harlem rented from a Moroccan woman he met on the flight, a threadbare job handing out leaflets in the cold, then a temp agency's referral to a place called Ohio—"I thought it was like another neighborhood or something, and I find myself taking the

264 / THE RIGHTS OF THE PEOPLE

bus for twelve hours." In Canton, he was paid six dollars an hour in cash to hang newly slaughtered chickens on a conveyor of hooks speeding by. "It was cold inside," he said, the chickens wet and slippery. "There are people working with the live chicken—I'm not gonna work there, the chicken is yellin' and stuff. I work with the dead one, all the day, ten hours. And I never work in my life!" He smiled and laughed all the way through the telling, as if the joke were on him.

He worked during the week, blew his money in bars and nightclubs on weekends, "and then when I'm broke I come back and work over again." Without the English that he later learned in prison, Koubriti gravitated to another Moroccan, Ahmed Hannan, the two of them practically alone as legal immigrants among the factory's battalions of undocumented aliens from Africa and Latin America. After five months in the hellish slaughterhouse, they followed a rumor that the Arab community in Dearborn, Michigan, could "help you out, especially the language—you don't speak the language, they may sympathize with you and give you a job."

They headed there with a third man, from Tunisia, but found few doors open. "No jobs, no English," was Koubriti's summary. "Go, look around, find a job. I was working busboy and dishwasher for seven-fifty. I'm working two jobs. I don't even have my lunchtime. I smoke my cigarette up. I eat up. Then he send me to clean the bathroom. I was pissed. He's Arab, too." Every position felt beneath him.

He and Hannan looked for something better through a community agency, which steered them to the midnight shift at Sky Chefs, a catering outfit at the Detroit airport. For months they washed trays and dishware from airliners, jobs that came with vague possibilities of promotion. More significantly, they came with employee ID badges. By the week after 9/11, when federal agents searching for terrorists were like prospectors delirious with gold fever, the ID cards glistened like nuggets of evidence.

Koubriti answered the knock at the door. He was about to learn some new rules: If you're an Arabic-speaking Muslim trying to make your way in America in a time of terrorism, you'd better work a long distance from an airport, do background checks on your housemates, make sure previous tenants aren't on watch lists, and scour your new apartment for any doodles and drawings and tapes left behind.

The places Koubriti and the others lived—first a basement apartment in Dearborn—had housed a rolling population of single young men, moving in and out as they struggled in one low-wage job after another. A couple of them left a faint legacy, the slightly sour whiff of something amiss. One, who had lived in the basement, was a mentally ill Yemeni,

Ali Ahmed, who had filled a day planner with demented scribbles and had committed suicide two months before Koubriti arrived. Another had taken videos of tourist sites in Las Vegas and Disneyland. A third, an Algerian, had bought audiotapes of sermons at an Islamic convention at a Ramada hotel; he was going to send them home to spread their message of nonviolence.

You don't get to choose your bedfellows in that kind of hardscrabble subculture, and one of Koubriti's fleeting housemates, a fraudster of many aliases, brought an air of discomfort into the basement. "His story didn't fit," Koubriti recalled. "In the beginning, he said he didn't have any money—'I need to live with you guys. I'm gonna find a job.'" Then he'd leave for most of the day, instruct them not to ask him any questions, and finally brag about "how he's good on the computer, how he can make fake documents for everybody."

Calling himself Yousef Hmimsa, he made the others nervous, and then downright hostile when he stole Hannan's Moroccan driver's license, they suspected, to duplicate in making forgeries. An interplay of mutual retaliation followed: They kicked Hmimsa out and moved to 2653 Norman Street in Detroit. Allegedly they pilfered some of his phony documents, either as leverage to retrieve Hannan's license or, as an indictment later charged, to use for themselves and extract a blackmail payment. Hmimsa, indicted for document fraud, took his revenge on them as a government informant possessed with a juicy story.

There were more twists and turns in the labyrinth, but suffice it to say that when FBI agents knocked on the door at Norman Street on September 17, 2001, they did not know anything about any of the men inside. They were looking for someone whose name was on the mailbox but hadn't lived there for two years: Nabil al-Marabh. He had surfaced in the frenetic investigation of the 9/11 attacks, in some piece of untested intelligence.[1] The team at the door comprised six agents from the FBI, the Immigration and Naturalization Service, and the State Department.

"I was taking shower," Koubriti recalled. "Knocking the door strongly, downstairs. . . . 'Nabil! Nabil!' They're yelling, 'Nabil!' Come downstairs, he told me. 'You know Nabil?' 'No know Nabil.' They have a translator with them."

In fact, Koubriti learned later, there had been two tenants between himself and Nabil. "An Egyptian man come after him, a family come after him, then we come." An FBI agent flashed a picture of Nabil, Koubriti said he didn't recognize the man, they didn't believe him, and they demanded his driver's license. As he turned upstairs to get it, they followed him inside—uninvited, he insisted—failing to observe the bureau's rule to inform him that he did not have to consent to a search. It never occurred to him that he had such an unimaginable right. "In my country you can't tell the police don't go to my house. They'll kick your ass."

Inside, the agents rudely woke Hannan and a third resident, Farouk Ali-Haimoud (at gunpoint, Koubriti said); inquired about Nabil; drew a blank, and asked the men where they worked. Technicolor, said Koubriti and Hannan. They had been fired by Sky Chefs for missing shifts after claiming injuries in a traffic accident, and were now packing videos for Technicolor. But in one of those random oversights that can mess up your life, they hadn't thrown away their old Sky Chefs badges. The agents spotted them "in plain view" during an initial search without a warrant. So here were airport IDs for jobs they didn't have. The men were handcuffed as the search continued.

The passes were nothing but fool's gold. They did not permit entry into secure parts of the airport—not to the tarmac or the planes, only to the one-story Sky Chefs building of gray, corrugated metal near the parking lots, a healthy bus ride at least a mile from the terminal. Anybody could drive up to it.

Nevertheless, the agents and prosecutors "would always bring up this Sky Chefs badge without ever explaining that it didn't allow access to the airport or to airplanes," said Koubriti's lawyer, Richard M. Helfrick. And the passes made the agents very interested in these three men, especially when Koubriti directed them to Hmimsa's forged documents.[2]

Then they came across a few items left over from the basement apartment, whose landlord had insisted it be cleared out entirely: the day planner with crooked lines, circles, and Arabic writing; the videotape of Disneyland and Las Vegas; and the audiotapes of an imam's sermons. Through the lens of suspicion, now polished and focused, these elements were arranged by investigators into "a covert underground support unit for terrorist attacks within and outside the United States," according to the indictment, "as well as a 'sleeper' operational combat cell," a "shadowy group" that "stayed in the weeds, planning, seeking direction, awaiting the call."[3] In shorthand, the three occupants of the Norman Street apartment, plus a fourth man, Abdel Elmardoudi, were dubbed the Detroit Sleeper Cell. American law enforcement was on the march.

The lead commando was Richard G. Convertino, a brash assistant U.S. attorney, a rising star among federal prosecutors. His investment in uprooting terrorism, shared with most Americans, came with the added depth of having lost a family friend in the 9/11 attack: a New York Fire

Department chaplain, Mychal Judge, who perished while helping a fire-fighter outside the World Trade Center. He was a Franciscan colleague of Convertino's brother, also a priest. Judge's family sent his ring to the prosecutor as a remembrance.

Convertino resented Washington's micromanagement of the high-profile case, stopped responding to incessant demands for reports and updates, and got so exasperated that he invited one official to meet him alone in an alley to duke it out, he told a reporter. The man was Barry Sabin, counterterrorism chief at the Justice Department, who had traveled to Detroit carrying concerns about the indictment. "I want to know where you got this theory," Sabin insisted.

"I pulled it out of my ass," Convertino snapped. "Is that what you want me to say?"[4] If so, Sabin would have been about right. The day planner, the linchpin of the case, seemed obscure and unconnected to the defendants. Leaf through its pages, and you see the Yemeni's full name, Ali Mohammed Ali Ahmed; the words "American Airbase in Turkey under the Leadership of Defense Minister"; "Queen Alia Jordan," a reference to the former wife of Jordan's late King Hussein, and numerous lines that make ninety-degree turns to the right, then to the left, each ending in a circle. From some circles, shorter lines radiate like misplaced spokes—or symbols of explosions. There are lines that jump and jiggle like tracings of an electrocardiogram, curved lines, lines that cross like intersections, and little stick figures that could be idle doodling or chicken feet or birds—or aircraft.

They were aircraft, decided Convertino, supported by an air force counterterrorism specialist, Lieutenant Colonel Mary Peterson. Joined by a couple of FBI agents, they also chose to believe that a shape resembling a map of the Arabian Peninsula, flanked by the Persian Gulf on one side and the Red Sea and the eastern coast of Egypt on the other, actually depicted a hangar at a U.S. airbase in Incirlik, Turkey—a hangar badly bent out of shape, apparently—and that the little chicken feet on one side were planes emerging and heading for a runway. Looking at this Rorschach test, Convertino also decided that some of the intersecting lines represented a diagram of the Queen Alia Military Hospital in Amman, Jordan—"casing sketches" that were part of the "tradecraft" of terrorists, in the lingo of the investigators. (Keith Corbett, a Justice Department cocounsel, conceded later that the drawings looked as if they'd been done by a three- or four-year-old child.)[5]

The films of Disneyland and Las Vegas were dubbed "casing videos" to prepare for attacks at the tourist spots. When the camera lingered on a trash container, the FBI argued that it was "an ideal location" for a bomb. When it panned to a cave at Disneyland, the Tunisian taking the video was heard saying, "This is a graveyard," according to the government translator, who was unfamiliar with the Arabic spoken in Tunisia. The defendants' interpreter, who knew the dialect, translated the line as "Here is a cave."[6] The audiotapes, never translated fully, were summarized and allegedly mischaracterized by an interpreter who was later revealed to be a violent criminal, compensated by federal prosecutors with a hefty fee and a reduced sentence.

Intriguing and terrifying tales were spun by the informant Hmimsa and believed, although in trial he displayed difficulty discerning truth from falsehood, saying of his many aliases, "None of them are lies to me." He claimed that the defendants were looking for vulnerabilities in security at Detroit and Chicago airports, that Koubriti wanted to poison food going onto airliners, that one defendant had called Las Vegas "the city of Satan," that the group wished to buy Stinger missiles to shoot down planes, that they communicated in code using the names of Moroccan soccer players, and that they all expressed admiration for Osama bin Laden.

Koubriti was angry at this and wanted to testify, but Helfrick was afraid that he'd lose his temper on the stand. Perhaps, but his rough naïveté might have played convincingly. "I was never getting involved in politics," he told me. "I used to ask my father, Why are you guys watching the news every day? I used to go find girls, drink, smoke hashish—honestly. I don't give a fuck about these politics, about this one killing this one, this one. I don't talk about religion. I wasn't religious. I'm a Muslim, I was born a Muslim, I do fast Ramadan, 'cause I think that's a big obligation. . . . I don't attend mosque. . . . I never heard the name Osama bin Laden that I heard after September 11. As a Muslim man, I never heard the name, but when I saw the picture I remember one day me and my mother and brother, everybody sitting at lunch and watching TV, showing this man with white stuff on his head asking all Muslims for jihad. Then we start laughing. I was like, What is this guy talking about? Jihad against who?"

The reporters covering the trial were also laughing, in disbelief, as they watched the government roll out its case. "We were all waiting for that climactic moment when we all said, 'Yes, that's it.' And it never happened," said David Ashenfelter, a Pulitzer Prize–winning reporter for the *Detroit Free Press*. "All we had was 'tradecraft.'" He pronounced the word in a conspiratorial whisper. "And we used to laugh in the back row about 'tradecraft.' There were so many things that we have in our homes that fall under the category of what [the FBI] called 'tradecraft'; we looked at that and said, 'Man, we're all guilty.'"

If the reporters could be so skeptical of the carefully sanitized case the government chose to put on, then perhaps the jurors would have been skeptical if they had seen what the government withheld. Behind each incriminating interpretation of the day planner and the videos ran a strong countercurrent of doubt, constituting exculpatory evidence required under the Supreme Court precedent in *Brady v. Maryland* to be turned over to the defense. Under that ruling, handed down in 1963, a conviction can be overturned if the prosecution fails to disclose information raising questions about the defendant's guilt.[7] And beneath Hmimsa's fluent storytelling lay evidence impeaching his credibility, required under *Giglio v. United States* to be revealed.[8] These are two pillars of criminal procedure, so Helfrick and the other defense attorneys appealed repeatedly to Judge Gerald E. Rosen, who was slow to recognize the prosecution's defiance of the law.

In exchange for his testimony against the "sleeper cell," Hmimsa was treated with kid gloves in a plea agreement that consolidated ten felony charges of credit-card and document fraud, and lowered the amount stolen to $70,000, producing a relatively light sentence of forty-six months. This is a chronic problem with criminals who become government informants. But prosecutors here went further: They also protected him from scrutiny by deporting witnesses and burying his boasts of lying, as reported in a letter from a fellow inmate.

The letter came from Milton "Butch" Jones, a notorious drug dealer in the cell next to Hmimsa's, who took copious notes of conversations as Hmimsa denounced the U.S. invasion of Afghanistan and bragged of fooling the FBI and the Secret Service. It was forwarded to Convertino well before the trial by another assistant U.S. attorney, Joe Allen, and by law should have been given to the defense. But it was not, and so the jury never knew of Hmimsa's boasts. The inconsistencies in the stories Hmimsa told were cloaked by Convertino's refusal to put him before a grand jury or allow FBI interviewers to take notes of their pretrial interviews.[9] That left no way for defense attorneys to compare his trial testimony with what he'd said before.

The government hid witnesses like peas in a shell game. Three men who could have thrown Hmimsa's testimony into question were deported before the trial. One of them, Brahim Sidi, "had been in government custody the entire time we were looking for him and the entire time the government said they didn't know where he was," complained William

Swor, one of the defense attorneys. "He had been deported three weeks before the original trial date."

Inconvenient facts were discarded, concealed, or manipulated to fit the theory of the crime. The defense and the jury never learned that FBI counterterrorism agents in Las Vegas had determined that the film purporting to prepare for a terrorist attack was not a "casing video."

Jurors didn't hear that the sinister interpretations of the doodles and drawings had been questioned by some intelligence and law enforcement officials. Convertino kept under wraps the CIA's conclusion that the supposed sketch of the base in Turkey was neither useful nor prepared by a terrorist cell—an assessment Convertino didn't seem interested in hearing, according to the senior CIA analyst who relayed the finding. A similar view by the Turkish police—that it didn't resemble any sketch they'd seen done by terrorists—was also kept from the jurors.

Neither defense nor jury knew of a dissenting report by an air force special agent contradicting Lieutenant Colonel Peterson's testimony that the sketch "was depicting airfield operations." The agent pointed out that the so-called hangar drawing showed it upside down, its door "opening from the rear" instead of the front. Yet in her testimony saying she'd circulated the sketch among other base officials, Peterson failed to mention the contrary opinion, thereby creating a "strong inference of unanimity," according to a later filing by the Justice Department, which called her testimony "inaccurate."[10]

Finally, despite promises to introduce pictures of the Queen Alia military hospital, Convertino did not do so, putting on the stand a State Department security officer from the embassy in Jordan, Harry Raymond Smith, who had taken aerial photos but testified that he had not, and insisted that he could not because of Jordanian security restrictions. Evidently, the pictures did not coincide with the sketch. Again, the jury never knew.

And so it convicted Koubriti and Elmardoudi of conspiring to provide "material support" to terrorists. They and Hannan were found guilty of document fraud, and Ali-Haimoud was acquitted of all counts.

Why did the jurors buy the story? "You start a terrorism trial on the day the United States invades Iraq, you select an anonymous jury," explained defense attorney Swor. "They assemble somewhere away from the courthouse at secret parking lots. They come on secret buses. They are escorted into the federal courthouse under guard. You don't think they are scared? One of the prospective jurors asked to be excused because she was absolutely convinced that our clients were going to find out who she was and where she lived and send someone to kill her." Defense attorneys got nowhere in their motions to postpone the trial so it didn't coincide with the invasion, to reduce the security hype so jurors would not be biased, and to force the prosecution to disclose evidence.

After the convictions and before sentencing, however, the case unraveled, thanks to persistent defense motions and a few honest Justice Department officials. Joe Allen presented the Butch Jones letter about Hmimsa to colleagues, who went to Judge Rosen, confirming the growing unease he had felt during the trial. Rosen ordered a full investigation of evidence withheld, "the most unpleasant task that I've had in almost fourteen years as a judge," he said, which resulted in the government's motion to dismiss the terrorism charges but to retry the fraud counts.

The epilogue was undramatic. Despite her "inaccurate" testimony under oath, Mary Peterson continued up the career ladder, suggesting that the air force saw nothing wrong with her behavior. She was put in charge of the counterterrorism branch at the Intelligence Fusion Center in Baghdad, then assigned to NATO, commanded a support group in England, was promoted to full colonel, and became the air attaché at the U.S. Embassy in Poland.[11]

Convertino and Smith of the State Department did not fare so well. Convertino, in long-standing conflicts with some of his bosses, was taken off the case before sentencing and pushed out of government into private practice.[12] But that wasn't the end. This had been the first terrorist trial after September 11, and senior officials found the withholding of exculpatory and impeachment evidence blatant and embarrassing. So the Justice Department took the rare step of indicting its own prosecutor, along with Smith, for conspiracy, obstruction of justice, and making false statements. A jury quickly found them not guilty, however, and so they walked free. Convertino sued the Justice Department for privacy violations and malicious prosecution; Koubriti did the same against Convertino and the government.[13]

Nabil al-Marabh, the man the FBI was looking for at the Norman Street apartment, was arrested a day or two later in a Chicago suburb but never prosecuted. After a plea agreement on immigration issues, the government assured a federal judge that he had no terrorist ties, contrary to the intelligence report that had set the entire case in motion, and he was deported to Syria.[14]

Hannan and Koubriti remained vulnerable to prosecution for faking injuries in the traffic accident to defraud an insurance company—the same accident that had brought their dismissals for missing work at

Sky Chefs. Hannan, tired of waiting in jail, pleaded guilty and accepted deportation back home to Morocco. Koubriti was released from jail on an electronic tether, hence the ankle bracelet. Helfrick worked to resolve the charge, and in 2009 the government finally agreed to drop it if Koubriti stayed out of trouble for six months.[15]

"There are a lot of dangerous guys out there," concluded the reporter David Ashenfelter. "These aren't among them."

TERRORISM AND THE BILL OF RIGHTS

How to deal with the dangerous and spare the innocent—and how to know the difference—are questions that have put the United States itself on trial since September 11, 2001. The constitutional culture has been unsettled by various methods used against terrorism suspects inside the country—not just the "detainees" at Guantánamo and those who disappeared into secret CIA prisons abroad. On U.S. soil, with insufficient evidence to bring criminal charges, the government has imposed preventive detention by locking people up as "material witnesses," jailing them for months pending deportation, or—in three cases—putting them in military prisons as enemy combatants. When the criminal courts have been used, solid investigation has been mixed with bumbling and overreaching.

Protections of the Bill of Rights are violated every day at the grassroots level of American life, but when the encroachments occur on the large stage of counterterrorism, the drama grips Americans' passions with special force. The country now thinks about civil liberties mainly in terms of the war on terrorism, not the war on crime, although the incursions into liberty are part of the same set of constitutional issues.

Because terrorism combines ideology and violence, authorities have trespassed on the First Amendment by considering speech and religion when targeting suspects. Because prevention is paramount, officials have tunneled beneath the Fourth Amendment's restrictions on search and surveillance, and have sometimes breached the Fifth Amendment's shield against self-incrimination to gather intelligence. Because state secrets need keeping and public trials are unpredictable, the protectors of national security have sporadically evaded the protections of due process in the Fifth and Sixth Amendments, including the right to counsel and the right to confront and summon witnesses.

As in certain cases of ordinary crime, the unconstitutional actions have damaged the reliability of the fact-finding process, whose accuracy depends on the strict observance of the principles. Some innocents have been convicted, some who are guilty have surely been missed, and egregious penalties have been imposed on hapless misfits who have fantasized more vigorously than they have plotted.

Unconstitutional expedience has coursed through one agency after another like a virus infecting a remarkable number of highly educated attorneys from the most prestigious law schools. Yet it has also activated the country's self-correcting immune system, leaving us ill but very much alive. The judicial branch did not stand passively aside as the Bush administration tried to imprison people in the United States indefinitely without access to the courts. And contrary to some conservative Republicans' fears that criminal courts could not handle terrorist cases, they have proved capable of doing so.

Outcries erupted on the right when President Obama initially moved the leading 9/11 plotters from Guantánamo into the civilian system, and when his Justice Department prosecuted in civilian federal court the al-Qaeda-trained Nigerian student Umar Farouk Abdulmutallab for trying to blow up a plane as it approached Detroit on Christmas Day 2009. Loud patriotism, it seemed, meant casting aspersions on the constitutional rights provided in the criminal justice system, a crown jewel of our democracy. The country could not agree on how to protect its own liberties.

One argument held that observing the rights (to counsel, against self-incrimination) for a non-American in an act of war would deprive the government of critical information, presumably accessible through tough interrogation. The assumption did not hold up. Abdulmutallab talked freely following his arrest about his associates in Yemen and, following a hiatus after being Mirandized, resumed cooperating at the urging of his family, presumably in the hope of a plea agreement.[16]

Similar arrangements had been achieved in numerous cases where suspects with attorneys had offered useful intelligence after being read their Miranda rights to silence and to counsel: An American in Chicago, David Coleman Headley, provided information on the 2008 attacks on a railroad station, hotels, and a Jewish center in Mumbai. A New Yorker, Bryant Neal Vinas, helped European prosecutions with details on al-Qaeda training camps. Mohammad Junaid Babar, an American who had given or received explosives instruction in the Afghan-Pakistani border region, pleaded guilty to conspiring to provide material support to al-Qaeda and testified in Canadian and British terrorism trials. Based on cooperating defendants in Minneapolis, the government acquired enough evidence to charge eight men with recruiting young immigrants to become suicide bombers in Somalia.[17] The would-be Times Square car bomber, Faisal Shahzad, talked helpfully before and after being read his rights, the Justice Department reported. He later pleaded guilty and received a life sentence.

Nothing indicated that military commissions, favored by critics on the right, would do better than civilian courts. In examining 123 prosecutions for terrorism, almost all of them since 2001, Human Rights First concluded that the criminal justice system had performed adequately, and that no alternative mechanism was needed—not an "enemy combatant" designation by the president, and not a national security court as advocated by George W. Bush's last attorney general, Michael B. Mukasey, where hearsay and coercion might be accepted, and evidence based on sensitive intelligence could be concealed from defendants.[18]

In advocating a security court, Mukasey cited his 1995 experience as a U.S. district judge trying a group led by Sheikh Omar Abdel Rahman for conspiring to blow up the United Nations headquarters, the Holland and Lincoln Tunnels, and other New York City landmarks. A list of nearly two hundred unindicted co-conspirators, representing considerable secret work by intelligence agencies, was disclosed to defense lawyers, and "that list was in downtown Khartoum within ten days," Mukasey said, alerting those named (including Osama bin Laden) that they were under U.S. surveillance.[19]

Mukasey's claim was misleading. The law contains a workable remedy, which the government never invoked to conceal the names in that case: the Classified Information Procedures Act (CIPA).[20] It was passed in 1980 after defendants accused of espionage and other crimes tried to "graymail" the government into dropping charges by threatening to divulge secrets or demand their disclosure in open court.[21] The ploy sometimes worked, and prosecutions were abandoned to avoid unwelcome revelations. Now, the CIPA procedures allow a judge to conduct a closed, in camera review of classified information to be introduced by the defense or sought from the government. If the judge finds the evidence relevant, the government says yes or no to disclosure.

If the answer is yes, then it's seen by the defense attorney, who must have a security clearance. But the defendant himself usually doesn't get a look at it, except possibly in a censored or summarized form called a "substantial equivalent," which conceals intelligence sources and methods. Some courts have extended this approach to live witnesses, who have been masked or assigned pseudonyms.

If the government says no to disclosure, the judge decides on a sanction, which could be as minor as removing all the factual evidence that the concealed material would address, or as stiff as the dismissal of a count or a charge. It rarely comes to that, though, for as anyone who has dealt with security-minded censors quickly learns, negotiation over language and detail usually forges a solution.[22] After its close study, Human Rights First concluded, "We are not aware of a single terrorism case in which CIPA procedures have failed and a serious security breach has occurred."[23]

The disadvantages for the defendant include his inability to see the raw material—to confront the evidence, which may contain an exculpatory flaw that his lawyer wouldn't notice. Even his lawyer doesn't participate in the initial examination of the classified material, and judges and prosecutors can't be expected to see relevance the same way as the defense.

Gathering intelligence and keeping it out of defendants' hands were among Bush's motives in designating two American citizens and one legal foreign resident as enemy combatants, subject to indefinite incarceration in military prisons without charge or trial. These might be called "internal combatants"—part of the family, so to speak, because they all had the legal right to live in the United States and were known in legal parlance as "U.S. persons" enjoying full constitutional protection. Two were actually arrested inside the country: the legal foreign resident and one of the American citizens; the second American was captured in Afghanistan. They were distinct from the external combatants, such as those in Guantánamo, who had been seized abroad and were not citizens.

Although the three were held incommunicado, lawyers managed to file habeas corpus petitions on their behalf, by which they invoked the venerable right to summon their jailers before a judge to justify the imprisonment. The Bush administration fought this vigorously, and ultimately lost. The framers had made the Great Writ of habeas corpus exceedingly resilient, first by placing it with legislative powers in Article I, suggesting that only the Congress could suspend it, and then only "when in Cases of Rebellion or Invasion the public Safety may require it." Consequently, the Bush strategy found little traction in the courts.

The chief justice had ruled during the Civil War that Lincoln had no power, as president alone, to suspend habeas corpus,[24] and, just after the war, the Supreme Court decided that military tribunals could not be used to try civilian citizens when civilian courts were functioning.[25] During World War II, however, the Court ruled that the president could declare a squad of German military infiltrators, including a naturalized American, enemy combatants and try them before military tribunals.[26]

These competing precedents carried the Court into the case of Yaser Esam Hamdi, raised in Saudi Arabia from the age of three, captured in Afghanistan, and transported to Guantánamo, where the military discovered his American citizenship when he mentioned that he'd been born in Louisiana. He was then transferred to American soil, first to the naval brig in Norfolk, Virginia, then to the brig in Charleston, South Carolina. The government alleged that he had fought with the Taliban, an assertion a federal district court judge found unsubstantiated, based on "little more than the government's say-so." His father contended in court papers that his twenty-year-old son, traveling for the first time alone, had gone to do "relief work" and had been "trapped in Afghanistan once that military campaign began."

Hamdi had no lawyer and got one only because of a brief newspaper report that he had been flown from Guantánamo to Norfolk via Virginia's Dulles Airport. The item was seen by the federal public defender in Virginia, Frank Dunham, Jr., who asked the court to be appointed counsel, then filed a habeas corpus petition on Hamdi's behalf. But Dunham was not allowed to see his client until the case had worked its way up to the Supreme Court, and the brief was due. That was the government's pattern: stall until the verge of embarrassment and defeat in the highest court, then yield as little as possible.

The conservative Fourth Circuit had ruled that Hamdi had no right to challenge, and the judiciary had no power to examine, his designation as an enemy combatant under which Bush claimed the authority to hold him indefinitely without charge, counsel, or trial. The government argued, remarkably, that such a detainee had sufficient opportunity during interrogation to deny that he was a combatant—that is, while possibly being tortured by the "enhanced interrogation techniques" that the government had secretly authorized.

In normal times, it could have been naturally assumed that no legitimate court could possibly have endorsed such an argument. But these were not normal times, and so those who cared about noble principles were reduced to awkward celebration when the Supreme Court reversed the Fourth Circuit and declared the obvious: that "due process demands that a citizen held in the United States as an enemy combatant be given a meaningful opportunity to contest the factual basis for that detention before a neutral decisionmaker."

It was a mixed opinion, however, interpreted by the left and the right to suit their own purposes. Two overlapping majorities of the justices ruled that American citizens could be held as enemy combatants, under the measure passed by Congress a week after September 11 authorizing the president to use "all necessary and appropriate force" against "nations, organizations, or persons" associated with the attacks. However, the other majority found that since Congress had not suspended habeas corpus, the Fifth Amendment's due process clause also gave a prisoner the right to challenge the detention. "There is no bar to this Nation's holding one of its own citizens as an enemy combatant," wrote Justice Sandra Day O'Connor, but only "once it is sufficiently clear that the individual is, in fact, an enemy combatant." That finding may be made with looser standards than in a criminal court, the opinion continued, including second-hand evidence and a presumption of guilt, standards that could be employed by military commissions.[27]

Some conservatives took heart from this, most notably John Yoo, author of the infamous torture memo, who said that he saw it as "a 50-percent win for the government," affirming its power to hold citizens as enemy combatants as long as some form of judicial review is accorded. By contrast, however, the most erudite conservative on the Court, Antonin Scalia, joined by the liberal John Paul Stevens, scoffed that the plurality of justices, "as though writing a new Constitution, comes up with an unheard-of system in which the citizen rather than the Government bears the burden of proof, testimony is by hearsay rather than live witnesses, and the presiding officer may well be a 'neutral' military officer rather than the judge and jury."

Liberals focused on the fact that Hamdi had won his right to contest his imprisonment, and they hailed the most widely quoted line in O'Connor's opinion: "We have long since made clear that a state of war is not a blank check for the President when it comes to the rights of the Nation's citizens."[28]

After the decision, Dunham went to the military to negotiate Hamdi's release, and four months later, the malignant enemy combatant turned suddenly benign, harmless enough to go free. With no solid evidence against him, the Bush administration dodged the Court-ordered fact-finding process by deporting him to Saudi Arabia. In exchange, Hamdi renounced the American citizenship that he had acquired automatically at birth in Louisiana, and which he'd never known was his until the military had told him so. Unlike Dunham, who called his own American citizenship "the most important and valuable thing to me in my life, the last thing I would give up," Hamdi felt that he was giving up nothing and gain-ing everything that mattered at that moment: an end to his imprisonment, which had lasted three years without charges. He also agreed to live in Saudi Arabia for five years; never travel to Afghanistan, Iraq, Israel, Syria, or Pakistan; and not sue the U.S. government.[29]

The Supreme Court's decision in *Hamdi v. Rumsfeld* set in motion a small cascade of government capitulation. Both other cases of internal enemy combatants were eventually transferred to the criminal courts, but only after years of further delays and maneuvers by the Bush administration's ideologues, who treated each Court opinion as if it set no precedent and carried no impact beyond the specific defendant. This was a kind of constitutional apostasy, a defiance of the intricate culture of willing compliance with the rule of law. It did not take a scholar to see that what the Court said about Hamdi's right to habeas corpus would apply to the two others seized as enemy combatants, but the president and his men ignored and evaded adverse rulings to the extent possible.

The other American, Jose Padilla, was arrested at Chicago's O'Hare Airport on May 8, 2002, after flying in from Zurich. His name had been mentioned during the interrogation of Abu Zubaydah, a training camp personnel clerk originally thought to be third or fourth in the al-Qaeda hierarchy,[30] who described Padilla as part of a plot to detonate a "dirty bomb" that would spread radioactivity somewhere inside the United States.[31]

Padilla had been convicted for murder as a juvenile and then for gun possession in Florida. He converted to Islam in prison, moved to Egypt after his release, and traveled to Saudi Arabia, Pakistan, and Afghanistan, where in 2000 he allegedly enrolled in an al-Qaeda camp.

He was held for a month in civilian custody as a material witness, which is why he was assigned a lawyer by the court, but was then designated an enemy combatant by Bush and spirited away to isolation in the navy brig in Charleston, as the White House asserted the president's power to keep him locked up indefinitely without charges or trial. Bush's declaration, "based on the information available to me from all sources," came in a censored one-page order completely devoid of evidence or specifics.[32] The "sources" turned out to be Zubaydah and at least one other captive whose information was tainted by torture. The unverified statements from interrogations kept Padilla in the brig for one year and eight months before he saw an attorney, and three years and eight months before finally being turned over to the criminal justice system for indictment and prosecution.

The decision to use the courts was effectively forced by the courts. While Padilla's habeas corpus petition was working its way through the federal judiciary, the Supreme Court granted Hamdi's habeas appeal. Rather than argue essentially the same case again, the government delayed, then finally transferred Padilla to the criminal justice system, though not until shortly before his appeal was to be heard by the Supreme Court.[33]

He claimed that he was tortured in the brig. But his statements, evidently coerced, were touted by officials as evidence of al-Qaeda plots foiled. These included the "dirty bomb" scheme, training by al-Qaeda in explosives, and a plan to "undertake a mission to blow up apartment buildings in the United States using natural gas," a Senate committee was told by Deputy Attorney General James Comey. During interrogations, he allegedly admitted to laying plans with Khalid Sheikh Mohammed and other prominent al-Qaeda figures.[34]

This may have been true, but it was impossible to know, since the information was given under duress, a process the military didn't want disrupted. "Anything that threatens the perceived dependency and trust between the subject and interrogator directly threatens the value of interrogation as an intelligence gathering tool," said the head of the Defense Intelligence Agency, Vice Admiral Lowell E. Jacoby, in arguing that Padilla should be denied access to a lawyer. "Even seemingly minor interruptions can have profound psychological impacts on the delicate subject-interrogator relationship. Any insertion of counsel into the subject-interrogator relationship, for example—even if only for a limited duration or for a specific purpose—can undo months of work and may permanently shut down the interrogation process."[35]

In the Charleston brig, Padilla was manipulated with threats of being sent to another country or to Guantánamo Bay, his attorney contended in a brief. Using various techniques, military interrogators maneuvered him into helplessness: a pillow and sheet would be provided, then removed; a mirror would be given, then taken away; he was kept in bright lights, then in complete darkness, locked in a cold cell, denied a shower for weeks, allowed to exercise only at night.

"He was threatened with being cut with a knife and having alcohol poured on the wounds," according to the brief. "He was also threatened with imminent execution. He was hooded and forced to stand in stress positions for long durations of time. He was forced to endure exceedingly long interrogation sessions, without adequate sleep, wherein he would be confronted with false information, scenarios, and documents to further disorient him. Often he had to endure multiple interrogators who would scream, shake, and otherwise assault Mr. Padilla. Additionally, Mr. Padilla was given drugs against his will, believed to be some form of lysergic acid diethylamide (LSD) or phencyclidine (PCP), to act as a sort of truth serum during his interrogations."[36] (Drugging was banned by the Justice Department guidelines on torture.)

This may have explained the military's restrictions when he finally got to see an attorney. Just before the Supreme Court was expected to decide whether to hear the case, the government suddenly defused a key issue by calling one of his lawyers, Andrew Patel, to say that he and his colleague could see their client. But there were conditions: They could not ask Padilla any questions about the conditions of his incarceration, and the entire conversation would be audiotaped and videotaped while an officer stayed in the room, a breach of attorney-client privilege.

This was hardly the way Patel was used to meeting with clients, even those accused of heinous crimes. Padilla had been isolated so completely that he did not even know that he had a case pending before the Supreme Court. He was about to find out. Patel shipped twenty pounds of transcripts and filings to the brig for Padilla to read, but because of the monitoring he had no intention of letting Padilla say anything during the session. Patel would do all the talking, explaining his case. "I will tell him that one day I'd like to ask him many questions, and I hope we can," Patel said before he met with Padilla. Then he added: "My career has been spent as a criminal defense attorney, which means I deal with aberrant human behavior. Usually it's aberrant behavior by my clients, not by the government."

Padilla's complaints of abuse seemed at least partly valid, judging by the government's inability to retain the gravest accusations against him as he was transferred to the civilian justice system. Had he confessed to the most egregious plots voluntarily and without coercion, his statements could have been put into evidence, and certainly would have been. But since coerced statements are inadmissible under the Fifth Amendment, the charges were peeled away layer by layer until a prosecutable crime could be found. The radiological bomb plot, for which his arrest had been trumpeted by Attorney General John Ashcroft and certified in an affidavit by a Defense Department official, mysteriously disappeared, with no announcement or explanation.[37] So did the plan to blow up apartment buildings. Both charges just vanished from government documents; neither was mentioned in his criminal indictment. Their reliability appeared to have been contaminated by their origins: torture of Padilla inside the country and of Zubaydah outside. The government evidently concluded that the allegations could not be sustained in a normal, constitutional court of law.

Instead, Padilla and several others were charged with membership in a cell that conspired to commit murder overseas. It didn't get much more specific, but the main evidence, his application form to attend an al-Qaeda training camp, convinced a Miami jury. The government asked for a life sentence, and the judge gave him less—seventeen years and four months—because of the "harsh" conditions of his imprisonment in the brig, and the fact that "there is no evidence that [Padilla] personally killed, maimed, or kidnapped."[38]

The third "internal combatant," Ali Saleh Kahlah al-Marri, a legal resident of Illinois from Qatar, was shifted to the civilian system by the Obama administration in February 2009 after the Supreme Court had agreed to take his case the previous December.

On September 10, 2001, he had come to the United States with his wife and children for a master's degree in computer science and was eventually accused of association with al-Qaeda. Like Hamdi, al-Marri had run afoul of the conservative Fourth Circuit, where a three-judge panel had first ruled in his favor, only to be overturned by the entire court sitting en banc, which decided narrowly that the president had the power to detain a "U.S. person" indefinitely. This defied the opinions in *Hamdi* and in cases brought by prisoners at Guantánamo, and so the Supreme Court, in declaring the al-Marri appeal moot after he was placed in the criminal justice system, also vacated the Fourth Circuit's opinion, fortunately. That cut off the attempt by the conservative appeals court to permit unlimited executive power to arrest and detain indefinitely. He was indicted, pleaded guilty, and was sentenced to eight years for "conspiracy to provide material support" to a foreign terrorist organization, a broad statute that has been used extensively against terrorist suspects.[39]

For years, an odd minuet was danced by the president, the Congress, the Supreme Court, and the prisoners. While internal enemy combatants were asking for a fair hearing in court, external combatants in Guantánamo were pursuing the same goal in parallel litigation. They succeeded on paper, winning protection from a slim majority of the justices, but hardly any received their objective, fact-finding trials. More significantly for the whole country and its long-term constitutional health, the extraordinary regime of executive power sought by Bush was not swept cleanly away. A series of rulings by the Supreme Court inspired a series of laws by Congress, together leaving a dangerous legacy that Obama has mitigated but declined to erase. Foreigners and American citizens inside the United States, as well as outside, remained susceptible to presidential designation as enemy combatants, with foreigners subject to military commissions lacking sufficient guarantees to minimize the chance of error. That these powers were not used inside the country—not yet—was small comfort.

The Bush administration had argued that the Constitution and the courts did not reach to Guantánamo Bay, leased perpetually from Cuba, because the base was not on American soil. But since the United States had complete authority over the territory, and Cuba had none at all, the Supreme Court declined to participate in the fiction and ruled in *Rasul v. Bush* in 2004 that Guantánamo prisoners retained their habeas right.[40] After *Hamdi* the same year, containing the Court's admonition that some meaningful finding of fact was required, the Pentagon established Combatant Status Review Tribunals with one-sided rules, not to "try" enemy combatants so much as to process them. Congress responded with the Detainee Treatment Act of 2005. (Although the terms "tribunals" and "commissions" were often used interchangeably, they were to have different roles, the tribunals to determine whether the prisoners could be labeled enemy combatants, the commissions to determine guilt and punishment.)

The 2005 law stripped Guantánamo inmates—mentioning them explicitly—of their habeas right granted in a federal statute.[41] It made no mention of the two remaining internal combatants, and it did not purport to activate the Constitution's suspension clause by a finding that the country was subject to "Rebellion or Invasion."

Consequently, the Court found the following year that Congress had not suspended habeas corpus, which remained available to the Guantánamo inmates. Ruling five to three in *Hamdan v. Rumsfeld,* a case brought by a Yemeni who had been a driver for bin Laden, the Court also struck down the Combatant Status Review Tribunals the executive branch had unilaterally created, finding that they violated both the four 1949 Geneva conventions and their incorporation into the Uniform Code of Military Justice (UCMJ), which provides that military trials, "insofar as practicable," follow court-martial procedures. This pleased many military lawyers in the judge advocates general's divisions, who argued publicly that the court-martial model, with constitutional protections resembling those in criminal court, should be used to try terrorism suspects held at Guantánamo.

The president had failed to make the required determination that following the UCMJ was not practicable, the Court noted, and the tribunals were "not expressly authorized by any congressional act." Four of the justices declared, "Nothing prevents the President from returning to Congress to seek the authority he believes necessary."[42]

So he did, and the resulting Military Commissions Act of 2006 awarded the president some of the most awesome powers in American history. Again it denied habeas corpus to foreigners detained as enemy combatants, but this time there was no geographical restriction; they could be seized and held anywhere, in Afghanistan or Alabama, Iraq or Indiana. It permitted violations of practically every critical right in the Fourth, Fifth, and Sixth Amendments, allowing evidence obtained through warrantless searches, coerced interrogations, and hearsay—which meant that a government agent could testify that a witness had said something, without the witness being brought for cross-examination.[43]

Again the Supreme Court had to weigh in, and in 2008 again ruled, five to four, that people did not lose their constitutional right to habeas corpus by being labeled enemy combatants or being jailed at Guantánamo. "To hold that the political branches may switch the Constitution on or off at will would lead to a regime in which they, not this court, say what the law is," Justice Anthony Kennedy wrote for the majority in *Boumediene v. Bush*. "The habeas writ is itself an indispensable mechanism for monitoring the separation of powers. . . . If that privilege is to be denied them, Congress must act in accordance with the Suspension Clause's requirements," which would mean a determination that the country faced "Rebellion or Invasion."[44] This the Congress stopped short of doing.

In considering whether an adequate fact-finding substitute for a habeas writ existed, the Court in *Boumediene* cast aspersions on the military tribunals, which were to decide whether a person could be held as an enemy combatant. The tribunals posed a "considerable risk of error" by limiting the defendant's ability to confront witnesses, rebut evidence, and introduce exculpatory material, the Court ruled. The justices did not explicitly evaluate the next step in the process—the military commissions that were to conduct full trials of suspects whom the tribunals designated "unlawful enemy combatants." But under the standards set by the Court, the commissions wouldn't have passed muster either.

To protests from human rights and civil liberties groups, Obama and the Democratic-led Congress retained military commissions as an option for trying foreign citizens seized in the United States or elsewhere and accused under a broad swath of thirty-two crimes. These included far more than terrorism and violations of the laws of war: also hijacking, rape, spying, and lesser offenses commonly tried in criminal courts. Even while patching up most of the rights that had been shredded by the 2006 law, the Military Commissions Act of 2009 created a parallel judicial system—located in the executive branch—to handle a vast array of cases involving "alien unprivileged enemy belligerents," the new name for "enemy combatants."[45] It could be used inside the United States, but not against American citizens, leading several senators to propose stripping accused terrorists of their citizenship. A president and his attorney general could choose whether to send such defendants to trial before civilian judges and citizen jurors in federal criminal courts, or before panels of military officers in commissions. This was an enormous grant of executive power to evade a court system whose procedures have been seasoned by generations of constitutional precedent.

The new law significantly protects defendants' rights, although with caveats not yet precisely defined. Appeals from the commissions would be heard by the federal circuit court in D.C., which could even second-guess a guilty verdict by reexamining the evidence.[46] Contrary to the Bush approach, statements by the accused or witnesses would be inadmissible if made under torture or "cruel, inhuman, or degrading treatment," but less severe coercion might be allowed during capture or combat if a military judge finds the information "reliable and possessing sufficient probative value." The Fourth Amendment is not suspended inside the country, as it was under Bush's commissions; evidence obtained without proper warrants would be admissible only if seized overseas.

As in a civilian court, the prosecution must disclose facts that impeach witnesses or support innocence. The accused may summon his own witnesses and confront those against him, but hearsay may also be admitted under highly restrictive conditions: if the defense is told how it was obtained, has time to counter it, and the live witness is unavailable. As in civilian courts, complex procedures governing classified evidence seem, on paper, to protect the accused against conviction by secret information he cannot challenge. A charge that relies on evidence the government doesn't want to declassify and disclose may be reduced or dismissed by the judge—a commissioned officer who is also an attorney.

And that is one of the problems. Some military judges demonstrated remarkable independence in the abortive Guantánamo proceedings.

Moreover, President Obama and his aides seemed initially inclined to use the commissions rarely and discreetly.[47] Staffed with good people, the revised commissions may produce honest fact-finding to determine guilt or innocence accurately. But American liberty cannot depend on individual goodness alone. Judges and presidents come and go; some have yielded the country's values to the stresses of emergency and crisis. Obama has done some of that himself. Our history contains no guarantee that one or another citizen who rises to authority will wield the immense power of the state with wisdom, fairness, and humaneness. The only guarantee, if it exists at all, is embedded in our messy, complicated system that fragments and restrains that power.

So, America's sixth major departure from its constitutional principles leaves a formidable tool in the hands of the executive branch.

Rights advocates had hoped that the entire commission system would be scrapped after Obama took office. They wanted all terrorism suspects tried in civilian courts, an admirable goal not easily achieved, since a lot of evidence had been extracted by torture under Bush. Coerced and therefore unreliable, such testimony or confession would not be admissible in either civilian courts or the revised military commissions. A graphic illustration came in 2010 when a federal judge excluded a key government witness from testifying in the civilian trial of Ahmed Khalfan Ghailani, a Tanzanian accused of conspiring in 1998 to bomb the American embassies in Tanzania and Kenya, killing 224 people. Ghailani claimed that he had named the witness—the man who allegedly sold him the explosives—under abusive interrogation that included torture. These "coerced statements," Judge Lewis A. Kaplan ruled, had been extracted by violating the Fifth Amendment. Without that witness, the jury saw sufficient evidence to convict Ghailani of only 1 of 286 charges: conspiracy to destroy government buildings and property. Nevertheless, the judge gave him a life sentence.

Where untainted evidence was unavailable, Obama settled for indefinite detention without charge or trial, spurring two rights organizations to muster 120 former legislators, judges, prosecutors, diplomats, military officers, and government officials to urge the use of federal courts instead of such a "sweeping and radical departure from an American constitutional tradition that has served us effectively for over two centuries."[48]

At first, the Obama administration decided to try five alleged 9/11 plotters in federal court in lower Manhattan, citing the courts' effectiveness in previous terrorism cases as a means of discovering facts, determining guilt, and setting punishment if warranted.[49] Then, in the face of fierce political opposition, the administration considered using military commissions. It would be a severe capitulation, for the criminal justice system had already worked, albeit unevenly.

CONSPIRATORS AND WANNABES

Judging by the major terrorism cases prosecuted from 2001 through 2010, nothing on the scale of 9/11 appears to have been seriously planned, and al-Qaeda seemed uninvolved in most of the fledgling conspiracies, except indirectly as an inspiration, often via the Internet. Perhaps the government was skillful at thwarting plots at very early stages. Perhaps the authorities cast their nets so widely that they scooped up suspicious deviants before they evolved from marginal threats into full-fledged terrorists. Perhaps that is why most of the alleged crimes failed to match the bloated rhetoric that accompanied each arrest. Down in the details of the case, it turned out that wholesale slaughter had not been imminent, and no rampage of Islamic militance had been heroically repelled at the gates.

Instead, a few bored young men had gone off to training camps, had played paintball to practice battlefield skills, had concocted schemes with government informants, had tried and failed to get into Afghanistan, had broached the sale of a missile to an undercover agent, and had talked delusionally about attacking the Sears Tower in Chicago and John F. Kennedy Airport in New York—embryonic plans without the means of being carried out. Occasionally a plot seemed real, most notably two intercepted bombs flown from Yemen; the attempted car-bombing in Times Square; the would-be airplane bomber from Nigeria, trained by an al-Qaeda offshoot in Yemen; and a Manhattan coffee vendor, Najibullah Zazi, who pleaded guilty to taking explosives training in Pakistan, then accumulating chemicals bought from hair salons to combine into potent bombs.

The bloodiest domestic incident through 2009 bore no sign of having been organized by al-Qaeda or any other movement. It was the assault on soldiers at Fort Hood, Texas, by an army psychiatrist, Major Nidal Malik Hasan, who killed thirteen in what seemed an individual act sparked, possibly, by a religious radicalization whose indicators had been overlooked by intelligence and army personnel.

Otherwise, most dire threats were posed by sad-sack wannabes who didn't seem capable of lighting the right end of a fuse. They might have tried, however, and federal authorities weren't about to wait and see. A band of immigrants from Albania, Turkey, and Jordan, convicted of plotting to attack the Fort Dix army base in New Jersey, had gone as far as to vidcotape themselves shouting about jihad and training with automatic weapons in the Poconos. They were undone when they took the tape to be transferred to a DVD; a store clerk alerted the police, who called the FBI, which then infiltrated the group with two informants. Their "plan," to get onto the base as pizza deliverymen, envisioned a shootout followed by a miraculous escape.

In other cases, the government stretched the statutes to criminalize behavior that might have been ignored before September 11. Using asset-forfeiture laws, the Justice Department shut down a few Islamic charities by seizing funds, and prosecuted individuals for funneling contributions to Hamas and other groups on the government's terrorist list—contributions that ostensibly had gone for the organizations' humanitarian programs.

The zone of free speech shrank somewhat, bringing unwelcome FBI interest in comments that might ordinarily have been heard as extreme but benign, as acerbic political statements or ideological preaching, but not as threatening. Several people used rhetoric that may or may not have incited fellow Muslims to violence, and federal authorities per-suaded courts that such exhortations lay outside the First Amendment's protections. The most dramatic case ended with a life sentence for Ali al-Timimi, a cancer researcher who had earned a reputation as an erudite lecturer on Islam. Five days after September 11, he had spoken about jihad, as holy war, at a small dinner of young Muslims, some of whom then went to training camps of Pakistan's Lashkar-e-Taiba (Army of the Pious), which had conducted attacks on the Indian presence in disputed Kashmir.[50]

Beneath the public trials and beyond America's international frontiers, the drone attacks near the Pakistani-Afghan border, along with clandestine kidnappings, captures, and "renditions," apparently disrupted al-Qaeda's capacity to organize. While terrorism exploded in other parts of the world, and the wars in Iraq and Afghanistan drew jihadi fighters like moths to the flame, American soil stayed mostly free of attacks in the seven and a half years from September 11, 2001, through the end of Bush's tenure. He and his subordinates used that fact to justify their extralegal measures.

Therefore, the relatively innocuous cases that juries saw may have distorted some larger, hidden reality that never got to court. Some defen-dants seemed more misguided than dangerous. Some of the conspira-cies exposed in public trials looked synthetic, staged by FBI undercover agents or facilitated by unsavory criminals who worked as informants on the FBI's payroll. In 2009, for instance, agents posing as al-Qaeda opera-tives performed two separate capers in Illinois and Texas on two men who

had been targeted after their online and written statements favoring terrorism had been picked up by surveillance. The FBI led the men to think
they were planting car bombs—one near a federal courthouse in Spring-
field, the other beneath an office building in Dallas—but the explosives
were fake, and when the men punched numbers into their cell phones to
trigger the detonators, there were no booms, just busts.[51]

To some jurors, more discerning than those who convicted the Detroit
"sleeper cell," evidence in certain prosecutions appeared thin and speculative. It took three trials and three juries for the government to win its
case against a Miami group in the impoverished neighborhood of Liberty
City. In his long robe and cap, the leader, Narseal Batiste, seemed more
of a poseur than a terrorist. He called men "brother" and recruited a following to a quasi-religious cult that met in a warehouse, with more than
religion in mind.

Most were Haitian-Americans or Haitian immigrants. They were
either approached, infiltrated, or manipulated by an Arabic-speaking FBI
informant pretending to be a representative of al-Qaeda. Around him
they wove a web of grandiose fantasies, and he recorded their blustering.
He led them in a pledge of allegiance to al-Qaeda and bin Laden. He
taped Batiste boasting that they would start a "full ground war" against
the United States by destroying Chicago's 110-story Sears Tower and
bombing FBI offices in five cities. "I want to fight some jihad," Batiste
was heard saying at one point, to "kill all the devils we can."[52]

A senior FBI official called the plot "more aspirational than operational," a phrase then frequently applied to other conspiracies.[53] It contained plenty of words but no weapons, no explosives, and no actual
contact with the real al-Qaeda, making the charge of agreeing to provide
material support to the organization "a manufactured crime," in the view
of Batiste's attorney.[54] The Chicago police superintendent, Philip J. Cline,
said that there was "never any imminent danger to the Sears Tower or to
the city of Chicago."[55] Attorney General Alberto Gonzales saw a larger
pattern, declaring ominously, "The convergence of globalization and technology has created a new brand of terrorism. Homegrown terrorists may
prove to be as dangerous as groups like al-Qaeda."[56]

To prove conspiracy, prosecutors have to show that the defendants
not only talk among themselves but take at least one overt action, which
can be as simple as picking up the phone or walking across the street
to a meeting. The actions in this case were numerous. The defendants
photographed government buildings and a synagogue as potential targets,
the government charged. They asked the "al-Qaeda representative" to

train their "soldiers" and requested that he provide them with boots, binoculars, uniforms, radios, vehicles, bulletproof vests, automatic weapons, and $50,000 in cash. Batiste, who testified in all three trials, insisted that the money was to be used for his construction business and community-improvement projects. He seemed to think he was fooling al-Qaeda when, in fact, the FBI was fooling him—a play within a play.

The first jury acquitted one of the seven defendants and could not agree on the other six. A year later, the second jury deadlocked too, forcing a second mistrial. In the third year, the third jury finally found unanimity, acquitting one and convicting the remaining five, including Batiste. He received thirteen and a half years, the others, four to eight.[57]

Sting operations, infiltrations, and informants have been responsible for a good many counterterrorism prosecutions, raising the possibility of entrapment. That happens when a crime is proposed either by a law enforcement officer working undercover or by a citizen informant—usually a criminal looking for leniency—who pretends to be one of the boys while wearing a wire or a tiny video camera. Informants are often ill-trained and sloppy. By contrast, sworn officers who infiltrate violent movements are supposedly trained to pose as willing participants but not as initiators—a careful balance to protect themselves from discovery and the legal case from collapse. "You have to let it happen in front of you and just be there as a collector of evidence," explained Mike German, the former FBI agent and lawyer, who infiltrated white supremacist groups in California and Washington. "Ninety-nine times out of a hundred, your average FBI agent is going to be more honorable than an informant," who may blur the line between observing and initiating. But arguing entrapment is a hard defense, because a lawyer must show that his client had no predisposition to commit the crime; if there is such predisposition, it is not entrapment when government agents merely provide the opportunity.

In 2006, in exchange for cash and a reduced sentence, a twice-convicted narcotics trafficker went to work as a government informant. He became intricately involved in wild talk by a circle of Muslim men from Guyana and Trinidad whose conspiracy amounted to a year's bragging, posturing, and failed efforts to assemble a plot to blow up jet-fuel tanks and pipelines at Kennedy Airport. Whether they would ever have acquired the skills and the explosives remained a question: Law enforcement, monitoring them attentively, closed them down before they advanced beyond the talking stage. Officials then celebrated the disclosure of the plot with a discordant combination of glee, alarm, and reassurance.

"The public was never at risk," U.S. Attorney Roslynn R. Mauskopf conceded even after she raised the specter of a fiery demise for the airport and adjacent neighborhoods of Queens. "Had the plot been carried out," she declared, "it could have resulted in unfathomable damage, deaths, and destruction." Police Commissioner Raymond W. Kelly chimed in ominously, "Once again, would-be terrorists have put New York City in their crosshairs." Finally, the assistant director of the FBI's New York office, Mark J. Mershon, distilled the case into its essential ambiguity: "The ambitions were horrific, the capacities were very limited, but they kept trying. Their signature was their persistence."[58]

The group was a loose assortment of men who barely knew one another, allegedly led by Russell Defreitas, who seemed incapable of leading much of anything. He was a sixty-three-year-old former cargo handler who had been incensed at seeing missile parts readied for shipment through Kennedy to Israel—to kill Muslims, he told the informant, who recorded about three hundred hours of conversation with him. Briefly homeless and sleeping in subway trains, Defreitas had no contact with most of his family, practically no money, no training, and no experience in subterfuge and terrorism. He was semiliterate, his lawyers said, and had a low I.Q. But he had a few contacts in Guyana and was so trusting that he put the informant in touch with them.

The informant recorded his own phone calls with conspirators there, and he flew down with Defreitas several times for meetings in Guyana, where various men boasted and fantasized about wanting to blow up U.S. helicopters at the airport in Georgetown, to smuggle mujahideen from Asia into the United States, and to fly into Kennedy to execute their attack. One claimed to have a close friendship with a leader of Jamaat Al Muslimeen, a Trinidanian Muslim group that had nearly succeeded in a 1990 coup attempt by attacking the parliament building and taking the prime minister and cabinet members hostage. Contact with the movement was facilitated by a former member of Guyana's parliament named Abdul Kadir, which made the plot look serious enough for the FBI to buy plane tickets to Trinidad for Defreitas, the informant, and a third man. But their trip failed to interest the group in the Kennedy operation.[59]

The informant seemed such a constant presence in the brainstorming and networking that one wonders if the conversations and travel and meetings would have happened without him. In his vehicle, the FBI installed video and audio equipment that recorded Defreitas in a surveillance tour as they drove around the airport, pointing out fuel tanks and escape routes and commenting on security. Defreitas claimed that underground pipelines would erupt in an explosion and damage much of Queens, a threat dismissed as unlikely by experts who noted that the pipes were cut off by safety valves and lacked the oxygen necessary for combustion.

"Anytime you hit Kennedy, it is the most hurtful thing to the United States," Defreitas was recorded as saying. "To hit John F. Kennedy, wow. . . . It's like you can kill the man twice." He remembered idle and angry thoughts echoing in his mind while seeing planes on the runway: "If I could get a rocket, then I could do a hit. By myself, I am thinking about these things."[60] Delusions? Perhaps. But since 9/11 revealed a failure to envision such attacks, even delusions seem real.

Two categories of laws have come in handy for preventive prosecutions aimed at stopping would-be terrorists and other criminals long before they do harm. One is the "conspiracy" to commit a future crime; the other, "material support" to an organization designated unilaterally by the Secretary of State as terrorist.[61] Conspiracy can be used only if there's more than one suspect.[62] If there's just one culpable individual preparing with an undercover agent or informant, there's no conspiracy, and federal prosecutors have brought charges under the "material support" statute, even where the "support" is abortive, fictitious, or hypothetical. If numerous suspects are involved, the two violations can be layered on top of each other: conspiracy to provide material support.

The trouble is, both these laws have snared people with little more than tenuous desires to join a cause, so far from the actual act that their schemes look ludicrous and prosecutions look merciless. If you can be jailed for agreeing to provide material support to al-Qaeda when you've never been in touch with al-Qaeda (and just thought you had), or when you try and fail to reach Afghanistan, or when you attempt to sell a missile you don't have to nobody other than an FBI undercover agent,[63] how dangerous can you be? Doesn't organized terrorism require a level of rational thinking and planning? "Conspiracy" can be nebulous, and "material support" is defined so broadly and vaguely that some lawyers doubted its constitutionality until the Supreme Court upheld it in 2010, rejecting the vagueness argument. The federal law states:

> The term "material support or resources" means currency or monetary instruments or financial securities, financial services, lodging, train-

ing, expert advice or assistance, safehouses, false documentation or identification, communications equipment, facilities, weapons, lethal substances, explosives, personnel, transportation, and other physical assets, except medicine or religious materials.[64]

Any noncitizen in the United States or elsewhere can be tried in a military commission for this crime, under the law as revised in 2009 by the Democratic Congress and signed by President Obama. A U.S. citizen can be tried in civilian court.

The least specific offenses—"training" and "expert advice or assistance"—could preclude any contact with groups listed as "terrorist," even beneficial activities, such as training and advice on building democracy following civil wars. When a Justice Department official explained the law at a meeting in Washington of nonprofit agencies that provide humanitarian aid abroad, the representatives were shaking their heads and rolling their eyes in despair. The official even warned them to check out everyone they did business with, such as painters and plumbers they hired in foreign countries, to be sure they weren't affiliated with "terrorist" organizations. He would not rule out prosecution for slipups. Although no such cases have surfaced, experience suggests the danger in granting government such powers. In 2010 the Supreme Court upheld the law against a constitutional challenge by nonprofit groups claiming a violation of their First Amendment right to free speech and association.

They wanted to provide training in peaceful conflict resolution and international law to the Kurdistan Workers' Party (PKK) and the Liberation Tigers of Tamil Eelam (LTTE), separatist groups in Turkey and Sri Lanka, respectively, and to help them appeal for relief from the United Nations and other international bodies. Both the PKK and the LTTE had done violence to civilians and had been listed by the State Department as terrorist organizations. A majority of six justices in *Holder v. Humanitarian Law Project* argued that even advice on nonviolent methodology could enhance the organizations' standing and further their activities, which included the tactic of terrorism.

"Such support frees up other resources within the organization that may be put to violent ends," wrote Chief Justice Roberts in an opinion that read more like a policy paper than a constitutional analysis. "It also importantly helps lend legitimacy to foreign terrorist groups—legitimacy that makes it easier for those groups to persist, to recruit members, and to raise funds—all of which facilitate more terrorist attacks." The skills the American organizations wanted to impart could be used by the PKK "as part of a broader strategy to promote terrorism," he said. "The PKK could, for example, pursue peaceful negotiation as a means of buying time to recover from short-term setbacks, lulling opponents into complacency, and ultimately preparing for renewed attacks."

Having made the case, however, Roberts then urged judicial deference to the other branches. "Congress and the Executive are uniquely positioned to make principled distinctions between activities that will further terrorist conduct and undermine United States foreign policy, and those that will not," he declared.

As we have seen, curbing Americans' speech and association during wartime has been a dishonorable tradition from the early days of the republic. This case continued the pattern. Although the decision affected only a few people and organizations, and focused narrowly on the specific training that they had proposed, the ruling illuminated the war mentality that had penetrated the country, and showed how embedded it remained nearly a decade after the 9/11 attacks.

The Court did draw some limits around its findings. It held out the possibility that future applications of the material-support statute could violate free speech, without saying what they might be. It found no First Amendment violation in this instance, because the law does not bar individuals from saying "anything they wish on any topic," as Chief Justice Roberts wrote. It criminalizes neither "independent advocacy" nor outright membership in such organizations, he said, unless the listed group directs or coordinates with the advocate.[65]

Yet the ruling precludes the peacebuilding that many American humanitarian groups attempt. It has been common for nongovernmental organizations based in the United States to work in countries torn by civil wars, usually as the conflicts show signs of ending, to promote democratization and civil society. This will now be legally risky, perhaps impossible, unless prosecutors look the other way and human rights advocates ignore the law, as both sides have mostly done in the past. The State Department has typically been slow to remove certain movements from the "terrorist" list after violence has subsided. The Nepali Maoists remained designated long after they had ceased fighting and had become the largest party in a freely elected government; being on the list hampered even American diplomats who needed to deal with Nepal's Maoist prime minister. Nelson Mandela's African National Congress was designated because of the violence to which it finally resorted in its struggle against apartheid in South Africa, notwithstanding Mandela's inspirational leadership in healing racial wounds.

Congress could fix the problem if it were so inclined. As the Court observed, to prove a violation under the existing statute, prosecutors must show only that the trainer or adviser knew that the organization appeared on the terrorist list, "without requiring the Government to prove that plaintiffs had a specific intent to further the unlawful ends of those organizations." If that requirement to show specific intent were added to the law, pro-democracy and conflict-resolution work could presumably go ahead.

The solution has a pitfall, however: To assess intentions, investigators would have to examine the content of speech, often very private speech. They have already done so in numerous cases to determine whether suspects have intended to support groups that engage in terrorism.

Suspicions about the Portland Seven were generated largely by inflammatory statements that one of the group, Jeffrey Battle, thought he was making in private, and which the government cited to characterize the men's intentions. It made you think that every kid in America should be Mirandized: Anything you say anytime, anywhere, can and will be used against you in a court of law. Sami Omar al-Hussayen, a Saudi, was tried for designing Web sites allegedly to recruit terrorists. The jury found him not guilty, but he agreed to deportation. Strident support of the Palestinian cause brought unwanted attention to a Florida computer science professor, Sami al-Arian, who was accused of giving material support to Palestine Islamic Jihad; the jury acquitted him on most of the charges and deadlocked on the rest.

Once speech is followed by action, federal authorities have been eager to move, as when young Muslim Americans have gone off to camps in Pakistan or Afghanistan. The FBI hasn't been charmed by their claims of charitable impulses or religious awakenings or even second thoughts, although their true objectives often seem murky and confused.

Some young people seek adversity as a challenge to test themselves or to find themselves. Some feel like outsiders in the United States, which they believe devalues their heritage. Some mix dogmatic ideology or divine purpose into a quest for identity that can take them into fierce pride, even violence, as they attach to a cause larger than themselves. So it has been for whites who join supremacist militias, African-Americans who espouse black separatism, American Jews who confront Arabs in the West Bank, and American Muslims who venture into the wars being waged on behalf of Islam.

These are not parallel behaviors, but they come from similar roots of disaffection. Militant black movements in the United States have been largely nonviolent, notwithstanding some of the rhetoric. American immigrants to Israel usually find fulfillment being Jewish in a Jewish state without attacking Palestinians, despite a scattering of zealots who define religious virtue by doing so. Similarly, only a tiny percentage of Muslims in America have been drawn to militant callings for jihad—meaning not just the inner struggle for purity that the word conveys, but also the outer struggle of arms. It is no accident that some of them, including most of the Portland Seven who tried to reach Afghanistan, are also African-American converts to Islam, carrying a double stigma and a dual mission.

If those who gravitate to terrorist movements begin as souls adrift, they may naturally seem lost and harmless. To prosecute them preventively before terrorism is committed can look faintly ridiculous, especially when they're so directionless that no self-respecting al-Qaeda cell would trust them. That does not mean that they cannot shoot a gun or plant a bomb, however, and vulnerable personalities seem drawn to the sense of purpose and belonging that a movement provides. So they have naturally become targets of the government's post-9/11 preventive efforts.

In the spring of 2001, a few months before al-Qaeda struck and the Taliban suddenly became the active enemy,[66] seven Yemeni-Americans from Lackawanna, New York, went to Afghanistan for six or seven weeks in search of something religious, something political, perhaps something violent. Then all but one came quietly home, raising intense suspicions that they had been molded into a sleeper cell. They had allegedly been recruited by a man who had trained in al-Qaeda camps and fought with Muslims in Bosnia.

Their motivations remained obscure, but according to the attorney Kenneth Ballen, who has researched terrorism, they may have been inspired partly by a sermon given by a confused soul with heroic dreams, Jumah al-Dossari. Recruited by a Saudi fighter from Bosnia, he reportedly told them, "Muslims are dying, and we're not doing anything about it. We must stand up for our brothers. We must stand up and defend Islam." Leaders of the mosque where he spoke, offended by his radical preaching, told him to get out of town. Unfortunately, some of his young listeners got out as well, ending up in Afghanistan.[67]

Weapons training excited some, and they received instruction in firearms, rocket-propelled grenades, land mines, plastic explosives, and camouflage. Sahim Alwan, who told *The New York Times* that he had been driven there by "a lot of curiosity," soon realized he was in too deep, and decided to leave. At first he wasn't allowed to go. Then he became determined to do so after hearing talk of martyrdom and threats to America from none other than Osama bin Laden, who was also curious and invited him for two private conversations. The al-Qaeda leader asked him how Muslims in the United States felt about suicide missions. "We don't even think about it," Alwan quoted himself as saying. Bin Laden smiled.

The FBI, tipped off by an anonymous letter reporting the arrival of terrorists to recruit young men in Lackawanna, zeroed in on the six who had returned, using FISA warrants to monitor them closely and interpreting every e-mail about weddings, meals, and soccer games as code. The CIA saw the group as the "most dangerous" cell in the country, and so the president, vice president, CIA chief, and FBI director were regularly briefed.[68] President Bush even considered a proposal by Vice President Cheney to have the military swarm into the Buffalo suburb, arrest the men, and hold them as enemy combatants. The idea, pressed by Cheney's counsel David Addington, took its authority from a memo by John Yoo of the Justice Department arguing that in wartime, such action was barred by neither the Constitution nor the Posse Comitatus Act of 1878, which usually prohibits the military from domestic law enforcement.

Bush turned down the suggestion after hearing objections from FBI Director Robert Mueller; Michael Chertoff, the head of the Justice Department's criminal division; and Condoleezza Rice, the national security adviser.[69] The FBI then made the arrests in September 2002 and, under the threat of being declared enemy combatants, the men pleaded guilty and were sentenced to about ten years. The recruiter, Kamal Derwish, was killed when a missile from a CIA drone hit his car in the Yemeni desert.

Matthew Purdy of *The New York Times* put the question nicely: "Were they a cell in a deep sleep, or had their trip to Afghanistan been a bad dream?"[70]

Dreams and nightmares occupy us now. After the terrorist attacks of 9/11, we accused ourselves of lacking imagination. Most of us had never pictured a few suicidal men armed with box cutters seizing jetliners and bringing down the tallest buildings in New York. We had never fantasized so darkly, and since then we have been encouraged to do so. Through our heads dance the specters of cities stricken by chemical, biological, or nuclear weapons. We imagine. We are wise to imagine, for the threats are not fantasies.

Aggressive investigation is legitimate and necessary, but it creates two hazards: the danger of error in a particular case, and the danger to the country's larger culture of liberty. As it happens, the framers left us a system both practical and principled, a set of guarantees that protect our rights and simultaneously provide the best possible accuracy in criminal justice. We don't have to choose, because there is no contradiction. Observing the rights leads to reliability in the process.

While we stay alert by imagining the worst scenarios of terrorism, we might also imagine the sacrifice of our liberties on the altar of security. We face both threats—the risk of being attacked and "the risk of being less free," in Hamilton's words. The first step toward preventing either tragedy is vigilance.

The High Court of History

We are the people of July 4th—not September 11th.

—Thomas L. Friedman

IN SEARCH OF a shocking metaphor, critics of American policies after 9/11 reached for a Soviet analogy. Harold Pinter, the Nobel Prize–winning playwright, lamented the millions of Americans "imprisoned in the vast gulag of prisons which extends across the U.S." The University of California Press in 2004 published *American Gulag,* a book on immigration prisons by Mark Dow. Amnesty International disregarded the cautionary advice of a former Soviet political prisoner, Pavel Litvinov, and in June 2005 called the American prison at Guantánamo Bay "the gulag of our times."

Later that month, Senator Richard Durbin of Illinois quoted an FBI agent's memo on seeing Guantánamo prisoners chained in fetal positions and subjected to extreme temperatures. "If I read this to you and did not tell you that it was an FBI agent describing what Americans had done to prisoners in their control," Durbin told the Senate, "you would most certainly believe this must have been done by Nazis, Soviets in their gulags, or some mad regime—Pol Pot or others—that had no concern for human beings." After a week of stormy protest, Durbin apologized, saying, "I have come to understand that was a very poor choice of words."

By the following fall, however, the words had been widely adopted in the wake of *The Washington Post*'s disclosure that the CIA was operating a global network of clandestine prisons. "Secret, ad hoc prisons that carry a whiff of the old Soviet-style gulags are not the solution," said *USA Today.*[1] "U.S. MUST DISMANTLE ITS SECRET CIA GULAG," declared a headline on a Minneapolis *Star Tribune* editorial.[2] In *The Oregonian,* an editorial called the prisons "America's gulag."[3] "Gulag," the Russian acronym for the Chief Administration of Corrective Labor Camps, was made famous by Aleksandr Solzhenitsyn's trilogy, *The Gulag Archipelago.*

It would be easier to dismiss these parallels if the Soviet Union still existed as the antithesis of America. The contrasts were profound and

obvious then: a dictatorship that filtered ideas, enforced political obedi-
ence, and grew from a long authoritarian history—compared with a free-
wheeling democracy that relished irreverent speech, decentralized its
government, and threw its doors open to the world. Russia was a useful
foil for America's virtues, enabling not just our fear but also our pride. We
were different, as we could see vividly every day.

Now we can only remember how different we were, and consider how
to stay that way. The line between dictatorship and democracy looks so
bold and bright. The culture of freedom looks so permanent, the system
of protections so unshakable. Americans might be forgiven their complacency, as if it were divinely ordained that the United States should forever
guard the liberties of its people.

Yet from time to time the shadows of autocracy flicker across our shining enterprise, casting doubt. Even judges and legal scholars take note and
reach for that analogy. After the American citizen Jose Padilla was imprisoned as an enemy combatant, the Yale law professor Bruce Ackerman
declared, "Three years of not even being told what the charge against you
is, is worthy of Stalin."[4] When Florida police looking for drugs adopted a
practice of doing sweeps of buses and trains, checking everyone's ID and
asking to search luggage, a state court said the tactic "evoked images of
other days, under other flags," then thundered: "This is not Hitler's Ber-
lin, nor Stalin's Moscow, nor is it white supremacist South Africa." Nonetheless, the police methods were later upheld by the Supreme Court.[5]

So when thinking about the Soviet system as a model of what we do
not want to become, it is worth asking ourselves what to watch out for.

Major Lev Kopelev of the Soviet Red Army spoke German, the language
of the enemy. Captain James Yee of the United States Army spoke Arabic,
the language of the enemy. Kopelev tried to stop fellow soldiers from
raping and robbing. Yee tried to stop fellow soldiers from abusing and
humiliating. Kopelev was arrested on April 5, 1945. Yee was arrested on
September 10, 2003.

What happened to each officer in the end, however, marks the distinction between dictatorship and democracy, one that lies less in the
impulses and attitudes of people in authority, which can be all too similar
in both systems, than in structural bulwarks against the abuse of power.
The Soviet Union had no such barricades. Those in the United States are
in place, but they wobble at times.

The Soviet major and the American captain both held significant
posts. As the Red Army swept westward toward the close of World War II,

Kopelev propagandized German troops with leaflets and loudspeaker broadcasts. He also reported and halted rapes of civilians and looting by his comrades, for which he was charged with showing "pity for the enemy" and being "friendly with spies."[6]

Early in the American war on terrorism, Yee served as the Muslim chaplain at the Guantánamo Bay camp holding nearly seven hundred Muslim prisoners. He attempted to stop guards' violence against inmates and desecration of their Korans. For that, he was accused of having "associated with known terrorist sympathizers."[7]

Both the Soviet and American officers were orthodox patriots. Kopelev, a steadfast Communist Party member who revered Stalin, had received a commendation shortly before his arrest. Yee, a West Point graduate in a military family, and a Bush voter in 2000, received the highest possible performance evaluation two days before being taken into custody.[8] Kopelev was convicted and spent nine years in the Gulag, where he met Solzhenitsyn. Yee was publicly smeared, spent seventy-six days shackled in solitary confinement, and was ultimately driven out of the army. Both men's innocent, humane actions, seen by superiors through the lens of wartime fervor, were refracted into behavior that looked suspicious, then subversive, and finally treasonous.

It is not quite enough to say that the American system worked in Yee's case. Checks and balances were somewhat effective—army prosecutors didn't have evidence and had to drop the serious charges. But vindictively, they began to try him for possessing pornography and for adultery, an offense for which hardly anyone in uniform is ever prosecuted unless it is accompanied by other criminal charges, such as rape. In full view of his parents, his wife, and his four-year-old daughter, the army put on a female officer who testified to their affair, provoking Yee's sobbing wife to confront the officer outside the courtroom and shout, "You happy now? Destroying a family?"[9]

Perhaps shamed by the spectacle it was making of itself, the army finally abandoned the prosecution and settled for Yee's departure from the service. The free press, the cleansing sunlight of publicity, had opened an escape never available to Kopelev in the Soviet Union's closed system of thinking.

The two men were both minorities: Yee a Chinese-American convert to Islam, and Kopelev a Jew, and so their superiors on each side saw them as standing apart, outside the patriotic mainstream. As a Jew, Kopelev was berated by a confused Soviet general: "How can you love the Germans? Don't you know what they've been doing to the Jews?" The general then reminded him of an axiom of war: "To pity the enemy is to betray your own."

Six decades later, American officers with narrow experience in the world grew suspicious over Yee's daytime prayers with Muslims and his explanatory lectures on the prisoners' religious culture. A junior security officer thought him overly sympathetic, as did Guantánamo's General Geoffrey Miller, who later gained infamy as commander of the abuse-ridden Abu Ghraib prison.[10] As Yee recalled: "One of the initial allegations made against me was, 'Who does this Chinese Taliban think he is, telling us how to treat our prisoners?'"[11]

Both Yee and Kopelev wrote memoirs about their experiences, and both were published in the United States. Kopelev's could not appear in the Soviet Union, which was closed to its own history.

Having known Kopelev well during my years in Moscow, and after two long interviews with Yee, I was struck by how similarly they described their commanders' and persecutors' anxieties and fantasies. The Communist Party was internationalist in name only. In reality, it served as a repository of Russians' complexes about the outside world, especially the West: mixed feelings of inferiority and superiority, resentment and envy, curiosity and chauvinism, all producing impulses of suspicion toward fellow citizens who registered too much interest in things non-Soviet. In that insular universe, Jews looked somewhat alien, therefore untrustworthy, and associations with foreigners raised dark questions of disloyalty. The toxic paranoia reached its height under Stalin, and ebbed but did not disappear as the Soviet Union headed toward collapse.

In milder form, Islam, Arabs, and the Muslim world have played the same role for some Americans, but within a system known for its fragmented power, diverse attitudes, and a scattered ethnocentrism that does not usually shape government policy. Accordingly, five or six years after the persecution of Yee, a different military subculture—medicine and psychiatry—failed to sound an alarm when Major Nidal Malik Hasan, an army psychiatrist, preached the Koran inappropriately at grand rounds, corresponded with a radical imam by e-mail, and worried colleagues with remarks of concern about Muslim Americans fighting Muslims in Iraq, all danger signs much clearer than anything done by Yee. It seemed that the pendulum of vigilance had swung to the opposite extreme, at least in the milieu of the Walter Reed Army Medical Center. Hasan later killed thirteen at Fort Hood in Texas.

The Yee and Hasan episodes together illustrate how far from an autocracy America remains. It might seem pointless and offensive, then, to speak of the old Soviet Union and the United States in the same breath, the structures are so at odds with each other. The only similarities are in the attitudes of certain officials and citizens, and those are worth some attention.

Uncomfortable reminders of Soviet thinking kept cropping up in the United States during the post-9/11 era. Periodically I checked my impressions with Americans who had also lived in Moscow as diplomats or correspondents, and with Russians who had grown up there and emigrated. Usually they nodded and agreed that they recognized some of the symptoms of the autocratic mind-set, while also recognizing the vast differences between the systems.

Much of the behavior has been written about in these pages and elsewhere. Bush administration lawyers, who interpreted statutes to suit the government's programs of torture and warrantless surveillance, manipulated the law as adroitly as Kremlin officials once constructed façades of legal-looking procedures for trying dissidents. The purposes were the same: to facilitate the machinations of the state. So in Washington, the rule of law was suspended at times, as it was all the time in Moscow.

Both right-wing American ideologues and left-wing Soviet ideologues believed fervently in expansive executive power against weak legislative and judicial branches. Executive-branch dominance was pressed by Bush officials who evaded Congress and the courts, and Kremlin officials kept authority away from the supine legislature (the Supreme Soviet) and the judges who rendered "telephone justice."

In certain periods, the Soviet regime also spun and suppressed science for political aims, and Republican officials tried as much during the Bush administration, censoring studies on global warming, stacking committees and research programs to achieve desired results, and putting conservative social policy ahead of scientists' recommendations on certain regulations.[12]

Russians were screened for political orthodoxy before placement in significant jobs. Bush apparatchiks did the same, politicizing agencies of government from the Food and Drug Administration to the Department of Education and the Justice Department's Civil Rights Division. As litmus tests, applicants were asked ideologically charged questions: "What is it about George W. Bush that makes you want to serve him?" "Tell us about your political philosophy," whether you're a "social conservative, fiscal conservative, [or] law and order Republican." The options did not include liberal Democrat or even libertarian conservative. These inquiries were put to candidates for law-enforcement and policy-making positions at the Justice Department by a devout conservative in her twenties, Monica Goodling, a graduate of Messiah College and of the evangelist Pat Robertson's Regent University School of Law. "Aside from the President, give us an example of someone currently or recently in public service who you admire," she would say, requesting the name of a favorite Supreme Court justice or legislator. She asked applicants about their positions on abortion and their voting histories, issues irrelevant to the work they would do. Candidates were also helped by belonging to the Federalist Society, a highly organized movement of conservatives (including libertarians) skilled in recruiting law students and mentoring them into legal positions and judgeships.[13] In the narrow world of politicized hiring, membership became a key credential.

This was a reminder that during Soviet days, membership in the Communist Party had been a prerequisite for many influential jobs, including factory manager, hospital director, history professor, and journalist. The party was exclusive, however, embracing only a small percentage of the population. Komsomol, the Communist Youth League, had much broader coverage, grooming virtually all Soviet citizens from their school years upward. Without that membership card, early careers were stymied, which was devastating in a system where government owned virtually everything, from restaurants to coal mines.

The Federalist Society is not Komsomol or the Communist Party, of course. Nothing in any of these comparisons is exactly the same. Not all members of the Federalist Society think alike, and they certainly aren't afraid to speak their minds. But they do tend to cluster around a like-minded ideology, and their doctrinal purity drives their organizing efforts. Komsomol was virtually mandatory and all-inclusive; the Federalist Society is optional and self-selective. Komsomol and the party tolerated no competitive ideas outside their own; the Federalist Society stands as one choice among a multitude of ideas and associations across the American spectrum. But there's no avoiding the hard fact that when membership in an ideological movement is used to ensure political conformity in government hiring, the culture of political pluralism is damaged, and so is governmental expertise. The Bush administration's filtering produced immigration judges with no experience in immigration law, regulatory officials without expertise in their areas of responsibility, and a Coalition Provisional Authority to run Iraq that was populated with young Republican zealots who were politically safe and professionally impaired. The disastrous results were well documented.

Enforcing "political correctness" (an old communist term), absolutists of all stripes legitimize only a single way of thinking, exclude those who deviate, and discredit their opponents with propaganda. These were hallmarks of Soviet methodology, which also included imprisonment and exile. More play entered the Soviet system in later years, but for most of its history, the apparatus removed or destroyed anyone who disagreed, all the way up to the Politburo. In milder form, Bush ideologues attempted that as well, successfully at times.

My colleague Christopher Wren in the *New York Times* Moscow bureau used to feel a sense of déjà vu about the bullying KGB and Communist Party officials he encountered: They reminded him of Southern segregationists he'd covered during the civil rights movement. Soviet authorities did not appreciate the analogy, just as hard-right Republicans will not applaud the ones I'm making here. But I'm not the first to note the circular nature of the political spectrum, a line whose extreme ends, left and right, are bent around until they meet at a place where they share some unattractive traits: an unyielding sense of certainty that they have a monopoly on truth, and a raging intolerance of those who differ. It's not hard to find these characteristics in the United States today.

In the American system, though, it's not easy to convert intolerance into government fiat. Soviet Communists were in tune with Russian history, but right-wing radicals are at odds with American history. They resemble each other in their ways of thinking, not in what they can do.

The Soviet structure subordinated the individual to institutions, and so would extreme American conservatives—despite their rhetoric to the contrary—by means of activist judges on the right, enhanced corporate powers, expanded police authority against crime, and extralegal tactics of counterterrorism. Consider how readily some Republican politicians would turn off the constitutional protections of civilian courts and put terror suspects—even those arrested inside the United States—into the hands of military interrogators and military commissions. That's where they wanted to see the Nigerian who tried to blow up a plane over Detroit in 2009, and they railed against President Obama for respecting his rights and trusting a criminal justice system based on the framers' principles. On both the Soviet left and the American right, policy did and does pivot on national security, which rationalizes practically every abuse and musters a crude patriotism against dissent. Like some Americans, Soviet Communists valued conformity of opinion and feared the disorder brought by liberty.

The opposite approach, embracing the risks of robust freedom, might be called courage. "Those who won our independence by revolution were not cowards," Justice Louis Brandeis wrote years ago: "They did not fear political change. They did not exalt order at the cost of liberty."

This conclusion is not a prediction, then, just a note of caution. Although we're certainly not becoming Soviet, when we see occasional traits of a dead dictatorship we relearn the fundamental lesson bequeathed by the framers: that liberty cannot rest only on the goodness of transitory officials and leaders, whoever they may be, but relies on a durable foundation of constitutional protections. Those protections need defending. Rights that are not exercised are lost. Some have been diminished not only under the chisel of the courts but also by the neglect of ordinary citizens who neither invoke them nor challenge their violators.

The Supreme Court has failed too frequently. It often divides along the lines of political allegiance rather than constitutional analysis, cheapening itself. Most justices don't grow and evolve into their awesome powers, but rather freeze themselves in place, wherever they began, as if they had a lifetime appointment to honor whatever political constituency placed them on the bench. They would honor the country by respecting the observation of Justice John Paul Stevens: "Learning on the job is essential to the process of judging."[14] Under Chief Justice Roberts, the high court has grown less attentive to the precious rights of the small and the weak, more eager to strengthen the already strong. Therefore, our rights are less robust than they were a decade ago, and may be even less so a decade hence.

Yet eventually it will be the judgment of the high court of history that matters. The decision will be favorable if we nurture our checks and balances, if we push back hard to maintain our constitutional liberties, empower the powerless, and recognize that the rights of the lowliest criminal are not his alone. They belong to us all.

NOTES

CHAPTER I: SAVING THE CONSTITUTION

1. Transcript, Madison Debates, Constitutional Convention, July 11, 1787, the Avalon Project, Lillian Goldman Law Library, Yale Law School, http://avalon .law.yale.edu/18th_century/debates_711.asp.
2. Steven Waldman, *Founding Faith* (New York: Random House, 2008), pp. 142–44.
3. "When the Sixth Amendment was written, English law forbade a criminal defendant to have the assistance of counsel unless his case presented abstruse questions of law. The framers wanted to do away with this prohibition." Judge Richard A. Posner, "Overcoming Law," at http://www.law.umkc.edu/faculty/ projects/ftrials/conlaw/interp.html.
4. David Cole, interview with author, June 24, 2003.
5. Thomas Jefferson, *The Works of Thomas Jefferson,* Vol. 12, ed. Paul Ford (New York: G. P. Putnam's Sons, 1904–1905), pp. 137–38. Cited in David M. O'Brien, *Constitutional Law and Politics,* Vol. 2, *Civil Rights and Civil Liberties* (New York: Norton, 2003), p. 30.
6. *Marbury v. Madison,* 1 Cr. (5 U.S.) 137 (1803).
7. To the dismay of some legal scholars, it has been the due process clause rather than the guarantee of "privileges and immunities" that has governed the application of the Bill of Rights to the states. That has worried some rights advocates who see a prospect that "due process" could someday be interpreted literally and narrowly enough, as Justice Antonin Scalia has indicated he would like to do, to undermine the incorporation of some amendments into rights at the state and local levels. See Robert Barnes, "Gun Case Presents Quandary for Court," *Washington Post,* March 1, 2010, p. A1.
8. *Gitlow v. New York,* 268 U.S. 652 (1925).
9. *Near v. Minnesota,* 283 U.S. 697 (1931).
10. *Brown v. Mississippi,* 297 U.S. 278 (1936).
11. *Wolf v. Colorado,* 338 U.S. 25 (1949).
12. *Malloy v. Hogan,* 378 U.S. 1 (1964).
13. *Mapp v. Ohio,* 367 U.S. 643 (1961).
14. *Gideon v. Wainwright,* 372 U.S. 335 (1963).

15. *Miranda v. Arizona,* 384 U.S. 436 (1966).

16. *Duncan v. Louisiana,* 391 U.S. 145 (1968).

17. David McCullough, *John Adams* (New York: Simon & Schuster, 2001), p. 504.

18. 50 U.S.C. § 21, which reads in part: "Whenever there is a declared war between the United States and any foreign nation or government, or any invasion or predatory incursion is perpetrated, attempted or threatened against the territory of the United States by any foreign nation or government, and the President makes public proclamation of the event, all natives, citizens, denizens, or subjects of the hostile nation or government, being of the age of fourteen years and upward, who shall be within the United States and not actually naturalized, shall be liable to be apprehended, restrained, secured, and removed as alien enemies."

19. Sedition Act, approved July 14, 1798, § 2.

20. Geoffrey R. Stone, *Perilous Times: Free Speech in Wartime* (New York: W. W. Norton, 2004), p. 19.

21. A collection was taken up to pay his fine. Contributors included Thomas Jefferson, James Madison, and James Monroe. Stone, *Perilous Times,* pp. 18, 50–52.

22. Thomas Jefferson, *First Inaugural Address,* March 4, 1801, the Avalon Project at Yale Law School, http://avalon.law.yale.edu/19th_century/jefinau1.asp.

23. An antiwar politician, former Congressman Clement Vallandigham, was charged with "treasonable utterances" for saying that the "wicked, cruel, and unnecessary" war was being waged "for the freedom of the blacks and the enslavement of the whites." Stone, *Perilous Times,* p. 82.

24. Stone, *Perilous Times,* pp. 84–86, 124, and *Ex parte Merryman,* 17 F. Cas 144 (D. Md. 1861), in which Taney sat as a Circuit Court judge of the Maryland District.

25. Act of Apr. 20, 1871, ch. 22, § 4, 17 Stat. 14; A Proclamation [of Oct. 17, 1871], 7. The Hawaiian Organic Act of 1900 authorized the governor of Hawaii to suspend habeas corpus in case of rebellion or invasion. Ch. 339, § 67, 31 Stat. 153. In 1902, Congress authorized a suspension by the governor of the Philippines, who invoked it in 1905 for nine months. Act of July 1, 1902, ch. 1369, § 5, 32 Stat. 691.

26. *Ex parte Milligan,* 71 U.S. 1 (1866). The Chase Court, 1864–1873, the Supreme Court Historical Society, http://www.supremecourthistory.org/02_history/subs_history/02_c06.html, and *Ex Parte Milligan: Trials in Wartime,* American Bar Association, Key Supreme Court Cases, http://www.abanet.org/publiced/youth/sia/holtcases/milligan.html.

27. Stone, *Perilous Times,* p. 137.

28. 40 Stat. 553.

29. David Cole, *Enemy Aliens* (New York: New Press, 2003), p. 112–13.

30. Vartan Gregorian, "The Relevance of Academic Freedom," Herbert Gutman Memorial Lecture, CUNY Graduate Center, Oct. 15, 2002.

31. Peter H. Buckingham, "'Red Tom' Hickey and the Suppression of the Texas *Rebel,*" unpublished paper. On post-Reconstruction slavery using convicts, see Douglas A. Blackmon, *Slavery by Another Name* (New York: Doubleday, 2008).

32. Stone, *Perilous Times,* p. 224.

33. Conversation between Goering and U.S. Army Captain G. M. Gilbert on Apr.

18, 1946, quoted in Edward Dolnick, *The Forger's Spell* (New York: HarperCollins, 2008), p. 80.

34. Alexander Hamilton, Federalist Paper 8.

35. The Alien Registration Act, which also required all noncitizens to register with the government, 54 Stat. 670, 671, title I, §§ 2, 3 (June 28, 1940), current version at 18 U.S.C. § 2385.

36. Following the death of the judge, the government dismissed the charges against the fascists, four months after the end of the war. Stone, *Perilous Times*, pp. 255, 273–75.

37. Ibid., p. 280.

38. Ibid., p. 278.

39. Cole, *Enemy Aliens*, p. 93.

40. The vote was 6–3 in *Korematsu v. United States*, 323 U.S. 214 (1944). The Court also upheld a curfew imposed on Americans of Japanese ancestry in *Hirabayashi v. United States*, 320 U.S. 81 (1943) and *Yasui v. United States*, 320 U.S. 115 (1943). It delayed a decision in *Ex parte Endo*, 323 U.S. 283 (1944), releasing a Japanese-American woman whose brother was serving in the U.S. Army, until a day after the government announced that all the detainees would be released. See also Stone, *Perilous Times*, pp. 297–303.

41. Cole, *Enemy Aliens*, pp. 129, 141.

42. Ibid., pp. 148–49.

43. The material in this section is drawn mostly from *Intelligence Activities and the Rights of Americans*, Book II. Final Report of the Select Committee to Study Governmental Operations with Respect to Intelligence Activities, United States Senate ("Church committee"), Apr. 26, 1976, pp. 5–15, 50, and from original documents linked to the report.

44. Jane Mayer, *The Dark Side* (New York: Doubleday, 2008), pp. 113–15. Jack Goldsmith, *The Terror Presidency* (New York: Norton, 2007), pp. 36–37.

45. The state secrets argument, aimed at thwarting a suit by four Brooklyn residents who claimed that their international phone calls were illegally intercepted, was made after Attorney General Eric Holder announced tighter rules for invoking the protection, which he claimed would not be used to mask government wrongdoing or embarrassment. Michael Isikoff, "Obama Secrecy Watch II: A State Secrets Affidavit Straight from the Bush Era," *Newsweek*, Declassified Blog, Nov. 2, 2009, at http://blog.newsweek.com/blogs/declassified/archive/2009/11/02/obama-secrecy-watch-ii-a-state-secrets affidavit straight-from-the-bush-era.aspx. The case was *Shubert v. Obama*, formerly *Shubert v. Bush*, C 07-0693 (DC No. D. Ca.).

46. Mayer, *The Dark Side*, pp. 146, 180.

47. Cole, *Enemy Aliens*, p. 25.

48. Eric Lichtblau, "Thousands from Muslim Nations Were Investigated Before '04 Election, Data Show," *New York Times*, Oct. 31, 2008, p. A17, based on internal reports obtained by the National Litigation Project at Yale Law School and the American-Arab Anti-Discrimination Committee.

49. Eric Schmitt and Mark Mazzetti, "Secret Order Lets U.S. Raid Al Qaeda in Many Countries," *New York Times*, Nov. 10, 2008, p. A1.

50. Mayer, *The Dark Side*, p. 110.

51. Ibid., pp. 105, 151, 152, 165, 168, 173, 274, 276, 309.
52. Obama ordered that all interrogations, by the CIA and other agencies, be performed in accordance with the Army Field Manual, which barred abuse and torture. But the order could be rescinded. Democratic Senator Dianne Feinstein, chair of the Senate Intelligence Committee, launched an investigation into torture, but most of its findings remained classified. A limited declassified document was released in Apr. 2009. "Release of Declassified Narrative Describing the Dept. of Justice Office of Legal Counsel's Opinions on the CIA's Detention and Interrogation Program," at http://intelligence.senate.gov/pdfs/olcopinion.pdf.
53. "Re: Standards for Conduct of Interrogation under 18 U.S.C. §§ 2340–2340A," Memorandum for Alberto R. Gonzales, Office of the Assistant Attorney General, Aug. 1, 2002, pp. 1, 36–37. After its contents became public, it was rescinded by the White House, but its stricter replacement guidelines were secretly loosened by a subsequent memo that effectively permitted the abuse to continue. See the detailed account in Mayer, *The Dark Side.*
54. John C. Yoo and Robert J. Delahunty, "Re: Authority for Use of Military Force to Combat Terrorist Activities Within the United States," Memorandum for Alberto R. Gonzales, Counsel to the President, and William J. Haynes II, General Counsel, Dept. of Defense, Oct. 23, 2001. The memo finds no obstacle in the Posse Comitatus Act, 18 U.S.C. § 1385 (1994), which prohibits the use of the military for law enforcement purposes inside the country. The memo argues that counterterrorism could qualify as a military function rather than law enforcement.
55. Yoo and Bybee were accused of "professional misconduct" by the Obama Justice Department's Office of Professional Responsibility, which might have led to disbarment proceedings, but the charge was downgraded by Associate Deputy Attorney General David Margolis, a career official who dealt with disciplinary matters. He called their legal reasoning "flawed," but not punishable. "While I have declined to adopt O.P.R.'s findings of misconduct," Margolis wrote, "I fear that John Yoo's loyalty to his own ideology and convictions clouded his view of his obligation to his client and led him to author opinions that reflected his own extreme, albeit sincerely held, view of executive power while speaking for an institutional client." Eric Lichtblau and Scott Shane, "Report Faults 2 Authors of Bush Terror Memos," *New York Times,* Feb. 19, 2010. David Margolis, Memorandum for the Attorney General, the Deputy Attorney General, Jan. 5, 2010.
56. Emil Constantinescu, address to the World Justice Forum, Vienna, July 3, 2008.
57. "The Rule of Law Index," World Justice Project, World Justice Forum, July 2–5, 2008, Vienna, p. 6.
58. David Rothkopf, *Superclass* (New York: Farrar, Straus and Giroux, 2008), p. 193.
59. Nicholas D. Kristof, "117 Deaths Each Day," *New York Times,* March 13, 2004, p. 17. Scott Shane, "A Year of Terror Plots: Through a Second Prism," *New York Times,* Jan. 13, 2010, p. A1.
60. This holds whether terrorism defendants are held inside or outside the criminal justice system. From Sept. 12, 2001, to Dec. 31, 2007, only 28 percent of criminal terrorism convictions came at trial; the rest were guilty pleas. Just 9 percent of those charged were acquitted or had charges dismissed. Richard B. Zabel and

James J. Benjamin, Jr., *In Pursuit of Justice: Prosecuting Terrorism Cases in the Federal Courts,* Human Rights First, May 2008, p. 26.

CHAPTER 2: ANOTHER COUNTRY

1. *Terry v. Ohio,* 392 U.S. 1 (1968).
2. In *Terry,* Chief Justice Earl Warren used the term "reasonable grounds," while "reasonable suspicion" was used by Justice William O. Douglas in his dissent. Writing for the Court in later cases, including *United States v. Sokolow,* 490 U.S. 1 (1989) and *Illinois v. Wardlow,* 528 U.S. 119 (2000), Chief Justice William H. Rehnquist used "reasonable suspicion," which has become the accepted phrase. If there is reasonable suspicion that someone has committed or is about to commit a crime, a stop is permitted. Something more is required for a frisk: reasonable suspicion that he is armed.
3. *United States v. Sokolow,* 490 U.S. 1 (1989).
4. *Illinois v. Gates,* 462 U.S. 213 (1983).
5. *United States v. Sokolow,* 490 U.S. 1 (1989).
6. Richard A. Hobson and Charles E. Collins, Jr., *Identifying Characteristics of the Armed Gunman,* Metropolitan (D.C.) Police Department, Patrol Services Division, Apr. 3, 1995.
7. *United States v. Askew,* 04-3092, D.C. Circuit, Apr. 6, 2007, reversed by *United States v. Askew,*, 04-3092, D.C. Circuit en banc, June 20, 2008. Kavanaugh and Sentelle were two of an original panel of three. To justify their novel interpretation, Kavanaugh and Sentelle seized on an aside in *Hayes v. Florida,* 470 U.S. 811 (1985), although it found for the defendant and involved no *Terry* stop. Without an arrest warrant, police went to the home of a suspect in a burglary and rape to take him to be fingerprinted at the station house. When he refused to go, and an officer offered the alternative of arrest, the suspect accompanied them, was fingerprinted, and was then arrested. The Court found that without probable cause for the investigative detention, the fingerprinting violated the Fourth Amendment. The majority hedged by adding that "none of the foregoing implies that a brief detention in the field for the purpose of fingerprinting, where there is only reasonable suspicion not amounting to probable cause, is necessarily impermissible under the Fourth Amendment." Although the Court was leaving the question open, Kavanaugh and Sentelle jumped to this conclusion: "The *Hayes* Court endorsed the *investigative* step of on-the-scene fingerprinting." The D.C. Circuit then decided to hear the appeal en banc, which means that the entire membership of the court, beyond the original three-member panel, considers the case. Interestingly, the majority of the D.C. Circuit that overruled Kavanaugh and Sentelle included a strong conservative, Janice Rogers Brown, who has followed a libertarian streak—rather than precedent—in restricting police searches.
8. *Chimel v. California,* 395 U.S. 752 (1969). The opinion overruled *Harris v. United States,* 331 U.S. 145 (1947) and *United States v. Rabinowitz,* 339 U.S. 56 (1950), which permitted the police to search an entire apartment and an entire office without a warrant but incident to an arrest. *Chimel* imposed the restriction that only what police saw "in plain view" could be seized without a search warrant. See also O'Brien, *Constitutional Law and Politics,* Vol. 2, pp. 839–40.

9. *Minnesota v. Dickerson,* 508 U.S. 366 (1993) established the "plain feel" exception only if the object is immediately identified during a pat-down as "non-threatening contraband." The Court suppressed the evidence in this case, however, because the officer, having determined that there was no weapon in Dickerson's jacket, did not identify a lump as cocaine until he had squeezed and manipulated it, which the Court decided had taken the search beyond the check for a gun that justified the *Terry* stop. See also *Michigan v. Long,* 463 U.S. 1032, at 1049 (1983).

10. *Illinois v. Wardlow,* 528 U.S. 119 (2000).

11. As formulated in *United States v. Cortez,* 449 U.S. 411 (1981) and then in *United States v. Sokolow,* 490 U.S. 1, 109 (1989).

12. District of Columbia Official Code, DC ST § 50-2207.02.

13. *United States v. Richard Spinner, Jr.,* 05-3160 (D.C. Cir. 2007).

14. FBI Uniform Crime Reports: Law Enforcement Officers Killed and Assaulted, 2009, Table 19, http://www.fbi.gov/ucr/killed/2009/data/table_19.html.

15. Concurring opinion in *Minnesota v. Dickerson,* 508 U.S. 366 (1993).

16. *District of Columbia v. Heller,* 07-290 (2008). Washington, D.C., had the strictest gun law in the country, a virtual ban on private handguns everywhere. The statute was challenged by an auxiliary policeman who guarded the federal courthouse and wanted a license to keep a gun at home. The Court also struck down the D.C. law requiring any licensed gun at home to be disassembled or disabled with a trigger lock, reasoning that such restrictions would make the weapon unusable for self-defense. The ruling applied the Second Amendment only to the federal government, which essentially governs D.C., and did not yet incorporate state law into its protection. That incorporation, citing the due-process clause of the Fourteenth Amendment, came in a 2010 Supreme Court ruling that struck down laws in Chicago and Oak Park, Illinois, against keeping handguns at home. The opinion repeated the qualifiers used in *Heller,* noting that the right to gun ownership in the home did not erase local governments' powers to restrict the sale and possession of firearms to certain people or in certain locations. *McDonald et al v. City of Chicago, Illinois, et al,* 08-1521 (2010). Majority opinion by Samuel Alito. In Congress, conservative Democrats and Republicans proposed eliminating most gun control in the District as a condition of awarding D.C. a voting Representative in the House, a Faustian bargain vigorously opposed by D.C. officials and liberals in Congress in the spring of 2010. For the time being, D.C. kept its gun control and lost its chance for voting representation in the House.

17. *Morning Edition,* National Public Radio, Oct. 21, 2007.

18. Based on interviews with 63,943 U.S. residents. Of those stopped for traffic-light or stop-sign violations, 56.8 percent of blacks and 77 percent of whites thought the stop was justified, and for a vehicle defect, the legitimacy rate was 66.5 percent of blacks and 90.5 percent of whites. The percentage of searches done with the consent of the driver was 57.6. "Contacts Between Police and the Public, 2005," Bureau of Justice Statistics, Apr. 2007, http://www.ojp.usdoj.gov/bjs/pub/pdf/cpp05.pdf.

19. *Carroll v. United States,* 267 U.S. 132 (1925), opinion by Chief Justice William Howard Taft. In *Chambers v. Maroney,* 399 U.S. 42 (1970), the Court extended the warrantless search to cars that were impounded, reasoning that if the police

could search immediately without a warrant, they could also do so once they got the vehicle to a station house.

20. *Alabama v. White*, 496 U.S. 325 (1990).
21. *Delaware v. Prouse*, 440 U.S. 648 (1979).
22. See *Whren v. United States*, 517 U.S. 806 (1996), decided unanimously, for a comprehensive discussion of this line of cases.
23. *Michigan Dept. of State Police v. Sitz*, 496 U.S. 444 (1990).
24. *United States v. Martinez-Fuerte*, 428 U.S. 543 (1976).
25. *Delaware v. Prouse*, 440 U.S. 648 (1979). The Court excluded marijuana as evidence from a vehicle chosen randomly for a stop, but White, for the majority, went out of his way to suggest roadblocks as an alternative, stating, "At traffic checkpoints the motorist can see that other vehicles are being stopped, he can see visible signs of the officers' authority, and he is much less likely to be frightened or annoyed by the intrusion." This brought a sardonic dissent from Rehnquist, who thought random stops were acceptable: "Because motorists, apparently like sheep, are much less likely to be 'frightened' or 'annoyed' when stopped en masse, a highway patrolman needs neither probable cause nor articulable suspicion to stop all motorists on a particular thoroughfare, but he cannot without articulable suspicion stop less than all motorists. The Court thus elevates the adage 'misery loves company' to a novel role in Fourth Amendment jurisprudence. . . . The whole point of enforcing motor vehicle safety regulations is to remove from the road the unlicensed driver before he demonstrates why he is unlicensed. The Court would apparently prefer that the State check licenses and vehicle registrations as the wreckage is being towed away. . . . The Court does not say that these interests can never be infringed by the State, just that the State must infringe them en masse rather than citizen by citizen. To comply with the Fourth Amendment, the State need only subject all citizens to the same 'anxiety' and 'inconvenien[ce]' to which it now subjects only a few."
26. *Indianapolis v. Edmond*, 531 U.S. 32 (2000), with a vigorous dissent by Rehnquist, Thomas, and Scalia. Writing for the majority, O'Connor referred to *Sitz*, *Martinez-Fuerte*, and *Prouse*, which authorized checkpoints: "In none of these cases, however, did we indicate approval of a checkpoint program whose primary purpose was to detect evidence of ordinary criminal wrongdoing."
27. *United States v. Haley*, 669 F. 2d 201, 203–4 (1982). At the time, circuit courts were in disagreement about the question. An earlier Supreme Court decision, in *Johnson v. United States*, 333 U.S. 10, 13 (1948), had decided that "odors alone do not authorize a search without warrant."
28. *Illinois v. Caballes*, 543 U.S. 405 (2005). The D.C. Circuit had come to a different conclusion where police, discovering stolen license plates on a car, searched the trunk using the rationale that original plates might be there. They found a pistol but no tags. By two to one, a panel ruled the search without probable cause and therefore unconstitutional. The lone dissenter, who upheld the search, was John G. Roberts, Jr., soon to become Chief Justice. *United States v. Jackson*, 02cr00328-01 (D.C. Cir. 2005).
29. *United States v. Chadwick*, 433 U.S. 1 (1977).
30. *Arkansas v. Sanders*, 442 U.S. 753 (1979). On a tip, police followed a taxi carrying Lonnie Sanders from the Little Rock Airport, stopped the taxi, and opened his suitcase, which contained marijuana. Blackmun and Rehnquist dissented.

31. *Robbins v. California*, 453 U.S. 420 (1981). Police pulled over a car being driven erratically, and smelled marijuana, which gave them probable cause to search the passenger compartment. But then they crossed the line by opening two garbage bags. Even though they had probable cause to search them, the Court ruled, they could not do so without a warrant.

32. *United States v. Ross*, 456 U.S. 798 (1982).

33. *United States v. Johns*, 469 U.S. 478 (1985).

34. *California v. Acevedo*, 500 U.S. 565 (1991). After a Drug Enforcement agent in Hawaii intercepted a Federal Express package containing marijuana and addressed to a resident of Santa Ana, California, he arranged to have it sent to a police officer in Santa Ana, who took it to the FedEx office and waited for the addressee to pick it up. Officers followed the man home. When he emerged from his apartment to drop the box into the trash, an officer went to get a search warrant. Twenty minutes later, other officers saw a second man leave the apartment with a knapsack; they stopped his car, searched the knapsack, and found marijuana. Twenty-five minutes after that, Acevedo arrived, spent ten minutes in the apartment, then emerged with a paper bag about the size of one of the packages sent from Hawaii. The lead officer had not yet returned with the warrant, so when Acevedo put the bag in the trunk and started to drive away, he was stopped.

35. The Court gave lip service to protecting privacy, writing, "The line between probable cause to search a vehicle and probable cause to search a package in that vehicle is not always clear. . . . At the moment when officers stop an automobile, it may be less than clear whether they suspect with a high degree of certainty that the vehicle contains drugs in a bag or simply contains drugs. If the police know that they may open a bag only if they are actually searching the entire car, they may search more extensively than they otherwise would in order to establish the general probable cause required by *Ross*, [which] may enable the police to broaden their power to make warrantless searches and disserve privacy interests. . . . We cannot see the benefit of a rule that requires law enforcement officers to conduct a more intrusive search in order to justify a less intrusive one."

36. *California v. Acevedo*, 500 U.S. 565 (1991), dissent.

37. Provided he follows a department's standard inventory procedures and doesn't make up rules as he goes along or use the inventory as a pretext for an investigation. *Colorado v. Bertine*, 479 U.S. 367 (1987).

38. *Colorado v. Bertine*, 479 U.S. 367 (1987). See also *South Dakota v. Opperman*, 428 U.S. 364 (1976), which authorized the use of evidence seized from the glove compartment, as opposed to containers, during an inventory search, and *New York v. Belton*, 453 U.S. 454 (1981), which authorized a warrantless search of a zipped jacket pocket on a seat of a car whose occupants were being arrested for marijuana possession. "[W]e hold that, when a policeman has made a lawful custodial arrest of the occupant of an automobile, he may, as a contemporaneous incident of that arrest, search the passenger compartment of that automobile. It follows from this conclusion that the police may also examine the contents of any containers found within the passenger compartment."

39. *Florida v. Wells*, 495 U.S. 1 (1990).

40. *Knowles v. Iowa*, 525 U.S. 113 (1998), with the opinion by Rehnquist.

41. *Atwater v. Lago Vista*, 121 S. Ct. 1536 (2001). The decision was 5–4, with Souter, Rehnquist, Scalia, Kennedy, and Thomas in an unusual majority coalition, and Sandra Day O'Connor, Stevens, Ginsburg, and Stephen G. Breyer in dissent. Details of the circumstances of the arrest come from the majority and minority opinions, and from *ABA Journal*, June 2001, 87 A.B.A.J. 38. See also *National Review*, May 3, 2001, where Robert A. George wrote, "Can an America whose citizens have to fear arbitrary incarceration ever truly be 'safe'? In short, how safe can we be when our liberty most assuredly isn't?"

42. *Virginia v. Moore*, 06-1082 (2008). The ruling overturned the opinion by the Virginia Supreme Court, excluding the evidence.

43. *Arizona v. Gant*, 07-542 (2009). The lineup of the justices was unusual, mixing the typical conservative-liberal divide. Citing *Chimel*, which permitted such searches in an area "within the arrestee's immediate control," the majority opinion was written by Stevens and joined by Scalia, Thomas, Souter, and Ginsberg. Breyer, Alito, Roberts, and Kennedy dissented, arguing that the Court had overruled a simple guideline permitting police to search a vehicle incident to a driver's arrest, as set forth in *New York v. Belton*, 453 U.S. 454 (1981). In that case, a policeman who had pulled over a car for speeding smelled marijuana, saw a marijuana wrapping, and searched the passenger compartment, where he found the drug in a jacket. Four men in the car were arrested. The Court held that the interior of the car met *Chimel's* test of being in the arrestees' immediate area, and, striving to establish an unequivocal rule, declared, "We hold that when a policeman has made a lawful custodial arrest of the occupant of an automobile, he may, as a contemporaneous incident of that arrest, search the passenger compartment of that automobile." In *Gant*, each group of justices charged the other with misinterpreting precedent, a testimony to the confused state of the law on automobile searches; the majority said that *Belton* had not addressed the authority to search once a scene was secure; the minority said that the Court was now overturning the *Belton* rule.

44. *Schneckloth v. Bustamonte*, 412 U.S. 218 (1973). In dissent, Justice Thurgood Marshall cited a letter from FBI Director J. Edgar Hoover requiring his agents to inform people of their right to refuse to be searched. The policy remains in force, according to the FBI's legal counsel. E-mail from Angela D. Bell, Nov. 30, 2005. In practice, however, it is not always observed, according to subjects of searches. In subsequent cases, the Court has considered whether or not such advice was given in determining if a person's consent was voluntary. See *Florida v. Royer*, 460 U.S. 491 (1983).

45. *Florida v. Bostick*, 501 U.S. 429 (1991). The Court divided 6–3 with Marshall, Blackmun, and Stevens in the minority.

46. *Florida v. Royer*, 460 U.S. 491 (1983), decided 5–4 with White writing the majority opinion. Detectives who thought the passenger fit the profile of a drug courier asked for his ticket and license, discovered that the names didn't match, kept the documents, and led him to a police room. Without either placing him under arrest (which would have required a Miranda warning) or telling him that he was free to leave, the officers informed him that he was suspected of transporting drugs. They retrieved his checked bags from the airline and asked for permission to search. He did not respond but opened one suitcase lock with a key. He said he did not know the combination to the other's lock but did

not object to their forcing it open. The Court found the confinement unlawful (because, as one of the officers testified, there was no probable cause for an arrest until after the marijuana was discovered in the bags), and that the detention exeeded the bounds of a *Terry* investigative stop. The illegal confinement meant that the subsequent consent—in the absence of a search warrant—was not voluntary, and so tainted the search. See also *United States v. Mendenhall*, 446 U.S. 544, 555 (1980), which upheld such a stop, 5–4, because the defendant's ticket and identification were not held, so she was free to leave, and she was told she could decline a search.

47. Dina Temple-Raston, "Lies as Plain as the Nose on Your Face?" *Morning Edition*, NPR, Oct. 31, 2007. The Homeland Security project Future Attribute Screening Technology (FAST) aims at sensing heart rate, respiration, eye movement, skin temperature, voice quality, and body language. Dept. of Homeland Security, "Privacy Impact Assessment for the Future Attribute Screening Technology," Dec. 15, 2008, at http://www.dhs.gov/xlibrary/assets/privacy/privacy_pia _st_fast.pdf.

48. *United States v. (Robin) Nurse*, 286 U.S. App. D.C. 303, 916 F.2d 20 (D.C. Cir. ·1990).

CHAPTER 3: DEFENDING THE SYSTEM

1. *United States v. Tyshaun Bullock*, CR. 02-010 (D. D.C. 2002). Conflicting accounts from the transcript of the hearing on a motion to suppress physical evidence, July 9–10, 2001, before U.S. District Court Judge Thomas Penfield Jackson. Judge's ruling on the suppression motion, Aug. 20, 2002.

2. The concept was applied to the Fourth Amendment in *Wong Sun v. United States*, 371 U.S. 471 (1963). The Court found that if the unlawful police action is exploited to produce evidence, the evidence must be suppressed. If the relationship between the unconstitutional action and the evidence is attenuated, however, the evidence is admissible.

3. *Whren v. United States*, 517 U.S. 806 (1996). Narcotics officers passed a truck stopped for an unusually long time at a stop sign in a high-drug-use area of Washington, D.C. When they did a U-turn to drive back toward the truck, it turned suddenly without signaling and took off at an "unreasonable" speed. The officers, suspecting drug activity, pulled the vehicle over for the minor traffic infraction and observed bags of crack inside. The Court ruled the stop legitimate, even for an ulterior purpose, and the narcotics evidence admissible.

4. *Lewis v. United States*, 408 A.2d 303, 306 (D.C. Cir. 1979).

5. Michael Janofsky, *New York Times*, Apr. 10, 1997, p. A14; Stephen Braun, *Chicago Sun-Times*, Oct. 23, 1995, p. 18; *Shielded from Justice: Police Brutality and Accountability in the United States* (New York: Human Rights Watch, 1998), http://hrw.org/english/docs/1998/07/07/usdom1224.htm.

6. Lou Cannon, "One Bad Cop," *New York Times Magazine*, Oct. 1, 2000, Section 6, p. 32.

7. Patrick McGreevy, *Los Angeles Times*, July 12, 2006, p. A1. In addition, the City Council approved a payment of $20.5 million to settle a jury award to four police officers who sued for false arrest and malicious prosecution after a drug-

dealing cop accused them of framing a gang member on a gun charge. Mueve Reston, *Los Angeles Times,* Jan. 29, 2009, p. B3.

8. *Rampart Reconsidered: The Search for Real Reform Seven Years Later* (Los Angeles: Blue Ribbon Rampart Review Panel, 2006), Executive Summary, p. 9.

9. Ibid.

10. David Simon, "In Baltimore, No One Left to Press the Police," *Washington Post,* Outlook, March 1, 2009, p. B1. Simon dug out the name: Traci McKissick, who shot Joseph Alfonso Forrest in a struggle for her gun during a domestic dispute. She had lost her gun previously, in 2005; when she pulled it, a suspect grabbed it and threw it out a car window.

11. Defenders refused to take new cases in various jurisdictions in Rhode Island, Connecticut, Maryland, Florida, Tennessee, Kentucky, Ohio, Minnesota, Arizona, Montana, and Washington State. David J. Carroll, research director, National Legal Aid & Defender Association, interview with author, Jan. 27, 2009.

12. Robbie Brown, "Long Held in Capital Case, Man Sues to Get a Lawyer," *New York Times,* Jan. 2, 2009, p. A13.

13. Erik Eckholm, "Citing Workload, Public Lawyers Reject New Cases," *New York Times,* Nov. 8, 2008. The states where public defenders refused to take more cases were Florida, Missouri, Kentucky, Tennessee, Minnesota, Maryland, and Arizona. See also "Resolution on Caseloads and Workloads," American Council of Chief Defenders, Aug. 24, 2007.

14. Pascal F. Calogero, Jr., chief justice, Supreme Court of Louisiana, State of the Judiciary Address to legislature, May 3, 2005.

15. Ken Armstrong, "Grant County Settles Defense Lawsuit," *Seattle Times,* Nov. 8, 2005. Settlement Agreement in *Best v. Grant County,* 04-2-00189-0, in Superior Court, State of Washington for Kittitas County, Oct. 31, 2005, at http://www .defender.org/files/archive/GrantCountyLitigationSettlementAgreement.pdf. The caseload is calculated as 150 "case equivalents," with more serious prosecutions, such as murder, counting as two cases, and less serious, such as probation violation, as one-third of a case.

16. Indigent defendants in D.C. Superior Court are represented by the Public Defenders Service, a team of lawyers separate from the Federal Public Defenders, who work only in federal courts. The U.S. Attorney's office in D.C. is the only one in the country to handle "arrest-generated" cases—the products of street arrests by local police rather than investigations and grand jury indictments. In general, the office refers drug cases to federal court if they involve at least one hundred grams of heroin or five hundred grams of powder cocaine, which carry a five-year mandatory minimum sentence, or fifty grams of crack, which has a ten-year minimum. If the drugs don't "make weight," in the prosecutors' parlance, the defendant may still be charged in federal court if he's a major narcotics or gang figure, or if the police want to press him to cooperate in a wider investigation.

17. *Giglio v. United States,* 405 U.S. 150 (1972).

18. Upon this finding, Cushenberry stopped the jury trial and granted the defendant's motion for a judgment of acquittal. *United States v. Tyrone Phillips,* F-3210-97, transcript, pp. 166, 172, 173.

19. *United States v. Gerald F. Whitmore,* 03-3022 (2004). From the appellant's brief and reply brief, and the opinion of the D.C. Court of Appeals, March 5, 2004. After the Cushenberry ruling, the U.S. Attorney's office investigated and declined to charge Soto with perjury.

20. *United States v. Vernon Wilson,* CR-04-28, before U.S. district judge Emmet G. Sullivan. The stop was based on a dubious claim by another officer, looking from an observation post through five chain-link fences, that he could see Wilson, after dark, hand something to a man and take something green from him before getting into his car. The judge found this insufficient to establish probable cause.

21. "Evidence of the habit of a person or of the routine practice of an organization, whether corroborated or not and regardless of the presence of eyewitnesses, is relevant to prove that the conduct of the person or organization on a particular occasion was in conformity with the habit or routine practice." *Rules of Federal Evidence,* 2006, ed., Article IV, Rule 406.

22. "Specific instances of the conduct of a witness, for the purpose of attacking or supporting the witness' character for truthfulness, other than conviction of crime as provided in rule 609, may not be proved by extrinsic evidence. They may, however, in the discretion of the court, if probative of truthfulness or untruthfulness, be inquired into on cross-examination of the witness (1) concerning the witness' character for truthfulness or untruthfulness, or (2) concerning the character for truthfulness or untruthfulness of another witness as to which character the witness being cross-examined has testified." *Rules of Federal Evidence,* 2006, ed., Article VI, Rule 608 (b). To avoid mini-trials of earlier cases, this provision would prevent the defense from introducing as evidence of falsehood a judge's previous finding that an officer's account was not credible, but would allow the officer to be cross-examined about that prior case. "A cross-examiner may inquire into specific incidents of conduct, but does so at the peril of not being able to rebut the witness's denials." *United States v. Bynum,* 3F.3d 769 (4th Cir. 1993).

23. The conviction or the release from confinement, whichever is later, must be within the last ten years unless the judge finds an older crime more probative than prejudicial. *Rules of Federal Evidence,* 2006, ed., Article VI, Rule 609.

24. Character evidence, however, can be presented by the accused about himself and an alleged victim, and can be rebutted by the prosecution. *Rules of Federal Evidence,* 2006, ed., Article IV, Rule 404 (a). Otherwise, "Evidence of other crimes, wrongs, or acts is not admissible to prove the character of a person in order to show action in conformity therewith. It may, however, be admissible for other purposes, such as proof of motive, opportunity, intent, preparation, plan, knowledge, identity, or absence of mistake or accident . . ." Article 404(b).

25. *Hatch Act,* 5 U.S.C. § 7323 (a) (1).

26. Each jurisdiction permits a number of peremptory challenges. In federal courts, the defense gets ten and the prosecution six in cases carrying more than a year in prison, and each side is given twenty in capital cases and three for crimes punishable by one year or less, plus additional challenges if alternate jurors are seated. *Federal Rules of Criminal Procedure,* Rule 24: Trial Jurors, (b) Peremptory Challenges.

27. *Batson v. Kentucky,* 476 U.S. 79 (1986).

28. *New York Times*, Apr. 4, 1997, p. A24.
29. From the Anglo-Norman, "to speak the truth." *The American Heritage Dictionary of the English Language*, Third Ed. (Boston: Houghton Mifflin, 1992), p. 2001.
30. *Crimes and Criminal Procedure*, 18 U.S.C. § 922 (g) (1). In addition, the federal ban on gun possession applies to nine categories of people, including drug addicts, fugitives, those dishonorably discharged from the military, anyone under a domestic restraining order or with a misdemeanor domestic-violence conviction, and people in the United States unlawfully or on nonimmigrant visas. The prohibition concerns firearms transported in interstate commerce, which applies to every gun in the District of Columbia, since none is manufactured there.
31. Defendant's motion *in limine* to compel discovery and permit cross-examination, *United States v. Franklin A. Dorn*, Crim. No. 05-13, Feb. 2006, pp. 7–8.
32. Government's omnibus opposition to defendant's motion *in limine* to compel discovery and to permit cross-examination, *United States v. Franklin A. Dorn*, Crim. No. 05-13, Feb. 2006, p. 11.
33. Memorandum opinion, *United States v. Franklin A. Dorn*, Crim. No. 05-13 (D. D.C. 2006).
34. *United States v. Santana*, 427 U.S. 38 (1976).
35. *Brigham City, Utah v. Stuart*, 05-502 (2006).

CHAPTER 4: WITH WARRANTS AND WITHOUT

1. *Michigan v. Summers*, 452 U.S. 692 (1981). Whether someone so detained is in custody for *Miranda* purposes is another question. When not physically restrained, some courts have held, the person may not be in custody and therefore may not need to be warned before questioned. See appellants' brief in *United States v. James Isaac Gaston*, 02-3062 and 02-3063 (D.C. Cir. 2003).
2. Under federal and state laws, assets may be forfeited even before a court has adjudicated the case if there is probable cause to believe either that they are the fruits of a crime, such as drug money, or have facilitated a crime, such as a car to transport narcotics or a house where drugs are manufactured or sold. If criminal charges are brought and the defendant is acquitted, the assets are returned. If no criminal case is filed, the owner must go through a civil action in court to get them back.
3. 18 U.S.C. § 922(g). Other categories include fugitives, drug users, those dishonorably discharged from the military, people convicted of misdemeanors involving domestic violence, those deemed dangerous under court restraining order for stalking or domestic violence, and anyone who has renounced his U.S. citizenship.
4. James Otis, in oral argument representing Boston merchants against British writs of assistance, Boston, 1761, http://www.u-s-history.com/pages/h1204.html. *Paxton's Case*, Quincy's *Mass. Rpts.* 51 (1761). The statement "A man's house is his castle" is first attributed to Sir Edward Coke in the seventeenth century. John Bartlett, *Bartlett's Familiar Quotations* (New York: Little, Brown, 1980), p. 172.
5. *United States v. James Isaac Gaston*, 02-3062 and 02-3063, (D.C. Cir. 2003), appel-

lants' brief to U.S. Court of Appeals for the District of Columbia, p. 13. The officer was an Alcohol, Tobacco, and Firearms agent of the Treasury Department, Frank Oliver, Jr.

6. The presence of evidence must be "so closely related to the time of the issuance of the warrant as to justify a finding of probable cause at that time." *Sgro v. United States,* 287 U.S. 206 (1932).

7. *Illinois v. Gates,* 462 U.S. 213 (1983). The dissenters were Brennan, Marshall, and Stevens.

8. *Aguilar v. Texas,* 378 U.S. 108 (1964), and *Spinelli v. United States,* 393 U.S. 410 (1969).

9. Joe Hallinan, "Misfires in War on Drugs," *Plain Dealer,* Sept. 26, 1993, p. 17A.

10. Sara Rimer, "Minister Who Sought Peace Dies in a Botched Drug Raid," *New York Times,* March 28, 1994, p. A1. James Bovard, "No-Knock Entries by Police Take Their Toll on Innocent," *Christian Science Monitor,* May 24, 1994, p. 18.

11. John Dillin, "It Was the Perfect Drug Raid . . . but the Wrong House," *Christian Science Monitor,* Oct. 1, 1993, p. 6. See also Hallinan, *Plain Dealer,* and Bob Ross, "War on Drugs Takes Toll on Innocent," *USA Today,* Jan. 11, 1993, p. 1A.

12. Michael D. Bradbury, "Report on the Death of Donald Scott," Office of the District Attorney, County of Ventura, March 30, 1993; Kevin G. De Noce, Deputy District Attorney, "Motive Involved in the Trail's End Ranch Search Warrant," Office of the District Attorney, County of Ventura, March 31, 1993; John Dillin, "Citizens Caught in the Cross-Fire," *Christian Science Monitor,* Oct. 1, 1993, p. 6; Dillin, "When Federal Drug Laws Create Havoc for Citizens," *Christian Science Monitor,* Sept. 28, 1993, p. 10; Debra J. Saunders, "Big Brother Gets Grabby," *San Francisco Chronicle,* June 25, 1993, p. A24; Haya El Nasser and Jonathan T. Lovitt, "Raid, Slain Recluse: Stuff of Mystery," *USA Today,* Oct. 19, 1992, p. 3A.

13. Bill Torpy, "Big Score Holy Grail for Drug Officers," *Atlanta Journal-Constitution,* Jan. 13, 2007, p. 1A; Torpy, "Cop Murder Charges Sought," *Journal-Constitution,* Feb. 8, 2007; Rhonda Cook, "Police Lied, Informant Says," *Journal-Constitution,* Nov. 28, 2006, p. 1A; "Web Extra: Gregg Junnier Quotes," WSBTV, March 6, 2009. All three, Jason R. Smith, Gregg Junnier, and Arthur Tesler, pleaded guilty to federal charges of conspiracy to violate civil rights resulting in death. The first two also pleaded guilty to state charges and were sentenced to concurrent jail terms. Two other officers pleaded guilty to federal charges. "Three Former Atlanta Police Officers Sentenced to Prison in Fatal Shooting of Elderly Atlanta Woman," Dept. of Justice, Feb. 24, 2009, http://www.usdoj.gov/opa/pr/2009/February/09-crt-159.html. "Former Atlanta Police Sergeant Sentenced to Federal Prison for Warrantless Break-in of Private Home," Dept. of Justice, http://atlanta.fbi.gov/dojpressrel/pressrel09/atl061909a.htm.

14. Radley Balko, *Overkill: The Rise of Paramilitary Police Raids in America* (Washington, D.C.: Cato Institute, 2006).

15. Bill Torpy, e-mail to author, Feb. 12, 2007.

16. *United States v. Luong,* 470 F.3d 898 (9th Cir. 2006). On appeal, the government conceded that the affidavit did not support probable cause but argued, unsuccessfully, that the evidence should be admitted under the "good faith" exception in *Leon,* discussed below. The Ninth Circuit stated, "The warrant in this case was so lacking in indicia of probable cause that a reasonably well-trained officer

could not have relied on it in good faith." The appeals court also held that oral statements by the officer to the issuing magistrate, supplementing the sworn affidavit, could not be considered, given the Fourth Amendment's requirement for "probable cause, supported by Oath or affirmation." The government had cited cases from other circuits allowing such consideration: *United States v. Legg,* 18 F.3d 240, 243–44 (4th Cir. 1994) and *United States v. Maggitt,* 778 F.2d 1029, 1036 (5th Cir. 1985).

17. *United States v. Martedis McPhearson,* 469 F.3d 518 (6th Cir. 2006).

18. *United States v. Leon,* 468 U.S. 897 (1984). White wrote for the majority; Brennan, Marshall, and Stevens dissented.

19. Potter Stewart, "The Road to *Mapp v. Ohio* and Beyond," *Columbia Law Review* 83, Oct. 1983, p. 1401.

20. Ibid., p. 1365.

21. Craig M. Bradley, ed., *Criminal Procedure: A Worldwide Study* (Durham, N.C.: Carolina Academic Press, 1999), pp. 85, 105, 195–96, 230, 259, 295. In Germany, evidence can be excluded at the court's discretion, but not if a judge would have authorized a search. In England, police can be sued for trespass.

22. Common law, "based on custom and usage," evolved into an amalgam of Anglo-Saxon and Norman law following William the Conqueror's invasion of England, in 1066. Though never written, it formed the foundation of court decisions and, most famously, the *Commentaries on the Laws of England* by Sir William Blackstone, from which it entered the statutes of virtually all states "except Louisiana, which is still influenced by the Napoleonic Code." http://dictionary .law.com/definition2.asp?selected=248.

23. *Commonwealth v. Dana,* 43 Mass. 329, 337 (1841). Quoted in Timothy Lynch, *In Defense of the Exclusionary Rule* (Washington, D.C.: Cato Institute, 1998), p. 28, http://www.cato.org/pubs/pas/pa-319.pdf.

24. *Weeks v. United States,* 232 U.S. 383 (1914). The unanimous opinion was written by Justice William Rufus Day. It had some antecedents in *Boyd v. United States,* 116 U.S. 616 (1886), a civil forfeiture case, and *Adams v. New York,* 192 U.S. 585 (1904). In *Boyd,* the Court excluded private books and papers illegally seized as a violation of the Fifth Amendment's bar on compulsory self-incrimination. That meant that personal papers could be suppressed, for example, but not guns or drugs. In *Adams,* however, Day rejected an appeal to suppress gambling evidence regardless of how it was obtained. A decade later in *Weeks* he granted the defendant's appeal on different grounds: that Weeks had moved for the return of his illegally seized papers rather than their exclusion from trial—a distinction with the same result.

25. The doctrine was broadened in *Silverthorne Lumber Co. v. United States,* 251 U.S. 385 (1920), which suppressed the entire chain of evidence, even when legally obtained but based on information originating in an illegal search, and in *Agnello v. United States,* 269 U.S. 20 (1925), which excluded evidence seized in a warrantless search of the home of a suspect arrested elsewhere; a warrantless search incident to arrest does not extend to other places.

26. *Wolf v. People of the State of Colorado,* 338 U.S. 25 (1949). The Court found that the Fourth Amendment applied to the states but the remedy of the exclusionary rule did not.

27. The tactic was ended by the Supreme Court in *Elkins v. United States,* 364 U.S

206 (1960), a year before applying the exclusionary rule to the states in *Mapp v. Ohio*.

28. Lynch, *In Defense of the Exclusionary Rule*, p. 26.

29. *Mapp v. Ohio*, 367 U.S. 643 (1961). The ruling was 6–3, with Tom C. Clark writing for the majority and John Marshall Harlan, Felix Frankfurter, and Charles Evans Whittaker in dissent. Police entered a house without a search warrant and found pornography. The appeal by Dollree Mapp argued that the law under which she was prosecuted violated the First Amendment. The Court took the opportunity, raised only in amicus briefs, to overturn *Wolf*. See David M. O'Brien, *Constitutional Law and Politics*, Vol. 2 (New York: Norton, 2003), p. 973, reproducing letter from Potter Stewart to Tom Clark.

30. Sidney E. Zion, "Detectives Get a Course in Law," *New York Times*, Apr. 28, 1965, p. 50.

31. "Evidence shall not be excluded from trial by military commission on the grounds that the evidence was not seized pursuant to a search warrant or other authorization." Military Commissions Act of 2006, 10 U.S. 47A, § 949a (2)(B). The provision was amended in 2009 to read, "Evidence *seized outside the United States* shall not be excluded" [emphasis added]. 10 U.S. 47A, § 949a (3)(A) of 2009.

32. *United States v. Calandra*, 414 U.S. 338 (1974).

33. *United States v. Janis*, 428 U.S. 433 (1976).

34. *United States v. Havens*, 446 U.S. 620 (1980). A decade later, in *James v. Illinois*, 493 U.S. 307 (1990), a 5–4 majority refused to extend the exception to all defense witnesses.

35. *Nix v. Williams*, 467 U.S. 431 (1984). A murder defendant in custody, but not warned of his right to remain silent, disclosed the location of his ten-year-old victim in a ditch. The condition of the body was the issue. His first trial was overturned because of the inadmissibility of his unwarned statement; his second trial, without the statement, was upheld on the grounds that the body's condition would have been observed when inevitably found by the police during the search of the area. Also, *Segura v. United States*, 468 U.S. 796 (1984), where evidence would have been obtained through independent sources.

36. *Stone v. Powell*, 428 U.S. 465 (1976).

37. *United States v. Leon*, 468 U.S. 897, 929 (1984). Jurisprudence never moves in a straight line, though. In a counterpoint, *Georgia v. Randolph*, 547 U.S. 103 (2006), held that police could not conduct a warrantless search where a resident who is present objects even though another resident consents. A man's estranged wife gave permission, her husband refused, the police entered anyway, and found cocaine. The Court applied the exclusionary rule, suppressing the evidence. Roberts, Scalia, and Thomas dissented. Alito did not participate.

38. *Arizona v. Evans*, 514 U.S. 1 (1995).

39. *Herring v. United States* 07-513 (2009).

40. *United States v. Banks*, 540 U. S. 31 (2003).

41. *Hudson v. Michigan*, 04-1360 (2006). Dissent by Breyer.

42. "The officer may break open any outer or inner door or window of a house, or any part of a house, or anything therein, to execute a search warrant, if, after notice of his authority and purpose, he is refused admittance or when necessary

to liberate himself or a person aiding him in the execution of the warrant." 18
U.S.C. § 3109.

43. 42 U.S.C. § 1983, 1988(a). Federal law also imposes up to a year in prison for an
official found guilty of depriving anyone of constitutional and statutory rights.
Prosecutions are rarely brought, however. 18 U.S.C. § 242.

44. Rowley tried and failed in the summer of 2001 to get headquarters to authorize
a search of the computer belonging to Zacarias Moussaoui, an unreliable al-
Qaeda operative who was taking flying lessons in Minnesota. FBI suspicions
prompted Moussaoui's arrest on Aug. 17 for overstaying his visa, but agents were
uncertain that they had sufficient probable cause to get an ordinary search warrant, so they never applied for one. They preferred a secret warrant under the
Foreign Intelligence Surveillance Act, which required probable cause to believe
that Moussaoui, a French citizen, was an agent of a "foreign power," whose definition included a terrorist organization. Although the Minneapolis FBI office
obtained information from France of his contacts with a Chechen leader, FBI
headquarters did not believe that was enough for a FISA application. See the
National Commission on Terrorist Attacks upon the United States, *The 9/11
Commission Report* (New York: W. W. Norton, 2004), pp. 273–76. Moussaoui
later pleaded guilty to being part of the 9/11 conspiracy and was sentenced to
life. His subsequent motion to withdraw his plea was denied.

45. *United States v. Calandra,* 414 U.S. 338 (1974).

46. 1 *Annals of Congress,* p. 439.

47. Lynch, *In Defense of the Exclusionary Rule,* p.1.

48. *People v. Defore,* 242 N.Y. 13, 21, 150 N.E. 585, 587 (1926).

49. Stewart, "The Road to *Mapp v. Ohio* and Beyond." Cited in Brennan's dissent.

50. *Treasury Employees v. Von Raab,* 489 U. S. 656 (1989).

51. *Skinner v. Railway Labor Executives' Association,* 489 U.S. 602 (1989).

52. O'Brien, *Constitutional Law and Politics,* Vol. 2, p. 913.

53. The Court denied certiorari in *Willner v. Barr,* 502 U.S. 1010 (1992), in which
the D.C. Circuit had allowed suspicionless testing of all public employees.

54. *Chandler v. Miller,* 520 U.S. 305 (1997). Ginsburg wrote the opinion. Rehnquist
was the lone dissenter.

55. *Ferguson v. Charleston,* 532 U.S. 67 (2001). In dissent were Rehnquist, Scalia,
and Thomas.

56. *Vernonia School District 47J v. Acton,* 515 U.S. 646 (1995). The vote was 6–3,
with Scalia—who had dissented in the U.S. Customs case—writing for the
majority, and O'Connor, Stevens, and Souter dissenting.

57. Linda Greenhouse, "Supreme Court Seems Ready to Extend School Drug
Tests," *New York Times,* March 20, 2002.

58. *Board of Education of Independent School District No. 92 of Pottawatomie
County et al. v. Earls et al.,* 536 U.S. 822 (2002). In the majority were Thomas,
Breyer, Kennedy, Scalia, and Rehnquist; in the minority, Stevens, Ginsburg,
Souter, and O'Connor.

59. Tamar Lewin, "Raid at High School Leads to Racial Divide, Not Drugs," *New
York Times,* Dec. 9, 2003, p. A16. *Alexander v. Goose Creek,* consent decree,
Exhibit C, cv-03845, filed March 27, 2006, found at http://www.aclu.org/images/
asset_upload_file313_24952.pdf. "Landmark Settlement Reached in Notorious

Drug Raid Caught on Tape," ACLU statement, July 11, 2006, at http://www.aclu
.org/drugpolicy/youth/26123prs20060711.html.

60. Eric Rich, "Rural Md. Drug Search Becomes a Sore Subject," *Washington Post*,
May 13, 2004, p. B1. "Students in Kent County School Drug Sweep Case Win
Landmark Settlement," ACLU statement, Aug. 6, 2007.

61. *Safford United School District v. Redding*, 08-479 (2009). Six justices—Souter,
Roberts, Scalia, Kennedy, Breyer, and Alito—signed the opinion. Stevens and
Ginsburg agreed that the search was unconstitutional but dissented on the
grant of immunity, arguing that the rules had been clearly established in a previous decision, *New Jersey v. T.L.O.*, 469 U.S. 325 (1985), which said that a
school search must not be "excessively intrusive in light of the age and sex of
the student and the nature of the infraction." Thomas agreed on immunity but
believed there was no violation of the Fourth Amendment.

62. Adam Liptak, "Strip-Search of Girl Tests Limit of School Policy," *New York
Times*, March 23, 2009.

63. *Samson v. California*, 547 U.S. 843 (2006). A policeman, who saw Donald Curtis
Samson walking down the street, searched him and found methamphetamine
inside a cigarette box. The Court found that parole was more akin to imprisonment than probation was. Previously, some suspicion had been necessary for
a warrantless search of a parolee, and in dissent, Stevens, Breyer, and Souter
wrote, "What the Court sanctions today is an unprecedented curtailment of liberty. Combining faulty syllogism with circular reasoning, the Court concludes
that parolees have no more legitimate an expectation of privacy in their persons
than do prisoners."

64. *Rocio Sanchez v. County of San Diego*, CV 00-1467 JYM (S.D. Cal. 2007). The
District Court judge had ruled in favor of the county, a Ninth Circuit panel
upheld the ruling 2–1, a majority of the Ninth Circuit refused to rehear the
appeal en banc (generating the dissent quoted), and the Supreme Court denied
certiorari.

65. *Wyman v. James*, 400 U.S. 309 (1971).

66. Editorial, "A Loss for Privacy Rights," *New York Times*, Nov. 28, 2007, p. A26.

CHAPTER 5: PATRIOTIC ACTS

1. "Judge Unseals Evidence for Lawyer Wrongly Arrested in Madrid Bombings,"
AP, Sept. 21, 2004, and letter to Elden Rosenthal, Mayfield's lawyer, from
Assistant U.S. Attorney Sara Clash-Drexler, March 24, 2005, quoted by Noelle
Crombie, "Mayfield Home Was Searched in Secret," *The Oregonian*, March 30,
2005, p. D01.

2. *Foreign Intelligence Surveillance Act*, 50 U.S.C. Chap. 36.

3. No. 103-359, 108 Stat. 3444 (Oct. 14, 1994). Previously, the attorney general
could authorize such secret searches, but their fruits were susceptible to suppression if a criminal case resulted.

4. Someone whose home has been searched under FISA may be notified later
if prosecuted or if the attorney general finds that "there is no national security interest in continuing to maintain the secrecy of the search." 50 U.S.C.
§ 1825(b). The Patriot Act also amended 18 U.S.C. § 3103(a), to give judges the

power to authorize a delay in notifying the target of any federal search warrant for a "reasonable period."

5. Richard B. Zabel and James J. Benjamin, Jr., *In Pursuit of Justice: Prosecuting Terrorism Cases in the Federal Courts,* Human Rights First, May 2008, pp. 95–96.

6. *In Re: All Matters Submitted to the Foreign Intelligence Surveillance Court,* 218 F.Supp2d 611 (FISC 2002), Multiple Docket Numbers, May 17, 2002, pp. 16–17.

7. FISA Amendments Act of 2008, H.R. 6304, incorporated into 50 U.S.C. § 1801. This opened the way to mass interception of huge quantities of phone calls and e-mail and other Internet traffic without specifying targets. The provision is not supposed to be used "intentionally" against anyone inside the United States or against "United States persons" abroad. A U.S. person is defined by 50 U.S.C. § 1801(i) as "a citizen of the United States, an alien lawfully admitted for permanent residence . . . an unincorporated association a substantial number of members of which are citizens of the United States or aliens lawfully admitted for permanent residence, or a corporation which is incorporated in the United States." But the FISA court has no role in monitoring ongoing surveillance it approves at the outset, so there is no oversight of whether intelligence agencies stop interception if they discover that a party is a U.S. person. For further discussion, see Chapter 6.

8. 50 U.S.C. § 1805(a)(3).

9. Glenn A. Fine, *A Review of the FBI's Handling of the Brandon Mayfield Case,* Office of the Inspector General, U.S. Department of Justice, March 2006, http://www.justice.gov/oig/. All references in the text to the Inspector General's report on Mayfield derive from this document.

10. To get a FISA warrant against a "non-U.S. person"—a foreigner in the U.S. illegally or for illegitimate purposes—authorities no longer have to show probable cause of his connection with a foreign organization, but merely that he alone "engages in international terrorism or activities in preparation thereof." This so-called "lone-wolf provision" was added to FISA, at 50 U.S.C. § 1801(b)(1)(C), by Section 6001 of the Intelligence Reform and Terrorism Prevention Act of 2004.

11. 50 U.S.C. § 1805(a)(3)(B).

12. For a history of the "wall," see Diane Carraway Piette and Jesselyn Radack, "Piercing the 'Historical Mists': The People and Events Behind the Passage of FISA and the Creation of the 'Wall,'" *Stanford Law and Policy Review,* Vol. 17:2, Spring 2006. Also, see *The 9/11 Commission Report* (New York: W. W. Norton, 2004), p. 539, n. 83. The commission found no legal reason that intelligence information on the potential hijackers who had entered the United States could not have been shared with criminal agents.

13. Michael E. Rolince, transcript, "Panel II of a Joint Hearing of the Senate and House Select Intelligence Committee," Federal News Service, Sept. 20, 2002.

14. The destroyer was attacked on Oct. 12, 2000, in Aden, Yemen, by a small boat laden with explosives. Seventeen crewmen were killed. The parallel investigations of Mihdhar—the criminal side for his alleged involvement and the intelligence side for his role as a suspected terrorist—never merged. The National Commission on Terrorist Attacks Upon the United States, *The 9/11 Commission Report,* pp. 266–72.

15. James Bamford, *The Shadow Factory* (New York: Doubleday, 2008), pp. 19–20.

16. *In Re: All Matters Submitted to the Foreign Intelligence Surveillance Court*, p. 17.
17. *The 911 Commission Report*, p. 539 n.
18. USA PATRIOT Act of 2001, Public Law 107-56, § 504, amending 50 U.S.C. § 1806(k)(2). The Foreign Intelligence Surveillance Court of Review, comprising three conservative semiretired judges who had never served on the FISA court, convened for the first time in history and heard secret oral argument from only the government side on Sept. 9, 2002. Although two amicus briefs were submitted from civil liberties groups, neither they nor anyone representing the opposing view was allowed to argue the case. The Court of Review, in an opinion riddled with factual errors that might have been caught in an adversary proceeding, upheld the removal of the wall and overturned a unanimous decision by the lower, seven-judge Foreign Intelligence Surveillance Court that had rejected the government's proposal, post–Patriot Act, to allow criminal investigators to direct the use of FISA for prosecutorial purposes. Finding a contradiction between the FISA statute and the government's interpretation, the lower court had sounded this warning: "Criminal prosecutors will tell the FBI when to use FISA (perhaps when they lack probable cause for a Title III electronic surveillance), what techniques to use, what information to look for, what information to keep as evidence and when use of FISA can cease because there is enough evidence to arrest and prosecute." The peculiar nature of the proceeding was illustrated by the fact that the court heard, in secret, from only one side of the argument: the government. *In Re: All Matters Submitted to the Foreign Intelligence Surveillance Court*, pp. 23–24. The Court of Review, however, found ample support in the 1978 legislative history of FISA for the concept that "intelligence and criminal law enforcement tend to merge in this area," as the Senate report on the law declared. Noting that practically all foreign intelligence also produces evidence of criminal conduct (except for the sheer monitoring of diplomatic communications between an embassy and its foreign ministry, for example), the Court of Review held that the Patriot Act's amendment to FISA, "by using the word 'significant,' eliminated any justification for the FISA court to balance the relative weight the government places on criminal prosecution as compared to other counterintelligence responses." The opinion stresses that FISA cannot be used in domestic criminal investigations lacking any foreign intelligence purpose whatsoever. The court concluded, "We think the procedures and government showings required under FISA, if they do not meet the minimum Fourth Amendment warrant standards, certainly come close." *In Re: Sealed Case No. 02-001*, 310 F.3d 717 (2002), decided Nov. 18, 2002, pp. 11, 29, 48. The presiding judge of the lower court, Royce Lamberth, had this acerbic reaction in a 2007 speech: "The Court of Review, in a very curious opinion, said that every attorney general in the last twenty-five years that had interpreted FISA had interpreted it wrong, and that all seven judges on the FISA Court were wrong, and here's the new interpretation. They're final because they're above me, but that doesn't make them right." Royce Lamberth, American Library Association, June 20, 2007, at http://www.ala.org/ala/washoff/washevents/woannual/annualconfwo.cfm#events.
19. Patriot Act, § 218, and 50 U.S.C. § 1804(a)(7)(B). In a memorandum dated March 6, 2002, Attorney General John Ashcroft interpreted this amendment to

mean that FISA could now "be used *primarily* for a law enforcement purpose, so long as a significant foreign intelligence purpose remains." *In Re: All Matters Submitted to the Foreign Intelligence Surveillance Court.*

20. Eric Lichtblau, "U.S. Uses Terror Law to Pursue Crimes from Drugs to Swindling," *New York Times*, Sept. 28, 2003, p. A1.

21. The lone dissenter was Senator Russ Feingold, Democrat of Wisconsin.

22. ACLU, "Year-Long Extension Contains No Privacy or Civil Liberties Safeguards," Feb. 25, 2010, http://www.aclu.org/national-security/congress-reauthorizes-overbroad-patriot-act-provisions.

23. Thomas Frank, *What's the Matter with Kansas?: How Conservatives Won the Heart of America* (New York: Metropolitan Books, 2005).

24. Bullets are usually made from lead batteries that are melted down. Two assumptions have proven incorrect: first, that the composition of the molten lead is consistent throughout, when in fact the beginning, middle, and end of the pour can contain different mixtures of elements, and second, that each batch is unique, when in fact multiple batches can be nearly identical. The first known use of the technique came in an attempt to analyze fragments of bullets in John F. Kennedy's assassination, but in 1964 the FBI director J. Edgar Hoover informed the Warren Commission, which was looking into the assassination, that the lab was unable to distinguish among the pieces of lead. John Solomon, "FBI Forensic Test Full of Holes," and "A Murder Conviction Torn Apart by a Bullet," *Washington Post*, Nov. 18 and 19, 2007, p. A1.

25. *Melendez-Diaz v. Massachusetts*, 07-591 (2009). The decision was 5–4, the opinion by Scalia.

26. Office of the Inspector General (OIG), *The FBI Laboratory: An Investigation into Laboratory Practices and Alleged Misconduct in Explosives-Related and Other Cases*, Apr. 1997.

27. The account of the lab's work is drawn from the Office of the Inspector General (OIG). See Fine, *A Review of the FBI's Handling of the Brandon Mayfield Case.*

28. Melissa Anne Smrz et al., "Review of FBI Latent Print Unit Processes and Recommendations to Improve Practices and Quality," *Journal of Forensic Identification*, 56 (3) 2006, p. 416.

29. *Brandon Mayfield et al. v. John Ashcroft et al.*, Complaint for Violation of Civil Rights, CV-04-1427-PA, Oct. 2004, p. 6. Details of the investigation are drawn from both the Mayfield complaint and the OIG report.

30. Robert B. Stacey, "Report on the Erroneous Fingerprint Individualization in the Madrid Train Bombing Case," *Forensic Science Communications*, Jan. 2005, Vol. 7, No. 1, at http://www.fbi.gov/hq/lab/fsc/backissu/jan2005/special_report/2005_special_report.htm.

31. E-mail from Angela Bell, FBI Office of Public Affairs, March 22, 2007.

32. Sarah Kershaw et al., "Spain and U.S. at Odds on Mistaken Terror Arrest," *New York Times*, June 3, 2004, p. A1.

33. Mayfield complaint, p. 15.

34. The CIA, the National Security Council, the Defense Department, the Department of Homeland Security, the Justice Department, the FBI, the Treasury Department, and the National Security Agency.

35. "Judge Unseals Evidence for Lawyer Wrongly Arrested in Madrid Bombings," AP, Sept. 21, 2004.

36. "Judge Unseals Evidence" and Fine, *A Review of the FBI's Handling of the Brandon Mayfield Case,* p. 82.

37. Fine, quoting material witness arrest-warrant affidavit, pp. 66, 252–53.

38. Judge Ann Aiken, opinion of Sept. 26, 2007, in *Brandon Mayfield et al. v. United States of America,* Civil No. 04-1427-AA (D. Or. 2007).

39. Mayfield complaint, p. 12.

40. Fine, p. 59.

41. Mayfield complaint, p. 10.

42. Fine, p. 56.

43. E-mail from Beth Anne Steele of the FBI Portland office to a colleague, quoted in Eric Lichtblau, *Bush's Law: The Remaking of American Justice* (New York: Pantheon, 2008), p. 72.

44. Smrz et al., *Journal of Forensic Identification,* 56(3)2006, pp. 418–33.

45. Richard Willing, "FBI Checking Prints in Death Row Cases," *USA Today,* Jan. 11, 2006, p. 3A. After Special Agent Ann R. Todd, assigned to speak for the lab, failed to respond to the queries, Angela D. Bell, FBI Office of Public Affairs, said, "Unfortunately, the management at the FBI has determined that we can not provide any additional comment and/or information." E-mail, March 22, 2007.

46. Sarah Skidmore, "Wrongly Accused Man Settles Bomb Suit," AP, Nov. 29, 2006. The comment was so obtuse that I wondered if Jordan had been misquoted, so I called him three times and left offers with his assistant and his press officer to receive a clarification or correction, if one was warranted. They didn't provide one and so let the statement stand.

47. 50 U.S.C. §§ 1805 (a) (5), 1824 (a) (5); H.R. Rep. No. 95-1283, Part I, 95th Congress. 2d Session (1978), at 80–81.

48. *Brandon Mayfield et al. v. United States of America,* Civil No. 04-1427-AA (D. Or., Sept. 27, 2007). The statutes amended by the Patriot Act, 50 U.S.C. §§ 1804 and 1823, were found unconstitutional by the District Court judge, before the Ninth Circuit refused to let the suit go forward.

49. *Mayfield et al. v. United States of America,* No. 07-35865 (9th Cir., 2009). Mayfield had argued that the government's retention of private materials unconstitutionally seized under FISA constituted an ongoing injury to him, but the appeals court found that even if that were the case, a finding that the seizure violated the Fourth Amendment would not require the government to return or destroy the materials. Therefore, no redress was possible. Mayfield's petition asking that the full membership of the appeals court rehear the case en banc was denied. The Supreme Court refused to review the decision.

50. *United States v. Battle,* CR 02-399-JO (D. Or.), Government's sentencing memorandum, Nov. 19, 2003. It wasn't the first target practice, according to the government. They had been to indoor firing ranges and rural areas in the spring and summer of 2001 as well.

51. Ron Gluckman, e-mail to author, Apr. 27, 2006.

52. *Battle,* sentencing memorandum.

53. *Battle,* motion to suppress foreign intelligence surveillance evidence, Aug. 1, 2003.

54. *Battle,* motion to suppress, pp. 26–27.

55. Charles Gorder memo to author.

56. Gorder, interview with author, Feb. 15, 2006.
57. *Battle*, motion to suppress, p. 30.
58. Sharing FISA intelligence with criminal investigators was less free during the period of investigation than now. Although the Patriot Act had effectively removed the wall between them, the Foreign Intelligence Surveillance Court had issued an opinion requiring that any discussion between the intelligence and criminal sides of the FBI be monitored by a high-ranking Justice Department official. *In Re: All Matters Submitted to the Foreign Intelligence Surveillance Court*, May 17, 2002. This was reversed by the Foreign Intelligence Surveillance Court of Review, in *In Re: Sealed Case No.* 02-001, Nov. 18, 2002, issued after the Portland Seven surveillance had been completed.
59. 18 U.S.C. § 2384: "If two or more persons in any State or Territory, or in any place subject to the jurisdiction of the United States, conspire to overthrow, put down or destroy by force the Government of the United States, or to levy war against them . . . they shall be fined under this title or imprisoned not more than twenty years or both." Defense lawyers argued, in a motion to dismiss, that the act of war had to occur in territory under U.S. jurisdiction. In rebuttal, the government countered that the geographical limitation applied to the conspiracy, not to the contemplated conduct. *Battle*, memorandum in support of defendants' motion to dismiss the indictment, May 2, 2003; opposition of the United States to defendants' motion to dismiss the indictment, June 6, 2003.

CHAPTER 6: THE LAW FALLS SILENT

1. For a detailed matrix of governmental powers to conduct searches and their codification in law, see "Current Legal Standards for Access to Papers, Records, and Communications," Center for Democracy and Technology, http://www.cdt.org/wiretap/govaccess/govaccesschart-11x17.pdf.
2. Letter to Kenneth Sutton from Michael J. Wolf, special agent in charge, New Haven Division, FBI, May 19, 2005. Sutton, the systems and telecommunication manager of Library Connection, had told the FBI to deliver the letter to George Christian, the executive director.
3. U.S. District Court Judge Victor Marrero, 334 F. Supp 2d 471 S.D. N.Y. (2004). After the Patriot Act was revised in 2005, the Second Circuit sent the case back for reconsideration, and again, on Sept. 6, 2007, Marrero ruled the gag order in violation of the First Amendment. 04 Civ. 2614 (S.D. NY 2007). He was partly upheld by the Second Circuit in 2008, *Doe v. Mukasey* 07-4943-cv (2nd Cir. 2008). The three judge panel found the revised nondisclosure provision, which permitted a recipient to go to court to prove the gag order unlawful, an unconstitutional prior restraint of speech under the First Amendment, and the court shifted the burden of proof to the government to show in court why national security or an investigation would be harmed by disclosure. The Obama administration continued to defend the gag provision, then in 2010 settled the case by allowing the recipient, Nicholas Merrill, to identify himself.
4. "State Privacy Laws Regarding Library Records," American Library Association, http://www.ala.org/oif/stateprivacylaws.
5. 18 U.S.C. § 2709(c). Gag orders appear in all sections of federal law permitting the use of National Security Letters for obtaining various records. Although no

penalty for violation was mentioned in the original Patriot Act, its renewal and amendment added it to 18 U.S.C. § 1510, providing that anyone who "knowingly and with the intent to obstruct an investigation or judicial proceeding violates such prohibitions or requirements applicable by law to such person shall be imprisoned for not more than five years, fined under this title, or both."

6. Besides Christian, the three executive board members were Peter Chase, director of the Plainville Public Library; Barbara Bailey, director of the library in Glastonbury; and Janet Nocek, director of the Portland Library.

7. 18 U.S.C, § 1510. See also Charles Doyle, *CRS Report for Congress: National Security Letters in Foreign Intelligence Investigations: Legal Background and Recent Amendments,* Congressional Research Service, March 20, 2007, http://www.fas.org/sgp/crs/intel/RL33320.pdf.

8. Alison Leigh Cowan, "Librarians Must Stay Silent in Patriot Act Suit, Court Says," *New York Times,* Sept. 21, 2005, p. B2.

9. *John Doe et al. v. Alberto Gonzales,* 3:05-cv-1256 (JCH), (D. Conn. 2005), "Ruling on Plaintiffs' Motion for Preliminary Injunction," pp. 17, 23, 26. The ruling struck down 18 U.S.C. § 2709(c), but was stayed on appeal. Justice Ginsburg refused to vacate the stay, and the Appeals Court then dismissed the government's appeal as moot, given the Justice Department's permission for the library consortium to reveal its identity. *John Doe v. Gonzales,* 05-0570-cv(L), 05-4896-cv(CON) (2nd Cir. 2006).

10. Chase interview by Ray Hardman on *Front and Center,* CPTV, taped Oct. 4, 2006, aired Jan. 5, 2007.

11. Eric Lichtblau, "Libraries Say Yes, Officials Do Quiz Them About Users," *New York Times,* June 20, 2005, p. A11.

12. It is the League of Women Voters.

13. Only in a narrow technical sense were administration officials' statements correct: They were responding to concerns that Section 215 of the Patriot Act, which authorizes FISA warrants for "any tangible things (including books, records, papers, documents, and other items)," would be used against libraries, and apparently it had not been. They did not volunteer the fact that National Security Letters had been used instead. Patriot Act, Public Law 107-56, Sec. 215, amending 50 U.S.C. 1851 § 501.

14. O'Connor interview by Ray Hardman on *Front and Center,* CPTV, taped Oct. 4, 2006, broadcast Jan. 5, 2007.

15. The IP addresses are made anonymous after nine months, and cookies in Google's search-engine logs are made anonymous after eighteen months. "Why are search engine logs kept before being anonymized?" Google Privacy Center, http://www.google.com/intl/en/privacy_faq.html#toc-store.

16. "Resolution on the Retention of Library Usage Records," American Library Association, June 28, 2006, http://www.ala.org/Template.cfm?Section=ifresolutions &Template=/ContentManagement/ContentDisplay.cfm&ContentID=135888.

17. 47 U.S.C. § 1002 (a), as amended by the Communications Assistance for Law Enforcement Act of 1994, now 47 U.S.C. §§ 1001–21.

18. *American Council on Education v. Federal Communications Commission,* 451 F.3d 226 (D.C. Cir. 2006).

19. 12 U.S.C. 1829b (d). The act's constitutionality was upheld in *California Bankers Assn. v. Shultz,* 416 U.S. 21 (1974).

20. State legislatures can fall victim to the same syndrome. Massachusetts hastily passed a law in the fall of 2001 requiring Internet providers to turn over e-mails in response to administrative orders. John Laidler, "After Attacks, Senate Acts Swiftly," *Boston Globe,* Oct. 28, 2001, p. 5. The ACLU has filed complaints with most states' public utilities commissions over telecom companies' suspected disclosure of customer records to the government. See http://www.aclu.org/ puc-spying-map. But it is mostly a federal problem; little real-time electronic surveillance is done by states. "Forty-six states or territories have state wiretap laws, authorizing state and local police to intercept the content of voice or email communications, but in the average year, half of them make little or no use of those laws." Jim Dempsey, e-mail to author, June 8, 2007. Illinois did only one in 2009, and police did none in Virginia, Texas, Ohio, Louisiana, Washington, and smaller states. The leaders were California (586 wiretaps), New York (424), New Jersey (206), Colorado (115), and Florida (78). See http://www .uscourts.gov/wiretap09/Table1.pdf.

21. *United States v. United States District Court,* 407 U.S. 297 (1972). Data on time, cited by Douglas, are drawn from an investigation by Senator Edward Kennedy. In the case, one man was charged with bombing a CIA office in Ann Arbor, Michigan, the other two with conspiring to attack government facilities. Powell wrote the unanimous opinion. Rehnquist did not participate.

22. Nicholas M. Horrock, "National Security Agency Reported Eavesdropping on Most Private Cables," *New York Times,* Aug. 31, 1975, p. 1.

23. *United States v. Miller,* 425 U.S. 435 (1976). Mitch Miller was convicted of having an unregistered still and 175 gallons of whiskey, discovered during a fire at his warehouse, and of defrauding the government of taxes. Unlike documents in the nineteenth-century case *Boyd v. United States,* 116 U.S. 616, 622 (1886), in which the Court ruled against "compulsory production of a man's private papers to establish a criminal charge against him," the Court ruled in *Miller* that instruments held by a bank "are not respondent's 'private papers,'" and that he "can assert neither ownership nor possession." Majority opinion, 7–2, by Powell.

24. *Smith v. Maryland,* 442 U.S. 735 (1979). After a Baltimore woman was robbed and gave police a description of the thief's car, she received threatening phone calls from the man. In one call, he told her to step onto her porch. When she saw the car driving past her house, she reported the plate number to police, who traced it to Michael Lee Smith and—without a warrant or court order— asked the phone company to put a pen register on his phone, which captured a call to her number. On that basis, police obtained a search warrant of his home and put him in a lineup, where the victim identified him. Majority opinion, 5–3, by Blackmun.

25. Office of the Inspector General, *A Review of the Federal Bureau of Investigation's Use of National Security Letters,* Department of Justice, March 2007.

26. "Important Information Every Schwab Account Holder Needs to Know," Charles Schwab & Co., Inc., June 2007.

27. 15 U.S.C. § 1681.

28. 12 U.S.C. § 3414.

29. 18 U.S.C. § 2709.

30. 50 U.S.C. § 436.

31. The number of letters, as opposed to requests contained in letters, rose rapidly after the Patriot Act was passed in 2001. One letter may contain many requests, as in 2004, when nine letters requested information on 11,000 phone numbers, thereby causing the jump in figures for that year. Statistics, legal history, and data on FBI abuses derive from Office of the Inspector General, *A Review of the Federal Bureau of Investigation's Use of National Security Letters,* Department of Justice, March 2007, and Office of the Inspector General, *Report to Congress on Implementation of Section 1001 of the USA Patriot Act,* Department of Justice, Feb. 2010. After investigators found abuses, the FBI pulled back somewhat, issuing 16,804 in 2007 and 24,744 in 2008. Ronald Weich, assistant attorney general, letter to chairs of Senate and House Committees on Judiciary and Intelligence, May 14, 2009.

32. Mark Mazzetti and Eric Lichtblau, "Pentagon Review Faults Demands for Bank Records," *New York Times,* Oct. 14, 2007, p. A30. Based on heavily censored documents obtained by the ACLU under the FOIA. See http://www.aclu.org/safefree/nationalsecurityletters/32145prs20071014.html.

33. Patriot Act, § 505.

34. Additional officials are authorized under the Fair Credit Reporting Act, 15 U.S.C. § 1681(v), which empowers supervisory officials of an agency investigating or analyzing international terrorism, and the National Security Act, 50 U.S.C. § 436, empowering officials down to the level of assistant secretary or assistant director of agencies with employees with access to classified material.

35. "U.S. persons" also include U.S. corporations and associations containing a substantial membership of citizens or lawful permanent residents. 50 U.S.C. § 1801 (i).

36. The reason for the inaccurate FBI records was that the computer default for NSLs under the Electronic Communications Privacy and Right to Financial Privacy Acts was set to "non-U.S. person," meaning that if no information was entered, the NSL's target was recorded as a non-U.S. person. Twenty-six of 212 approvals found U.S. persons listed as non-U.S. persons. The default has since been changed to U.S. person. Office of Inspector General, *A Review of the Federal Bureau of Investigation's Use of National Security Letters,* p. 35.

37. Executive Order 12333, § 2.4 of Dec. 4, 1981.

38. Patriot Act, § 358(g), amending the Fair Credit Reporting Act.

39. OIG report, *National Security Letters,* p. 113 n. 150.

40. OIG report, *National Security Letters,* p. 114 nn. 151, 152.

41. James Bamford, *The Shadow Factory* (New York: Doubleday, 2008), pp. 19–20.

42. "Summary of the White House Review of the December 25, 2009 Attempted Terrorist Attack," White House, Jan. 8, 2010.

43. Lawrence Wright, "The Spymaster," *The New Yorker,* Jan. 21, 2008, p. 55.

44. Transactional Records Access Clearinghouse of Syracuse U., "Criminal Terrorism Enforcement in the United States During the Five Years Since the 9/11/01 Attacks," http://www.trac.syr.edu/tracreports/terrorism/169/ and "Who Is a Terrorist?" http:// www.trac.syr.edu:80/tracreports/terrorism/215/. The turndown rate jumped from 31 percent in fiscal year 2002 to 73 percent in fiscal year 2008.

45. Dina Temple-Raston, "Terrorism Case Shows Range of Investigators' Tools," NPR, Oct. 3, 2009.

46. *Report from the Field: USA Patriot Act at Work*, U.S. Dept. of Justice, March 2004, p. 7.
47. Ibid., p. 6.
48. Glenn A. Fine, Gordon S. Hedell, Patricia A. Lewis, George Ellard, and Roslyn A. Mazer, Inspectors General of the Dept. of Justice, Dept. of Defense, CIA, NSA, and Director of National Intelligence, "Unclassified Report on the President's Surveillance Program," July 10, 2009, p. 9.
49. Jack Goldsmith, *The Terror Presidency* (New York: W. W. Norton, 2007), p. 180.
50. Jane Mayer, *The Dark Side* (New York: Doubleday, 2008), pp. 68–69.
51. Goldsmith, *The Terror Presidency*, p. 181.
52. Deb Reichmann, "Bush Calls for Expansion of Spy Law," AP, Sept. 19, 2007.
53. James Risen and Eric Lichtblau, "Bush Lets U.S. Spy on Callers Without Courts," *New York Times*, Dec. 16, 2005, p. A1; Risen and Lichtblau, "Spying Program Snared U.S. Calls," *New York Times*, Dec. 21, 2005, p. A1. See also James Risen, *State of War* (New York: Free Press, 2006), and Eric Lichtblau, *Bush's Law: The Remaking of American Justice* (New York: Pantheon, 2008).
54. Eric Lichtblau, James Risen, and Scott Shane, "Wider Spying Fuels Aid Plan for Telecoms," *New York Times*, Dec. 16, 2007, p. A1.
55. Bamford, *The Shadow Factory*, pp. 189–94.
56. Lichtblau and Risen, "Spy Agency Mined Vast Data Trove, Officials Report," *New York Times*, Dec. 24, 2005, p. A1.
57. Bamford, *The Shadow Factory*, p. 194.
58. Ibid., pp. 130–31.
59. Lesley Cauley, "NSA Has Massive Database of Americans' Phone Calls," *USA Today*, May 11, 2006, p. A1.
60. Fine et al., "President's Surveillance Program," pp. 33, 34, 35.
61. Plea agreement, *United States v. Iyman Faris*, 03-189-A (E.D. Va. 2003). After pleading guilty to two counts of providing, and conspiracy to provide, material support to a foreign terrorist organization, Faris was sentenced to twenty years. Dept. of Justice, "Iyman Faris Sentenced for Providing Material Support to Al Qaeda," Oct. 28, 2003.
62. Dept. of Justice, "Legal Authorities Supporting the Activities of the National Security Agency Described by the President," Jan. 19, 2006.
63. James B. Comey, testimony, House Committee on the Judiciary, June 8, 2005.
64. Comey's account comes from his testimony before the Senate Judiciary Committee, May 15, 2007, plus his subsequent written answers.
65. Fine et al., "President's Surveillance Program," pp. 24–28. This report is used throughout to fill in gaps in Comey's testimony.
66. Comey, written answers to questions from Senator Patrick Leahy submitted May 22, 2007, released June 7, 2007, http://leahy.senate.gov/press/200705/052507ComeyResponse.pdf.
67. Besides the FBI director, those prepared to resign were Jack Goldsmith, Patrick Philbin, Chuck Rosenberg, Daniel Levin, James Baker, David Ayres, and David Israelite, plus "a large portion" of Comey's staff. Comey, written answers.
68. Fine et al., "President's Surveillance Program," p. 27.
69. Lichtblau, *Bush's Law*, p. 184.
70. Comey, written answers. Richard B. Schmitt, "Cheney Is Said to Have Halted Promotion," *Los Angeles Times*, June 7, 2007, A13.

71. Ruth Marcus, "Guilty of Insufficient Overreaching," *Washington Post,* May 23, 2007, p. A21.
72. The presiding judges were, first, Royce Lamberth, and then, Colleen Kollar-Kotelly.
73. Risen, *State of War,* p. 53.
74. Fine et al., "President's Surveillance Program," p. 18.
75. Bamford, *The Shadow Factory,* p. 113. Del Quentin Wilber, "Surveillance Court Quietly Moving," *Washington Post,* March 2, 2009. Weich, letter to chairs, May 14, 2009.
76. All Lamberth quotes from Royce Lamberth, American Library Association, June 20, 2007, at http://www.ala.org/ala/washoff/washevents/woannual/annualconfwo.cfm#events.
77. Wadih el-Hage, an American citizen, was sentenced to life.
78. Dept. of Justice, "Legal Authorities."
79. Authorization for Use of Military Force, Pub. L. No. 107-40, § 2(a), 115 Stat. 224, 224 (Sept. 18, 2001).
80. *Youngstown Sheet & Tube Co. v. Sawyer,* 343 U.S. 579 (1952).
81. Beth Nolan et al., "On NSA Spying: Letter to Congress," *The New York Review of Books,* Feb. 9, 2006. Signed by Beth Nolan, Curtis Bradley, David Cole, Geoffrey Stone, Harold Hongju Koh, Kathleen M. Sullivan, Laurence H. Tribe, Martin Lederman, Philip B. Heymann, Richard Epstein, Ronald Dworkin, Walter Dellinger, William S. Sessions, and William Van Alstyne.
82. 18 U.S.C. § 2511(3) (1976).
83. FISA § 201(c), 92 Stat. 1797.
84. FISA reads: "Notwithstanding any other law, the President, through the Attorney General, may authorize electronic surveillance without a court order under this subchapter to acquire foreign intelligence information for a period not to exceed fifteen calendar days following a declaration of war by the Congress." 50 U.S.C., § 1811. John Yoo omitted reference to this provision in his memos arguing that FISA did not address the president's wartime powers, and thus left them unimpeded. Yoo's omission gave weight to internal Bush administration criticisms of the legal rationale for the NSA program.
85. Alberto Gonzales, letter to Senators Patrick Leahy and Arlen Specter, Senate Committee on the Judiciary, Jan. 17, 2007, http://graphics8.nytimes.com/packages/pdf/politics/20060117gonzales_Letter.pdf.
86. Lawrence Wright, "The Spymaster," p. 46.
87. Despite the sunset provision, surveillance orders issued during the law's term remained in effect for a year.
88. George W. Bush, statement, Office of the Press Secretary, White House, July 10, 2008.
89. FISA Amendments Act of 2008, H.R. 6304, amending the Foreign Intelligence Surveillance Act of 1978, 50 U.S.C. § 1801.
90. Fine et al., "President's Surveillance Program," p. 31.
91. H.R. 6304. § 702 (b)(5).
92. Judge Anna Diggs Taylor, *ACLU et al. v. NSA et al.,* 06-CV-10204 (E.D. Mich. So. Div. Aug. 17, 2006).
93. *ACLU et al. v. NSA et al.,* 06-2095/2140 (6th Cir. 2007).
94. Complaint for Declaratory and Injunctive Relief, July 10, 2008, *Amnesty Inter-*

national et al. v. John M. McConnell et al., o8-cv-o6259 (S. D. N.Y. 2008). Plain-tiffs include Amnesty International, Global Fund for Women, Global Rights, Human Rights Watch, International Criminal Defence Attorneys Association, *The Nation*, PEN American Center, Service Employees International Union, Washington Office on Latin America, Daniel N. Arshack, David Nevin, Scott McKay, and Sylvia Royce. Judge John G. Koeltl dismissed on Aug. 20, 2009. Appealed to Second Circuit as *Amnesty International et al. v. John M. McConnell et al.*, o9-4112-cv. Another case proceeded thanks to a government slip-up. An Islamic charity, al-Haramain, won in federal district court after the government inadvertently revealed that the organization had been monitored without FISA warrants. The judge rejected the Obama administration's argument for dismissal on state-secrets grounds. The victory had limited application, both because of the unusual disclosure of monitoring and because the judgment of illegality related only to Bush's Terrorist Surveillance Program, which was superseded by the 2008 FISA amendments that legalized the secret surveillance. *Al-Haramain v. Obama*, o7-o109 (N.D. Cal. March 31, 2010).

95. George W. Bush, speech at the Alfalfa Club, Jan. 2007, quoted by Michael Gawenda, *The Age*, Jan. 31, 2006.

CHAPTER 7: THE RIGHT TO BE LET ALONE

1. *Olmstead v. United States*, 277 U.S. 438 (1928).
2. *Katz v. United States*, 389 U.S. 347 (1967). From Harlan's concurring opinion. Stewart framed the concept more generally in his majority opinion.
3. Thomas L. Friedman, "Naked Air," *New York Times*, Dec. 26, 2001, p. A29.
4. Jonathan Starkey, "Quick Airport Screening Service Shuts Down," *Washington Post*, June 24, 2009. Several other companies made bids to buy the customer lists and revive the program.
5. Katie Hafner, "Internet Users Thinking Twice Before a Search," *New York Times*, Jan. 25, 2006, p. A1.
6. *City of Ontario v. Quon*, o8-1332 (2010).
7. *Griswold v. Connecticut*, 381 U.S. 479 (1965) and *Roe v. Wade*, 410 U.S. 113 (1973).
8. *Olmstead v. United States*, 277 U.S. 438 (1928). Author's emphasis.
9. http://blogs.abcnews.com/theblotter/2006/12/can_you_hear_me.html.
10. Brandon C. Welsh and David P. Farrington, "Crime Prevention Effects of Closed Circuit Television," Home Office Research Study 252, Aug. 2002, http://www.homeoffice.gov.uk/rds/pdfs2/hors252.pdf.
11. Jeffrey Rosen, *The Naked Crowd* (New York: Random House, 2004), p. 47.
12. Ibid., p. 48.
13. Dana Canedy, "Tampa Scans the Faces in Its Crowds for Criminals," *New York Times*, July 4, 2001, and "About Face," *St. Petersburg Times*, Aug. 23, 2003, p. 16A.
14. Allison Klein, "Gunshot Sensors Are Giving D.C. Police Jump on Suspects," *Washington Post*, Oct. 22, 2006, p. A1.
15. ACLU, "Closure of DHS Domestic Spy Satellite Program a Positive Step, Says ACLU," June 24, 2009.

16. Rick Weiss, "Dragonfly or Insect Spy? Scientists at Work on Robobugs," *Washington Post,* Oct. 9, 2007, p. A3.

17. The technology was first used by the military to determine if a wounded soldier was alive before risking a medic to save him. "It can detect the respiration signature of an individual standing up to 5 meters behind a 20 centimeter hollow core concrete block wall and wooden doors typical of those found on most homes and which are almost transparent to the system." Eugene F. Greneker, "Radar Flashlight for Through-the-Wall Detection of Humans," Georgia Tech Research Institute, http://gtresearchnews.gatech.edu/newsrelease/FLASH _SP.html. Greneker and others were awarded a patent in 2007. http://www .patentstorm.us/patents/7199749.html.

18. Dept. of Homeland Security, "Privacy Impact Assessment for the Future Attribute Screening Technology," Dec. 15, 2008, at http://www.dhs.gov/xlibrary/ assets/privacy/privacy_pia_st_fast.pdf.

19. 47 C.F.R. § 20.18(h)(1). See also *In the Matter of the Application of the United States of America for an Order Authorizing the Installation and Use of a Pen Register and a Caller Identification System on Telephone Numbers [Sealed] and [Sealed] and the Production of Real Time Cell Site Information,* 05-4486 JKB, (D. Md. 2005) (Magistrate Judge Bredar).

20. Stored Wire and Electronic Communications and Transactional Records Access, or "Stored Communications Act," 18 U.S.C. § 2703 (d).

21. Pen/Trap Statute, 18 U.S.C. § 3121.

22. *In Re Application for Pen Register and Trap/Trace Device with Cell Site Location Authority,* 2005 WL 2656621 (S.D. Tex. Oct. 14, 2005) (Magistrate Judge Smith).

23. *In the Matter of the Application* (Magistrate Judge Bredar), pp. 12–13.

24. Ellen Nakashima, "Cellphone Tracking Powers on Request," *Washington Post,* Nov. 23, 2007, p. A1.

25. *In Re Application of the United States of America for an Order for Disclosure of Telecommunications Records and Authorizing the Use of a Pen Register and Trap and Trace,* 05 Mag. 1763 (S.D. N.Y. 2005) (Magistrate Judge Gorenstein).

26. Charlie Savage, "Judges Divided Over Growing GPS Surveillance," *The New York Times,* Aug. 14, 2010. See *United States v. Maynard,* 08-3030 (D.C. Cir., 2010).

27. Chris L. Jenkins, "Stalkers Go High Tech to Intimidate Victims," *Washington Post,* Apr. 14, 2007, p. A1.

28. Rosen, *The Naked Crowd,* p. 61.

29. Joshua D. Wright, "The Constitutional Failure of Gang Databases," *Stanford Journal of Civil Rights & Civil Liberties,* Vol. 2, 2005, p. 115. See also Molly Bruder, "Say Cheese! Examining the Constitutionality of Photostops," *American University Law Review,* Vol. 57, p. 1693.

30. *United States v. United States District Court,* 407 U.S. 297 (1972). The Supreme Court ruled 8–0 that the Fourth Amendment precluded warrantless surveillance of Americans for national security purposes when they were not agents of foreign powers. Wiretaps authorized only by Attorney General John N. Mitchell, not a judge, were used against three political dissidents accused of conspiring to destroy government property, one of whom allegedly bombed a CIA office in Michigan. The Supreme Court upheld the lower courts, which had ordered the contents of the overheard conversations disclosed to the defendants.

31. Newton Minow et al., Technology and Privacy Advisory Committee, Department of Defense, *Safeguarding Privacy in the Fight Against Terrorism,* March 1, 2004, p. 35. Quotes from Jeremy Bentham, *The Panopticon Writings,* Miran Bozovic, ed. (London, New York: Verso, 1995). Christopher Slobogin, "Symposium: Public Privacy; Camera Surveillance of Public Places and the Right to Anonymity," *Mississippi Law Journal* 213, p. 240 (2002).

32. "Learning to Live with Big Brother," *The Economist,* Sept. 27, 2007.

33. Rachel L. Swarns, "Senator? Terrorist? A Watch List Stops Kennedy at Airport," *New York Times,* Aug. 20, 2004, p. A1.

34. "TSA and FBI Ordered to Pay $200,000 to Settle 'No Fly' Lawsuit," ACLU press release, Jan. 24, 2006, http://www.aclu.org/safefree/general/23926prs20060124.html.

35. Glenn A. Fine, Statement before the House Committee on Homeland Security, Nov. 8, 2007.

36. Dennis C. Blair, director of national intelligence, and Michael E. Leiter said that tighter controls had come in 2009. "I should not have given in to that pressure," said Blair. Eric Lipton, "Officials Regret Curbs on Adding to Terror Watch List," *New York Times,* Jan. 21, 2010, p. A18.

37. Julia Preston, "Judge Suspends Key Bush Effort in Immigration," *New York Times,* Oct. 11, 2007, p. A1. The Bush administration decided not to appeal the judge's order, and the Obama administration rescinded the matching requirement. ACLU, "Government Terminates 'No Match' Rule Harmful to Legal Workers," Oct. 7, 2009.

38. Editorial, "Watching Orwell," *New York Times,* Sept. 6, 2007.

39. *Brinegar v. United States,* 338 U.S. 160 (1949).

40. Ryan Singel, "Newly Declassified Files Detail Massive FBI Data-Mining Project," *Wired,* Sept. 23, 2009. ACLU, "FBI Data Mining and Collection Program Threaten Privacy of Innocent Americans," Sept. 24, 2009. FBI, "The National Security Analysis Center," white paper draft of Apr. 21, 2006, at http://www.wired.com/images_blogs/threatlevel/2009/09/nsac_data_sets.pdf

41. Minow et al., *Safeguarding Privacy,* p. 39.

42. Markle Foundation, *Creating a Trusted Network for Homeland Security,* 2003, pp. 33, 38, 71, and 73. The panel, chaired by Zoë Baird and James Barksdale, included Michael A. Vatis, Robert D. Atkinson, Stewart Baker, Jerry Berman, Ashton Carter, Wesley P. Clark, Esther Dyson, Amitai Etzioni, Slade Gorton, Morton H. Halperin, Eric Holder, Abraham D. Sofaer, Mary McCarthy, and others.

43. Unauthorized access to private information: Jenna Wortham, "Facebook Glitch Brings New Privacy Worries," *New York Times,* May 5, 2010. Shopping information: Initially, users had no choice; the messages about buying activities were sent automatically. After 50,000 members signed a petition of protest, Facebook began asking users for approval after each purchase made through Facebook's shopping portal, called My Shopping. Louise Story and Brad Stone, "Facebook Retreats on Online Tracking," *New York Times,* Nov. 30, 2007, p. C1.

44. Electronic Privacy Information Center, http://www.epic.org/privacy/iei/attachment_a.pdf.

45. Markle Foundation, *Creating a Trusted Network,* Appendix H.

46. Timothy Lynch, at Federalist Society annual conference, Mayflower Hotel,

Washington, D.C., Nov. 10, 2004. The requirement is to file Suspicious Activities Reports to the Treasury Department's Financial Crimes Enforcement Network. Section 314(a) of the Patriot Act also authorizes government agents to request information about individuals suspected of terrorism.

47. Don Van Natta, Jr., and Jo Becker, "Spitzer Fall Began with Bank Reports," *New York Times,* March 13, 2008.

48. Markle Foundation, *Creating a Trusted Network,* p. 146.

49. "Important Information Every Schwab Account Holder Needs to Know: Privacy Policy, 2007 Annual Notification," Charles Schwab & Co., June 2007, p. 3.

50. See Chapter 6. Office of Inspector General, *A Review of the Federal Bureau of Investigation's Use of National Security Letters,* Department of Justice, March 2007.

51. Markle Foundation, *Creating a Trusted Network,* p. 164.

52. Ibid., Vignette 4, p. 126.

53. Minow et al., *Safeguarding Privacy,* pp. vii–viii, citing Department of Defense Appropriations Act, 2004, Pub. L. No. 108-84, § 8183 (Sept. 25, 2003), and p. 19.

54. Minow et al., *Safeguarding Privacy,* p. viii.

55. Visible Technologies, "Visible Technologies Announces Strategic Partnership with In-Q-Tel," press release, Oct. 16, 2009. Noah Shachtman, "Exclusive: U.S. Spies Buy Stake in Firm That Monitors Blogs, Tweets," *Wired,* Oct. 19, 2009.

56. Lara Jakes Jordan, "Data on Americans Mined for Terror Risk," AP, July 11, 2007.

57. Minow et al., *Safeguarding Privacy,* p. 5.

58. "Data Mining and Homeland Security: An Overview," Congressional Research Service, Jan. 18, 2007, p. 21.

59. "The 2007 International Privacy Ranking," Privacy International, http://www .privacyinternational.org/article.shtml?cmd[347]=x-347-559597.

60. The Hanover Police Department has 20 full-time officers; Dartmouth Safety and Security has 28, including supervisors. In 2008, drug violations on campus resulted in 6 arrests and 21 referrals for disciplinary action, compared with 3 and 18 respectively, the previous year. Town of Hanover, Police Department Web site, http://www.hanovernh.org/police; "Annual Security and Fire Safety Report September 2009 Dartmouth College," pp. 5, 14. http://www.dartmouth .edu/~security/docs/Dartmouth%202009%20Annual%20Clery%20Report-3.pdf.

61. *The State of New Hampshire v. Adam Nemser,* 2000-443, Oct. 25, 2002. The opinion reports that when the college's proctor asked the Hanover police chief for an opinion on whether DSS officers "being private citizens, risked arrest if they took possession of contraband in the course of their duties," the police chief replied that while they were not legally exempt from prosecution, in practice he would not arrest college security officers.

62. *Piazzola v. Watkins,* 442 F.2d 284 (5th Cir., 1971) and *State v. Hunter,* 831 P.2d 1033 (Utah App. 1992).

63. *Camara v. Municipal Court,* 387 U.S. 523 (1967). The Court ruled that a resident's refusal to permit city inspectors to conduct a code-enforcement inspection without a warrant cannot be grounds for prosecution, but that the warrant can be issued on the grounds of "reasonable legislative or administrative standards for conducting an area inspection."

64. Government's opening brief, *United States v. Ronald C. Kline*, 03 50349, 03-50585 (9th Cir. 2004), p. 10.
65. Ibid., p. 7.
66. Ibid., p. 8.
67. Ibid., pp. 31–32. The earlier case, *United States v. Walther*, 652 F.2d 788, 790 (9th Cir. 1981), involved an airline employee who routinely opened suspicious cartons on behalf of the Drug Enforcement Administration, and was paid for finding significant amounts of narcotics. He was ruled an agent of government, subject to Fourth Amendment restrictions. See also *United States v. Sherwin*, 539 F.2d 1, 6 (9th Cir. 1976): "A private person cannot act unilaterally as an agent or instrument of the state; there must be some degree of governmental knowledge and acquiescence. In the absence of such official involvement, a search is not governmental."
68. Appellee's brief, *United States v. Ronald C. Kline*, 03-50349, 03-50585 (9th Cir. 2004), pp. 12, 19. See also Gary Dimmock, "Canada's Hero Unmasked," *Ottawa Citizen*, June 29, 2002, p. A1.
69. Appellee's brief, *Kline*, p. 12. Carr portrayed Willman as a "citizen tipster," not an "informant," to help place him beyond the reach of the Fourth Amendment.
70. Government's opening brief, *Kline*, p. 12.
71. Unpublished opinion, *Kline*.
72. Christine Hanley, "Ex-Judge Collapses at Sentencing," *Los Angeles Times*, Feb. 21, 2007, p.B3.
73. Posted by KhayotIK, Feb. 23, 2007, on Download.com.

CHAPTER 8: LIFE, LIBERTY, AND THE PURSUIT OF TERRORISTS

1. Nabil al-Marabh "had once roomed with a known al Qaeda operative, and he himself was now number 27 on the FBI's terrorist watchlist," writes Erich Lichtblau in *Bush's Law: The Remaking of American Justice* (New York: Pantheon, 2008), p. x. In the end, however, the intelligence was deemed incorrect, and the government determined that al-Marabh was no threat and had no ties to terrorist groups.
2. The fraudulent documents included a passport, a Social Security card, a U.S. Immigration form, a U.S. visa, and a U.S. green card, most in the name of Michael Saisa. *United States v. Karim Koubriti*, Olm80779 (E. D. Mich.) Criminal Complaint, Sept. 17, 2001.
3. *United States v. Karim Koubriti et al.*, 01-80778, Second Superseding Indictment, Aug. 28, 2002. The initial search was based on an FBI claim that Koubriti had given consent, although he recalled only signing something in English, which he couldn't read. Later, a warrant was obtained for a more thorough search.
4. The account of the Sabin-Convertino clash was confirmed by one other participant. Paul Egan, "Cleared of Misconduct, Former U.S. Prosecutor in Terror Case Seeks Redress from the Government," *Detroit News*, at http://www.mail-archive.com/osint@yahoogroups.com/msg54606.html.
5. Norman Sinclair, "Fed Terror Trial Faced Probems," *Detroit News*, Oct. 17, 2007.

6. William Swor, attorney for Abdel Elmardoudi, interview with author, May 11, 2006.
7. *Brady v. Maryland,* 373 U.S. 83 (1963).
8. *Giglio v. United States,* 405 U.S. 150 (1972).
9. The tactic raised objections from one FBI agent, Jim Brennan, and some Justice Department officials in Washington. *United States v. Karim Koubriti et al.,* 01-80778 (E.D. Mich.), Government's consolidated response concurring in the defendants' motions for a new trial and Government's motion to dismiss count one without prejudice and memorandum of law in support thereof, Aug. 31, 2004, p. 46.
10. Government's motion to dismiss, *Koubriti et al.,* p. 30.
11. "Colonel Mary Peterson—U.S. Air Attache to Poland," U.S. Diplomatic Mission, Warsaw, Poland, March 5, 2009, http://poland.usembassy.gov/embassy -events/embassy-events-2009/colonel-mary-peterson--u.s.-air-attach-to-poland -5-march-2009. Peterson did not respond to an invitation to offer her viewpoint. E-mail to Peterson from author, May 8, 2009.
12. For details on Convertino's clashes with senior Justice Department officials, see Egan, *Detroit News,* at http://www.mail-archive.com/osint@yahoogroups.com/ msg54606.html.
13. In his suit, Convertino subpoenaed David Ashenfelter, the reporter, to learn which officials had leaked the information that he was under investigation. Ashenfelter prevailed in federal court in resisting the disclosure based on his Fifth Amendment right against self-incrimination, a novel defense for a journalist. *Convertino v. United States Department of Justice,* 07-CV-13842-DT (D.C. E.D. Mich., So. Div. 2009). Convertino's suit against the Justice Department was still pending at the time of this writing. Koubriti's, allowed to go forward by a federal district court, was dismissed by the Sixth Circuit on the ground that Convertino had absolute prosecutorial immunity since his failure to disclose exculpatory evidence was committed as an integral part of the judicial process, which is not susceptible to civil liability. *Koubriti v. Convertino,* 09-1016 (6th Cir. 2010).
14. John Solomon, "Despite Evidence, Man Deported," AP, June 3, 2004, http://www.boston.com/news/nation/articles/2004/06/03/despite_evidence _man_deported/.
15. Ed White, "U.S. Willing to Drop Fraud Charge Against Man at Center of 2003 Botched Detroit Terror Trial," AP, July 28, 2009.
16. Since the penalty for failing to Mirandize someone in custody is the exclusion of his statements from evidence, Abdulmutallab did not have to be read his Miranda rights, one argument held, because his statements would not be necessary to convict him, given that a planeload of witnesses saw him try to detonate the explosives. He could have been questioned for intelligence purposes. In 2010, Attorney General Eric Holder proposed legislation to expand Miranda's public-safety exception so that suspected terrorists could be questioned before being read their rights, and their statements used in trial. Charlie Savage, "Holder Supports a Miranda Limit," *New York Times,* May 10, 2010, p. A1.
17. Carrie Johnson, "Airliner Plot Being Prosecuted 'In Wrong Place,' Giuliani Says," *Washington Post,* Jan. 9, 2010, p. A3.

18. Richard B. Zabel and James J. Benjamin, Jr., *In Pursuit of Justice: Prosecuting Terrorism Cases in the Federal Courts* (New York: Human Rights First, 2008).

19. Stuart Taylor, Jr., "The Case for a National Security Court," *National Journal,* Feb. 27, 2007. Five of the plotters were arrested while mixing two hundred gallons of gasoline with fertilizer in a Queens garage; eight others were arrested subsequently. Mukasey also alleged, incorrectly, that the disclosure of bin Laden's satellite phone records in another case alerted him to the fact that his phone was monitored, and he stopped using it. Actually, he had stopped using it years earlier. Zabel and Benjamin, *In Pursuit of Justice,* p. 89. Mukasey also rescinded the 2001 and 2002 memo from the Justice Department's Office of Legal Counsel authorizing the domestic use of the military against suspected terrorists. Steven G. Bradbury, "Re: October 23, 2001 OLC Opinion Addressing the Domestic Use of Military Force to Combat Terrorist Activities," Memorandum for the Files, Office of Legal Counsel, U.S. Dept. of Justice, Oct. 6, 2008.

20. Classified Information Procedures Act, Pub. L. No. 96-456, 94 Stat. 2025, 2025-31 (1980), at 18 U.S.C. app. 3.

21. The term "graymail" may come from L. Patrick Gray, an FBI director who was prosecuted under the Civil Rights Act for ordering agents to wiretap without warrants and break into homes and photograph diaries, letters, and various documents belonging to friends and relatives of the Weather Underground, a violent antiwar group. His lawyers, arguing that the surveillance was legal because it was aimed at gathering foreign intelligence, not criminal evidence, demanded discovery of classified information showing the Weather Underground's connections to Cuba and East Germany. The assumption was that the government would drop the case, which it did against Gray but not against two other FBI officials, Edward S. Miller, head of intelligence, and Mark Felt, deputy director, who had become Deep Throat, the *Washington Post's* key source in the exposure of the Watergate break-in. They were convicted and fined but pardoned by President Ronald Reagan. Frank Dunham, Jr., Felt's attorney, interview with author, Jan. 4, 2005.

22. One approach, used in the Moussaoui and Abu Ali cases, is the "silent witness rule," in which a witness may refer to Country A, Person 1, page 14, and the like; only the judge, jury, prosecution, and defense counsel would have keys to this simple code. The specifics would not be disclosed to the public. Zabel and Benjamin, *In Pursuit of Justice,* pp. 86–87.

23. Ibid., p. 9.

24. *Ex parte Merryman,* 17 F Cases 144 (D. Md. 1861), in which Chief Justice Roger Taney, sitting as a circuit court judge, found that since the power to suspend was located in Article I, creating the legislative branch, only Congress could do so, and only "when in Cases of Rebellion or Invasion the public Safety may require it." U.S. Constitution, Article I, Section 9, Paragraph 2.

25. *Ex parte Milligan,* 71 U.S. 1 (1866).

26. *Ex parte Quirin,* 317 U.S. 1 (1942). Two German submarines had landed them in Florida and Long Island. The American citizen, Herbert Hans Haupt, could have been held for the duration of the conflict without trial, the Court ruled. The military trial had begun before the Court heard the case, and shortly after the decision upholding the military tribunals, six of the eight, including Haupt,

were executed in the electric chair. The other two, who had confessed and cooperated, received life terms and were deported to Germany after the war.

27. *Hamdi v. Rumsfeld*, 542 U.S. 507 (2004). The Fourth Circuit had dismissed Padilla's habeas petition, ruling that the president could hold him without factual inquiry or evidentiary hearing. 296 F3d 278 (4th Cir. 2002). Rather than try Hamdi, the government agreed to release him to Saudi Arabia in exchange for his renunciation of American citizenship. The dire threat he posed suddenly evaporated.

28. *Hamdi v. Rumsfeld*, 542 U.S. 507 (2004). The decision was by plurality, with two pairs of dissenters. Souter and Ginsburg found no congressional authorization for an enemy-combatant designation. They denied that the federal statute on detentions, 18 U.S.C. § 4001(a), had been satisfied by the post-9/11 Authorization for Use of Military Force, 115 Stat. 224, which they said was insufficiently clear and robust. And they noted that thirty-eight days after adopting that resolution, the same Congress passed the Patriot Act, which set a seven-day limit on detention of alien terrorist suspects without criminal charges or deportation proceedings. 8 U.S.C. § 1226a(a)(5). Scalia and Stevens noted that in longstanding English tradition, inherited by the framers, aliens had been interned until the end of wars, but citizens who fought on the enemy's side had been prosecuted criminally for treason. The plurality (O'Connor, Rehnquist, Kennedy, and Breyer), having found congressional authorization for the enemy-combatant designation, did not reach the question of whether, as the Bush administration asserted, the president's powers as commander in chief, in Article II of the Constitution, also constituted authorization. (Souter acerbically cited Justice Robert Jackson's observation in 1952 that the president is not commander in chief of the country, only of the military.) *Youngstown Sheet & Tube Co. v. Sawyer*, 343 U.S. 579 (1952). Thomas was the only justice to find unfettered executive power to detain Hamdi indefinitely as an enemy combatant.

29. Frank Dunham, interview with author, Jan. 4, 2005. Dunham doubted that the renunciation of citizenship, which by law is supposed to be voluntary, was valid in that it was coerced in exchange for release. Terri Nelson, "Hamdi Returned to Saudi Arabia," AP, Oct. 11, 2004.

30. Scott Shane, "Divisions Arose on Rough Tactics for Qaeda Figure," *New York Times*, Apr. 18, 2009, p. A1.

31. Jane Mayer, *The Dark Side* (New York: Doubleday, 2008), pp. 155-56; interviews with Andrew Patel, one of Padilla's attorneys.

32. George W. Bush, "To the Secretary of Defense," June 9, 2002.

33. The Court had rejected Padilla's petition earlier on the argument that it had been brought in the wrong jurisdiction—the Second Circuit, covering New York, where he had first been jailed as a material witness, rather than the Fourth Circuit, covering South Carolina, where he was currently held in the Navy Brig. *Rumsfeld v. Padilla*, 542 U.S. 426 (2004). The Second Circuit had found no presidential authority to hold him; the Fourth Circuit later recognized the authority. Miffed that the government was unwilling to test its ruling in the highest court, the judges refused to approve Padilla's transfer to civilian courts. *Padilla v. Hanft*, 05-6396, Order, Dec. 21, 2005. The Supreme Court then approved the transfer and vacated the Fourth Circuit's opinion without giving full consideration to the question of whether a U.S. citizen could be seized on American soil

(as opposed to the battlefield) as an enemy combatant under the September 11 congressional authorization.

34. Deputy Attorney General James Comey, testimony, Senate Judiciary Committee, June 1, 2004.

35. Declaration of Vice Admiral Lowell E. Jacoby (USN), Director of the Defense Intelligence Agency, in *Padilla v. Bush,* 02 Civ. 4445 (S. D. N.Y 2003), Jan. 9, 2003.

36. Motion to dismiss for outrageous government conduct, *United States v. Padilla,* 04-60001 (S. D. Fla., Miami Div. 2006), Oct. 4, 2006.

37. Michael Mobbs, "Declaration of Michael H. Mobbs," affidavit in *Padilla v. Bush,* 02 Civ. 4445 (D.C. S. D. N.Y. 2002), Aug. 27, 2002.

38. Judge Marcia Cooke, in Kirk Semple and Carmen Gentile, "Padilla Sentenced to More Than 17 Years in Prison," *New York Times,* Jan. 22, 2008.

39. *Al-Marri v. Hanft,* 2-04-2257-26AJ (D.C. S.C.), Petition for Writ of Habeas Corpus, July 8, 2004; Respondent's Answer to the Petition for Writ of Habeas Corpus, Sept. 9, 2004; *United States v. Al-Marri,* 09-CR-100-30 (D.C., Cent. Dist., Ill., Peoria Div.), indictment, Feb. 26, 2009. He was initially arrested as a material witness, then indicted for counterfeit credit cards, then charged with making false statements to a bank and to the FBI. He moved to suppress statements he claimed were made under torture, and the day before the hearing was transferred to military custody. See also ACLU, "Al-Marri Sentence Proves Federal Courts Can Handle Terrorism Cases," Nov. 2, 2009.

40. *Rasul v. Bush,* 542 U.S. 466 (2004), by a 6–3 majority.

41. 28 U.S.C. § 2241.

42. *Hamdan v. Rumsfeld,* 05-184 (2006). See also UCMJ, Art. 21, 36. The majority found that the Geneva conventions were judicially enforceable because of their Common Article 3, which applied to the Guantánamo prisoners as nonmembers of any duly constituted military force. The article applies to a conflict not of an international character occurring in the territory of one of the conventions' signatories, meaning that it protects individuals in such territory, whether or not they are affiliated with a signatory or a nonsignatory. The Geneva conventions provide for a regularly constituted court, which can include courts-martial or military commissions, if deviations from court-martial procedures are required for practical reasons. Hamdan's lawyer, Neal Katyal, took the opposite side in a similar 2010 case, arguing on behalf of the government, as principal deputy solicitor general, that habeas corpus should not be extended to the U.S.-run prison at Bagram in Afghanistan, to which suspected terrorists seized elsewhere had been taken. The D.C. circuit ruled that the Bagram prisoners were not entitled to the habeas right. *Maqaleh v. Gates,* 09-5265 (D.C. Cir. 2010).

43. Military Commissions Act of 2006, § 3930.

44. *Boumediene v. Bush,* 553 U.S. 723 (2008).

45. "Unprivileged" meant people not listed in any of the eight categories covered by the Geneva conventions. Military Commissions Act of 2009, 10 U.S. § 47A.

46. Each conviction would get an automatic review by a U.S. court of military commissions review, comprising panels of military lawyers, and could then be appealed to the federal Court of Appeals for the D.C. Circuit, followed by the Supreme Court.

47. In 2009, Attorney General Eric Holder referred five Guantánamo detainees,

one of whom allegedly orchestrated the attack on the destroyer USS *Cole* in Yemen, for trial in the new military commissions. He sent five accused organizers of the 9/11 attacks for trial in federal criminal court in Manhattan but decided to change venues after an uproar of fear from the political right about security in New York City. Faced with intense political opposition, the White House considered sending them to military commissions as well.

48. "Beyond Guantanamo: A Bipartisan Declaration," The Constitution Project and Human Rights First, Nov. 4, 2009. List of signatories at http://www .constitutionproject.org/manage/file/348.pdf.

49. The five were Khalid Sheikh Mohammed, Walid Muhammad Salih Mubarak Bin Attash, Ramzi Bin al-Shibh, Ali Abdul-Aziz Ali, and Mustafa Ahmed al-Hawsawi. Attorney General Eric Holder, statement, Nov. 13, 2009.

50. For an insightful account of the Timimi case, see Milton Viorst, "The Education of Ali Al-Timimi," *The Atlantic,* June 2006.

51. The would-be bombers were Michael C. Finton, an American, and Hosam Maher Husein Smadi, a Jordanian. Mike Robinson, "Men Accused of Unrelated Bomb Plots in Ill., Texas," AP, Sept. 25, 2009.

52. *United States v. Batiste et al.,* 06-20373 (S.D. Fla. 2006), Indictment; "Seven Florida Men Charged with Conspiring to Support al Qaeda, Attack Targets in the United States," press release, Dept. of Justice, June 23, 2006.

53. Scott Shane and Andrea Zarate, "FBI Killed Plot in Talking Stage," *New York Times,* June 24, 2006.

54. The attorney was Ana M. Jhones. "Five Miami Men Convicted of Sears Tower Attack Plot," AP, May 12, 2009.

55. Shane and Zarate, *New York Times,* June 24, 2006.

56. DOJ press release, June 23, 2006.

57. "Florida: Sentencing in Tower Plot," *New York Times,* Nov. 21, 2009.

58. Michael Powell and William K. Rashbaum, "Papers Portray Plot as More Talk Than Action," *New York Times,* June 4, 2007.

59. Contact with the group had been facilitated by Abdul Kadir, a former member of Guyana's parliament, who was extradited along with two others to face trial in the United States. He and Defreitas were convicted; two pleaded guilty.

60. *United States v. Defreitas et al.* (E.D. N.Y.), complaint, June 1, 2007.

61. Defense lawyers have argued that without an adversary proceeding to contest the designation, such organizations are deprived of due process under the Sixth Amendment, and those convicted of providing support are similarly violated. See *United States v. Ford,* CR-02-399 HA (D. Or. 2002), Memorandum in Support of Defendants' Motion to Dismiss the Indictment.

62. *United States v. Arbane,* 446 F.3d 1223 (11th Cir. 2006).

63. *United States v. Lakhani,* 03-cr-00880, Criminal Complaint (D. N.J. Aug. 11, 2003) (Dkt. No. 1).

64. 18 U.S.C. 2339A(b).

65. *Holder v. Humanitarian Law Project,* 08-1498 (2010).

66. Although the United States did not enter combat against the Taliban until 2001, President Bill Clinton issued Executive Order 13129 on July 4, 1999, declaring a national emergency that prohibited U.S. persons from making or receiving any contribution of funds, goods, or services to benefit the Taliban.

67. Kenneth Ballen, *Terrorists in Love: Hope and Fear from Inside the World of Islamist Extremism* (New York: Free Press, 2011).

68. Matthew Purdy and Lowell Bergman, "Where the Trail Led," *New York Times,* Oct. 12, 2003.

69. Mark Mazzetti and David Johnston, "Bush Weighed Using Military in Arrests," *New York Times,* July 24, 2009.

70. Matthew Purdy, "Our Towns: Puzzling Over Motives of the Men in the Lackawanna Qaeda Case," *New York Times,* March 30, 2003.

EPILOGUE: THE HIGH COURT OF HISTORY

1. *USA Today,* Nov. 14, 2005, p. 20A.

2. Minneapolis *Star Tribune,* Nov. 4, 2005.

3. *The Oregonian,* Nov. 3, 2005, p. B06.

4. *Diane Rehm Show,* WAMU, Apr. 6, 2006.

5. *Florida v. Kerwick,* 512 So.2d 347, 348–49 (Fla. App. 1987), quoted in Thurgood Marshall's dissent in *Florida v. Bostick,* 501 U.S. 429 (1991). Police boarded buses, checked IDs and tickets, and asked to search bags.

6. Lev Kopelev, *To Be Preserved Forever* (New York: Lippincott, 1977), pp. 10, 87.

7. James Yee, *For God and Country* (New York: Public Affairs, 2005), p. 145. The formal charge was "failing to obey a lawful general order" by taking classified documents home and "wrongfully transporting classified material without the proper security containers or covers." But the documents allegedly in Yee's possession were never determined to have been classified. Neil A. Lewis, "Charges Dropped Against Chaplain," *New York Times,* March 20, 2004.

8. "Captain Yee's performance during this rating period has been truly exemplary in every measure," read the evaluation. The highest box was checked: "Outstanding Performance. Must Promote." Ray Rivera, "Suspicion in the Ranks," *Seattle Times,* Jan. 9–16, 2005, attached documents.

9. Neil A. Lewis, "Case Against Ex-Chaplain Opens Focusing on Affair," *New York Times,* Dec. 9, 2003.

10. General Miller's spokesman conveyed my request for an interview or e-mail exchange, but Miller was unwilling.

11. Interview with Yee, Beliefnet, Nov. 22, 2005, http://www.alternet.org/story/28586/.

12. Most notable was the FDA's refusal to approve over-the-counter sales of the morning-after contraceptive pill, despite scientists' assessment that access was safe for women seventeen and older. The decision, ultimately reversed, was a sop to the antiabortion lobby. Gardiner Harris, "Morning-After Pill: Politics and the F.D.A.," *New York Times,* Aug. 28, 2005.

13. "An Investigation of Allegations of Politicized Hiring by Monica Goodling and Other Staff in the Office of the Attorney General," Office of Inspector General, Dept. of Justice, July 2008, Chap. 3. http://www.justice.gov/oig/special/s0807/.

14. John Paul Stevens, remarks, Fordham U. Law School, 2005, quoted by Linda Greenhouse, "One Man, Two Courts," *New York Times,* Apr. 10, 2010.

INDEX

A NOTE ABOUT THE AUTHOR

David K. Shipler worked for *The New York Times* from 1966 to 1988, reporting from New York, Saigon, Moscow, and Jerusalem before serving as chief diplomatic correspondent in Washington. He shared a George Polk Award for his coverage of the 1982 war in Lebanon and was executive producer, writer, and narrator of two PBS documentaries on the Israeli-Palestinian conflict, one of which won an Alfred I. duPont–Columbia University Award for excellence in broadcast journalism. He is the author of four other books: *Russia: Broken Idols, Solemn Dreams; Arab and Jew: Wounded Spirits in a Promised Land* (which won a Pulitzer Prize); *A Country of Strangers: Blacks and Whites in America;* and *The Working Poor: Invisible in America.* He has been a guest scholar at the Brookings Institution, a senior associate at the Carnegie Endowment for International Peace, a trustee of Dartmouth College, chair of the Pulitzer jury on general nonfiction, a writer-in-residence at the University of Southern California, and a Woodrow Wilson Visiting Fellow. He has taught at Princeton University, at American University in Washington, D.C., and at Dartmouth College.

A NOTE ON THE TYPE

This book was set in Fairfield, the first typeface from the hand of the distinguished American artist and engraver Rudolph Ruzicka (1883–1978). In its structure Fairfield displays the sober and sane qualities of the master craftsman whose talent has long been dedicated to clarity. It is this trait that accounts for the trim grace and vigor, the spirited design and sensitive balance, of this original typeface.

Rudolph Ruzicka was born in Bohemia and came to America in 1894. He set up his own shop, devoted to wood engraving and printing, in New York in 1913 after a varied career working as a wood engraver, in photoengraving and banknote printing plants, and as an art director and freelance artist. He designed and illustrated many books, and was the creator of a considerable list of individual prints—wood engravings, line engravings on copper, and aquatints.

COMPOSED BY CREATIVE GRAPHICS, ALLENTOWN, PENNSYLVANIA

PRINTED AND BOUND BY BERRYVILLE GRAPHICS,

BERRYVILLE, VIRGINIA

BOOK DESIGN BY ROBERT C. OLSSON